The Complete
GORDON SETTER

Dedication

COMPILING HISTORY of the modern Gordon Setter in America, 1945 forward, had the immediacy of an autobiography. As I came across names of dozens of splendid dogs and their dedicated, intelligent, strong minded owners, the memories (half-forgotten) came to life and brought realization of and pride in what was a concerted effort.

That the breed could progress to its present success is a tribute to these people and their lovely dogs.

Having viewed almost forty years of activity in the breed makes it possible for me to perceive definite patterns as kennels came and went and outstanding dogs changed the type—an on-going state of affairs.

Tracing "roots" of current Gordons will be possible at last for today's fanciers through this first inclusive history of the Gordon Setter in America.

Jean Sanger Look
East Randolph, New York

THE COMPLETE
GORDON SETTER

by JEAN SANGER LOOK

and ANITA LUSTENBERGER

First Edition, Second Printing

1985

HOWELL BOOK HOUSE Inc.
230 Park Avenue, New York, N.Y. 10169

Library of Congress Cataloging in Publication Data

Look, Jean Sanger.
   The complete Gordon setter.

   1. Gordon setters.   I. Lustenberger, Anita.
II. Title.
SF429.G67L66   1984   636.7'52   84-9071
ISBN 0-87605-158-1

Contents

Acknowledgments

I OWE most sincere thanks to those people who offered information, assistance and encouragement vital to the writing of this book:

Margaret Sanger
Fred Itzenplitz
Anita Lustenberger
Muriel Clement
Mrs. Mildred Adams (England)
Mrs. Dawn Ferguson (Australia)
Mrs. Janice Stomp (Canada)

Special appreciation goes to Elsworth Howell. His skillful editing has brought welcome improvement to this book.

—*Jean Sanger Look*

Foreword

GORDON SETTER FANCIERS are most fortunate to have this highly authoritative book on their fine Black and Tans. It is the definitive and dedicated work of two of the finest scholars in the breed, Jean Sanger Look and Anita Lustenberger.

JEAN SANGER LOOK began her dog activities with Basset Hounds. She became a Director of the Basset Hound Club of America and helped to establish the first breed field trials to be held in western Pennsylvania. She initiated the Basset column in the American Kennel Club *Gazette* which she wrote for ten years.

In 1949 she became an active supporter of the Gordon Setter Club of America's field trial program. She supplied photos and reports for trials of Gordons and Bassets which appeared in the Field Trial section of AKC's *Gazette* at the time.

Jean became Secretary of the Gordon Setter Club of America in 1952. For twenty years she had stints as Director, Vice President, AKC *Gazette* columnist and GSCA Treasurer from 1962 to 1972. In the mid '50s she was also Treasurer of the former National Gordon Setter Field Trial Club. She helped to organize the Gordon Setter Field Trial Club of Western New York in the late '60s.

The successful breeders George and Myrtle Heslop provided Sangerfield with all its foundation stock beginning in 1945. In 1950 Sangerfield leased Ch. Heslop's Burnvale Duchess in whelp to Ch. Heslop's Courageous. From this litter the Sangers made five champions whose names Heslop's Burnvale Christopher, H.B. Laird, H.B. Edie, H.B. Symons and H.B. Sarah Jane are well remembered.

JEAN SANGER LOOK

ANITA LUSTENBERGER

10

In the late '50s, Jean and her sister Margaret established a kennel of Gordons in East Randolph, New York.

Am./Can. Ch. Sangerfield Jed born in 1957 became the first top winning Gordon for 1960-64 and the first American champion Gordon to win his Canadian title in 35 years. Owner-handled by Fred Itzenplitz, Jed was also the top breed winner in the breed's history to 1960. He won 35 group placements including six firsts and seven GSCA Specialties, four in 1963.

Other Sangerfield champions were Am./Can. Ch. Sporting Look, sire of 14 champions one of which, Ch. Sportin' Life, in turn sired 25 champions, including Ch. Sangerfield Bonnie of Ru-Bern, dam of Ch. Daron Rebel with a Cause, a great breed and group winner, and Am./Can. Ch. Sangerfield Patsy with Am./Can. CD in obedience and a great producing bitch. In fact, Sangerfield Gordons won CDX and T (tracking) titles.

In 1960 the GSCA asked Jean to put together a Club Yearbook. Jean's first effort, dated 1963 and covering 1939 through 1960, was a small paperback but well received. It was followed by hardcover editions for the years 1960-66, 1967-69, 1970-72, and the latest edition 1973-78 for which Jean was co-editor.

In nearly 40 years of existence, Sangerfield has produced 75 Gordon litters and won more than 100 show titles.

Currently, Jean, an Honorary Member of the GSCA, is in charge of its publicity materials and serves as Associate Editor and columnist for the new *Gordon Setter Quarterly* published by Hoflin Pub. Ltd. in Denver, Colorado.

ANITA ANDERSON LUSTENBERGER joined the Gordon Setter Club of America as a junior member in 1952. She was attracted to the breed because of its temperament, Scottish background, sensible and functional build, and the black and tan color which was familiar to her because her father owned Doberman Pinschers.

As a Navy junior, she went to 16 schools in twelve years, lived in many countries and saw Gordons at shows and kennels in Italy, Great Britain, USSR and other lands.

She has contributed to all the GSCA publications since 1970, wrote the chapter covering the breed in the U.S.A. for *The Gordon Setter,* by G. Gompertz, published in Great Britain, contributed the article on the breed in *The Encyclopedia Americana,* and—like Jean Look—writes columns for the *Gordon Setter Quarterly.*

Anita served the GSCA as Secretary (for six years), Vice President, member of its Board of Directors and Show Chairman of New York Specialty Show. She has also served as Newsletter Editor and member of

11

the Board for the Port Chester (N.Y.) Obedience Training Club. She is a member of the TarTan Gordon Setter Club and the British Gordon Setter Club. She has judged Sweepstakes and Fun Matches. She has a B.A. in zoology, an MEd. in Education, and a M.S. in Human Genetics. She is a Diplomate of the American Society for Medical Genetics and a Genetic Counselor in birth defects. She is currently a project director in clinical genetics at Columbia University.

Few books covering individual breeds of dogs can boast authors and compilers of such distinguished and long-term experience as Jean Sanger Look and Anita Anderson Lustenberger possess.

I am most deeply honored to publish and present this masterwork to the Gordon Setter fancy.

— Elsworth Howell

1

Origin and History of the Gordon Setter

Great Britain (1000-1900)

To the British goes credit for having developed Pointers, Setters and Spaniels to strong entities. But, one finds little precise information on this evolution.

From the early days the owning of hunting dogs was confined to the wealthy class. Under the feudal system established by William the Conquerer, property qualifications for killing game existed, as did the requirement of a franchise for keeping hounds and other hunting dogs.

Those privileged persons often exchanged prized dogs, horses, livestock with their peers in England and with their foreign counterparts. Thus they maintained the best quality.

Unfortunately, the details of breedings lodged only in the memories of owners, kennel managers and game keepers.

This feudal system continued for nearly seven hundred years. However, it was steadily eroded by the many political and economic changes which swept over the British Isles in the wake of wars for the Crown, civil wars, wars with foreign countries, and the growth of population and industry. The steady upward mobility of the lower classes entitled more and more people to at least a limited form of these special hunting rights.

By 1600 the sporting method of taking game was to go into the fields with a brace of "Setting Dogges." Since this was before guns, nets were used and the dogs were trained to point, then crouch low so that the net could be spread over them and the game birds. Today some Setters will drop on point, surely a marvelous example of the persistence of certain instincts.

With the coming of the Industrial Revolution in the 1700's the face of Britain changed completely. The middle class had both money and some leisure and almost complete freedom from the forestry and franchise laws.

The 1700's are said to have been the Golden Age of field sports. In Britain, it was the age of the Squire, and he most certainly was a sportsman with his own dogs. By this time Setters had become a distinct breed and, while not yet fully separated, each was taking shape as indicated by contemporary paintings.

At the end of the Jacobite Rebellion in 1745 the Scottish Highlands were opened up because of the military roads which had been built. Soon the wonderful sporting opportunities there became known to the English and for the next century grouse hunting, deer stalking and salmon fishing absorbed their attention.

By the early 1800's as guns became more efficient, netting birds became obsolete and pointing dogs were expected to range more freely.

Under the reign of William IV (1830-1837) almost the last barrier between the common man and freedom to hunt was removed when the franchise laws were permitted to lapse.

After Queen Victoria took the throne, a long and peaceful period existed (1837-1901). A benevolent Monarch, she saw to improvements in the conditions of the lower classes. Her love of dogs and sports encouraged the development of kennels, shows and field trials. Better transportation and communication meant that breeders could benefit by the freedom to exchange ideas and bloodlines.

The founding of the British Kennel Club in 1873 added momentum to this growing industry because the recording of pedigrees created a demand for purebred dogs. Exporting became big business, and the quality of dogs improved steadily.

Britain became a nation of dog fanciers and they remain so today, producing quality stock in all breeds.

Some Clues as to the Origin of the Gordon Setter

One of the earliest books on methods of hunting various types of game was *Livre de la Chasse*. Written during the middle of the 1300's by a world famous sportsman, Gaston de Foix, Vicomte de Bearn, it was a best seller.

The Second Duke of York, imprisoned on political grounds from 1406 to 1413, spent his time on the worthy project of translating this well known book into English. Herein we find the first references to the Spaniel. "Another kind of dog there is that is called falcon-dog or spaniel because it comes from Spain, not withstanding that there are many in other countries.

When they are taught to be couchers they are good for taking partridges and quail with a net . . ."

Far better known is the book first published in Latin by Dr. Johannes Caius, titled *De Canibus Britannicis* (1570). The early English translation of this says, in part, "another sort of Dogges (called Setter) be there, serviceable for fowling, making no noise with foote or tounge whiles they followe the game." By the early 1600's the well informed Gervase Markham had this to say: "There is also another sort of land spannyels, which are called Setters, and they differ nothing from the former, but in instruction or obedience; . . . and when they come upon the haunt of that they hunt: they shall sodainly stop and fall downe upon their bellies, and so leisurely creepe by degrees to the game, till . . . so neere that they cannot press neerer without danger of retriving, then shall your Setter sticke . . ."

Three hundred years later, William Arkwright, a dog writer, wrote that he felt the setting Spaniels originated in Spain, were taken to France and thence to England.

One of the earliest writers to mention our breed as an entity is Rev. B. Symonds. Writing in 1818, he states: ". . . fifty years ago (there were) two distinct tribes,—the black tanned—and the orange or lemon and white."

A portrait of the three Setters done in 1805 by Sydenham Edwards is considered proof positive that, by then, each Setter was a definite entity, and it is the first such painting to be published in a dog book. It shows a white Setter in the foreground, crouched as though on point. Behind it, standing boldly, is a much larger Setter, deep red with white face blaze. In the rear, in a position one might call "backing," is a black and tan Setter. This dog has generous tan markings, curls on the top of its head, a curly coat and not so much as a spot of white. Of special interest is that each dog has big, round, bright yellow eyes!

H.D. Richardson's book, *Dogs: Their Origin and Varieties,* published in 1847, refers to English, Irish and Scotch Setters.

Other writers refer casually to several well established black and tan strains both in England and Scotland. Opinion is that they were a development of careful breeding for color from what once was considered just another marking for the English Setter.

Considerable variation existed amongst these early Gordons. Some are described as small and wiry; others as tall and bony, or coarse and clumsy. Curly, straight, silky and short coats are all mentioned. Hunting style varied as well, from the slow moving to the wide ranging. Regardless, great respect was expressed for the hardiness, willingness to hunt any cover or game bird, and the liking for water and retrieving displayed by Black and Tan Setters.

It is possible that certain qualities were, indeed, color linked, which led to the development of each Setter by color. Certainly cross-breeding of the three varieties took place nonetheless, but this led to better development of

"Two Spaniels in a Landscape," Charles Towne, c. 1780-1850.

Gordon Castle at Fochabers.

each. Not until the Kennel Club was formed and the purity of blood became popular did this practice lessen and the distinctive conformation and style of hunting of each breed became more pronounced.

The Black and Tan Setter at Castle Gordon (1800-1900)

At the time Alexander, 4th Duke of Gordon, was born in 1743 the Scottish Deerhound was the special breed at the Castle. But, by the end of the century the kennel was reduced and by 1825 there were no hounds left.

By then an elderly man, the Duke may have found the rigors of deerstalking on the Scottish moors too much for him. Also, overhunting had sadly reduced the deer population. One can speculate that the Duke turned to Setters and bird hunting as a sport within his capabilities.

Writings of the period which refer to visits to Castle Gordon would indicate that Alexander must have begun raising Setters in earnest between 1800 and 1820. Visitors to the Castle make mention of black and tan dogs, as well as various other colorings such as black and white, black tan and white, or orange and white.

Rumors are quoted in various publications of the times that Gordon Castle had resorted to a cross with a Collie as part of its breeding program. At first this seems an absurd combination, but upon investigation we find that the Collie referred to was black and tan with a gleaming flat coat, beautiful tan markings, drop ears; nothing like what we think of as a Collie today.

Verification of this came in an interview made in the 1940's with Mr. Alex MacLachlan. A native born Scot who by then was living in Missouri, he recollected that all his family were stockmen and gamekeepers on the great estates of Gordon and Richmond. His father was gamekeeper at Richmond. Alex agreed that the black and tan Collie had a part in the development of the Gordon Castle Setter and that the Gordons he knew in Scotland bore little resemblance to the Gordons he saw in the American shows in 1940. He felt that those he remembered were more like the field English Setters.

Other comments reveal that these Scotch Collies were sagacious, docile, and beautiful. The Setter cross was useful to the farmers and shepherds since it produced handsome dogs that could hunt birds as well as herd sheep. There are enough reports of such breedings to give the matter credence. It should be added that these crosses were not confined to Gordon Setters; any setter would do. But, whether such crossbred stock was ever incorporated into the long range breeding program of the Duke is quite another story.

Other Gordon breeders were said to have tried crosses with Bloodhounds, black Pointers, and solid black Setters, and given the times, anything was possible. The breed was still being developed and most

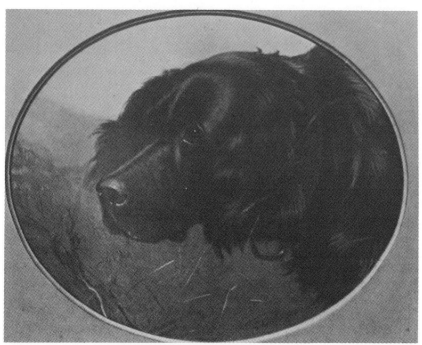

"Old Kent" — painting by George Earl.

Modern English Setters in U.S. which bear remarkable resemblance to Gordon Castle setters as they were in the early 1900's.

owners aimed only for the best possible hunting dog. Experiments must surely have taken place.

At the death of Alexander in 1827 at the age of 84, the 5th Duke of Gordon succeeded him, but survived only until 1836. The title of Duke of Gordon became extinct since he left no heirs, and the property passed to a nephew, the Duke of Richmond.

The kennels had been greatly reduced after the death of Alexander, so by the time the famous dispersal sale was held at Tattersalls in 1836, only eleven dogs were offered. One of the purchasers was the Duke of Richmond who bought a five year old black and white bitch named Juno.

During the next forty years the Castle kennel was built up with excellent working setters, most of which were tricolor.

In 1875 the 6th Duke of Richmond succeeded. The title of Duke of Gordon was restored and he thus became the 6th Duke of Richmond *and* Gordon.

One of the more intriguing puzzles in the history of the Setters at Gordon Castle is how come the 5th and 6th Dukes went blithely on their way, doing their own thing, raising tricolor Setters while at shows, by 1880, Black and Tan classification predominated.

No mention has been made that the Castle kennels showed their dogs so perhaps it was a simple matter of sticking with what they liked.

In 1862 dog show classes had been established for English, Irish, and Black and Tan Setters.

In 1873, "Black and Tan Setter" became the official breed classification by the British Kennel Club. The reason given was that this body felt the Gordon Setter was tricolored, and that many Black and Tan Setters were not related to the Castle strain. Therefore, this classification should be defined for Black and Tans, whether Gordon or not. Obviously, tricolor dogs would not be welcome in a Black and Tan class, and by 1879 they had pretty well been crowded out of the show scene.

In 1890 Vero Shaw in *The Illustrated Book of the Dog* pointed out that a Gordon Setter marked with white would have no chance in the show ring as the judges were very hostile to it.

When the new standard was written by the fledgling Gordon Setter Club of England in 1891, no ruling was made on white except to mention that little was seen of it on show dogs.

After the 6th Duke died in 1903 the kennel was slowly phased out and by 1907 it was closed. The remaining dogs were purchased by Isaac Sharpe. Kennel records do not seem to have survived, possibly destroyed by a fire at the Castle.

One last word on setters at Castle Gordon appears in *The Complete Dog Book* by Dr. William A. Bruette, published in 1925. He speaks of tricolor Setters at the Gordon estates which, while similar in appearance to the old Gordons, were in truth of the Laverack English Setter strain.

Mounted head of "Dandie."

"Grouse and Rock" woodcut, source and date not known. Dogs the property of the Duchess of Bedford (c. 1880).

In 1955 the Castle, perhaps damaged beyond repair, was demolished, leaving only the tower.

All in all, the various residents of Gordon Castle had maintained their own strain of Setters for nearly one hundred years, far longer than anyone else has ever done. This strain at its best was held in high regard as a working Setter, and the bloodlines were widely dispersed.

Important Events in the Gordon Setter World (1850-1930)

Many interesting events took place in the last part of the 1800's which greatly affected the progress of Setters and dogs in general.

The first dog show held in England was at New Castle, in June of 1859. Only Pointers and Setters were exhibited. It was a private affair arranged by a few shooting men to settle an old argument as to which of the dogs in that particular district most closely resembled the ideal conformation of its breed.

Only one class for Setters was provided. In an entry of 36, a Black and Tan named Dandie placed first. At this show the judges alternately showed and judged. Fair enough.

No photographer dashed into the ring to take Dandie's picture, but when he died years later, his owner did mount his head. A photo of this shows him to be somewhat slant eyed, dish faced, and well marked. (It wasn't uncommon to mount famous dogs of those days, and some of them still can be found in the British Museum.)

By 1861 separate classes for each Setter were provided. For show purposes, Gordons were known as Black and Tan Setters.

The first field trial for Setters was held in 1865. Once again this was a small affair. Black and Tans did well, the winner of the first prize was a grandson of Dandie, whose owner showed great imagination and named him Dandy.

As is so often the case in studying the history of dogs, we find that the British established another "first" by creating the Kennel Club of England in 1873. This body quickly began publishing both a stud book and the *English Kennel Gazette*.

Having a registry helped put an end to the bewildering habit of changing a dog's name at will, as well as of duplicating names. However, it was not compulsory to register whole litters, only the individuals the breeder felt were the best.

At last, pedigrees and kennel names were available, as well as information on shows, judges and trials. Standards were accepted by the various breed clubs. All this gave impetus to the growth of raising, showing and field trialing the Setters.

In England, a Gordon Setter Club was formed in 1890 with a handful of members. After much effort this Club held a breed field trial in 1893.

Only five dogs appeared, and since they performed with something less than star quality, the membership was discouraged from trying again.

It is worth noting that although these seemed to be great times for dogs, the mortality rate was very high. No such thing as dog food existed, each breeder made up his own brew. Illnesses and injuries made inroads, especially on puppies. Edward Laverack, of English Setter fame, had this warning in 1872, revealing the depth of the problem: "It is almost a certainty that any young dog who has not had distemper will catch it at an exhibition . . . having lost numbers of very valuable young dogs by sending them to show before over distemper, I am resolved never to do so again until they have safely passed through this dangerous malady."

In 1924 the British Kennel Club saw fit to change the breed classification from Black and Tan Setters to Gordon Setters. The reasons given were that by then all Black and Tans had some blood ties to the Castle Gordon Setters and the breed had become commonly known as Gordon Setters, regardless of markings. (In America, the Kennel Club had changed the name in 1892.)

Encouraged by this move, the British Gordon Setter Club was re-established in 1927. By 1931 the Kennel Club accepted a new breed standard as presented by the club.

In this standard allowance is made for a white spot on the chest, but the smaller the better. Under "Faults" were listed white feet and too much white on the chest.

Since then the British standard has had one more revision though it remains similar to the 1931 version. The change was in the "General Impression" where the reference to a weight bearing hunter was added.

Kennel Profiles 1850-1900

The Gordon Setter was a highly successful breed during these years. Many kennels shared breeding stock with each other, some with Gordon Castle. Dates given are for the kennels.

Rev. T. Pearce (c. 1860-1880)

Owner of the most famous and controversial early setter, Ch. Kent, (pedigree not authenticated), Rev. Pearce purchased this dog and began showing him extensively in 1864. Kent must have been what we call a flashy showman for he won with ease and became all the rage as a stud dog, servicing as many as 60 bitches a year at the height of his popularity. He produced some outstanding stock, but breeders worried because the breed became overbalanced with Kent offspring.

Because of his fame, this dog was subject to considerable criticism, often in print, so that we can read for ourselves the comments that his head

Dr. John H. Salter, D.L., J.P. Member of the Kennel Club 1875-1932. Vice-President 1901-1932. Avid Sportsman, active breeder of Gordons; author; and dog show judge extraordinaire, travelling world wide.

Ch. Rex II; Dr. Salter's homebred. Painting by R. Nightingale 1881. (Collection of Carriage House Antiques)

was too big; he was thick in shoulder, weak in hindquarters. His height was 25½ inches, big for those days. Those who liked him referred to his beautiful black coat, bright tan, white vest, and his intelligent, animated presence.

Among his famous get were Ch. Rex, Young Kent, La Reine, and Silk.

Dr. John Salter (1873-1881)

Ch. Rex, an excellent field dog, was given to Dr. Salter in 1873. A handsome dog, he soon became a popular stud. At this time it was not uncommon for Gordon breeders to use an Irish Setter cross now and then to maintain a faster, lighter type. Dr. Salter was one of those breeders, and through a mating with his Irish Setter, Sal, Rex gave him Rex II, Regent II. Rex II became a well known show winner both in England and Germany, and was a prolific sire.

From 1881 to 1920, Dr. Salter turned his attention to judging shows and field trials both in England and abroad. He was very popular and had many assignments which kept him busy travelling.

Mr. Parson of Taunton (c. 1880-?)

A number of Gordons whose names are well known in America were exported by Mr. Parson. Ch. Beaumont (1883) and a bitch, Ch. Belmont (1885) both of superior quality, were sent to Mr. Morris of New York who named his kennel Beaumont. In 1889 these two dogs and the kennel name were sold to Dr. John Meyer, and subsequently Beaumont ended up with Mr. James Blossom.

Another fine dog from Mr. Parson was Ch. Bob who was bought by Mr. A.A. Moore of Philadelphia.

One has to feel sorry for these dogs, sold and resold as they were. This was the fate of many imports.

Mr. Robert Chapman, Sen., Glenboig; Heather Kennels (1875-1900)

While smaller kennels continued to breed and show quality stock, the Gordon Setter scene was, for the last 25 years of the century, dominated by this kennel. Chapman was a long time breeder of gun dogs for hire maintaining nearly two hundred, of which about sixty were Gordons. All his adult dogs were field trained, including those he showed.

Not overly fond of the heavy type of Gordon he saw at the shows, Chapman set about to develop a more graceful, light weight dog by incorporating Irish Setter blood.

His first famous show dog was Ch. Heather Grouse (1886), regarded as one of the best Gordons of all time. Chapman's dogs were noteworthy for their flat, silky coats, plenty of feathering, excellent tan markings and

24

Ch. Belmont (bitch) considered the best in Britain in 1885. Exported to Beaumont Kennels of Dr. Morris, USA.

GORDON-SETTER. CH. "MARQUIS". T. JACOBS. OWNER.

Ch. Marquis, winner of all championship classes at shows in the early 1880's.

attractive heads. Their critics noted that they were slab sided and needed stronger hindquarters.

Mr. Chapman made it a point to exhibit as many dogs as would account for all the breed prizes, and this tactic made him almost unbeatable. It is said that other breeders became discouraged and gave up showing.

Among the many dogs exported to the United States we find the names of Ch. Heather Crack, Heather Roy, Harold, Lad, Donald, Bee and York.

To Australia went Heather Bloom, Bounce, Bess and Spark.

Norway received the sisters, Heather Bride and Kate, as well as Earl, Norway Prince and Leah.

Still others went to the continent, especially France.

In 1902 a scandal broke which led to Mr. Chapman's suspension from the Kennel Club for ten years. He was said to have falsified a registration (for a Flat Coat) and bribed a clerk. This gave his critics a great chance to cast aspersions on all his pedigrees and the purity of his stock. But, these matters are not to be given too much weight.

After Mr. Chapman was forced to stop breeding, he exported many Gordons to Norway. From there they spread to Denmark where the Rask Strain was well established. Eventually, in the thirties, dogs carrying these bloodlines came to the United States and the Inglehurst Kennels.

Breeding of the Heather Gordons was continued by Chapman's son using the kennel name of Johnstone during the early 1900's. Later he switched to Scottish Terriers and used the Heather name for his outstanding kennel.

David Baillie, Garbet (c. 1888-1910)

Baillie came to the United States in 1888 to manage the Meadowthorpe Kennels in Kentucky, bringing with him many Heather Gordons. Upon the death of his wife, he returned to Scotland and took over management of the Heather Kennel. Baillie was in charge of showing the dogs all over Great Britain and the continent.

In 1897 he started his own Gordon Kennel, later buying most of Chapman's kennel when it closed. He was said to have paid eight pounds apiece for one hundred dogs (all breeds).

Major Cornelius Schilbred of Norway purchased Garbet Vera and this name is often found in Scandinavian pedigrees. Other familiar names are Ch. Garbet Nap, and Crack.

Isaac Sharpe of Keith, in Banffshire; Stylish Kennels (1875-1938)

A fine sportsman, Mr. Sharpe maintained a kennel of up to seven hundred dogs, mostly Pointers and Setters, of which about fifty were

Ch. Heather Lad. Sent to America where he became a big winner.

Ch. Stylish Scorcher. Big winner in the early 1900's.
Dominant sire in the Stylish Kennels.

Gordons. It is hard to imagine a kennel of this magnitude, especially since all the adult dogs were fully field trained and leased to sportsmen.

For twenty years he supplied sporting dogs to King George V when the Royal party visited Balmoral.

Sharpe's kennel was near Gordon Castle and he rented a grouse moor from the Duke of Richmond. When the Castle kennel closed in 1907, Mr. Sharpe bought the last of those dogs.

Very active in showing and field trialing his Gordons, Mr. Sharpe soon made the name Stylish as famous as the Heather name had been. (Much of his basic stock came from the Heather kennel.)

One of his first winners was Stylish Ranger, said to be the best Gordon ever to appear at field trials. He won this Kennel Club Derby in 1901 and the All-Age in 1902. Sharpe sent him to Norway where the dog became an influential stud.

Ch. Stylish Scorcher and his brother S. Barney, direct descendants of Ranger, were whelped in 1922. Scorcher was thought to be the model of a dual type Gordon. He proved to be prepotent, and as a result, headed the Stylish kennel for many years.

Exported to the United States were dogs with these familiar names: Stylish Ben, Saffron, Madame, Stagestruck, among many others.

Like Chapman, Sharpe exported to countries around the world. Given transportation as it must have been in those days, is it not amazing that these dogs ever survived to reach their destinations?

At the onset of World War I Sharpe bought up all the best gun dogs he could from those who were unable to keep them under wartime conditions. He was able to weather it, and remained in business throughout the War.

For many breeders conditions worsened steadily. By 1917 dog shows were prohibited in England. Dog food was rationed and hard to come by. One breeder recalls feeding her dogs boiled fish heads, snails from the garden, home grown carrots and onions, with what biscuit she could get. By her own words, the dogs suffered malnutrition. No doubt the people did as well.

At War's end in 1918 breeding stock was dangerously low and Gordons made a slow recovery. Less than six per year had been registered from 1914-1918.

Fortunately, Sharpe's kennel had managed to hang onto a few good ones as had a few other small kennels and they provided stock for recovery. By 1923 Gordon registrations had risen to a grand total of 54 for the year. This was one of the reasons Mr. Inglee imported Scandinavian dogs in 1920—nothing was available elsewhere.

Mr. Sharpe died in 1938 at an advanced age. Disaster struck the kennel (and thus the breed) at the outbreak of World War II. A large number of the dogs, including all the Gordons, had to be destroyed by order of the Government.

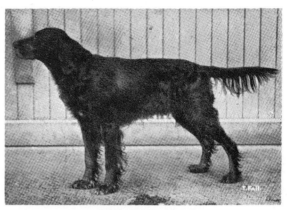

Burnvale Ranger, whelped 1914.

Ch. Crombie King. Date of birth and breeding unknown.

chess of Dendy. One of the all time great bitches. During the 1950's she was winner of 21 CCs, five of them at Owner, Miss I. Hoffman, field trained her and handled her to her full championship. Duchess was also of the Brood Bitch trophy for 1958-59. Breeder, Miss Sadler of Dendy Kennels.

Though the Stylish name continued a few years while Sharpe's daughter, Mrs. A. Ricketts, remained active, most of the Gordons registered by her were purchased, not bred in her kennels.

1920-1940 Recovery

Professor L. Turton Price, Crombie (1920-1933)

This kennel name is more famous for English Setters than for its Gordons. It is said that no kennel ever had better stock of both varieties at one time. Prof. Price began his Gordon kennel with Crombie King (pedigree unknown), purchased in 1920. This dog did well both in the field and at shows and became his foundation stud.

Another great dog, Burnvale Ranger, was purchased in 1921. He traced back to Heather stock as well as that of Gordon Castle. Price added several Stylish bitches to his kennel.

A grandson of Ranger and Crombie King became this kennel's most successful producer, Peter of Crombie. The names of his get familiar to Gordon breeders include Ch. Dawn of Daven, Ch. Valiant Sheila, Ch. Lomond Lion, Bydand Fast Set, Dalnaglar Hector, Major of Ardale, and the famous bitch, Silver Lining, dam of Barnlake Brutus and Downside Bonnie. Silver Lining was later sold to T.E. Davis (Barnlake) as his foundation bitch.

Prof. Price served as the first President of the British Gordon Setter Club (revived in 1927) and was on the standards committee. His death in 1933 brought an end to a kennel which greatly influenced both the English and the Gordon Setter in Britain and America.

William Murray Stewart: Bydand (1920-1938)

Mr. Stewart was largely responsible for reviving the breed club. He served on the standard committee along with Isaac Sharpe, Allenwood Nielson, and Prof. Price.

Dogs produced by the kennel include such notables as Bydand Miss Sport, Painter's Nancy, Bydand Clansman, Ch. Lomond Lion, and Bydand Coronach, Braw Lass, Blue Bonnet, Fast Set, many of which appear in extended American pedigrees.

Coronach was sold to Mrs. Kitty Grey (Frith); Clansman, Braw Lass and Blue Bonnet to Miss Sadler (Dendy); Donald Dhu and Fast Set to Mrs. A.E. Wright (Winsdon), all successful small kennels. From them came Premier of Dendy, Ch. Duchess of Dendy (all time top winning bitch, with 21 CC to her credit) and Ch. Wossen of Winsdon.

Miss E.C. Sharpe, Dalnaglar (1920-1940)

Miss Sharpe had no connection with Isaac Sharpe. Her famous kennel was founded on Crombie stock, and was committed to producing a true dual purpose Gordon. Dalnaglar Hector was an outstanding sire and a good winner at field trials. His son, Ch. Dalnaglar Peer, was a prepotent stud and the name is a familiar one in America primarily through his son, Barnlake Brutus.

Mrs. A.V.C. Bromley, Calbrie (1927-1960)

A firm believer that show dogs can be field trial winners, Mrs. Bromley consistently bred with this in mind, and in her long career she produced a notable strain. Her first Gordon was Ch. Cornwallis Critic, a son of Stylish Scorcher. Mated to Bydand Blackgown, he produced Ch. Bouncer of Calbrie, exported to America. Bouncer had a long career, living to be 16.

After World War II Mrs. Bromley resumed her activities with Gordons and from two litters out of Ch. Duchess of Dendy she obtained some of her finest dogs. Sired by Ch. Game Sassenach, they were Gay Bouncer of Calbrie, Sh. Ch. Gemma of Dendy, Sh. Ch. Salter's Blakke Shadow of Calbrie (6CC) and the outstanding field trial and show winner, Ch. Blackgown of Calbrie.

Mrs. Mildred K. Adams, Salters (1933-   )

Mrs. Adams' long career with Gordons and her talent for writing about them has made hers a familiar name to all fanciers.

Her kennel name is a tribute to her great Uncle, Dr. Salter, well known breeder-judge of the 1880's.

In 1934 Mrs. Adams bred one of the better known Gordons in England and the United States, Ch. Great Scot (of Blakeen). Sold in 1938 to Mrs. Sherman Hoyt, this dog had a successful show career in America during the 1940's, and sired many fine dogs, including six champions. Probably the best known of his offspring is Ch. Blakeen Saegryte, owned by George Thompson of Loch Ridge Kennels.

After World War II, Mrs. Adams returned to the breeding of Gordons and has produced such notables as Sh. Ch. Game Sassenach, Sh. Ch. Salters Adam Gordon, and Sh. Ch. Salters Black Tulip of Calbrie.

In 1967 under the aegis of the Gordon Setter Association Mrs. Adams published her splendid monograph, *The Story of the Gordon Setter,* which has been helpful in providing information for this chapter.

Mrs. M.M.C. Rowe, Cairlie (1940-   )

Cairlie has been a strong and successful supporter of Gordons since the end of the War. From her foundation bitch, Canny Lass of Dendy, Mrs.

Sh. Ch. Yodel of the Speygrounds (show 1958). Bred by Mrs. F. Van Dam (Holland).

Thompson

Jack, Judy and Jill of Cromlix, breeder, J. MacDonald. Owner, Lady Aukland. All dogs with field trial placements. (c. 1940).

Fall

Field Trial Champion Rowney of Crafnant, w. 1950. Winner of one CC, six Reserves, almost became the Dual Ch. for which the breed is still waiting. The third of seven Gordons to become Field Trial Champions since Stylish Ranger (early 1900's).

Rowe obtained the famous producer, Ch. Dignity of Cairlie, founder of a long line of grand bitches. Among them, Ch. Elegance of Cairlie, Ch. Gretel of C., Ch. Pride of C. and more recently, Quality, Unity, Vanity, Xella, Zet and Cannie Lass, all carrying her kennel name. Mrs. Rowe's accomplishment of producing eleven show champions is a record.

Mention must be made of the kennels which concentrated on breeding Gordons for hunting. While the British Gordon Setter Club does not sponsor breed field trials, there are available various gun dog trials, open to all Setters.

As it is in America, smaller dogs are favored, and bloodlines are shared among those breeders interested only in hunting or trials.

Again, as it is in America, several kennels manage to straddle the fence and produce good field dogs which can be shown with success. Among them we find the names

Alderberry; Major and Mrs. Harvey-Bathurst

Fearn; Mrs. E.J. Brooke Buist (well known field trial judge)

Wassetfell; E.B.D. Johnson

Biggin; Mr. J.T. Flowers

Cromlix; Lady Auckland

Boyndie; Miss I. MacIntosh
        (F.T. Ch. Boyndie Ruadh)

Crafnant; Mr. George Burgess
            (F.T. Ch. Rowney of Crafnant)

Mr. E.H. Waide

F.T. Ch. Highdown Nadine, bred by Capt. Rich but taken to her title by Mr. Bailey in 1950, was the first Gordon to win a F.T. title since Stylish Scorcher.

The Gordon Setter in the United Kingdom 1960-1982 is covered in Chapter 4.

2

The Breed
Comes to America

1600-1900

THE FIRST SETTLERS to land on American shores must have been surprised to find no dogs like the ones they left behind nor any large farm animals or agriculture.

The only domesticated animal maintained by the eastern Indians was the dog, but it was given solely a utilitarian role. Shown in early drawings, this dog resembled most a coyote or spitz type. It earned its keep by pulling sleds; carrying loads; helping to round up game such as bear, deer and moose for the kill; acting as clean-up squads around the camps; and as watch dogs.

Other small dogs, often with white long coats, were kept for use in rituals, for hair for weaving or, in some instances, for food.

References to dogs belonging to the settlers are meager. The Mayflower log lists as cargo one spaniel and one mastiff. One man's diary does refer to these two as a "great Mastiffe bitch and a Spannell" and he indicates they accompanied their owners in their roamings.

By 1635, however, from somewhere came plenty of dogs as the Village of Salem had to pass a dog ordinance. There is no indication that the native Indian dogs were ever adopted by the Pilgrims, which is rather surprising.

The Colony of Massachusetts Bay authorized each town to purchase Wolf hounds to use against the wolves in 1648 and by 1656 native bred Mastiffs were available for use with the Militia. By the next century individuals had become prosperous land owners and their diaries contain comments about packs of hounds. Hunting for sport and recreation was not acceptable in the Puritan settlements but in the southern colonies where life was pursued more graciously it was a big part of each day's activity. Surely Spaniels and Setters must have made their way to this area—though once again no specific references are found.

Because of the ever increasing emigration from Great Britain of well to do merchants, it seems reasonable to assume that the development of Setters in America must have been based on the dogs that these people brought with them, and must have followed along the same lines as did the development of the dogs in the Old Country. But, as in Great Britain, our country was embroiled in a constant battle with some country somewhere. Trying to survive in America and develop new areas occupied the attention of these early settlers and it is doubtful if they spent much time worrying about pedigrees and breeds of dogs.

Peace and prosperity in America reflected good times in Great Britain under Queen Victoria. More and more attention was paid to the sport of hunting birds with dogs except in the last strongholds of the Puritans where any recreation was considered a sinful waste of time.

Good dogs of specific breeds with British Kennel Club registration numbers became increasingly popular and while there was not as yet a registration body in America, records were kept and efforts made to sustain breed quality.

The first well documented importation of dogs from Gordon Castle is dated 1842 when George Blunt of New York bought Rake and Rachel. A photo of a drawing of Rake by the famous A. Pope shows a very curly dog, white with black saddle. He was said to have tan markings as well. Rachel, who was given to Daniel Webster, was black and tan only. Mr. Blunt's grandson wrote Freeman Lloyd in 1931 to say that until 1906 they and Webster raised hunting dogs descended directly from these two imports.

The Civil War (1861-1865) followed by twelve years of Reconstruction of the South wreaked havoc on the American economy and lifestyle. Not until the late 1870's was life normal enough to encourage resumption of leisure sports, with emphasis on sporting dogs.

The earliest registration body was National American Kennel Club Stud Book, published in St. Louis, Mo. 1879. The first Gordon Setter listed was Bang—owner J. W. White; whelped Dec. 1875, by Jerome Marble's (later Copeland's) imported Shot (E.1630) x White's Nell by Stockton's imported Dash White's Fly by Belmont's imported Robin. The second dog was Baron—bred by Belmont from his brace imported from Lord Rothschild's kennels in England. Baron had been sold to Mr. Isaac Bingham of Galveston, Texas. The third dog was Ben—bred by the Baltimore Kennel Club, July 1874, by Jenkins' imported Hero (by Idstone's Kent) x Cassard's Maggie No. 903. Ben was a big winner at the first shows.

Bee (F) in background, Grouse (D) imported about 1880 from
U.K. to America. Both were extremely successful show dogs.

Ch. Florence H. Photo taken in 1905 carries the notation "Mrs. F. Howe, Jr's cele-
brated setter, a quality Gordon showing great character and eminently typical."

In 1886 this registry was merged into what is now the American Kennel Club.

One of the first prominent Americans to espouse the cause of the native Gordon Setter was Harry Malcolm of Maryland. A great sportsman and dog man, he had a sizable kennel where he bred Black and Tan Setters strictly for hunting. Unquestionably his efforts to promote the breed contributed to its success during the last of the 1800's.

Malcolm was a great believer in clubs, formed a number of them including the first Gordon Setter Club of America (sometimes referred to as the American Gordon Setter Club). He served as first President. This club was one of the charter members of the newly formed American Kennel Club.

In 1891 The Gordon Setter Club wrote the first breed standard based in part on one written by Mr. Malcolm at an earlier date. It left lasting improvements in judging which had, up to this time, been carried on without specific guidelines.

The first dog show recorded was held at Chicago in 1874 and had a small entry of 21 sporting dogs. Competitive placings were not given; judges merely commented on the dogs. A pair of black and steel setters won highest praise. Too bad our curiosity as to what they looked like will never be satisfied.

The first show with placements and awards was held in the fall of 1874 at Mineola, N.Y. Classes were offered for Irish Setters, Gordon Setters, Setters of Any Breed, and Pointers. No best in show was awarded.

From this modest start shows took off and by 1877 the first Westminster Kennel Club show was held in New York City with entries totalling 1194. This was a three day show with 45 breeds represented. Only nine sporting breeds; the three Setters, two Pointers (any weight, or over 50 pounds), Chesapeakes, Irish Water Spaniels, Retrieving Spaniels other than pure Irish, Cocker Spaniels, Field Spaniels of Any Other Breed. Breed totals of interest were: 145 English Setters, 171 Irish and 79 Gordons, (both Native and Imported listings for all three).

By today's standards trophies were elegant: $150 silver cups; bamboo flyrods; pearl handled 32 revolver; silver dog collar.

As interest in dog shows increased so did the formation of clubs to promote a special breed. The importation of top quality Gordons from Great Britain reached a peak during the last of the 1800's. Such clubs as Toledo, Quaker City, St. Louis, Baltimore and Westminster all had Gordons.

The list of noteworthy imports included such names as Grouse, Bee, Blossom, Beaumont, Bellmont, Heather Bee and Heather Roy, Heather Lad, Duke of Edgeworth, all of which did consistent winning. Competition was keen, money no object and the victim was the native Gordon Setter and its supporters who could not win against such strong competition.

Finally, in 1892 the American Kennel Club officially changed the name of the breed from Black and Tan Setter to Gordon Setter. This was 25 years before the British Kennel Club followed suit.

Many prominent citizens of those days became fanciers of the Gordon Setters: doctors, businessmen, bankers, all importing the best: i.e., August Belmont; Dr. J. S. Niven of London, Onatrio; Dr. S. G. Dixon of Philadelphia; James Blossom, President of the Gordon Setter Club; C. Cass Hendee, famous wildlife artist of the times, owner of the Highland Kennels, the only one to last into the 1940's; J. B. Vandergrift and William Allison of Pittsburgh; Mr. and Mrs. B. W. Andrews (the "A" Kennels).

The first recorded field trial took place at Memphis, Tenn. in 1874. Dogs were placed by a system of points: nose, 30; pace and style, 20; breaking, 15; and so on. Nearly all the entries were listed merely as Setters.

In 1893 and 1894 trials were held by the Gordon Setter Club but poor support and mediocre performance by the dogs ended this endeavor. How surprising it is to find that the British Gordon Setter Club also had their first trial in 1893 with the same lack of support.

As interest grew in the hunting opportunities of the sparsely populated South and West where vast flat acreage and abundant native gamebirds existed, more and more sportsmen became intrigued with field trials in these areas. Truly an American development, these trials soon became all the rage. Professional dog breeders, trainers and handlers got busy turning out dogs suitable for the warm weather, the three hour heats. Speed and stamina were the two most important elements. The Gordon and the Irish soon vanished from the field trial scene, totally unfitted for this activity. We can be grateful.

The English Pointer developed rapidly as the perfect field trial dog, a position it has held to this day.

For a few years the English Setter, often a crossbred, put up a good show but it lost out numerically as well as in performance. Strains of the English Setter bred for field trials became a travesty of a true breed, and the show and field strains were soon sharply divided. How fortunate it is that no one cared to do this to the Gordon or Irish.

At the same time an end was put to the business of market hunting. Alarmed at the rapid eradication of one species after another of game birds, the Government began its conservation efforts. The hunting style of Americans changed and field trial-bred Pointers and English Setters became all the rage even for personal gun dogs. By the early 1900's only a handful of Gordons and Irish were shown at the Garden and most of the Gordon kennels were closed.

The business climate of America centered around New York City and Wall Street and was a "Boom and Bust" affair. The Panic of 1893 bankrupted over 15,000 Banks and businesses in the East. Not long after, in 1907 the Stock Market crashed; hundreds of businesses failed in the wake

1914

Black Beauty A, owner Ralph Mace. An American bred, typical of Gordons of the period about 1912. Great-granddaughter of Florence H.

Charles T. Inglee, the founder
e modern US Gordon Setter.

Mr. Inglee's first Danish import and stellar show dog and producer, Ch. Inglehurst Joker.
(This picture is also identified as Ch. Inglehurst Pollyanna. It is of interest regardless of who it is).

of the collapse of the Knickerbocker Trust Company. Since a majority of Gordon Setter exhibitors were persons of wealth and prominence it is most likely that many of them suffered financial reverses which ended their involvement with the breed. This would help account for the puzzling abruptness with which the appearance of Gordons at dog shows ended.

From 1910 until 1920 there was little show activity for Gordons. Though still found as hunting dogs and family pets, the tally for show champions between 1884 and 1918 stood at a meager 60—most of them made before 1900. World War I further reduced the dog population and show activity. Not until 1920 were Americans in good enough shape financially to encourage raising and showing purebred dogs once more.

Charles T. Inglee who had a lifelong involvement with Setters as hunting and show dogs set about reviving the Gordon Setter about 1920. At first he attempted to locate enough good specimens in America.

He found two on Long Island, one of which became his first Gordon show champion. This was Governor Edwards by imported Stylish Ben out of Am. & Can. Ch. Trampus Shannon, a popular winner of the time.

Not finding enough stock in America, Mr. Inglee had to turn to imports. Little was available from Great Britain so he chose to go to Norway, Denmark and Sweden where the hunting Gordon was of good type and readily available. Inglee liked their strong, rather racy build, their dark coloring and their hunting ability. These dogs had the added virtue of stemming from a combination of British and Scandinavian bloodlines so that they blended well with the dogs Mr. Inglee already had.

His first import to carry the Inglehurst name was Joker, born in 1920 and sired by Duke Rask out of Cora of Brobygaard. Others soon followed: Petra (B) Soeraegen's Campan x Hera; Inglehurst Lunny (B) Pan x Stjerne; and Inglehurst Gieb (D) Duke Rask x Hera. All became American show champions.

Joker proved to be the most valuable Gordon in the Inglehurst kennel which soon numbered about 40 of the breed. In 1922 Joker finished his show championship with three five point wins in eight days. He was shown as a special and had a most successful career, especially considering he was about the first Gordon to appear in the ring consistently since the turn of the century.

Mr. Inglee's records attribute to Joker 78 litters, more than 300 puppies and 20 show champions, a record not equalled for another twenty years. His offspring were at home in the field or in the show ring.

Described by Hugh McLaughlin, a contemporary of Inglee's, Joker was not over 25" with a square muzzle, high forehead, deep chest, good bone and strong, straight tail. He was a splendid hunter and an imperious show dog.

Ch. Petra produced nine of Joker's show champions. One of the better known was Ch. Inglehurst Joker, Jr., owned by Donald Fordyce. This was a great big dog, splendid conformation, put together tight as a drum. An elegant bird dog, with an impulsive, dominating personality, he, too, was an excellent producer. Few dogs were bred during these years so that this fine dog had limited opportunities.

Another Joker x Petra winner, born in 1928, was Am. and Can. Ch. Leitchvale Marksman, the second to hold both titles, also said to have won a Best in Show, though details are lacking.

Inglehurst Marie (Joker x Petra) finished in 1928. Mr. Inglee kept her and showed her extensively. Her record of 32 wins, 25 Best of Breeds, 2 Sporting Group first, 6 seconds, and one fourth place is a fine record for any Gordon bitch then or now.

Other names like Ch. Inglehurst Gillette, Guardsman, Poppy, Scout, Ch. Marcella's Bud and Ch. Marcella's Joe, pop up in pedigrees from the kennels active at that time. In turn, they are found back of today's Gordons.

Fortunately for us, Mr. Inglee kept meticulous records of his dogs. Even more fortunately, his ledgers containing this information have been carefully preserved by Charles Meyer, current dog show judge who, as a young lad, helped Mr. Inglee show his dogs. In his beautiful handwriting, Mr. Inglee included much information on the litters and pups. Each litter was numbered. When he closed the book in 1935 it was with his 300th litter and a total of 40 show champion Gordon Setters.

During these years Mr. Inglee had maintained training grounds in North Carolina where he sent all his young dogs in the winter for field work.

Probably the most influential person in the breed, owner of one of the most influential dogs, it is fitting that Inglee had Ch. Inglehurst Joker mounted when the dog died at age of 12. Joker can now be seen at the Peabody Museum in New Haven, Conn.

Aside from the dogs, Mr. Inglee was very club oriented and in 1924 he and a few friends organized the new Gordon Setter Club of America which soon became a member of the American Kennel Club. The founders were Frank Burke, Donald Fordyce, Howard Huntington, William Cary Duncan, James Neville, and Hugh McLaughlin. Four of these officers served until after 1940.

Many kennels owed their start to dogs from the Inglehurst strain.

One of the earliest was the Svane Kennels owned by Dr. A. P. Evans. His interests lay entirely with hunting and field trials where he was eminently successful. He also served as Field Trial Chairman for the new Gordon Setter Club.

His most famous two field trial winners were bitches, mother and daughter, Svane June and Svane June's Baby, whose careers are discussed in some detail in the Field Trial chapter.

Others were Svane Llockie, Svane Judy, Svane Nell, Svane Black Douglas.

Ch. Petra. First Danish bitch imported by Mr. Inglee; dam of 9 champions.

Rare photo taken at N. Westchester Kennel Club show at Katonah, N.Y. June 1940. All the Gordon Setter bigwigs were there. Left to right: Cornelius McGlynn, Dr. Evans, William Howell, Donald Fordyce, Hugh McLaughlin, and Mr. Briggs.

Though the trials sponsored by the Gordon Setter Club were not especially successful, Gordons continued to compete in All Pointing Breed Trials with a fair share of placements. Nearly all these dogs came from Inglehurst stock. On the West Coast Dr. Rixford whose estate was in Stockton, Ca. established a winning kennel of dual Gordons based on Ch. Rex of Rixford (Ch. Inglehurst Gunnar x Ch. Inglehurst Joy). John Taafe in San Rafael, whose kennel name was Marinero, was also active in both field and show. Later on both Ch. Great Scot of Blakeen and Ch. E.E.G's Scotia Lancer were added to this kennel.

These bloodlines continued in California through the Rhythm Kennels of Alec Laurence, of the Bay area. Today they can be found back of such active field trial breeders as Springset and St. Andrew's, as discussed in the Field Trial chapter.

Donald Fordyce, for many years Secretary of the American Kennel Club, gave full support to the Gordon Setter Club and the breed and served in various capacities from 1924 until his death in 1952. His kennel name of Clonmellerslie is found on winning dogs of the 30's. His best dog was Ch. Inglehurst Joker, Jr. Another nice one was the lovely bitch used to illustrate the GSCA standard, Ch. Clonmellerslie Royal Flush.

William Cary Duncan, best known for his 22 years as Gazette breed columnist, kennel Editor of *Outdoor Life,* and as a Director of the American Kennel Club, raised show Gordons under the kennel name of Thistlerock.

Another kennel based on Inglehurst was that of Prof. James Munn whose Gregorach Kennels were active from the late 20's well into the 1940's. One of the earliest winners was a male, Ch. Ginger (Inglehurst Gillette x Inglehurst Minnie Ha Ha) who won many groups and placements. His picture represented the breed in one of the earlier American Kennel Club standards books.

Ginger produced 7 champions, among the best known being Ch. Gregorach Fast x Prof. Munn's English import, Stylish Madame. Fast, along with several kennel mates, was sold to Jake and Dottie Poisker in the mid 40's as foundation for their famous Windy Hills Kennel in Pennsylvania.

Marcella Kennels (James Powell and Frank Morgan) produced Ch. Marcella's Bud (Ch. Inglehurst Joker x Marcella Belle). His best known son was Ch. Larrabee's Pietro, out of Stylish Fannie. Not an import, as the name would imply, Fannie was—you guessed it—mostly Inglehurst stock.

Mr. A. N. Nichter, Avalon Kennels, Canal Fulton, Ohio, had joined the ranks of Gordon breeders in 1930. About 1934 he imported from England the bitch, Dochfour Beauty (Eng. Ch. Stylish Scorcher x Dorius). When she was bred to Ch. Larrabee's Pietro, they produced a number of winning Gordons, the best being Ch. Prince of Avalon, owned by the Royal Hall Kennels of California.

Prince was shown extensively in 1941. His owner, Pat Hall, took him on a grand tour of 9,700 miles and 9 shows! His wins included group 3 at St. Petersburg, Fla. and Richmond, Indiana; group 2 at Clearwater, Fla. and group first and Best American Bred in Show at Miami, a stellar win for a Gordon.

Other Pietro x Beauty stars were Ch. Buck Lou of Avalon and Ch. Larrabee's Avalon Beauty, Mrs. Girardot's famous bitch.

Gordon Setter breeders of this era made up in loyalty what they lacked in numbers. Several made such significant contributions to the breed affecting the whole future that a more detailed account of their efforts is in order.

Charles and Edna Girardot began their involvement with Gordons in the early 30's. Their large kennel was located in Scotia, New York, just outside of Schenectady. For kennel names they used EEG's, also Scotia, and sometimes both. Their first champion bitch was Ch. Larrabee's Avalon Beauty (c. 1934).

Always an active G.S.C.A. member, Mrs. Girardot recalls that when she first set about planning her Gordon breedings she obtained a pedigree of every one registered with the AKC between 1928-1938. She began by tracing Beauty's pedigree and became so intrigued with the work that she went on to follow Beauty's family back to the Gordon Castle strain—a huge undertaking. The worth of this project then and now cannot be overstated.

This fascinating study was first presented in the 1939 Gordon Setter Club Yearbook—the one and only ever published until 1963. This informative, nicely put together little book was edited by Mr. J. E. Bentinck-Smith; other contributors included Mrs. J. E. Larrabee; Dr. Henry Rixford; a French breeder by name of Busnell-Vallee; and Richard Cooper, the handler, on grooming dogs for show.

Mrs. Girardot chose Ch. Lancer of Serlway to be the sire of her first litter from Beauty. From this litter came one of the best known Gordons, Ch. EEG's Scotia Nodrog Rettes, foundation stud for Afternod Kennels, and for whom the kennel was named.

Some of the prominent dogs coming from Girardot's kennels during the 40's were EEG's Old Faithful Lass, foundation bitch for the Milestone Kennels; Ch. Scotia Darling; Ch. EEG's Scotia Lancer (Ch. Lancer of Serlway x Scotia Moor Queen). This dog was top Gordon in 1946 with 30 Best of Breeds and four group placings.

Another winner was Ch. Scotia Lancer's Son (Ch. EEG's Scotia Lancer x Ch. Loch Ridge Stylish Lady) owned by the Browers. Owner-handled he won Best of Breed at Westminster in 1949 and 1950. His brother, Ch. EEG's Scotia Atom Bomb, served as stud dog for the kennel along with Ch. Larrabee's Jock (Marcella's Bud x Dochfour Beauty).

When Gordon Setter Club Field Trials began, Edna was an active

44

supporter of the effort handling her own dog, Deacon Dawson, a big going hard hunting contender.

By 1948 poor health forced the Girardots to greatly reduce their kennel activities. By then they had a huge multi-breed spread plus a boarding kennel, kennel shop and grooming service.

Mrs. Girardot was made an Honorary Member of the Gordon Setter Club during the early 50's. As of 1981 she was living in Florida, still active with her famous Pomeranians.

About 1936 Dr. Claude Searle of Serlway Kennels in Chicago began his short but influential career as a Gordon breeder by importing two British adult specimens, both of which became successful show dogs and producers.

The male with a bitch's name, Downside Bonnie of Serlway, caused endless confusion during his years as an active show dog because of it. He was a lovely dog, sired by Bydand Coronach x Silver Lining, imported from Miss D. Purdey.

Valiant Nutmeg of Serlway (Valiant Captain x Valiant Meg) was imported in whelp to Dalnaglar Hector (Peter of Crombie x Belle of Crombie). Her breeder was Mrs. E. M. R. Reoch.

These two dogs carried the best bloodlines that Great Britain had to offer and as a result, their produce was excellent. Many Serlway dogs went as foundation stock for kennels in the East.

Nutmeg was the first bitch in Gordon Setter history to be the dam of 12 show champions. All carried the Serlway kennel name except for one, Ch. Valiant Captain of Eastcourt.

Bonnie produced eight show champions in America. After he had completed his show championship (handled by Dick Cooper) in the Chicago area, the dog was sold to George Van Ostoff of Eastcourt Kennels in New York State. Bonnie was campaigned extensively on the East Coast from 1938 to 1942 and set quite a record: Best of Breed, Westminster 1939-40-41 (always a prestigious win). In 1940 he had 34 Best of Breeds and 12 group firsts. In 1941 he garnered 17 Best of Breeds and ended his career with a total of 27 group placements. This was the best record since that set by Ch. Inglehurst Joker in the 1920's.

The most important producers from this kennel were:

1) Ch. Brutus of Serlway (Ch. Barnlake Brutus of Salmagundi x Nutmeg) who was the sire of the second Field Trial champion in America, Ebony Sultan. The dam was Ch. Audley of Serlway (Ch. Downside Bonnie of Serlway x Nutmeg).

2) Ch. Black Rogue of Serlway (Ch. Downside Bonnie x Ch. Meg of Serlway) bred to Ch. Rita of Avalon sired Loch Ridge Major Rogue. In turn, Major Rogue when bred to Ch. Blakeen Saegyte produced three important dogs: Loch Ridge Reckless Lady, Loch Ridge Rogue's Ace II and Ch. Loch Ridge Rogue's Don.

Ch. Downside Bonnie of Serlway with Dick Cooper.

Ch. Barnlake Brutus of Salmagundi.

3) Ch. Kent of Serlway bred to Halenfred Cinderella sired Ch. Halenfred Bright Deil, top Gordon of the early 1950's.

4) Ch. Lancer of Serlway (Bonnie x Nutmeg), bred to Ch. Larrabee's Avalon Beauty, sired Ch. EEG's Scotia Nodrog Rettes.

5) Loch Ridge Vagabond King (Ch. Downside Bonnie of Serlway x Ch. Loch Ridge Liza Jane) sired four champions, the most important of which was Ch. Heslop's Stylish Lad. Through Lad's granddaughter Fld. Ch. Denida's Bonnie Velvet, the breed got Can. & Am. Ch. and Fld. Ch. Chance's National Velvet, CD, and Ch. Bonnie's Mac's MacGeowls, CD, sire of two Dual Champions and six show champions.

Loch Ridge Major Rogue was the sire of Canada's first and only dual champion, Vagabond Jean of Glentanar, and Vagabond King was one of her grandsires.

This Serlway strain left a lasting contribution to the Gordon Setter, especially strengthening the dual purpose qualities.

1936-1940: War Clouds Form

Fearing the results of the War they now perceived to be inevitable, British Gordon Setter breeders parted with their best dogs, sending them to America in the hope that this way these bloodlines could be continued. Their experiences during World War I made them panicky. Americans thus had access to superb breeding stock. Combined with each other and the good dogs already in the US, these imports had a lasting impact on the breed and changed it from the original Inglehurst type.

One of the imports which left a strong imprint was Barnlake Brutus of Salmagundi (Ch. Dalnaglar Peer x Silver Lining). Brought here in 1936 by Mrs. J. W. Griess of Salmagundi Poodle fame, Brutus was shown to his title by Percy Roberts, later the well known judge.

Ch. Valiant Nutmeg of Serlway had four champions sired by Brutus, all carrying the "of Serlway" name: Brutus, Spirit, Janet and Lorna.

Ch. Larrabee's Cricket had eight champions from Brutus which constituted the foundation stock for the Heslop Kennels.

Also in 1936 Mrs. Sherman Hoyt became an active Gordon Setter exhibitor under her kennel name of Blakeen. She had purchased Eng. and Am. Ch. Bouncer of Calbrie (Bounder of Serlway x Bydand Black Gown) from his American owner, and her next acquisition was Blakeen Belle (Ch. Clonmellerslie Joker x Gunman's Moll), an American bred bitch. Later she imported Eng. Sh. Ch. Great Scot of Blakeen and Stylish Stagestruck of Blakeen.

With the advent of WW II Mrs. Hoyt ceased raising Gordons. A number of her best dogs went to George Thompson of Baltimore whose Loch Ridge Kennels soon became a leader.

With so many kennels closing up shop, the number of active Gordon

Ch. Great Scot of Blakeen.

Ch. EEG's Scotia Lancer (w. 1941).

breeders was reduced to a handful. Those that were left worked together and, by sharing bloodlines and supporting various shows, they kept the breed afloat.

The Heslop Gordon Setter Kennels (1936-1955)—George and Myrtle Heslop, Jonesville, New York.

Mr. Heslop was born in Scotland where he and his family operated a horse farm, raising and training Irish Hunters. They also bred various hunting dogs, mostly terriers. The principles of livestock breeding were instilled, serving George well when he started raising Gordons in the U.S.

In the early 1920's at the age of 19, George came to the United States alone. He went to work for General Electric in Schenectady, and stayed with them until retirement.

After his marriage to Myrtle in the 30's, raising Gordons became their hobby. They chose this breed because it was ideally suited to hunt the grouse and woodcock cover of that part of New York State.

In 1936 Heslops bought their first show prospect. Larrabee's Cricket (Ch. Larrabee's Avalon Boy x Inglehurst Lady Belle) was linebred: Ch. Larrabee's Pietro, the sire of Avalon Boy, was a brother of Lady Belle.

Cricket turned out to be a great success, finishing her championship handily.

In 1938 Heslops purchased imported Tarras of Shawk (Ch. Stylish Scorcher x Trix of Shawk).

Their last import, made in 1939, was Highland Queen of Tweedvale (Ch. Lomond Lion x Blackberry of Tweedvale).

For Cricket's first litter George chose Ch. Barnlake Brutus, who was linebred on the Crombie strain, and a half brother of Downside Bonnie.

Born in April 1939, Cricket's litter proved to be everything the Heslops had hoped for. Not in a hurry to sell these ten pups, George kept a number of them, and as they matured and showed promise, he sold them to other breeders. As a result their influence became far reaching.

The Heslops kept two famous males, Courageous and Crusader, the top winners and producers of this period.

Three lovely bitches, Heather Lassie, Merry Maid, and Loch Ridge Liza Jane, produced quality pups however they were bred. Lassie went to Phil Canfield (Nodak Kennels), Merry Maid to Tirvelda Kennels, later to Parkwood, and Liza Jane went to George Thompson.

Courageous finished with a group four when he was 19 months old. Merry Maid and Crusader were slightly over two when they finished.

From a litter born in April 1943 (Crusader x Highland Queen) came Ch. Heslop's Burnvale Duchess. She was a big, sturdy bitch. When bred to Courageous, she produced excellent pups, so good, in fact, that Heslops repeated the breeding several times. All in all Duchess had 13 champions.

The most influential members of this tribe were: Ch. Heslop's Burnvale Bonnie, CD, foundation bitch for Gordon Hill Kennels of Muriel

Ch. Heslop's Courageous with breeder-
handler George Heslop. 1948.

Miriam Steyer Mincieli with her Ch. Milestone Monarch as a young dog.

Clement; Champions Heslop's Stylish Charm II and Heslop's Burnvale Piper (Osborne); Ch. Heslop's Burnvale Laird (Fletcher). Five more provided foundation stock for the Sangerfield Kennels of Margaret Sanger and Jean Look, and Janet produced 7 champions for the Windy Hill Kennels (Poisker).

Highland Queen had one more litter before she was stolen, this one sired by Loch Ridge Vagabond King (Ch. Downside Bonnie x Ch. Loch Ridge Liza Jane).

From this litter came Ch. Heslop's Stylish Lad, Ch. Heslop's Stylish Beauty (Sanger) and Stylish Queen. Bred back to Courageous, Queen produced the all-time winning bitch, Ch. Heslop's Dorvius (Thompson).

In the late 40's Myrtle's health failed and kennel activities were slowly phased out. By then they had produced 29 champions. George had served as a Gordon Setter Club Director, and as its President in 1947 and 48, and had become an AKC judge. They were chosen to be Honorary Members of the club.

In the mid 1950's, a dog they had sold to Americans was taken to England where he became integrated into their bloodlines. This was Ch. Heslop's Burnvale Dash (Matson' Robin x Heslop's Lucious Pixie), the first and only American show champion Gordon ever bred from in Great Britain.

The Heslops were a hospitable couple who liked nothing better than to have a house full of Gordon Setter people, which they often did. They attended all the shows and field trials they could until the death of George in 1955. Myrtle died in 1980.

Loch Ridge Kennels (1940-1955—George Thompson, Baltimore, Md.

When Mr. Thompson decided to add Gordon Setters to his kennel, he was the most fortunate of mortals. Never had so many topflight dogs been available for sale or at stud.

He was quick to recognize them and as a result, his kennel was successful from the first. He hired the best handlers, showed as much as possible during those lean years and planned his breeding program with great care. He, George Heslop and Mrs. Girardot exchanged breeding stock and, no doubt, many discussions on the breed which aided them all.

He bought one of the Brutus-Cricket bitch pups, named her Loch Ridge Liza Jane and finished her show title when she was two. Bred to Downside Bonnie, she produced Ch. Loch Ridge Dalnaglar Jane (Eldredge) and Loch Ridge Vagabond King.

From Ch. Rita of Avalon, CD, bred to Ch. Black Rogue of Serlway, Mr. Thompson got another of his foundation studs, Loch Ridge Major Rogue.

When Mrs. Hoyt discontinued her Gordon kennel, Thompson

obtained Ch. Blakeen Talisman (Ch. Bouncer O'Calbrie O'Marlu x Ch. Stylish Stagestruck of Blakeen). Talisman was his main stud. This dog was Best of Breed at the Garden and the GSCA Specialty in 1946. He sired ten champions.

Thompson's special pride, however, was Ch. Blakeen Saegryte (Ch. Great Scot of Blakeen x Blakeen Belle), 1940. He bought her as a young dog and by age of three years she was on a winning streak. In a matter of months she had frequent Bests of Breed and four group placements in a row. In the spring of 1944 Saegryte was hit by a car in a freak accident. She survived but was not again showable. This was a real loss to the breed as she was on her way to big things.

By good fortune Saegryte turned out to be an excellent producer. She was the dam of seven champions. One, sired by Ch. Black Rogue of Serlway, was Ch. Loch Ridge Rogue's Don. The other six were sired by Ch. Blakeen Talisman: Loch Ridge Saegryte's Judy, Loch Ridge Winsome Lass, Talisman's Chip, Major Talisman, Tally's Rip, and Dual Ch. Loch Ridge Saegryte's Tibby.

Thompson sent a number of Gordons to California where the breed was rare. Major Talisman went to Firmin Flohr (Dunvegan Kennels) while Winsome Lass and Rogue's Don went to Porter Washington (Briarcliff Kennels).

Major Rogue went to the Glentanar Kennels of James Forbes in Saskatoon. He sired the first and only Canadian Dual Champion, Vagabond Jean of Glentanar.

Before Rogue left he had sired Ch. Wilson's Corrie, out of Ch. Loch Ridge Victoria. Corrie was foundation bitch for the Afternod Kennels.

Eng. and Am. Ch. Great Scot of Blakeen, by then in Mr. Thompson's kennel, sired six champions. Ch. Milestone Monarch out of Loch Ridge Reckless Lady became the foundation stud for the Milestone Kennels of Miriam Steyer Mincielli. Others were Ch. Vale of Tirvelda (Eldredge, later Afternod), out of Ch. Heslop's Merry Maid; Heslop's Burnvale Scot, brother of Vale, sire of six champions including Ch. Thurston's Scot who won Best American Bred in Show, the first Gordon to do so since the 1930's.

George Thompson's good luck continued with his purchase of Heslop's Dorvius (Courageous x Heslop's Burnvale Queen). This was a large, heavy coated bitch who loved to show. Handled by Tom Gately, she finished in 1946 and went on to rack up a show record not yet equalled by a Gordon bitch: 34 Bests of Breed, 3 Best Opposites, two group first, five group second, 7 group third, and five fourth places.

Mr. Thompson served as Secretary-Treasurer, then Director, and finally in 1949-1950 as President of the Gordon Setter Club of America. He turned his attention to being an AKC judge and phased out his Gordon activities in the early 50's.

Ch. Blakeen Saegryte.

Ch. Blakeen Talisman.

For his many contributions to the breed, he was made an Honorary Member of the Gordon Setter Club of America, Inc.

Life During the War Years 1941-1945

No one under 50 has clear memories of these grim years. Everybody ought to know what it was like.

By 1942 we were fighting a war on two fronts. In the highly industrialized sections of the United States, factories were running 24 hours a day, 7 days a week. Many women had joined the work force to replace the men that had been called up. Everyone worked at least full time; more often than not, many hours overtime.

The Government scooped up every suitable dog it could find, breeders turned to raising Shepherds above all other breeds.

Dog food was scarce and not of good quality. Young veterinarians were inducted, creating a scarcity only partially filled by elderly men who came out of retirement to help out. Distemper was rife, and all medication went to the Armed Forces Canine Corps.

While a few dog shows continued to be held, gasoline was rationed, and how far could you get on five gallons a week? Heating oil and natural gas were constantly short, buildings were either closed or in use by the Government, shutting out dog shows.

Blackouts along the East Coast were routine. Enemy submarines were sighted in the waters off the East Coast. The West Coast was shelled by the Japanese.

It was a poor time to raise show dogs and pursue a hobby, to say the least, and many people could not continue.

Everything was rationed, and standing in line for some foods was the order of the day.

It wasn't long before a flourishing Black Market developed. Money would buy anything. Perhaps this was the origin of the Underground Economy that came in for so much attention in 1982.

When the hostilities ended in May of 1945, the pent up demand for dogs and hobbies burst out, and registrations for Gordons in 1945 was exactly double what it had been in 1944—to a total of 250.

Fortunately, most of the good dogs had lived through these years and while they were no longer youngsters, they were still useful for breeding.

The next five years saw a rapid increase in owners and breeders of Gordons. Dog show activity picked up quickly, and by 1949, Field Trials for Gordons had become a reality.

1940-1945—Show Activity

At first, Americans felt secure that they would not be drawn into the War in Europe. Dog shows and dog breeding continued unabated throughout 1940. The Gordon Setter was progressing rapidly, 135 registrations and 16 champions in this year; among them were: Great Scot of Blakeen, Highland Queen of Tweedvale, Cornwallis of Avalon, Lancer of Serlway, Captain Ike of Charlemar, Kent of Serlway, Stylish Stagestruck of Blakeen, Black Rogue of Serlway, Larrabee's Jock and Audley of Serlway.

The Annual Specialty of the Gordon Setter Club was held as usual at North Westchester in July, with an entry of 24. Best of Breed went to Ch. Downside Bonnie of Serlway, Best Opposite to Ch. Brenda of Serlway.

1941

This year 172 registrations and ten champions were recorded. More famous producers finished: five littermates, Heslop's Courageous, Merry Maid, Crusader, Mac and Loch Ridge Liza Jane. Others were General Mike of Charlemar and General Mercer. Ch. Timberdoodle Dan of Avalon won the breed's first CDX.

Ch. Captain Ike of Charlemar topped an entry of ten at the Garden, with Best Opposite to Heather Adeline, one of the last imports. At the Gordon Setter Club Annual Meeting the top show Gordon award was given to Downside Bonnie of Serlway for 1940. He had a splendid record of Best of Breed at 34 shows, and 12 Sporting groups.

(*Author's note:* it should be pointed out that the Gordon Setter Club was entirely responsible for ratings, and the dogs had to belong to club members. Top Producers were based on the aggregate number of points won by offspring, not just the champions made. There was nothing in existence even faintly like the various systems used at present.)

The October, 1941 *American Kennel Gazette*'s lead article was titled, "If War Comes, What About Dogs? American Red Star Plans Helping Like Animal Defense Society in British Isles."

Gordon Setter Club members made arrangements among themselves to render mutual aid in case of an invasion on the East Coast—not as far fetched as it sounds.

1942

A dramatic drop in show activity took place, with only three dogs completing their show titles: Heslop's Black Knight, Blakeen Saegryte and Loch Ridge Stylish Lady. Show entries totalled only 179 for the entire year.

Westminster was held anyway, with greatly reduced entries. Ch. Heslop's Courageous was Best of Breed for the first of four consecutive such wins. BOS was won by Ch. Brenda of Serlway.

1943

The February *Gazette* reported exactly *three* shows and *one* Field

Trial. Once again three Gordons won their championships, Loch Ridge Victoria, Lynn's Werrie, and Heslop's Heather Lassie. Best Opposite at the Garden was Ch. Blakeen Saegryte. A junior Handler, Walter Wilson, won first place showing his Gordon Setter—something new for the breed.

A small entry of seven turned out for the annual club specialty. Courageous was Best of Breed; his sister, Heather Lassie, Best Opposite.

From May to September 45 shows were held, but Gordons were entered at only 12 with a total of only 30 exhibits.

1944

This was THE bad year. Registrations dropped to 124, with Duke of Monmouth II, EEG's Scotia Lancer, Loch Ridge Rogue's Don and Sonia of Avalon being the only new champions.

At the Garden, Saegryte was again BOS. Courageous and Heather Lassie were awarded Top Show wins for the year.

1945

With the end of the War, dog shows and breedings bounced back so that by the end of the year registrations totalled 250, but only Blakeen Annie Laurie and Blakeen Talisman made their championships. EEG's Scotia Heather placed BOS at the Garden. At the club meeting, Porter Washington's Ch. Loch Ridge Rogue's Don was named top Gordon.

There were 15 entries at the Fall Specialty at Rye, N.Y. Courageous won this one, too, and Ch. Heslop's Stylish Beauty (Loch Ridge Vagabond King x Heslop's Burnvale Queen) was BOS.

1946-1950

While registrations remained about the same, during 1946 13 Gordons made their titles. Of note were: Heslop's Stylish Lad, Loch Ridge Dalnaglar Jane, Heslop's Dorvius, Valiant Captain of East Court, Heslop's Stylish Charm II and Heslop's Burnvale Duchess.

At the Garden, Ch. Blakeen Talisman won the breed with Best Opposite to EEG's Scotia Heather. No report on the Meeting and who got the top awards was published.

The specialty was held in Baltimore for the first time, and drew a record breaking 47 entries. Talisman was top dog, with Brenda of Serlway as Best Opposite.

The club was emboldened by this success to hold a Fall Specialty in Schenectady, where the entry was 48. Best of Breed and third in the group (a big event) went to Ch. Heslop's Crusader, while Dorvius was BOS.

1947

Registrations soared to 353, with new champions totalling 28. Best

56

known of them were: Wilson's Corrie, CD, Loch Ridge Winsome Lass, EEG's Scotia Nodrog Rettes, Heslop's Courageous, Jr., Laddie of Parkwood (Heslop's Burnvale Ranger x Ch. Heslop's Merry Maid) owned by *Gazette* columnist, Eva Camp, Black Beauty's Duke (Pride of Avalon x Comrade Black Beauty), Porter Washington, Gregorach Fast, Milestone Monarch and Heslop's Burnvale Piper.

Annual Awards announced at the club meeting held at the Garden were: Top Producers, Courageous and Duchess. Top Winner went to the bitch, Ch. Heslop's Dorvius, whose record remains among the best, if not THE best for her sex: 34 Best of Breed, 19 Group placements plus one Specialty Best of Breed. Other outstanding dogs of the year were another bitch, Ch. Heslop's Burnvale Charm II, and Laddie of Parkwood with a group three.

Talisman won the breed at Westminster, with BOS to Charm II. At the only club Specialty, held again at Baltimore, entry totalled 42 with Dorvius taking the breed, Crusader BOS.

1948

This was a slow year, registrations dropped to 271, new champions to a modest 11. Among those 11 we find Ch. Halenfred Scorched Gold, Ch. Fast's Firebrand, Ch. Milestone Magnificent, and Heslop's Burnvale Jean.

At the Garden, Dorvius won the breed with Best Opposite to a newcomer, Ch. Milestone Monarch (Steyer).

Top Producer was again Courageous, while three bitches shared the honors: Saegryte, Duchess and Scotia Heather. Other top producing males were Talisman and Gregorach Fast.

Top winner was Ch. Colonel's Duke of Mercer (Ch. General Mercer x Ch. Rita of Avalon, CD), Johnson. Two dogs each won a single group four: Ch. Heslop's Courageous, Jr. (Ch. Heslop's Courageous x Ch. Heslop's Burnvale Duchess) and Ch. Loch Ridge Tally's Rip (Ch. Blakeen Talisman x Ch. Blakeen Saegryte).

At the September Club Specialty at Westchester, Ch. Heslop's Burnvale Jean (a bitch by Ch. Heslop's Courageous x Ch. Heslop's Burnvale Duchess) won the honors, with Best Opposite to Ch. Milestone Monarch. The meeting was made lively by a discussion of how to handle the alarming increase of solid red pups in Gordon Setter litters. This matter is still under discussion, 34 years later.

Alec Laurence (Rhythm Kennels, California) reported Gordons were being shown much more often on the Coast, and that there had been six to 15 at every central California show. Plans were being made by West Coast Gordonites to hold a gundog trial in February of 1949.

1949

Registrations rose to 354, with 12 new champions: EEG's Scotia

Ch. Fast's Firebrand of Windy Hill with owner-handler Jean Lathlaen, judge George Thompson. Firebrand was a littermate of Ch. Fast's Falcon of Windy Hill and resembled him closely, though Falcon was larger. No good photo of Falcon exists.

Ch. EEG's Scotia Nodrog Rettes, fi
dog at Afternod Kennels.

Rare photo of Vincent Wilcox, shown going BOS at the GSCA Specialty in 1951 with Ch. Afterno Fidelia. CC, Ch. Heslop's Burnvale Piper with Dorothy D. Hardy.

Another uncommon photograph, this one of Marion Wilcox with Ch. Sternod Sue, a dog which was pivotal in the Sternod breeding program. Her name appears in pedigrees repeatedly. *Shafer*

1960 Gordon Setter Club Specialty at Trenton, N.J. BB and Gp. 4, Ch. Heslop's Burnvale Piper with Dorothy Hardy. BOS, Ch. Heslop's Burnvale Charm II with Tom Gately, prominent Eastern handler. Judge Eldred. *Brown*

Lancer, Fast's Falcon of Windy Hill, Milestone Bruce, Ravenscroft Jean's Debutante among the best known. The Gordon Setter Club had 87 members. Isn't it rather striking that they could engender all this activity?

The breed took another surge forward. The first all-Gordon field trial was held by the parent club, a highly successful event which established an activity that has flourished ever since.

Suddenly there were ten group placements for the year.

Ch. Heslop's Burnvale Piper, one second and one fourth.

Briarcliffe Vagabond, at his first show, group two (Ch. Black Beauty's Duke x Ch. Loch Ridge Windsome Lass), owner, Green.

Laddie of Limerick (Ch. Lancer of Serlway x Ch. Heslop's Heather Lassie) went on the Florida Circuit and was the only Gordon, yet won two thirds and one fourth. Owner, Gavagan.

Osborne's Stylish Tammerlane, bitch, (Osborne's Iron Mike x Osborne's Alabama Style), owner, Bill Osborne, two fourths.

Ch. Fast's Falcon of Windy Hill, owner, Poisker, one fourth.

Courageous was once again Top Producer, followed by Talisman. Heslop's Burnvale Duchess was top bitch.

Twenty-one Gordons were entered at the Garden. Best of Breed to a newcomer, Ch. EEG's Scotia Lancer's Son (EEG's Scotia Lancer x Ch. Loch Ridge Stylish Lady), Brower. BOS to Dorvius. Marion Wilcox in reporting this show said that all the specials were shown by professional handlers, a first for Gordons which had been mostly owner-handled up 'til now.

Forty-nine entries made up the September Club Specialty, with brother and sister winning, Ch. Heslop's Burnvale Piper, BB and Charm II, BOS.

Kennel Profiles: Newcomers, 1945-1950

A number of kennels had their start between 1944 and 1948. Several deserve more than a passing comment because of the leadership demonstrated by the owners. There is no question but that the breed would have faltered once more had it not been for the steadying influence of these breeders. Their ambitions were aimed at the survival and improvement of the Gordon Setter. Staunch supporters of shows, field trials and a strong Gordon Setter Club, they were friends, and helpful with newcomers. They kept going through the up and down career of the breed during the 50's and well into the 60's, when survival finally appeared assured.

By the mid 40's most of the old supportive kennels had closed, for reasons best known to their owners. Loch Ridge, Heslop, and EEG kept going until the 50's but on a steadily declining basis.

Newcomers utilizing the excellent stock available at that time filled the gaps and soon created their own styles of Gordons.

Milestone (1937-1975) Miriam Steyer Mincieli, Bronx, N.Y.

By 1947 Miriam was serving as Gordon Setter Club Secretary. She was inspired to start a small, monthly club newsletter which received such a warm welcome that after a year, the work on it became more than she could handle. It passed to Marion Wilcox, with whom it became closely associated over the years.

Never a large kennel, Milestone was, even so, a prominent one during the next ten years, with Miriam showing and field trialing all her own dogs.

The first two Gordons at Milestone were EEG's Old Faithful Lass (EEG's Laddie Boy x EEG's Scotia Huntress) and Ch. Milestone Monarch (Ch. Great Scot of Blakeen x Loch Ridge Reckless Lady). When these two were bred they produced Champions Milestone Grand Duke and Magnificent.

Bred to Ch. Milestone Majestic (brother to Monarch), Magnificent gave Miriam Ch. Milestone Matriarch. Sent to the West Coast, she became the property of the Sunderlands and produced a number of fine Gordons carrying the Sun-Yak kennel name. This line is found in today's West Coast Gordons through the Springset line.

Ch. Milestone Meg of Redchico, an early member of this prominent kennel owned by Bernard Chevalier, was sired by a son of Magnificent (Milestone Favorite), out of Star Farm Belle.

One of Milestone Monarch's best known get, Ch. Afternod Fidelia (out of Ch. Wilson's Corrie, CD) became the property of Don and Carol Chevalier, Loch Adair Kennels. (See L.A. profile).

The Milestone Gordons were known for their large size, big bone, rich tan markings, dark eyes, and bold temperaments. At field trials they showed admirable speed and style.

In 1965, in recognition of the many years of support given the breed and the club, Miriam was made Honorary Member.

Arelyn Thurston (1945-1965) Thurston's or Thor's Hill, New York State

Thurston's Cricket, born 1946, was Arelyn's first Gordon. Prior to that Arelyn had raised Cocker Spaniels. Cricket represented the old American Gordon line. Sired by Beau Rustic x Bissell's Midnight Spook, she was purely hunting stock.

Next came Lady Beth of Parkwood (Loch Ridge Vagabond King x Ch. Heslop's Merry Maid). Bred to Heslop's Burnvale Scot (Ch. Great Scot of Blakeen x Heslop's Burnvale Maid), Lady Beth produced a top winner, Ch. Thurston's Scot. His win as Best American Bred in Show was the first in 20 years for a Gordon.

Arelyn served as *American Kennel Gazette* columnist for the Gordon Setter Club from 1955 to 1965—a long, successful stint. She gave this up when she became an AKC judge for Setters.

Ch. Loch Adair Blair, first Loch Adair champion with Art Baines, popular handler of the times. Judge George Thompson of Loch Ridge Kennels.

Ch. Osborne's Stylish Maurauder, top Gordon for 1950. One of the biggest Gordons ever shown. Died very young. Profuse coat was not a problem in those days! *Brown*

Morris and Essex winners 1952. Harold Sydney with BB Ch. Halenfred's Scorched Gold, BOS, Ch. Heslop's Burnvale Sarah Jane with Dorothy D. Hardy. *Brown*

Donald Sunderland with Ch. Sun-Yak Chief Joseph, Celeste Sunderland with Ch. Rural Rhythm, 1954. Judge Max Riddle. Yakima, Wash. show. *Roberts*

During her career she raised 40 litters. Among the better known of her dogs were Champions Thurston's Valiant Cordelia and Spring Squire; Ch. Thor's Hill Artist; Ch. Thurston's Stylish Angus who won Best of Breed at Westminster, shown by his Junior Handler-Owner, Kim Cameron.

Arelyn acquired Roevalley Duke (Eng. Show Ch. Blaze of Westerdale x Eng. Show Ch. Angela of Gramerci) when he was about four years old. This handsome, friendly dog refused to show; otherwise the story might have been different. As it was he sired some nice Gordons, among them Angus, mentioned above; and the winner of the Combined Setter Specialty in 1969, one of the most titled Gordons. This was Am. & Can. Ch. Cyn-Dan's MacTavish (dam, Lady of Ancastle), Am. and Can. CD, owned and trained by Denise Conway.

The club is fortunate to have in its archives Arelyn's kennel records and her *Gazette* columns.

Halenfred (1946-1960) Harold Sydney, Rhode Island

This elite hobby kennel produced a string of successful Gordons. Mr. Sydney did not neglect the hunting aspects of the breed. His own dogs were field trained and often participated in Gordon Setter Club trials.

The two foundation dogs, purchased in 1946, were littermates, Halenfred Cinderella and Ch. Halenfred Scorched Gold (Ch. Heslop's Courageous x Ch. EEG's Scotia Heather).

"Scorchy" finished in 1949 and in 1950 and '51 he was top winning Gordon. He produced four champions carrying the kennel name: Scamp, Dusty Gold, Scorcher, and Robin Adair, CD. This last dog, out of Ch. Heslop's Burnvale Bonnie, CD, became one of the first males in the Loch Adair kennels.

Ch. Halenfred Bright Deil (Ch. Kent of Serlway x Cinderella), born in 1951, won two Gordon Setter Club specialties, Best of Breed three times at Morris and Essex, was top Gordon in 1953, 1954 (with a group 3) and 1955.

Mr. Sydney turned his attention from raising dogs to judging them and is currently an active AKC judge, especially of Sporting Dogs.

Sun-Yak (1948-   ) Donald and Celeste Sunderland, Yakima, Wash.

The Sunderlands were introduced to the breed by Ch. King of The Palouse (Ch. Lancer of Serlway x Ch. Heslop's Heather Lassie). He was so successful as a pet and companion, show dog and hunter that they became interested in raising Gordons. A bitch from Alec Laurence, Ch. Rural Rhythm (Scot's Heather Lad x Ch. Ravenscroft Jean's Debutante) bred to King gave them Ch. Sun-Yak Chief Joseph, a top West Coast show dog with group placements. Sun-Yak Medicine Man (Chief's brother), owned by Alec Laurence, was used extensively for breeding.

Ch. Milestone Matriarch (Ch. Milestone Majestic x Ch. Milestone

Gordon Setter Club Specialty of 1956 at Trenton. BB Ch. Windy Hill's Ablaze of Gunbar with Jake Poisker. Judge, Cornelius McGlynn.   *Brown*

Star Farm Best Bet at Trenton Specialty 1956, going Winners Dog. The late Harold Correll, handler, at the top of his profession in those days. Judge Cornelius McGlynn.
Brown

Best of Breed (left) and BOS at Gordon Setter Club Specialty held in Indianapolis, Ind. in 1957. BB: Ch. Scotch Burr of Gunbar, CD with prominent midwest handler, Dick Cooper. BOS Ch. Blarney Stone's Tartan Doll with owner-breeder, Ridgely Reichardt. Both dogs top winners in the late 50's.

Frasie

Ch. Windy Hill's Satan with breeder-handler, Jake Poisker. Satan was top winner for 1958.

Magnificent) was a valued addition to the kennel. Bred to Chief she produced Can. Ch. Sun-Yak Forty-Niner, who died just before finishing in the US, and Sun-Yak Thunderhead, not shown but used extensively for breeding.

These older Sun-Yak dogs appear in extended pedigrees of native California Gordons carrying the Springset kennel name.

During his most active years in the breed, Don Sunderland served as a Director of the Gordon Setter Club. After 1955, because of business and family commitments, the Sunderlands curtailed their activity with Gordons, though they continued to own them. In 1975 they were able to pick up where they left off, now have two Can. and Am. show champions, and a third Gordon destined for field trials and shows.

Windy Hill (c. 1943-1966) John T. (Jake) and Dorothy (Dottie) Poisker, Souderton, Pa.

Also, Windy Hill...B; Mrs. William (Margot) Bradbury

When the Poiskers began their Gordon Setter kennel they made a wise move and purchased adults from the Gregorach Kennels of Professor Munn, located in New Jersey. This well established, successful endeavor, dating back to the late 1920's, had started (like everyone else at the time) with Inglehurst stock. Munn's Ch. Ginger (Inglehurst Gillette, Jr. x Inglehurst Minnie Ha Ha) was a winner of many variety groups and placings. An imported bitch, Stylish Madame (Stylish Lion x Stylish Mine) produced a number of Gregorach champions when bred to Ginger.

By the early 1940's Prof. Munn began phasing out his kennel, and this is when the Poiskers entered the picture. Gregorach Fast (Ch. Ginger x Stylish Madame) was purchased as a hunting dog. A bitch, Delaware Belle, granddaughter of Ch. Downside Bonnie of Serlway and Ch. Spirit of Serlway, was selected for breeding.

Fast and Belle produced Jill and Ch. Bonnie Belle of Windy Hill, foundation bitches.

Early on, the Poiskers had settled for line or inbreeding, and they had also planned never to repeat a breeding.

When it came time to breed Jill, they went back to the Serlway line through Loch Ridge Rogue's Ace II (Ch. Black Rogue of Serlway x Ch. Blakeen Saegryte). This mating gave them two of their foundation studs, Blake and Duncan of Windy Hill.

In 1945 they brought in Heslop's Burnvale Janet (Courageous x Duchess). Her first litter sired by Ch. Gregorach Fast resulted in the famous "F" litter: Champions Fast's Falcon of Windy Hill (sire of 13 champions including one Dual); Fast's Firebrand, Flash and the bitch, Faith.

Bred to Blake of Windy Hill, Janet gave them Ch. Blake's Rogue of

Windy Hill, special pet of Margot Bradbury. Rogue sired seven champions, carefully linebred, most of them carrying the Windy Hill...B name.

With these outstanding dogs to work with, Poiskers continued to produce many champions, whose names will appear in the story of the 50's and 60's.

Jake, Dottie and Margot all contributed generously to the activities of the Gordon Setter Club. Jake was on the Field Trial Committee, later served as a Director, then President for 1953 and 1954. Dottie was always busy gathering support for shows and trials and serving on committees. She was club Secretary in 1955 and '56, and edited the Newsletter in 1957.

Margot Bradbury supported the trials and shows, and often won! She took on the Newsletter in 1951 and stayed with it until 1956, a long time for a difficult task. Eventually Margot turned her full attention to her sheep farm, at which she became an expert.

In 1965 Jake and Dottie were made Honorary members of the Gordon Setter Club, in appreciation of their many years of support for the breed and club, and contribution thereto.

Kennels which owed their success to stock obtained from Windy Hill were numerous: Star Farm (Fleishman, Pa.); Gunbar (Platt, Ill.); Sycamore Lodge (Keiffer, Pa.); Fastline (Lathlaen, Pa.); Laurel Lane (Lefkowitz, Pa.); Braw Clan (Kunkle, Delaware); Hacasak (Christine, Pa.); The Glen (Levy, Pa.); Blarneystone (Reichardt, St. Louis); Chance (Putchat, Pa.).

The influence of this strain is profound and continues today. Just for fun, I traced a 1981 pedigree and found the name of Fast's Falcon 26 times. Each modern breeding increases this concentration because there are so few individuals back of the present American Gordon. Considering that the breed was rebuilt from scratch in 1924 and that no new blood of any significance has been introduced since 1945, this is not surprising.

Today's breeders, presented with a three or four generation pedigree are seldom aware of the close breeding back of their dogs.

The Windy Hill dogs were distinctive. Not as large as most of the earlier Gordons, they were brightly marked, heavily feathered with silky straight coat. Heads were blocky, with square cut muzzle, strong stop. These dogs were lively and aggressive, showing with flash and dash. They brought to the breed two innovations: tails carried high and wide rear movement. Many Windy Hill dogs showed exceptional enthusiasm for hunting, epitomized by Dual Ch. Windy Hill's Lucky Chance, owned and trained by Nate Putchat.

In the late 60's Ch. Legend of Gael, CD (Ch. Chance's Lucky Buck x Chance's Lady Perfidia) began his sensational career. "Valor," as he was known, represented all the Poiskers had bred for. Given an opportunity, it is quite possible that Valor would have completed his Field Championship. His pedigree carries a concentration of the best of the Windy Hill stock.

Three other kennels had their start during the mid-forties. Because of their long association with the breed, only the stories of how they started will be given here. The names of dogs from these kennels will appear throughout the ensuing history of the breed, while the names of the owners are woven into the fabric of the Gordon Setter Club of America.

Gordon Hill (1946-   ) Mrs. Roland (Muriel) Clement, Conn.

Muriel began her career as a dog enthusiast when only 11 years old. After studying dog books and magazines, she settled for the Gordon. Not until she graduated from collegiate nursing school was she able to fulfill her dream by the purchase of Heslop's Burnvale Bonnie (Courageous x Duchess) in 1946.

Bonnie went on to become a show champion and the first of many of Muriel's Gordons to obtain her CD degree. This is thought to be only the second degree won by a Gordon in America.

Bonnie also produced a number of litters, many members of which found their way into the mainstream of Gordon breedings of the period.

Muriel has bred 26 litters, and bred or owned 26 champions. Her list of CD winners is long, and few dogs in her pedigrees are untitled. Many of her pups have competed with success at field trials. The achievement of a Dual Championship by her Gordon Hill Lollipop (Ch. Yorkley Hawk of Gunbar x Ch. Gordon Hill Holly, CD) is one shared by a small, elite group of dogs and breeders.

Never one to fear the unknown, Muriel has bred to different dogs of different strains, though always keeping the thread of her own bloodline. She was one of the few lucky breeders to have a litter sired by Ch. Legend of Gael, CD. This was her "Q" litter which has had considerable success.

Because of three children, a full time job and an invalid mother, Muriel's "kennel" has had to consist of two house dogs (at Roland's request). But, careful planning and supervision of pups has given her many satisfactory co-ownerships.

Now, a new partnership with Susan De Silver has opened up a more active future. With her own kennel, and great enthusiasm for shows and field trials, Susan is sharing the Gordon Hill name and stock.

Since her earliest connection with the breed Muriel has been an active member of the Gordon Setter Club, serving in many capacities: *Gazette* columnist; Secretary; Director, and since 1975, the club Delegate to the American Kennel Club. She has also served the regional Tartan Gordon Setter Club in a number of positions.

Afternod Kennels (1946-1975) Vincent and Marion K. Wilcox, Conn.

The first two Gordons at this famous kennel were purchased as adults:

EEG's Scotia Nodrog Rettes (Ch. Lancer of Serlway x Ch. Larrabee's Avalon Beauty) and Wilson's Corrie (Loch Ridge Major Rogue x Loch Ridge Victoria). The Wilcoxes showed both these dogs to their championships, and Marion took Corrie to her CD—the third Gordon to win this title.

Before long, raising Gordons, shows, and the club became their major interests. Independent means meant that they could pursue their hobby without financial restrictions.

They built a beautiful country home especially adapted for their dogs. Here they bred many litters per year, and concentrated on their goal of a strong female line.

Various other lines were added to their original ones, then blended into their own special type.

By the 1960's the Afternod strain was well established and exhibited from coast to coast with much success. The Top Producers Section of this book carries the pedigrees and photos of many of these dogs.

Kennels owing their start to the generous help from the Wilcoxes include: Loch Adair (Chevalier); Idlenot (R. Noren); Sutherland (J. Lawrence); MacAlder (Stephenson); Kris (R. Christianson); Stilmeadows (Gidday). The Wheel of Fortune brought together Mrs. Elizabeth Clark and Afternod Yank of Rockaplenty (Ch. Wee Jock Adair x Ch. Afternod Ripple) in 1969. His success in the show ring and as a stud dog solidified the position of the Afternod strain as a leader.

The Gordon Setter Club is indebted to the Wilcoxes for many years of support. Marion served repeatedly as Newsletter Editor, also as Treasurer, and Director. Vincent, who died suddenly in 1953, had been President and AKC Delegate. He loved field trials, and was the world's best marshall.

In 1975 Marion's death brought to an end this remarkable kennel which had produced over 200 litters, and at least 200 champions. In 1981, the strain continues unabated in the hands of many breeders throughout the United States.

Sangerfield (1945-   ) Margaret Sanger, Jean Sanger Look and (1960-   ) Fred Itzenplitz. Upper New York State

In 1945 we indulged in a long held ambition to own a boarding kennel, especially in North Carolina. This meant room for dogs of our own, and by then we had chosen the Gordon as our first breed. At that time the idea of raising pups was not uppermost.

Our first champion was Heslop's Criss Cross (Ch. Heslop's Courageous x Inglehurst Ingenue). We added on Ch. Heslop's Stylish Beauty (Loch Ridge Vagabond King x Ch. Highland Queen of Tweedvale) and later, Judge Palmer (Courageous x Tam O'Shanter). Through his mother, Judge Palmer traced directly to the Svane June line.

Several Courageous x Duchess pups were added.

We enjoyed field training on quail and woodcock in our North Carolina precinct. But, boarding was our business.

From 1950 to 1960 we added Basset Hounds to our kennel. In 1956 Jean wrote the first book on that breed, published by All-Pets Books.

Forced to move our kennel when zoning laws changed, we took the hint and moved back to beautiful Western New York State.

Jean has served the Gordon Setter Club of America in many capacities: Secretary, *Gazette* columnist, Director, Vice-President and lastly Treasurer for 11 years, Yearbook Editor from 1960 to 1972. Margaret was breed columnist for *Popular Dogs* and the *Gazette*.

Fred Itzenplitz has served many years as a GSCA Director; show chairman and club representative for the Combined Setter Specialties; on the committee for the Midwest Specialty and as a member of the GSCA Yearbook Committee.

It should be mentioned that in the first few years we raised Gordons we used three other kennel names: Look, Sanger and Greymount.

1950-1959

The early part of this decade saw each of the new breeders consolidating his own strain. Working with stock obtained in the late 40's but without the guidance of the "old timers" it was every man for himself.

No doubt the Korean War (1950-1963) coming as it did only five years after the dreadful World War II put a damper on dog activities. Not until the end of the decade did show attendance equal that of the late 40's.

Nonetheless, these were important years in Gordon Setter history.

Hip dysplasia was identified in Gordon Setters for the first time in 1950 though it had been recognized in a few breeds as early as 1935. Attempts by the Gordon Setter Club of America to establish effective policies to meet this problem were met with a lack of consensus among Veterinarians on key issues: X-ray positioning, diagnosis, breeding recommendations, and causes, making positive action impossible. (Almost the same conditions exist even in 1983).

Good things happened, too. The revival of Field Trials for the breed was extremely successful. Though confined to the East Coast at first trials were well supported and attracted a crowd of young breeder-owners. Because they had no choice but to start with dual purpose bloodlines, they kept on with the philosophy and produced show dogs, field dogs, and Dual Champions from all the same stock.

While the Gordon made no surge numerically it began to be seen in areas from which it had been absent since before WW II. On the West Coast entries at shows slowly began to increase. These dogs, closely related to the older Eastern stock, were also dual purpose. Sparked by Alec Laurence, Don and Celeste Sunderland, a few shows with major points became available.

In the Chicago area renewed show activity and the start of breed Field Trials were brought about when Bill and Marge Platt moved to Palatine along with their string of excellent Gunbar Gordons. They soon attracted supporters for both activities. (See Field Trial chapter.)

Such were Cal and Elsye Calvert (Denida Kennels) of Moline, Ill., who stayed with the breed long enough to produce some influential dogs. Their first bitch, Ch. Calvert's Highland Queen (Ch. Heslop's Stylish Lad x Mississippi Valley Jet) bred to Ch. Pell-Mell's Bonnie Bruce (Gabriel of Serlway x Ch. Pell-Mell Penelope) produced a couple of litters of excellent field dogs, the best known being Fld. Ch. Denida's Bonnie Velvet (Steve Gaydos); also, Ch. Denida's Bonnie Rebel, CD, of Terlo Kennels (Walter and Lois Ellis) and the Calvert's own Ch. Denida's Gallant Knight. Both Queen and Knight had trial placements.

In St. Louis, Ridgely and Pat Reichardt began their Blarney Stone Gordon kennel with Windy Hill's Weir of Kay and Blarney Stone's Deluxe Baby (Bing of Parkwood and Lady of Cliffhaven), a sister of Mississippi Valley Jet. For a number of years their Ch. Blarney Stone's Banshire (Wier of Kay x Deluxe Baby), with his son Lancelot (out of Windy Hill's Claudia B) and daughter, Ch. Blarney Stone's Tartan Doll (out of Blarney Stone the Piper), were consistent winners both in the Mid West and on the East Coast.

Another small but quality kennel was that of Warren and Stephanie Malvick with their bitch, Ch. Pell-Mell Penelope (O'Tail x Nelson's Heather Beauty) who produced five champions. The best known are Ch. Pell-Mell Bonnie Bruce, sired by Gabriel of Serlway and Ch. Brian Courageous (Klarer), sired by Ch. Sangerfield Ben.

Along the East Coast where activity was well supported by Halenfred, Afternod, and Gordon Hill in New England, several newcomers joined the ranks. They deserve mention.

Ken Lasher (MacGregor) hit the jackpot with his first Gordon puppy, Ch. Page's Captain MacGregor (Ch. Page's MacDonegal II x Fld. Ch. Page's Shuriridge Liz). Sire of five champions, winner of over 50 Bests of Breed, many group placements, he produced the Lasher's subsequent winners, MacGregor's Michael Lad and Braeburn Flash, both out of that fine bitch, Ch. Windy Hill's Lorna B. Ch. Windy Hill's MacGregor, another son, went to Lillian Carson in California and became one of the earliest Gordons to win a Mexican Championship. Mary Creamer subsequently owned MacGregor. His name appears in current West Coast pedigrees.

Jack Page was going from win to win with his Fld. Ch. Page's Shuriridge Liz. He also was producing successful show dogs from his field stock such as Page's MacDonegal II and Lasher's dog. (Jack's career will be discussed more fully in the chapter on Field Trials).

Art Fletcher began his kennel about 1952 with the purchase of two sisters, Kitty Lightfoot and Sanger's Cindy (O'Field's Ready Response x Ch. Heslop's Burnvale Edie). Art soon became involved in Gordon field trials with Kitty and dog shows with Cindy. His addition of Ch. Heslop's Burnvale Laird rounded out his small hobby kennel. Over the next few years a number of Gordons carrying the name Fletcher made their appearance, among them Dark Belle (Tinnie), Scotch Lorelei, Dixie Rebel, and from a mating of Roevalley Duke and Ch. Fletcher's Dark Belle, Ch. Donnie Brae Eric Knight. Art continued his interest and activities until hampered by failing health in the late 60's. He served terms as a Director of the Gordon Setter Club of America and on field trial committees.

Loch Adair, Loch Adair Redchico (1951-   ) Donald and Carol Chevalier, Bernard Chevalier

Carol Parsons Chevalier purchased her first Gordon Setter in 1951, Halenfred Robin Adair (Ch. Halenfred Scorched Gold x Ch. Heslop's Burnvale Bonnie, CD). He soon became a show champion and earned his CD. In 1952 Carol acquired as foundation bitch Ch. Afternod Fidelia (Ch. Milestone Monarch x Ch. Wilson's Corrie, CD).

From a mating of these two came Ch. Loch Adair Blair who produced Allspice of Redchico when bred to Ch. Afternod Kate.

In 1959 Spice was bred to Ch. Afternod Drambuie. From this litter came Ch. Afternod Redchico Cutty Sark, Ch. Afternod Curry and Ch. Afternod Clove. Also in that year Fidelia, bred to Afternod Sumac, whelped the famous Afternod Fidemac.

By 1967 Loch Adair Diana of Redchico (Ch. Afternod Hickory x Allspice of Redchico) had become the second bitch in breed history to produce 13 Champions. She also won the award for Top Producing Bitch, All Breeds.

One of her sons sired by Drambuie was Ch. Wee Geordie Adair. When bred to Ch. Afternod Curry he produced Ch. Loch Adair Kate. Kate, bred to Hugh's Sir Gordie of Windy Hill, gave the world those famous litter mates, MacNeil of Ellicott, Torrance of Ellicott, and Kadon's Katie Did.

Diana bred to Ch. Afternod Callant (Ch. Afternod Drambuie x Ch. Afternod Woodbine) produced three very influential Gordons:

1) Loch Adair Monarch became a Dual Champion in 1974, a dream come true for any Gordon breeder. "Monty" was largely trained and handled by his amateur owner, Leonard Smith. Monty also became a Top Producer with 12 champions to his credit. Among the better known are Ch. Mygatt's Dugan, Ch. MacLeod's Electra O'Chaparral, and Ch. Sutherland MacDuff.

2) Ch. Wee Jock Adair, CD, had an excellent show career and is listed in Top Producers with 33 champions to his credit. Certainly the

best known and most influential is the legendary Ch. Afternod Yank of Rockaplenty, CD, out of Ch. Afternod Ripple.

3) Ch. Wee Laurie Adair also had a successful show career and is a Top Producer of seven champions. One of them was Ch. Loch Adair Peer of Sutherland, a foundation stud for the kennels of Judith Lawrence in Washington State. Peer became a CD, a Top Producer of 12 champions including Sutherland Vanessa, Odds On and Lass of Chambray.

The sudden death of Donald Chevalier in 1979 changed the picture at Loch Adair. Though no longer as active in the breed as she was, Carol continues her interest in Gordons.

(1950-1959) Top Producers and Winners

Until 1953, two years after his death, Ch. Heslop's Courageous remained the Top Producer. His lifetime total of 19 champions seems modest by today's standards so it must be judged in perspective. Other Top Producers of this decade with totals of five champions or over were:

Males

Ch. Blakeen Talisman	10
Ch. Fast's Falcon of Windy Hill	13 (one Dual)
Ch. Blake's Rogue of Windy Hill	7
Ch. Heslop's Burnvale Piper	5
Judge Palmer	6
(Ch. Heslop's Courageous x Tam O'Shanter)	
Heslop's Burnvale Scot	6
Ch. Blarney Stone's Banshire	5
Ch. Page's Captain MacGregor	5

Bitches

Ch. Heslop's Burnvale Duchess	13
Heslop's Burnvale Janet	6
Ch. Pell-Mell Penelope	5
Ch. Calvert's Highland Queen	4 (one Dual)

1950

Activity was highlighted by exactly two shows: Westminster with an entry of 14 Gordons where Ch. Scotia Lancer's Son repeated his Best of Breed win, as did Ch. Heslop's Dorvius with Best Opposite, and — The Gordon Setter Club Specialty at the Trenton, N.J. show. In an entry of 41, Ch. Heslop's Burnvale Piper won again, and his sister, Ch. Heslop's Burnvale Charm II, was BOS. Piper went on to a group IV, a big event.

The most consistent winners continued to be the dogs from the late 40's. A young male, Ch. Osborne's Stylish Maurauder (Ch. Blakeen

74

Talisman x. Ch. Heslop's Burnvale Charm II) was the top winner with a record of 27 Bests of Breed, two group III and two group IV. Besides Piper's placement, there was only one other, a fourth place.

1951

The first big (13) entry of Gordons at a California show in 20 years was won by an owner-handled American-bred dog who went on to a group II, Balero's Own (El Principe Valiente x Wee Oregon Lass).

Page's Shuriridge Liz, then just a yearling, made history by winning the Open Puppy Stake at the Germantown Field Trial Club Trials. This was the first time a Gordon had won an Open Stake since the 1930's.

For this year two kennel mates shared top honors as winners. Ch. Halenfred Scorched Gold or Ch. Halenfred Bright Deil took Best of Breed at the larger Gordon entries, and Deil had two group placements.

1953

The first Gordon Setter brace to be shown at the Garden was trained and handled by Margot Bradbury (Windy Hill-B) with her Ch. Blake's Rogue of Windy Hill and his son, Ch. Windy Hill MacTavish.

Top Winner was a bitch for the first time in many years: Ch. Loch Adair Annie Laurie (Ch. Heslop's Burnvale Piper x Ch. Afternod Fidelia) was owned and handled by Larry Davidson.

1954 & 1955

The first Gordon Setter Club Specialty to be held in the Midwest was won by Ch. Windy Hill's Doreen B (Ch. Blake's Rogue of Windy Hill x Windy Hill's Heidi O'Shuriridge) Bradbury, with BOS to another frequent winner, Ch. Windy Hill's Ablaze of Gunbar (Ch. Fast's Firebrand of Windy Hill x Windy Hill The Soulful Lass), owned by the Platts.

The May club Specialty held with the Trenton show had 39 entries. Bright Deil was Best of Breed, and Doreen B, Best Bitch.

1956

Ch. Windy Hill Witch of Kay (Ch. Fast's Falcon of Windy Hill x Belinda of Windy Hill) Poisker won two club specialties. Ablaze won Trenton. Ch. Page's Captain MacGregor was top winner for the year with three group III. Five other dogs had single placements.

1957

In keeping with the Gordon Setter Club's plan to move the Midwest Specialty around the area, a Specialty was held in Indianapolis with 16 entries. Best of Breed went to the consistent winner, Ch. Scotch Burr of

Gunbar (Platt) and BOS to another steady winner, Ch. Blarney Stone's Tartan Doll (Reichardt).

For the first time a Puppy Sweepstake was held by the GSCA in connection with their Specialty at Trenton. There were 17 puppies, 49 in the regular classes. Dual Ch. Windy Hill's Lucky Chance was Best of Breed with Ch. Windy Hill's Lorna B, Best Opposite.

Five group placements were won by Scotch Burr and this gave him the top awards for the year. Star Farm Best Bet won a group I. MacGregor's Michael Lad completed his championship at the age of 11 months 3 days, plus a group III—a record. Three other dogs each won a single group III.

1958

There were 24 Gordons at the Garden, the biggest of the postwar entries at that show. Breed was won by the dog of the year, Ch. Windy Hill's Satan (Ch. Windy Hill's Ablaze of Gunbar x Seitz's Devil of Shiloh), owned by the Cooleys, with BOS to Tartan Doll. Later, Satan won two GSCA Specialties, and by the year's end he had 14 Bests of Breed, 8 group placements including a first, and he was never defeated in the breed. Tartan Doll was the top bitch with five Bests of Breed.

1959

Tartan Gordon Setter Club held its first Specialty at Hartford Conn. with a good entry of 30. Since this was a February show, this number was surprisingly large. The breed win went to Ch. Afternod Hickory (Buhler), and BOS to Banshire's Heather (Ch. Heslop's Burnvale Piper x Sycamore Lodge Black Arrow) Mullin.

This year three Field Champions were made, Shuriridge Hummingbird (Penterman), Ch. Windy Hill's Lucky Chance (Putchat), and Ch. Gunbar's Dare Devil, CD (Platt).

Two dogs began their careers late in 1959 which were to extend through the first half of the 1960's. Sangerfield Jed (Ch. Sangerfield Peter x Ch. Sangerfield Tillie) won a group IV at his second show, handled by his owner, Fred Itzenplitz. Sangerfield Smokey (Judge Palmer x Holt's Dolly of Greymount), owned by J. Look, completed his title in 14 shows with nine Bests of Breed and one each group I, II, III, and IV.

Am. Can. Ch. Sangerfield Smokey with Margaret Sanger. Marion Wilcox with trophy; judge the legendary Frank Foster Davis. This was Smokey's first Specialty win—1960, the Tartan Gordon Setter Club event, held in Hartford, Conn.

Shafer

3

The Modern Gordon
Setter in America

1960-1969

THIS DECADE was an exciting one for breeders who had
spent the past years watching good Gordons being relatively ignored at
shows.

Several things had improved the Gordon image. The obvious success
of the breed in the field manifested by a number of handsome Dual
Champions; improved numbers at shows as well as more widespread
exhibition of top animals; and interest by professional handlers in showing
the better dogs.

No surge in registrations took place. Beginning with 292 in 1960, the
number grew modestly year by year to 726 in 1969.

The Vietnam War lasting from 1964 to 1973 cast a pall on the United
States, though the economy was not as severely affected as in World War
II.

Dog shows were small, Gordon entries few and far between except for
a few at Eastern shows. Exhibitors were by and large the older group.

Looking back at events which affected the dog game, we find that the
sudden introduction of jet aircraft in 1959 and 1960 was tremendously
important. Not only did these planes dramatically increase the speed of
flights for people, they made shipping dogs vastly safer. Hundreds of new
flights were instituted, long distance non-stop flights became common so

that eastern Gordon breeders (still the center of activity at that time) were able to reach markets that had been out of range.

In discussing the interesting events of these years the Top Producers will not be mentioned unless they also figure as Top Winners since they have been featured in the last section of this book. Because of the proliferation of Awards systems, each based on a slightly different method, space does not permit reporting all of them. Breeding and ownership of the dogs are given the first time only.

As mentioned at the conclusion of Chapter 2, Ch. Sangerfield Smokey and Ch. Sangerfield Jed were the Top Winners from 1960-1965. By winning consistently all over the northeast and midwest these dogs brought about a change in the attitude of judges and exhibitors. More good dogs were campaigned past their championship, more people stayed for the Group judging, and the judges ceased to turn a blind eye to the Gordon in their groups. More and more, Gordons became a truly competitive member of the Sporting Group.

After Jed retired in 1965, John Lawreck began showing Ch. Afternod MacAlder Tyr in 1967. In a short time Tyr had a highly successful career ending with 25 Best of Breeds, many group placements including a first. Following on his heels, Ch. Legend of Gael, CD, then owned by Mrs. Cheever Porter, shown by Jane Forsyth, launched a career which spanned the 1967-1972 period. "Valor" became the then top all time Gordon Setter winner with multiple Bests In Show. His success had much to do with the increase of interest in the breed by owners of other sporting dogs.

Two Bests In Show (besides Valor's) were recorded in the early 60's: one for a bitch, Am. & Can. Ch. Gunbar's Flapper, and one for a male, Am. & Can. Ch. Ger-Don's Ambrose Hobkirk, CD, both wins being in Canada. The tide was indeed turning, though even by the end of the decade only a half dozen or so Gordons placed in groups each year, usually at the end of the line. We were happy with what we got, believe me! It was progress.

1960

The first Combined Setter Specialty, long in process, took place Sunday before the Westminster show. Dr. Wolfgang Casper, well known Irish Setter breeder, had struggled for years with the problem of finding a show site. We ended up in a small high school gym with far more dogs than expected—60 English Setters, 40 Gordons, and 85 Irish. It was pandemonium but fun. For the first and only time in my memory of New York in February, the sun shone and it was like summer.

A gorgeous class bitch, Smokey Cinder of Glenarm (Afternod Ian Smokey x My Girl of Brookview, owned by Pusey, took the breed over many of the best specials in the country. Best Opposite to Ch. Windy Hill's Satan, owned by Klenk.

Westminster saw Smokey Cinder going Best Opposite, while a Junior handler-owner, Kim Cameron, won the breed with Ch. Thurston's Stylish Angus (Roevalley Duke x Osborne's Stylish Tammerlane II).

The spring Gordon Setter Club Midwest Specialty moved to Indianapolis, with an entry of 23. Am. & Can. Ch. Sangerfield Smokey won the breed and a group III, while Am. & Can. Ch. Gunbar Flapper went Best Opposite.

The Eastern Club Specialty at Trenton, New Jersey, had 14 in Sweepstakes, 38 in the classes. Once again Smokey Cinder came from Open to go Best of Breed, a rare win for a bitch. Best Opposite to Winners Dog, Chance's Lucky Ace (Dual Ch. Windy Hill's Lucky Chance x Ch. Aberdeen Artemis), Klenk.

Tartan Gordon Setter Club (Connecticut) had 22, another Specialty win for Sangerfield Smokey, and BOS to Ch. Gordon Hill Holly, CD (Gordon Hill Peg's Angus x Ch. Chips Chum of Gordon Hill, CD).

Group Placements

Ch. Sangerfield Jed: one I, three III, two IV in the U.S.; his Canadian Championship and two group II, two III. Jed was the first American Gordon to win a Canadian title in 35 years. Shortly thereafter, Ch. Sangerfield Smokey followed suit. His wins for the year, two group II in the U.S.; three group II, one IV in Canada.

Ch. Smokey Cinder of Glenarm had a group I, a fine win for a bitch, also a group IV. Others with one placement, Ch. Chance's Lucky Ace and Can. Ch. Sun-Yak Forty-Niner, owner Sunderland.

1961

An unusually severe winter with deep snows along the East Coast held down entries at all the shows.

Combined Setter Specialty had half as many Gordons. Best of Breed to a lovely bitch, Ch. Windy Hill Caryn B (Ch. Blake's Rogue of Windy Hill x Ch. Sycamore Lodge Sue), Vickers, and BOS to Windy Hill Stephen B (Dual Ch. Windy Hill's Lucky Chance x Ch. Windy Hill's Drusie B), Bradbury.

Westminster was way off, too. Muriel Clement handled her handsome bitch, Ch. Gordon Hill Holly, CD, to Best of Breed, with BOS to Ch. Dew-E's Douglas MacA. (Thurston's Thors Hill Artist x Thurston's Thors Hill Delight).

At Tartan, exhibitors were either snowed in or out, only four entries made it, but couldn't leave. Best of Breed went to Ch. Lazy Oaks Halenfred Amos (Ch. Halenfred Dusty Gold x Ch. Loch Adair Annie Laurie), Kaplan, and Best Opposite to Milestone Meg of Redchico (Milestone Favorite Star x Star Farm Belle), Chevalier.

Am. Can. Ch. Gunbar's Flapper shown winning Best Opposite at Gordon Setter Club Specialty, Indianapolis, Ind. in 1960. Judge Fred Hunt; Marge Platt owner-handler, Bill Platt presenting trophy. In 1961 Flapper won a BIS. She was the first and to date the only bitch to do so. *Frasie*

May 6, 1962, Gordon Setter Club of Am. Specialty at Trenton, N.J. Brood bitch class winner, left: Muriel Clement with Ch. Gordon Hill Holly, CD; center: Carol Chevalier with Glascott's Gordon Hill Ivy, Reserve bitch; and Jennie James with Sweepstakes winner, Gordon Hill Jelly Bean. Judge Ray Beale. *Brown*

The Midwest Club Specialty was held in St. Louis. Best of Breed to the consistent Midwest winner, Ch. Blarney Stone's Lancelot (Ch. Blarney Stone's Banshire x Ch. Windy Hill Claudia B). BOS to Blarney Stone's Bonnie Lassie.

At Trenton in May, Caryn B won her second Specialty, with BOS going to Ch. Brandywine of River's Edge (Shuriridge MacDuff x Windy Hill Nutmeg), Bradley.

The Big Event of the year came in September when Gunbar Flapper went Best in Show at the Winnipeg, Sask. show. This was the first big win for a bitch since 1928 when US/Can. Ch. Inglehurst Barberry did it, and the first BIS since the early 1950's when Thurston's Scot won Best American Bred In Show.

Group Placements

Am. & Can. Ch. Sangerfield Jed one II, one III, four IV; Am. & Can. Ch. Sangerfield Smokey two IV; Am. & Can. Ch. Gunbar Flapper BIS and two III (Canada); one I.

1962

Ch. Sangerfield Smokey won the Combined Setter Specialty and Westminster. Best Opposite at the Specialty was won by Ch. Windy Hill's Shiloh Gypsy (Butch's Chris of Shiloh x Stylish Black Lady), Levy, and Ch. Gordon Hill's Holly, CD, won at the Garden.

Once again a Gordon was invited to participate in the Field Exhibition held at the Garden. This time Pete Glass and his Fld. Ch. Page's Johnny Walker did the honors. This was great fun. An area was set up with corn stalks, etc. and a few birds (deceased if I remember correctly) planted here and there. All pointing breeds were eligible. Most entries were rather flurried.

February brought another round of very bad storms, and once again Tartan got smacked. Best of Breed to Sangerfield Jed, Best Opposite to Ch. Milestone Meg of Redchico. A serious virus made its appearance along the east coast this winter. Many dogs left this show to become seriously ill, and not a few died.

The Midwest Specialty was moved to Detroit. A sheet of ice covered the City. Roads were so hazardous that exhibitors were not allowed to leave town. Sangerfield Smokey won his fourth Specialty, and retired not long after as he was now over eight years old. BOS at Detroit went to that consistent winner Ch. Gunbar's Flapper who wasn't getting any younger either, being seven!

The May Specialty at Trenton was a repeat win for Ch. Chance's Lucky Ace, with BOS to a rising star, Ch. Afternod Alder (Ch. Afternod Drambuie x Afternod Kalmia), Wilcox.

Am. Can. Ch. Sangerfield Jed winning Best of Breed at the Garden under Judge Dr. Redden. F. Itzenplitz, owner-handler. 1963. This year Jed won four Specialties, three group firsts, among others.   *Brown*

Am. Can. Ch. Hickory Smoke Wild 'N Wully, CD, owner-breeder-handler Joyce Ruess. Shown going Best of Breed at the Gordon Setter Club of America Specialty at Trenton, N.J. 1965. Judge Clark Thompson. This dog was a prominent stud dog of the times.   *Shafer*

1962 group placements set no records. Sangerfield Jed won two II and one IV in the US, and one I, one II in Canada (making 25 placements to date). Sangerfield Smokey won one group IV.

1963

A good sized entry at the Combined Setter Specialty was topped by Ch. Sangerfield Jed and Ch. Gordon Hill Holly, CD, as Best Opposite. Jed also won Westminster but the small entry had no bitches.

The Tartan winter show had but ten entries, again plagued by bad weather. Best of Breed to Ch. Gunbar Repeater (Ch. Scotch Burr of Gunbar x Gunbar Jigger), Langsam; BOS to Breadalbane Nutmeg Laurel (Ch. Scotch Burr of Gunbar x Vagabond Gal), Campbell.

The Trenton Specialty had a good entry of 16 Sweeps and 40 in the regular classes. Sangerfield Jed was on a winning streak and won this Specialty, the Ohio Specialty, and Tartan in June. BOS at Trenton was Ch. Aberdeen Artemis (Ch. Fast's Falcon of Windy Hill x Windy Hill Ginger Boots), Lefkowitz. At Ohio, Jed's nine-year-old mother, Ch. Sangerfield Tillie, came from Veteran's Class to go BOS. Tillie was sired by Judge Palmer x Ch. Heslop's Burnvale Dawn. Jed won the group, as well.

At Tartan Ch. Meghan Maguire (Ch. Matson's Robin x Fletcher's Scotch Lorelei), Windus, was Best Opposite.

Group Placements

Sangerfield Jed had three group I, two group II, and two group III.

English's Little Joe (Thurston's Farmer Boy Jeff x Thurston's Stylish Lady), English; Ch. Afternod Alder and Ch. Star Farm's Rocket (Ch. Star Farm Best Bet x Banshire's Heather), Fleischman; all had single placements. Ch. Gunbar Repeater had two III and one IV.

1964

Ch. Afternod Alder ran off with Best of Breed at the Combined Setter Specialty and Westminster, a noteworthy effort for a bitch. At the Combined Setter Specialty Ch. Afternod Redchico Cutty Sark (Ch. Afternod Drambuie x Allspice of Redchico), Silk, was BOS.

The Trenton entry rose to 24 Sweeps and 55 in the classes, the biggest show yet. Best of Breed was won by Ch. Star Farm Rocket, while Ch. Afternod Wishbone (Ch. Afternod Hickory x Ch. Afternod Elgin II) went BOS, Chavkin.

The Ohio Specialty was larger, too, with an entry of 36, the largest in the Sporting Group. Sangerfield Jed won the breed and group I for a second year. BOS to Ch. Afternod Curry (Ch. Afternod Drambuie x Allspice of Redchico), Chevalier & R. Wilcox.

Ch. Afternod Wishbone was Best of Breed at the Tartan Specialty

84

proving that bitches were getting their fair share of attention; BOS to Ch. Chance's Lucky Buck (Dual Ch. Windy Hill's Lucky Chance x Ch. Windy Hill's Regina), Putchat.

Group Placements

Jed won two group I, two group II, and one IV. This was his last year in the ring. His career had eclipsed that of any other American Gordon with a record of 35 group placements. Seven Specialty Best of Breeds, four in 1963, set another record.

1965

No clear leader emerged this year. Ch. Buddy D of Han-Mar (Windy Hill's Davey B x Dixie Means), Christine, won the Combined Setter Specialty while Ch. Afternod Abbie of Aberfoyle went BOS.

At the Garden Ch. Afternod Callant (Ch. Afternod Drambuie x Ch. Afternod Woodbine), West, was Best of Breed, and Best Opposite was won by Ch. Ger-Don's Bridget Motherwell (Ch. Afternod Wallace x Dual Ch. Glascott's Scottish Majesty), Corbett.

Abbie of Aberfoyle went Best Opposite at the Trenton show, while Best of Breed to Am. & Can. Ch. Hickory Smoke Wild 'n Wully (Sergeant's Colorful Major x Windy Hill's Zoe), J. Reuss.

Warren, Ohio Specialty had an entry of 34, with Best of Breed to Ch. Brian Courageous, Klarer, and Ch. Sangerfield Tillie, now eleven years old, captured Best Opposite.

The Fall Tartan show had a good entry of 44. Ch. Afternod Wishbone repeated her win here, and BOS went to Ch. Buddy D of Han-Mar.

Only three dogs had group placements, Ch. Afternod Cutty Sark (Ch. Afternod Drambuie x Ch. Afternod Woodbine), Wilcox, had one IV, as did Ch. Ger-Don's Bartholomew Tweed (Ch. Afternod Wallace x Dual Ch. Glascott's Scottish Majesty), Rost.

Am. & Can. Ch. Ger-Don's Ambrose Hobkirk (Am. & Can. Ch. Hickory Smoke Wild 'n Wully x Dual Ch. Glascott's Scottish Majesty) placed once, group I, once, group III, and once group IV in Canada.

1966

Combined Setter Specialty with 42 entered was won by Ch. Wee Geordie Adair (Ch. Afternod Drambuie x Loch Adair Diana of Redchico), Chevalier. Best Opposite was a repeat win by that most successful bitch, Ch. Afternod Abbie of Aberfoyle.

At Westminster, English Show Champion and American Champion The Boss (Gay Hunter x Roevalley Teal) made his debut in the East. He was the first English Show Champion to be imported to America since the

Ch. Wee Geordie Adair with breeder, Carol Chevalier handler. BB at Combined Setter Specialty New York, 1966. Judge Langdon Skarda. Awarding trophy, owner Ken Lotker, a generous patron and worker for this show during the 60's.

Best Opposite at Combined Setter Specialty 1966, Ch. Afternod Abbie of Aberfoyle with breeder owner Wally Chavkin. Abbie was a top bitch of these years. She won BOS at this show in 1965 and 1967; BOS at Trenton GSCA Specialty in 1965 and BB at Tartan Specialty in 1966 plus a group III.

Ch. Afternod MacAlder Tyr, owners Stephenson and Lawreck. In 1966, handled by John Lawreck, Tyr had 27 BB and seven group spots including a first. He was named Top Gordon for the year. He is listed in Top Producers.

Imported Eng., Bermudian, and American Champion The Boss shown with Walter Shellenbarger handler, owners Bill and Marge Platt (Gunbar Kennels). The Boss was Best of Breed at Westminster in 1966, had many other breed wins and group placements on the west coast.

1940's and ran up an impressive show record on the West Coast for his owners, Bill and Marge Platt. BOS went to Brandywine's Heather, De Rossiers.

The Trenton Specialty in May was growing by leaps and bounds. This year's entry of 23 in Sweeps, 87 total, was a record. The proud winner, Ch. Afternod Cutty Sark, with BOS to Ch. Afternod Caramel (Ch. Afternod Drambuie x Ch. Afternod Woodbine), Recht & Wilcox.

At the Ohio Gordon Setter Specialty Ch. Afternod MacAlder Tyr (Afternod Fidemac x Ch. Afternod Alder) began a busy summer by going Best of Breed. Following a trend which has persisted until today, the Veteran Bitch went BOS. At age 11, Ch. Sangerfield Tracy (Look's Black Daniel x Ch. Heslop's Burnvale Edie) "wowed 'em."

Ch. Afternod Abbie of Aberfoyle topped an entry of 52 at Tartan, Best Opposite to Ch. Legend of Gael, CD (Ch. Chance's Lucky Buck x Lady Perfidia), Ann Tessler Rich.

The first Pacific Region Gordon Setter Club Specialty was held in September, with an entry of 24. Best of Breed was won by Ch. Wildfire Black Watch (Afternod Fidemac x Ch. Afternod Woodbine), Martin, who went on to a group III. Best Opposite was Ch. Afternod Ivy III (Afternod Fidemac x Ch. Afternod Alder), Sykes, a sister of MacAlder Tyr.

Group Placements

The second Gordon male to win Best in Show was Ger-Don's Ambrose Hobkirk at the Winnipeg, Sask. show, owned and handled by Angela Salter. He also had two group II in Canada.

English, American and Bermudian Ch. The Boss had 22 Best of Breeds, one group II, one III, and three IV.

Ch. Wildfire Windfall (Afternod Fidemac x Ch. Afternod Woodbine) garnered two group II and two IV shown in the Gulf Coast area, Freedman.

Ch. Afternod MacAlder Tyr ended a busy summer with 25 Best of Breed, one group I, two group II, two group III, and two group IV.

Single placements were given to Hickory Smoke Neil Cameron (Ch. George Gordon Sangerfield x Heslop's Hickory Huntress), Scholtz; Legend of Gael; Afternod Cutty Sark; Star Farm Rocket and Afternod Abbie of Aberfoyle.

1967

Ch. Legend of Gael, CD, won the Combined Setter Specialty while Best Opposite went to Ch. Hacasak's Sioux's Chance (Dual Ch. Windy Hill's Lucky Chance x Ch. Windy Hill's Regina), Christine. At the Garden only three bitches showed up, with the win going to Ch. Bonnie Gay of RuBern (Ch. Sangerfield Index x Ch. Alice of Achnacarry), Kurz.

The Trenton show was a disaster, with the grounds a sea of mud. On

First Specialty win for Ch. Legend of Gael, CD (w. 1965) came in 1967 at the Combined Setter Specialty, handled by his owner, Ann Tessler Rich. Judge P.C. Tuttle, trophy donor, George Pugh. *Klein*

Am. Can. Ch. Rogheath Ben MacDhui shown with John Lawreck, handler, owner Mrs. Robert Stahl. In 1968 this dog won the Pacific Regional Gordon Setter Club Specialty, repeating this win in 1969, 1970. Shown extensively until 1972 he had many group placements. He became one of the breed's top producers.

Can. Am. Ch. Cyn-Dan's Mister McTavish, Can. & Am. CD, became the oldest Gordon to win the Combined Setter Specialty in 1969 at age of nine. Shown with trophy, breeder-owner Dr. Danice Conway. Judge, John Stocker (Yorkley Kennels). John Lindsay, handler.

top of that it was cold, cars got stuck, you name it. The sodden winners were: Best of Breed, Am. & Can. Sporting Look (Ch. George Gordon Sangerfield x Am. & Can. Ch. Sangerfield Patsy, Am. & Can. CD) and Ch. Afternod Aberdeen (Ch. Afternod Drambuie x Ch. Afternod Ivy III), Kugelmas.

The Midwest Specialty, now a fixture at Warren, Ohio, had 21 Sweeps and 32 in the classes. Best of Breed went to a stylish bitch, Ch. Saturday Farm Killiedrum Eve (Ch. Sangerfield Smokey x Sangerfield Sybil), Cook, while her half brother Ch. PinePatch Palmer (Smokey x Ch. Sangerfield Tillie), Pugh, was given BOS.

Tartan had a big entry of 21 Sweeps, and 66 in the classes. Another member of a famous litter won Best of Breed, Ch. Afternod Scot of Blackbay (Afternod Fidemac x Ch. Afternod Alder), C. Dunham. Best Opposite to Ch. Windrock Hickory Paean (Ch. Hickory Smoke Wild 'n Wully x Meghan Maguire), A. Lustenberger.

The second show for the Pacific Regional found Black Watch repeating his win in 1966, with a consistent winner, Ch. Weaver's Tam O'Shanter (Stylish Rhythm x Livermore Lollipop), Weaver, taking the honors for Best Opposite.

Group Placements

Ch. Legend of Gael, CD, had one I, two IV.

Ch. Braun MacCumhal of Brookview (Bud O'Field Brookview x Prairie's Black Cinders) one group I, Walker.

Am. & Can. Ch. Cyn-Dan's Mister MacTavish (Roevally Duke x Lady of Ancastle) two group I, Conway.

Ch. Wildfire Black Watch; Ch. Mac's Casey of Camino (Am. and Mexican Ch. Windy Hill's MacGregor x Heatheridge Cinder Baby); Am. & Can. Ch. Chance's Lucky Lady (Dual Ch. Windy Hill's Lucky Chance x Ch. Windy Hill's Regina), Althaus, all had one group placement.

Mister MacTavish deserves special mention. He was the first Gordon to win both his obedience and show titles in Canada and the United States, plus the fact that he was about seven years old when he did it.

Loch Adair Diana of Redchico (Ch. Afternod Hickory x Allspice of Redchico) became the Top Producing Dam, All Breeds, having eight of her get finish in 1967. She went on to a total of 13, tying the previous record for the breed—owner, C. Chevalier.

1968

This year saw a whole new cast of characters. Best of Breed at the Combined Setter Specialty was the successful bitch, Ch. Wee Laurie Adair (Ch. Afternod Callant x Loch Adair Diana of Redchico), Chevalier. Best Opposite to Can. & Am. Ch. Sporting Look.

At the Garden, Laurie was Best Opposite, while Ch. Afternod Gallant Adair (Ch. Afternod Drambuie x Ch. Afternod Woodbine), Goepfert, won the breed.

At Trenton, Gallant Adair was Best Opposite to his sister, Ch. Afternod Gwen Adair, Bowen.

The Warren, Ohio Specialty held their first Sweepstakes with an entry of 16. Gallant Adair was Best of Breed, and the Sweeps winner, Sangerfield Portrait (Am. & Can. Ch. Sporting Look x Ch. Terlo's Lady of Clan Cameron), F. Itzenplitz, went BOS.

Mr. Ronald Butterworth from England judged the Tartan Specialty where they had an entry of 58. He liked Ch. Afternod Angus of Aberfoyle (Drambuie and Wishbone), Chavkin, for Best of Breed, and the group judge liked him for group I. Best Opposite went to OakLynn's Bonnie Bridget (Bud O'Field of Brookview x Imp. Borderland Taupie), McLean and Reynolds.

The Pacific Regional Specialty, now up to 37 entries, was won by the highly successful Ch. Rogheath Ben MacDhui (Ch. Afternod Anagram x Ch. Afternod Ivy III), Stahl, who also won a group IV. BOS was Weaver's Tam O'Shanter, repeating her 1967 win at this show.

Group Placements

Ch. Legend of Gael, CD, one group I, two group II, one group IV.

Ch. Wee Jock Adair (Ch. Afternod Callant x Loch Adair Diana of Redchico), Chevalier, group I.

Am. & Can. Ch. Afternod Sybilla (Afternod Fidemac x Ch. Afternod Alder) Canadian group IV, Gidday.

Ch. Loch Adair Merri Mac (Ch. Afternod Callant x Loch Adair Diana of Redchico), Altott, group IV.

1969

A snowstorm buried New York City for the February Combined Setter Specialty and Westminster. As a result, Gordon entries at the first show were down to 30, and only 10 made it to the Garden.

Best of Breed at the Specialty was Am. & Can. Ch. Cyn-Dan's Mister MacTavish, Am. & Can. CD. At age of nine, he made like a puppy, full of life and joy at being a show dog. Best Opposite was won by Ch. Terlo's Lady of Clan Cameron (Ch. Sangerfield Index x Ch. Terlo's Andrea), Ellis.

Ch. Afternod Scot of Blackbay was Best of Breed at the Garden and Ch. Saturday Farm Killiedrum Eve was the best bitch.

The Club Specialty, held for so many years at Trenton, was moved to the Penn-Treaty Kennel Club show, where there was a good entry of 17 Sweepstakes and 43 regular classes. Terlo's Lady of Clan Cameron was Best Opposite while Ch. Legend of Gael took the breed. By now going full

This photo represents a milestone in Gordon Setter history. Ch. Legend of Gael, CD, owned by
Cheever Porter and handled by the Forsyths won his first Best in Show at Vacationland Dog Club, C
1969. Breed judge Mrs. Beatrice Godsol. Then four years old, note the dramatic change since his v
1967. Truly, good Gordons mature at four years or better.

steam, Valor (Legend's kennel name) also won the GSCA Specialty at Warren, with Best Opposite to Ch. Gordon Hill Bydand Bonnie (Afternod Drambuie x Gordon Hill Happy Chum), Mattox.

Legend of Gael also won the Tartan Specialty where there were 10 Sweeps and 46 Regular clssses. BOS went to Ch. Afternod Gwen Adair.

Ben MacDhui repeated his win at the Pacific Regional, and Can. Ch. Heathero Amber Velvet was Winners Bitch and Best of Winners (Althaus-Metzler). Ch. Wildfire Wendy was BOS (Slocombe).

Group Placements

Ch. Legend of Gael, CD, had a total of three specialties, nine group I, six group II, two group III, and five group IV. He won his first Best In Show in the Fall.

Ch. Rogheath Ben MacDhui won one group I, one group II.

Ch. Dandy Dan of Blackmore (Afternod Rockingham x Hewitt's Duchess), Foulk, two group IV.

Single placements went to Ch. Loch Adair Merri Mac, Hickory Smoke Neil Cameron, and Pinerow's Stormy Forecast (Ch. Pinerow's Duncan of Redchico x Oak Lynn's Bonnie Bridget), Rose.

This year saw the first CDX since 1964, Steeleawae Wildfire Weesmokee, Bill Steele, and a Best Brace in Show was won by Ch. Terlo's Gordon Brus O'Melrose and Terlo's Jennifer O'Melrose, handled by Tom Rogers.

This decade was one with confusing statistics. Membership soared from 185 in 1960 to nearly 500 by 1969. The number of champions made per year also rose dramatically from a low of nine in 1961 to a high of 48 in 1967. Dozens of new enthusiasts began breeding and showing Gordon Setters, yet registrations poked along sometimes up, sometimes down, averaging about 45 per year increase (four or five litters).

Some Leading New Kennels and Owners

1960-1963

Walter and Lois Ellis	TERLO	PA
Charles Stephenson	MACALDER	SD
Charles and Judy Levy	GYPSY GLEN	PA
Dr. Edward and Phyllis Blasser	MACGEOWLS	PA
Sam and Kit Christine	HACASAK	PA
Mary Frances deLamerens	BRIARPATCH	OH
Gerry Windus	WINDROCK	NY
David B. Cook	KILLIEDRUM	NY
Bill and Mary Schultz	DUNHAM'S CORNER	NJ
John P. (Pete) and Kay Campbell	BREADALBANE	CT
Dewey and Elizabeth Thomas	DEW-E'S	NY

Al Rost	GER-DON	NY
Frank and Marilyn Fetchet	BLACKMORE	OH
Ralph Langsham		NY
William Van Ormer	VA-OR'S	MO
Susan de Silver (Junior member GSCA)		NY
Robert Rose	PINEROW	CT
Frances and Pete Glass	GLASCOT'S	CT
Peter Haerle	SUNBURST	
John and Phyllis Lawreck	HIGHLANDER	NJ

1964-1967

Jean Althaus Metzler and Mr. and Mrs. Robert Althaus	HEATHERO	CA
Keith Bechler	ST. ANDREW	CA
Judith Lawrence	SUTHERLAND	CA
Marilyn Slocombe	LOCH TAY	CA
Norm and Sue Sorby	SPRINGSET	CA
Lillian Sykes	ROGHEATH	CA
Theron Weaver	TAM O'SHANTER	CA
John Ansley	TOMARCAN	PA
Steve Gaydos		PA
Allan and Joyce Ruess	HICKORY SMOKE	PA
Ken Lotker	THORNYBURN	NY
Jacqueline Freundel	ELLICOTT	MD
Dolores Gidday	STILMEADOW	MI
Waldo Proctor	BROOKVIEW	MI
Arthur and Frances Anderson	VIKING HILL	NJ
Thoburn Kilmer	BONNIEBAIRN	NJ
Eric Bachman		NY
William Steele	STEELEAWAE	TX
Joel and Barbara Morris	BELMOR	VA

Canadian

Thomas and Margaret Bocking	GRIANAN	Ont.

Australia

Julie Dickinson	LORROY	Parkes NSW

1967-1969

Mary Ellen Hill	HI-LAWAY	CT
Mrs. Rosemary Stahl	OAK RIDGE	CA
Suzanne Freedman	WILDFIRE	TX
Sarah M. Muckerman	GLENMOORE	MO

94

William and Jeanine Dwelly	BERRIDALE	SC
William and Sandra Allis	ENTERPRISE	NY

1967-1969

George Bennett	BEN-WEN	NY
Roger Lapp	MCKEVIN	NY
Pam McLean	WILSCOT	CT
Harry Metzger	CAMERON	PA
Robert and Ruth Noren	IDLENOT	WI
Roy Thomas	KILTKLAN	CA
Cynthia and Seth Austin	PEACHAM	NY
Bobbie Jones	HYTYME	MO
Mrs. Elizabeth Clark	ROCKAPLENTY	VA
Kay Monaghan	KADON	MD
Judge Martin Pence		HI
Mrs. Bettie Cott	GLENALDER	IA

1970-1982 (Oct.)

Registrations grew steadily until they reached a peak in 1976 of 1383, a total not yet surpassed. Oddly, the number of pups per litter had been dropping steadily. Perhaps there are many Gordons out there whose papers are not going through the AKC?

This decade brought a steady increase in the extensive campaigning of Gordons by professional handlers. Figures show the difference this can make. In 1970, for instance, over one hundred group placements were made by 12 dogs, but three dogs accounted for 80% of the total. The end result was that more and more Gordon owners stayed for the Sporting Group judging as their confidence in the breed's chances continued to rise.

Another change has been that many small kennels have sprung up in areas where Gordons were never seen before—the southwest, southeast, the plains states, upper peninsula, until by the end of 1981 we find the population center for the breed has left the east coast.

The early 1970's continued to be dominated by Ch. Legend of Gael, CD, whose enormously successful career did not end until 1972. When he retired he had a lifetime total of 17 Bests in Show, 78 group firsts, and a total of seven Specialties.

Following closely on his heels were several top contenders: Ch. Torrance of Ellicott, handled by George Alston; Ch. MacNeal of Ellicott, handled by Ross Petruzzo, both dogs sired by Sir Gordie of Windy Hill x Ch. Loch Adair Kate, and soon after them came Ch. Afternod Yank of Rockaplenty (Ch. Wee Jock Adair, CD, x Ch. Afternod Ripple), handled by George Alston. All had much success as we shall see when we review the years.

95

In 1975 a two-year-old from California began a meteoric career ranging from coast to coast: Ch. Daron Rebel with a Cause (handled by Patti Grant). Sired by Ch. Rogheath Ben MacDhui x Ch. Ru-Bern's Sangerfield Bonnie, Rebel ended his career in 1977 with a record breaking 24 Best in Show awards, nine specialties in the East, midwest and on the coast.

In 1977 Ch. Ben-Wen's Benjy McDee (Ch. Windrock's Tory Claymore x Ch. Ben-Wen Dee's Bonnie Lass), handled by Ross Petruzzo, started a career that didn't end until 1982 with an incredible record of 27 Best in Show awards, 74 Group firsts, 49 other placements, *twenty* Specialties and a mind boggling 286 Bests of Breed out of 298 times shown.

One must acknowledge the dedication and ability of the handlers involved. To keep a dog in show condition and *show minded* for careers such as these takes genius.

1970

There were three Gordon Setter Club Specialties, plus the Combined Setter Specialty and the Tartan GSC Specialty.

Best of Breed at the Combined Setter Specialty went to Ch. PinePatch Lucky Ace of Spades (Ch. PinePatch Palmer x Chance's Lucky Duchess), Zimmer, while the class bitch took Best Opposite—Wee Bonnie CoriSue (Windrock's Skye McQueen x B. Bonnie Breigh) owned by Bill Dwelly.

Legend of Gael won the breed at the Garden, with the class bitch Afternod Heiress of Sark going Best Opposite, Reynolds.

The entry at the Midwest Specialty at Warren, Ohio climbed to 56. It was an exciting event as the Best of Breed winner, Ch. Briarpatch's Rob Roy, CD (Ch. Brian Courageous x Betelgeuse of Suffolk) was owner-handled by M. deLamerens to a group first. Best Opposite to Ch. Bonnie Lass of Blackmore (Afternod Rockingham x Dark Eyes Meg of Blackmore).

Ch. Legend of Gael, CD, won Tartan and went group I, while Best Opposite went to Ch. Afternod Heiress of Sark.

The Spring Gordon Setter Club Specialty was moved from Trenton, New Jersey to the Sand and Sea Show in August. Here again, Legend of Gael won the Breed and went on to a group II. Best Opposite was that consistent winner, Ch. Windrock's Aberdare Meghan (Windrock's Skye McQueen x Page's Gingerbread Jenny), Windus.

The Pacific Regional Specialty was for the first time held as a separate show. Entries were well up and everyone reported enjoying the relaxed atmosphere. Best of Breed went to Ch. Rogheath Ben McDhui, Stahl, with Best Opposite to Ch. Wildfire Wendy (Ch. Afternod Fidemac x Ch. Afternod Woodbine).

96

Ch. Windrock's Aberdare Meghan shown winning group III 1971. Handled by Ross Petruzzo, she became the top winning bitch in breed history.

Ch. Sutherland Vanessa with owner Chuck Palm, 1971.

Mrs. Elizabeth Clark with Ch. Rockaplenty's Pit-A-Pat which became the all time top producing Gordon bitch with 16 champions. 1971 photo.

Ch. Afternod Yank of Rockaplenty (1971) two years old, winning the group at Northwestern Indiana K.C. under Dr. Richard Gaetz. Handler, George Alston.

Group Placements

Ch. Legend of Gael, CD nine BIS; 29 group I, over 40 placements. Ch. Torrance of Ellicott one BIS, two group II, nine placements. First in Groups to: Ch. Dandy Dan of Blackmore plus one placement. Am. & Can. Ch. Afternod Scot of Blackbay, plus two placements. Ch. Briarpatch's Rob Roy, one group I. Ch. MacNeal of Ellicot had four placements; Can. Ch. Grianan Morag McTay, a bitch owned by Margaret Bocking, placed three times, a special event in Canada; Ch. Hickory Smoke Neil Cameron, one fourth; Ch. Rogheath Ben McDhui, three placements; and single placings to Ch. Anniversary Andrew (Cutty Sark of Brookview x Anniversary's Mac's Peaches), Platt; Am. & Can. Ch. Pinerow's Stormy Forecast; Am. & Can. Ch. Jock of Inwood (Heathero A'Highwayman x Proud Piper of Blackmore), Martin.

1971

Ch. Legend of Gael, CD, won the breed at the Combined Setter Specialty, Westminster, and the Tartan Specialty. Ch. Afternod Yank of Rockaplenty (Mrs. W.W. Clark) made his debut at the Ohio Specialty and went on to a nice group II. In California, Ch. Ebony Sunburst Tartan Lad (Ch. Afternod MacAlder Tyr x Sunburst Cheyenne Autumn), Sexton, won the Pacific Regional.

Best Opposite at the Combined Setter Specialty went to Ch. Terlo's Inverness Thistle (Am. & Can. Ch. Sporting Look x Ch. Terlo's Lady of Clan Cameron), Mattrews; at the Garden, that frequent winner, Ch. Windrock's Aberdare Meghan; at Ohio, the class bitch Rockaplenty's Pit-A-Pat (Ch. Torrance of Ellicott x Ch. MacAlder Alcy, CD), Clark.

At Tartan, Ch. Wee Bonnie Cori-Sue bested the bitches, and Ch. Sutherland Vanessa (Ch. Loch Adair Peer of Sutherland x Ch. Afternod Karma), Palm, did likewise at the Fall California Specialty.

Group Placements

Ch. Legend of Gael had seven Bests in Show, 39 group I, 40 other placements. He was named *Number One Sporting Dog,* something no Gordon owner would have dared dream of a few years back.

Ch. MacNeal of Ellicott had one group I plus nine placings. Once again Can. Ch. Grianan Morag MacTay had a fine year with six placings. Ch. Afternod Yank of Rockaplenty had eight group spots. Single group placements went to Ch. Windrock's Aberdare Meghan; Ch. Rogheath Ben McDhui; Ch. Sportin' Life (Can. & Am. Ch. Sporting Look x Ch. Terlo's Lady of Clan Cameron); Ch. PinePatch Lucky Ace of Spades; Ch. Highlander's MacAlder Brutus (Ch. Afternod MacAlder Tyr x Afternod Babbie of Aberfoyle, Jones.

Ch. Torrance of Ellicott (Clark/Freundel), shown with handler George Alston. Torrance won 3 Specialties in 1973. Judge, Mrs. Nancy Frey.

US. Can. Mex. and Int. Ch. Briarpatch's Rob Roy, CD, shown with junior handler-owner Maria Cecilia de Lamerens in Mexico, early 70's.

1972

Combined Setter Specialty: BB, Ch. Legend of Gael, CD; BOS, Ch. Windrock's Aberdare Meghan.

Westminster: BB, Ch. Afternod Yank of Rockaplenty; BOS, Ch. Afternod Adair of Ballantrae (Afternod Fidemac x Loch Adair Kimberley).

Midwest at Cortland, Ohio this time, with a big entry of 27 Sweeps and 65 class entries, with a triumph for Ch. Afternod Yank, going on to Best in Show. BOS, Ch. Windrock's Aberdare Meghan.

In July Tartan had an entry of 32 at the Farmington Valley Show in Connecticut. BB to Ch. Forecast Tradewinds, Cohan, BOS to the class bitch, Windrock's Miss Gale (Ch. Legend of Gael x Windrock's Aberdare Meghan), Scovil and Windus.

Sand and Sea hosted another GSCA Specialty, with an entry of 56 in the regular classes. Ch. MacNeal of Ellicott won the breed and a group III, to the delight of the Gordon clan. BOS a class bitch, Viking Hills Tammi (Ch. Afternod Scot of Blackbay, CD, x Glenraven Ambush), Anderson.

The Pacific Specialty had an entry of 77, won by a relative newcomer Ch. Daron Make Mine Scotch (Ch. Rogheath Ben McDhui x Ch. Ru-Bern's Sangerfield Bonnie) with BOS to Ch. Wildfire Wendy, who was making a habit of this.

Legend of Gael retired early in 1972 after establishing a record.

Ch. Windrock's Aberdare Meghan also retired after a career making her the top winning bitch of all time with over one hundred Bests of Breed, many group placements, always handled by Ross Petruzzo.

Group Placements

Wins in Canada and widely scattered areas of the US were a good sign.

Ch. Afternod Yank of Rockaplenty had three Bests in Show, seven group I, 22 others. Ch. MacNeal of Ellicott, a group I and 11 other placements. Can. Ch. Deerswood Pintail (Ch. Crakehall Lionhart x Borderland Olivia), an English import, had two group firsts in Canada. Am./Can. Ch. Kil-Mur-EE's Seonaid O'Grianan (Can. Ch. Loch Adair Nabob's Flip x Grianan Rachel McTay); Bocking won two group I, plus four additional placements; nice going for a bitch. Ch. PinePatch Lucky Ace of Spades—eight placements. Ch. Sportin' Life—four placements.

Others: Ch. Gunbar Anniversary Andrew (2); Ch. Torrance of Ellicott (1); Can. Ch. Grianan Morag McTay (1); Am. & Can. Ch. Grianan Victoria Balfour (2); Ch. VonReisenhof Wildfire Blaze (2); and Ch. Highlander's MacAlder Brutus (1).

1973

Ch. Torrance of Ellicott won Best of Breed at the Combined Setter

Ch. Cricket of Cromarty (B), owner-handler, Bob Chambers, judge Hollis Wilson. Top winning bitch for 1973.

Ch. Wee Bonnie Cori-Sue, CD, with owner Jeanine Dwelly (about 1973). Frequent BOS winner.   *Ritter*

Specialty and the Midwest Specialty in Ohio. Ch. MacNeal of Ellicott was Best of Breed at Westminster and the Mid-Atlantic Specialty. Best Opposite at the Combined Setter Specialty was Ledgewood's Adsum Action (Ch. Rogheath Ben MacDhui x Ch. Loch Adair Quentina, CD); Ch. Afternod Robena of Aberdeen (Ch. Afternod Simon x Afternod Nora Beinn Bhreagh) owned by California breeder Roy Thomas won Best Opposite at Westminster and later in Southern California at their first Far West Combined Setter Specialty she was again BOS. At that show Best of Breed was Ch. Stillmeadows Aragant Alfie (Ch. Afternod Callant x Am./Can. Ch. Afternod Sybilla), Pringle.

The Tartan Club Best of Breed was Ch. Pinepatch Lucky Ace of Spades, with Afternod Alexandra (Ch. Afternod Simon x Ch. Afternod Aberdeen) Best Opposite. Ace went on to a group III.

In Ohio, Best Opposite was Ch. Windrock's Miss Gale (Scovil). At Mid-Atlantic, Ch. MacAlder Hacasak Jasmine (Ch. Afternod MacAlder Tyr x Ch. Hacasak Pocahontas), Lawreck, took this win.

The Pacific Regional had an entry of 59. Best of Breed to Ch. Daron Monarch (Ch. Rogheath Ben McDhui x Ch. Ru-Bern's Sangerfield Bonnie), Wedeman, with BOS going to Ch. Heathero Amber Velvet (Ch. Wildfire Black Watch x Dual Ch. Chance's National Velvet), Althaus / Lanning / Metzler.

Group Placements

No BIS this year. How soon we become accustomed to the unaccustomed! Just a few years ago a BIS for a Gordon seemed a dream.

The winning bitch this year was Ch. Bo-Cham's Cricket of Cromarty (Crestland's Duncan's Fancy x Ch. Brookforest April Dancer), Bob and Joan Chambers. In 36 shows she amassed 28 Bests of Breed, six Best Opposite, a group II and IV.

Ch. MacNeil of Ellicott had one group I, five additional placements.

Ch. Pinepatch Lucky Ace of Spades had one group I, 11 other placements.

Ch. Torrance of Ellicott won three placements.

Others with singles were: Ch. Page's M'Lord Royal Scot (Dual Ch. Glenraven Autumn Smoke x Page's Bit-O-Liz Betsy), DeFalco; Ch. Tomarcan Yair Linn of Gowdie (Dual Ch. MacGeowl's MacDougal x Yair of Drevaburn), Severance; Ch. VonReisenhof Wildfire Blaze; Ch. Windrock's Briarcliffe Brandy (Ch. Windrock's Smokey MacLean x Ch. Lady Jane of Markham), Rivellese; Ch. Windrock's Kelly MacLeod (B) (Ch. Hickory Smoke Black Douglas x Jon's Majestic Lady), Corcoran.

1974

This year saw an increase to seven Specialties, plus five so-called

Booster shows all under the egis of the Gordon Setter Club of America, Inc. New areas represented were Atlanta, Georgia; Santa Ana, California; Chicago, Milwaukee and Des Moines.

Gordons were again in the limelight. Ch. MacAlder Alcy, CD, was the *Top Producer All Breeds* with a record of 15 champions. This also topped the previous Gordon Setter record of 13. Mrs. W.W. Clark of Rockaplenty Kennels was the proud owner.

Ch. Afternod Yank of Rockaplenty (also owned by Mrs. Clark) had a most successful year winning Best of Breed at the Combined Setter Specialty, Westminster and the Midwest Specialty in Ohio. Best Opposites were: at Combined Setter Specialty, Ch. Afternod Ember V (Afternod Profile of Sark x Ch. Afternod Maud MacKenzie), Wilcox; at the Garden, Ch. Loch Adair Ripple's Regal Aire (Ch. Wee Jock Adair x Ch. Afternod Ripple), Chevalier; and in Ohio, Ch. Windrock's Miss Gale repeated her win of 1973.

In California at the Far West Combined Setter Specialts Best of Breed was won by Ch. Sutherland Dunnideer Waltz (Ch. Afternod Anagram x Ch. Hi-Laway's Calopin), Buletza, with BOS going to Ch. Daron Monarch, Wedeman.

In April the Southern California Regional group had their first Specialty. Best of Breed was Ch. Oakridge Mr. Mike of Shinfayne (Ch. Rogheath Ben MacDhui x Ch. Afternod Octavia III), Fantin. Bos went to a sister, Ch. Oakridge Trick or Treat, Lanskron.

The Mid Atlantic Specialty was held for the first time at Staten Island and won honors for being the most rained on show of the year, plus having a strong cold wind off the ocean. The dogs slogged around cheerfully even though they soon were soaking wet. Ch. Torrance of Ellicott, by now a Veteran, showed at his best and topped the breed, with the Best Bitch being the elegant Ch. Windrock's Miss Gale.

July saw a Specialty at Waukesha, Wisconsin with a good entry of 79. Best of Breed went to Ch. Rockaplenty's Hang Em High (Ch. Afternod Yank of Rockaplenty x Ch. Rockaplenty's Pit-A-Pat), Carden, with Best Opposite to Am. & Can. Ch. Sangerfield Patsy, CD (Am. & Can. Ch. Sporting Look x Ru-Bern's Miss Pepper), Sanderson/Itzenplitz.

The Pacific Regional was won by an eastern dog, Ch. Johnston's Highland Storm (Hacasak Encorce x Hacasak Chicasaw), Carden. BOS went to Ch. Sutherland Sparkling Claret (Ch. Stilmeadows Aragant Alfie x MacAlder Clare of Sutherland), Thompson.

Group Placements

Fifteen Gordons placed in the Sporting Group but only Yank won a Best in Show with 41 other placements.

Ch. Daron Rebel With a Cause won a group I plus three other spots. Ch. Forecast Tradewinds had one group I, one IV. Am. & Can. Ch.

104

Brother and sister going Best of Breed and Best Opposite at Southern Cal. GSCA Specialty, 1974. Judge Robert Kelton. At left, Patti Grant with Ch. Daron Rebel With a Cause, Ch. Daron Rainbows 'N Roses on right. *Bergman*

US. Can. Ch. Johnston's Highland Storm (about 1974). Winner of more than 100 Bests of Breed, many group placements. Handler, Dennis Kniola.

Am. Mex. Ch. KiltKlan's Robbie Mac Ben shown winning the Group at Club Canofilo de Baja California A.C. under judge Derek Rayne. The next day Robbie won group II. Handler-owner Doug Toomey.

Johnston's Highland Storm had three group I, ten additional placings. Ch. Rockaplenty's Celebration (Ch. Afternod Yank of Rockaplenty x Ch. Rockaplenty's Rack On), Pharr, had four placements. Ch. Windrock's Briarcliffe Brandy placed four times, while Ch. Pinepatch Lucky Ace of Spades placed three times.

Single placements went to: Ch. Afternod Ember V; Am. & Can. Ch. Afternod Nimrod Nuggets (Ch. Wee Jock Adair, CD, x Ch. Afternod Wendee), Mitchell; Ch. Daron Make Mine Scotch; Ch. Daron Monarch; Ch. Dew-EE's Sangerfield Alfresco (Am. & Can. Ch. Sporting Look x Sangerfield Jayne), Sanger; Ch. MacNeal of Ellicott; Ch. Sutherland Odds On (Ch. Loch Adair Peer of Sutherland, CD, x Ch. Afternod Karma), Palm, and Ch. Windrock's Miss Gale.

1975

Combined Setter Specialty was held once more at the Statler-Hilton. It was lovely for exhibitors, but not so hot for the hotel. One more year and they had had it. In 1977 we were again looking for a show site. Exhibitors also had had it. Unable to exercise their dogs outside, many found the confines of exercise pens in a small anteroom too much of a change for their dogs. The Boys In Blue were waiting at the hotel door to nab those desperate souls who attempted to sneak their dogs out for some fresh air.

The Statler was crammed with dogs, breed specialties were on every floor, it seemed. It was a whirl of social activity involving everybody who was anybody in any breed plus judges and AKC personnel. Too bad it had to end.

The Gordon entry of 67 was off quite a bit. Best of Breed went to Ch. Rockaplenty's Celebration, with BOS to Ch. Afternod Ember V.

Westminster had 22 Gordons, quite good. It was a wonderful day for the breed when Yank went First in the Sporting Group! Best Opposite was won by Ch. Boldbrook's Miss Holly (Ch. Afternod Yank of Rockaplenty x Ch. Rockaplenty's Band Wagon), Owens/Swanson.

The bad weather that began earlier culminated in a real blizzard in the Big Apple, marooning many dog people for several days.

The Far West Combined Setter Specialty was won by a brother-sister team, Ch. Daron Rebel with a Cause and Ch. Daron Rainbows and Roses. This pair repeated their wins at the Southern Cal. Specialty.

Rebel also won the Midwest Specialty, held this time in Springfield, Ohio, with Best Opposite to Ch. Idlenot's Lady Guinevere (Ch. Afternod Advocate x Ebony Lady), Zak. Ohio's first independent show, it was a great success with 81 entries from 18 states.

Mid-Atlantic Specialty saw Am., Can. & Bda. Ch. MacNeal of Ellicott topping the breed, while Best Opposite went to Ch. Afternod Penny (Dual Ch. Glenraven Autumn Smoke x Ch. Afternod Ellen of TeeQuinn), Matteis.

Waukesha show had a good entry of 74 in the classes, 26 Sweeps. Best of Breed was won by Ch. Laird Duncan of Berridale (Ch. Rogheath Ben MacDhui x Ch. Wee Bonnie Cori-Sue, CD), Dwelly. Am. & Can. Ch. MacAlder Lona (Ch. Rogheath Ben MacDhui x MacAlder Beauty), Stomp, was the best bitch.

The Northern California Specialty had a big entry of 79 topped by Ch. Daron Rebel With a Cause, while BOS went to Ch. Oakridge Magic Marker, CD (Ch. Rogheath Ben MacDhui x Ch. Afternod Octavia III), Herschler.

Group Placements

Ch. Daron Rebel With a Cause had six Best In Show awards, 16 group firsts, and twenty other placements. Ch. Afternod Yank of Rockaplenty, CD, had one group first, and what a splendid one at Westminster, the first Gordon to win it. Am. & Can. Ch. Johnston's Highland Storm placed nine times. Am., Can. & Bda. Ch. Rockaplenty's Celebration garnered eight placements. Ch. Rockaplenty's Hang Em High won five placements. Ch. Laird Duncan of Berridale placed three times. Ch. Windrock's Briarcliffe Brandy also had three wins. Am., Can. & Bda. Ch. MacNeal of Ellicott won a group I and a II.

Others included: Ch. Jayels Midnight Cowboy (Heathero Arran Ben Ayr x Heathero's Windsong), Buckley & Long; Ch. MacAlder's Collin (Ch. Afternod MacAlder Tyr x Afternod Babbie of Aberfoyle), Stephenson; Am. & Can. Ch. MacAlder Mr. Chips, Stephenson; Ch. McMac's O'Dorsey's Lamont (Ch. Torrance of Ellicott x Ch. Timberdoodle Thistledown), White; Ch. Sevshun's Tracy MacKnight (Ch. Windrock's Tory Claymore x Page's Meghan of Glomora, CD), J. Schultz; Ch. Sutherland Odds On.

The youngest Gordon Setter show champion ever recorded would appear to be Ch. Blakader's Brandywine, a bitch who finished at eight months of age. Her sire is Ch. Rockaplenty's Celebration, the dam is Gael's Bonnie Lass, owner, Kitty Pharr.

Am., Can. & Bda. Ch. MacNeil of Ellicott (1966-1980) had his last big win at age of nine when he went Best of Breed from the Veteran Class at the Paumanauk Booster, and then on to a group II. His illustrious career included over 200 Bests of Breed, 60 group placements, and a record of 45 champion get (by 1982).

Ch. Rockaplenty's Celebration completed his Bermudian show championship in three shows with a group I and III.

Frau Waldtraut Venz wrote from Germany that her Am. & German Ch. Gordon Hill Wilscot Lektor had again won Champion of the State of Rhineland, and Best In Show in a combined Setter Specialty with 175 entries.

108

Ch. Daron Rebel With a Cause continued to lead the pack. He was Best of Breed at the Combined Setter Specialty, Westminster, Far West Combined Setter Specialty, Southern Cal. Specialty, and the Northern Cal. Specialty.

The Midwest Specialty at Springfield, Ohio had a bigger entry, this time 86 class dogs and 37 Sweepstakes entries. Best of Breed to a handsome Class dog, Rockaplenty's Real McCoy (Ch. Afternod Yank of Rockaplenty, CD x Ch. Rockaplenty's Pit-A-Pat), Robinson.

Mid-Atlantic at New Brunswick, N.J. this year had a small entry of 34 in the classes, 20 in Sweeps. Best of Breed to Ch. McMac's George (Ch. Torrance of Ellicott x Ch. Timberdoodle Thistledown), Watson.

Great Lakes held their first independent specialty at the home of Rudy and Nancy Zak with the huge entry of 92 in the classes, 34 in Sweepstakes. Best of Breed to Am. & Can. Ch. MacAlder Mr. Chips.

Best Opposite Sex went to a different bitch at each show. At the Statler where the Combined Setter Specialty was held for the first time, that consistent winner, Ch. Sevshun's Tracy MacKnight won the award. Far West went to another consistent winner; from the Veteran's class it was Ch. Wildfire Heather. In Ohio, Am. & Can. Ch. Vagabond Lark of Rockaplenty, CD (Ch. Afternod Yank of Rockaplenty, CD, x Ch. Rockaplenty's Rugged but Right), Scott, was owner handled to her win. Ch. Windrock's Miss Gale, another frequent winner, took Mid-Atlantic. At the 10th Annual Northern Cal. Specialty at San Rafael on beautiful, lakeside grounds, BOS to Ch. Kendelee Pearl of a Girl (Ch. Sutherland MacDuff x Ch. Afternod Nighean Kendelee), Ellen Bruck. Ch. Inwood Kerrie On (Ch. Jock of Inwood x Ch. Cricket of Macalester), Martin, topped the big entry of bitches at Great Lakes.

Group Placements

Ch. Daron Rebel With a Cause had another highly successful year with five Bests in Show, 33 Group I and 40 additional placements. Am. & Can. Ch. Laird Duncan of Berridale had three group I, four group III. Ch. Kris' Black Bart (Ch. Afternod Yank of Rockaplenty, CD, x Ch. MacAlder Ingenue of Chris) had one group I, one IV. Ch. Forecast Tradewinds, a group I. Am. & Can. Ch. McMac's George, four placements. Am. & Can. Ch. Rockaplenty's Hang Em High, six placements. Am. & Can. Ch. MacAlder Mr. Chips, three placements. Ch. Windrock's Briarcliffe Brandy, two placements. Ch. McMac's O'Dorsey's Lamont, two placements.

Those with single placements include: Ch. Boldbrook's Yankie Junior (Ch. Afternod Yank of Rockaplenty, CD, x Ch. Rockaplenty's Band Wagon), Pickell; Ch. Gordon Hill Run For Daylight (Hacasak Metacom x

Am. Can. Bermudian Ch. MacNeal of Ellicott with owner, Kay Monaghan. MacNeal was named stud dog of the year 1976.

The late, very popular Sarah Muckerman, GSCA Membership Chairman, with Ch. Mickthea' Sporting Lass, CD, finishing under Judge Brodie at the 1976 club Regional Specialty near Chicago

Ch. Sevshun's Tracy MacKnight—top winning bitch for 1975, 1976 and 1977 with owner-handler, Donald Schultz.

Am. & Can. Ch. Rockaplenty's Hang Em High with handler Loree Ragano, (about 1976). Judge Hobbs.

Am. Can. Ch. MacAlder Mr. Chips, BB at Far West Specialty of the GSCA, 2/19/77. Handler Joyce Nilsen, judge the late, popular Winifred Heckmann.   *Jayne Langdon*

Ch. Gordon Hill Tyrelle MacAlder), Perrelli; Ch. MacAlder Nike Angel Baejacs (Ch. Rogheath Ben MacDhui x Ch. MacAlder Flame), Young/Miller; Ch. Sevshun's Tracy MacKnight; Ch. Sir Duncan of Glen Alder (Ch. Kirkaldy King x Glenalder Bonnie Brooke), Barker; Ch. Tarbaby's Candidate (Ch. Afternod Yank of Rockaplenty x Ch. Tarbaby's Midnight Sapphire), Faengi/Tenaglia.

One of the more interesting careers was that of Ch. Daron Majestic Jet (Ch. Rogheath Ben MacDhui x Ch. Ru-Bern's Sangerfield Bonnie), owned by Lt. Col. and Mrs. Edward Grabman of New Mexico. Jet went to Germany with his owners while Col. Grabman was stationed there. Shown until 1976 he won eleven CACIBs at shows in Belgium, Luxembourg, Austria, Germany and France. He became a VDH Sieger. Only the second American-bred Gordon to be shown on the continent, he returned here with his owners and as of 1982 is living a happy life back in New Mexico.

1977

The Combined Setter Specialty, looking for a home, tried Upsala College in New Jersey. Access was easy, parking roomy, but the building too small for so many dogs and rings. Gordons had an entry of 85, with Best of Breed going to Ch. Daron Rebel With a Cause, BOS to Ch. Stumpy Acres Blandwagin Kate (Ch. Afternod Yank of Rockaplenty x Ch. Stumpy Acres Kadon Katie), Zoll.

The Far West Combined Setter Specialty also had a good entry with 62 in the classes, 23 in Sweepstakes. Best of Breed went to Am. & Can. Ch. MacAlder Mr. Chips, handled by Joyce Nilsen and BOS to Ch. Wildfire Heather.

Midwest Gordon Setter Specialty held at Springfield, Ohio had an entry of 99, the best so far. Best of Breed to that fast-rising star, Ch. Ben-Wen's Benjy McDee (Ch. Windrock's Tory Claymore x Ben-Wen's Dee's Bonnie Lass), Annello/Pearlstein. BOS to another fast rising star, Rockaplenty's Sunshine (Am. Can. Ch. Rockaplenty's Hang Em High x Ch. Rockaplenty's Miss Kitty), Vines/Clark.

For the first time a program was provided for the GSCA membership. Following the dinner Saturday night, Rachel Page Elliott presented her interesting lecture on gait. This was well attended, suggesting that more could be done at Specialties in the way of informative programs for the members.

The Mid-Atlantic Specialty, also looking for a home, tried the Penn-Ridge show. With an entry of 53, Benjy topped not only the breed, but went on to a Best In Show, something he did often for the next three years, truly a record.

Ch. Rockaplenty's Sunshine bested the bitches at this show, something she continued to do with frequency.

Ch. Wildfire Heather, BOS at Far West Specialty. Judge W. Heckmann. One of many wins for thi lovely bitch.

At the Pacific Regional, there was a fine entry of 83 to make 123 entries. For once, there was heavy rain in sunny California. Best of Breed to Ch. Ben-Wen's Benjy McDee, and BOS to Ch. Wildfire Heather, the youthful Veteran.

The Midwest All Setter Specialty held in Chicago had a big Gordon entry of 95 with a total of 122 entries. Best of Breed to Am. & Can. Ch. Laird Duncan of Berridale, with Best Opposite to Ch. Rockaplenty's Mish Mash (Ch. Afternod Yank of Rockaplenty x Ch. Rockaplenty's Pit-A-Pat, Crabtree.

Southern California held their first independent Specialty October 22 at Arleta, California, with an entry of 60. Mr. Chips was Best of Breed, with Best Opposite to Ch. Sutherland Peeress (Ch. Sutherland Odds On x Sutherland Katrine), Lawrence/Green.

Booster shows were held at Salem, Oregon; Atlanta, Georgia; Minneapolis; Battleground, Washington; Denver, Colorado, and Des Moines.

Group Placements

Ch. Ben-Wen's Benjy McDee, three Bests in Show, seven group I and 25 other placements. Ch. Daron Rebel With a Cause, two Bests in Show, ten group I and seven other placements. Am. & Can. Ch. MacAlder Mr. Chips, seven group firsts, nine other placements. Ch. Boldbrook Minnesota Fats (Ch. Afternod Yank of Rockaplenty x Rockaplenty Band Wagon), Collins, one group I, five additional placements. Ch. Norcoaster's MacManus (Ch. Norcoaster's Glen Plaid x Rockaplenty's Good News), Grimm, one group I, three other placements. Am. & Can. Ch. Laird Duncan of Berridale, three placements. Ch. Caesar of Berridale (Ch. Laird Duncan of Berridale x Ch. Duchess of Windy Hill), Walker, two placements. Ch. Kris' Black Bart, two placements. Ch. Rossdhu Brae Ceanannus (Ch. Sutherland Odds On x Ch. Sutherland Ullapool Piper), Cowset, two placements.

Those with single placements: Am. & Can. Ch. McMac's George; Am. & Can. Ch. Rockaplenty's Pride and Joy (Ch. Afternod Yank of Rockaplenty, CD, x Ch. Rockaplenty's Pit-A-Pat), Jordan: Ch. Rockaplenty's Sunshine.

1978

This year the Combined Setter Specialty tried holding its show at a Holiday Inn at the Newark Airport. There were plenty of negative aspects which could not have been predicted. The innkeeper provided abominable service and was rude beyond belief. No provision had been made to accommodate the many people using the dining room so that two harried waitresses, and one hysterical chef were left to cope.

The conference room was so small that only two breeds could be judged at a time. Even so, the Gordon entry was 92. Best of Breed, Ch. Daron Rebel With a Cause; BOS, Ch. Rockaplenty's Sunshine.

Seventeen dogs were entered at the Garden, with Best of Breed to Ch. Ben-Wen's Benjy McDee, and Sunshine, Best Opposite.

At the Far West Combined Setter Specialty, Ch. MacAlder Mr. Chips took the Breed, and Ch. Wildfire Heather Best Opposite.

The Midwest show at Springfield, Ohio, now a lovely outdoor event, had 130 entries, with brother and sister champions taking top spots: Rockaplenty's Real McCoy, CD, Best of Breed, and little sister, Rockaplenty's Peaches 'N Cream (Clark), best bitch.

Twenty-two entries appeared at the Paumanauk Gordon Setter Club Specialty on Long Island. Best of Breed went to Ch. Ben-Wen's Benjy McDee, with Best Opposite to Ch. Sevshun's Tracy MacKnight.

The Mid-Atlantic GSCA Specialty, held again at the Penn Ridge show, saw Benjy win his second Specialty and Best In Show there. Melissa White's lovely bitch, Ch. Rockaplenty's Salute to Erik (Ch. Rockaplenty's Hang Em High x Ch. Rockaplenty's Miss Kitty), won Best Opposite.

In September, the Pacific Regional had an entry of 66, with Ch. Daron Rebel With a Cause winning the breed, Ch. Sutherland Lass of Shambray (Ch. Loch Adair Peer of Sutherland x Ch. Afternod Karma) going Best Opposite.

October saw the Southern California GSCA Regional with an entry of 14 Sweepstakes, 70 in regular classes. Best of Breed, Ch. McGehee's The Piper (Ch. Daron Monarch x HGL's Bydand Lass) and BOS to the class bitch, McGehee's Hi-Jinx (Ch. Daron Monarch x MacAlder Queen of Scots), both dogs the property of John and Betty McGhee.

Group Placements

, Ch. Ben-Wen's Benjy McDee had seven Bests in Show, two Specialties, 12 group I and 33 other placements. Ch. Daron Rebel With a Cause, three group I, four other placements. Ch. Rockaplenty's Real McCoy, CD, one Best in Show, seven placements. Ch. Blossomaire's Believe It or Not (Ch. Dunnideer Easy Does It x Ch. Daron Highland Fling), Yates, three placings. Ch. Boldbrook's Yankie Junior also with three placings.

Having two placements were: Norcoaster's MacManus, MacAlder Mr. Chips; Caesar of Berridale; McMac's George; Ch. O'Eire's Lord Blak Magic Jason (Ch. McMac's Return to Ravenscraig x Ch. Idlenot's Lady Guinevere), Ashburn; Rockaplenty's Hang Em High; and Boldbrook's Minnesota Fats.

Single spots went to: Ch. McMac's Hawkeye of Cameron (Ch. McMac's George x Ch. Viking Hills Lady Bea), Watson; Sutherland

116

Am. & Can. Ch. Rocka-plenty's Real McCoy, CDX, shown with handler Karen Prickett winning BIS at Mad River K.C. Ohio, 1978. Judge Bernard McGivern. *Martin Booth*

Ch. Caesar of Berridale with owner-handler, B. Walker. Winner of numerous breeds and group placements. *Missy Yuhl*

Ogilvy Bran (Ch. Sutherland MacDuff x Ch. Sutherland Lass of Shambray), Maounis; Sutherland Odds On; Kris' Black Bart; McGehee's The Piper; Ch. Bo-Cham's Byline on Sports (Ch. Sportin' Life x Ch. Bo-Cham's Cricket of Cromarty), Chambers; Loch Loin's Excalibur (Ch. Sutherland MacDuff x Ch. Sutherland Vaillance Gilda), Gabbert, from the classes.

1979

A few dogs did a lot of winning. Ch. Ben-Wen's Benjy McDee had his best year, copping the Combined Setter Specialty; Westminster breed, Midwest, Ohio Specialty; Paumanauk Specialty; and Mid-Atlantic Specialty where he once more went on to Best In Show.

Ch. Rockaplenty's Salute to Erik also had a most successful year. She took Best Opposite at the Combined Setter Specialty, Westminster, and Peach Blossom (Atlanta), and Best of Breed at the Tartan GS Specialty.

Am. & Can. Ch. MacAlder Mr. Chips won the Northwest Specialty. Southern California went to Ch. Chapparal Ace's High (Ch. MacAlder Mr. Chips x Ch. MacLeod's Electra O'Chaparral), L. Sanders. Am. & Can. Ch. Rockaplenty's Real McCoy won the Far West Combined Setter breed Specialty, Great Lakes (Ill.), and Peach Blossom Specialties. Ch. Rockaplenty's Nomad (Ch. Afternod Yank of Rockaplenty x Ch. Rockaplenty's Pit-A-Pat), Cohen, was Best of Breed at the Northern California Specialty.

Other Best of Opposite Sex winners were: Ch. Don-D's Gillian (Ch. Daron's Rebel With a Cause x Ch. Don-D's Miss Mischief), Selle, at Far West; in Ohio Ch. Scothill's Goode Faithe, Veteran bitch entry owned by Jack Page; Mid-Atlantic, Ch. Rockaplenty's Sunshine; Tartan, Ch. Glenwood's Damn Yankee (Ch. Afternod Yank of Rockaplenty x Ch. Glenwood's Heavenly Body), E. Schuster; Ch. Claymore's Autumn Aria (Ch. Loch Adair Redchico Othello x Ch. Ledgewood's Camura), Del Buono, at Paumanauk, and at Great Lakes Am. & Can. Ch. O'Hillock's Divine Sarah (Ch. Rockaplenty's Hang Em High x Jennifer Gay Lady), S. Walter.

A veteran bitch, no newcomer to the Winners Circle, Ch. Sutherland Lass of Shambray, J. Lawrence, took Best Opposite at Northwest, Southern California and Northern California Specialties.

Group Placements

Ch. Ben-Wen's Benjy McDee made a record number of Best in Show and group wins: seven BIS, 27 Group I, and 38 additional. Am. & Can. Ch. Rockaplenty's Real McCoy was also successful with ten group I, and 18 others. Am. & Can. Ch. Blossomaire Believe It or Not had a group I, plus

Ch. Rockaplenty's Nomad with handler Patti Grant taking the breed at the Pacific Regional Specialty of the GSCA in 1979. Nomad is now owned by Mrs. Elizabeth Clark. *Jayne Langdon*

Ch. Rockaplenty's Sunshine with handler, Mary A. Alston, going BOS at Mid-Atlantic Specialty, 1979. Judge W. E. Tipton.

Ch. Loch Loin's Finn McCoul, CD, with owner Pierre Brun at the GSCA Northwest Specialty, 1979. *Lindemaier*

Ch. Loch Loin's Ebisu Ginger, CD, going BOS, Northwest Regional GSCA Specialty, Washington, 1980. *Lindemaier*

GROUP
FIRST

WESTMINSTER
KENNEL CLUB
1980

Ch. Ben-Wen's Benjy McDee winning Group I at Westminster in 1980, judge Peter Thomsen. Only the second Gordon to do this. *Gilbert*

two other spots. Ch. O'Eire's Lord Blak Magic Jason had two group I, six others. Ch. Rockaplenty's Sooner Victory (B), (Am. & Can. Ch. Rockaplenty's Hang 'Em High x Ch. Rockaplenty's Miss Kitty), Regano, had four placements.

Other placements in the Sporting Group were: Ch. Kris' Black Bart (2); Ch. McMac's George (2); Ch. Caesar of Berridale (3); Ch. Kendelee Pendragon (Ch. Sutherland MacDuff x Ch. Afternod Nighean Kendellee (1), Sorenson/Buck; Am. & Can. Ch. Laird Duncan of Berridale (1); Ch. Sutherland Odds On (1); Ch. Smokey Islay Peat of Delta (Ch. Loch Adair Titan of Tedmar x Ch. Smokey Island Mist of Delta), Currie (1); Ch. Rockaplenty's Nomad (2); Ch. Boldbrook's Yankee Junior (3) and Ch. Don-D's Gillian (1).

1980

The statistics for this year are most unusual. While thirty Gordon Setters won group placements only Ch. Ben-Wen's Benjy McDee won Bests in Show (2) in the U.S. In Canada, the first Canadian bred, owner-handled Gordon to go BIS was Am. & Can. Ch. Clansman Colourguard, owned by Jim and Janice Stomp. (See Canadian chapter for details.)

There were ten Gordon Setter Club sponsored Specialties, with one dog, Benjy, winning two, plus the breed at Westminster. From the standpoint of prestige, Benjy's group I at the Garden was *IT* for 1980. Many truly great Gordons have appeared in the Sporting group at this show dating back to the late 1800's, yet they are usually passed over. Benjy is only the third Gordon to be lucky, and the second to win the group. But, I'm betting it won't be long before a Gordon goes Best in Show at Westminster. In this year MacNeal of Ellicott, truly a legendary Gordon with a wonderful record of wins and of successful progeny, died at age of 14. To own a dog like that is a career in itself, and Kay Moneghan was wise to realize early what a gem she had.

The Combined Setter Specialty was held for the first time at the Field House at Rockland Community College, Suffern, N.Y. Not a flake of snow fell on New York, but those exhibitors driving up from the Southeast had to struggle through heavy storms in the area of Washington, D.C. This was a huge building. The three setters were judged at one time and there was still room for more. Plans were all set to go back there for 1981 when a conflict in schedules made this impossible. Fortunately we located the Civic Center at White Plains, an equally satisfactory site for the event.

In an entry of 91, Benjy was Best of Breed, with BOS to Ch. Rivermist Tigerlily (Ch. Kadon's Riff Raff x Hickory Smoke Molly MacQueen), Goodman.

The Garden had 24 Gordons, quite a large entry. Benjy again won BB and as mentioned before, he went on to a Group I. BOS went to Ch. Rockaplenty's Salute to Erik.

There were 57 entered at the Far West Combined Setter Specialty. Ch. Warlock's Calypso Dancer (Ch. Afternod Yank of Rockaplenty, CD, x Ch. Kadon's Blue Tango of Warlock), K. Monaghan, won the breed, while Ch. Rockaplenty's Sooner Victory, Ragano/Fulger/Avery, was Best Bitch.

The entry at Springfield, Ohio soared to 119. There was a five minute cloudburst during almost every class combined with strong, cold winds which continued all the next day as well. Ch. Warlock's Windjammer (Ch. Afternod Yank of Rockaplenty, CD, x Ch. Kadon's Blue Tango of Warlock), Goodman, Best of Breed and that glamorous bitch Ch. Rockaplenty's Sooner Victory went Best Opposite.

The Southern California Regional Specialty had a small entry of 37. Ch. McGehee's The Piper topped the breed, BOS to Dunsmuir Molly of Kiloh (Ch. Sutherland Lexington x Ch. Sutherland Daer of Dunsmuir), Luty.

Paumanauk Gordon Setter Club Specialty had 23 entries. Ch. Claymore's Autumn MacGregor (Ch. Loch Adair Redchico Othello x Ch. Ledgewood's Camura), Berlind, went Best of Breed. Ch. Afternod Ember VI (Ch. Forecast Tradewinds x Ch. Afternod Ember V), Zirolli, took Best Opposite.

Fifty-seven Gordons showed up for the Tartan Gordon Setter Club Specialty and Best of Breed was won by Ch. Gordon Hill Run for Daylight (Hacasak Metacom x Ch. Gordon Hill Tyrelle MacAlder), Perrelli. Ch. Rivermist Tiger Lily topped the bitches.

The Northwest Regional held at Battleground, Washington, had a good entry of 59. Best of Breed was won by a flashy class dog, Chapparal Ablaze Aglory (Can. & Am. Ch. MacAlder Mr. Chips x Ch. MacLeod's Electra O'Chapparal), Johnson. Best Bitch was Ch. Loch Loin's Ebisu Ginger, CD (Ch. Sutherland MacDuff x Ch. Sutherland Vaillance Gilda), M. Zeemin.

Once again the Mid-Atlantic Specialty was held with Penn Ridge, N.J. show, and once again Ch. Ben-Wen's Benjy McDee won the breed, the group and Best In Show for his fourth unprecedented clean sweep. Ch. Rivermist Tiger Lily was top bitch. The Pacific Regional was held again at San Rafael with 94 class entries, 24 sweepstakes, their largest show to date. The dashing young dog that won the Northwest Specialty won this one too, Ch. Chaparral Ablaze Aglory, CD. Best bitch was Ch. Lipe's Princess Anna (St. Andrew Heberdes x Coalinga Lady), Mattox.

The Great Lakes Specialty Show and Obedience trial, held in the early Fall near Chicago, had a big entry of 80. Best of Breed was won by Can. & Am. Ch. MacAlder Mr. Chips, while Ch. Rockaplenty's Salute to Erik, Curtis/White, went Best Opposite.

Ch. Speedwell's Buck Rogers,
owner H. Shelly, shown with judge
Mrs. Anne Clark and handler
George Alston. 1980. Frequent
Breed winner with many group
placements. *Gilbert*

Ch. Rockaplenty's Salute to Erik with Judge Tom Bradley III in 19
Frequent BOS and BB winning bitch with group placements.

BEST OF BREED
PETRULIS

. Can. Ch. Blossomaire Believe It Or Not, winner of multiple Breeds and group placements. h handler-owner Shirley Yates. Judge, Eldredge.

Group Placements

Ch. Ben-Wen's Benjy McDee, two Bests In Show, five additional Group I, nine other placements; Can./Am. Ch. Clansmen Colourguard, Canadian BIS, three group I, 17 additional placements; Am./Can. Ch. Rockaplenty Nomad, four group I, four others; Ch. Glenwood's Damn Yankee, CD, one group I, two others; Ch. Balcone's Gaelic Judd, CD (Corlyn's Oban Arran O'Balcones x Rockaplenty's Kissing Cousin), Collins, four group I, four others; Ch. Norcoaster's MacManus, one group I, one II; Ch. MacAlder Phoenix (Am./Can. Ch. Rockaplenty's Hang Em High x Ch. MacAlder Lara), Stephenson, one group I; Ch. Boldbrook's Yankie Junior, one group I, two others; Ch. MacAlder Sterling (Ch. MacAlder Phoenix x Ch. MacAlder Melody), Stephenson, one group I; Ch. Gentry's Beauregard (Ch. Tarbaby's Colorguard x Gentry's Tarnation), Boyer, three group I, eight others; Am./Can. Ch. McMac's Hawkeye of Cameron one group I, one IV (Can.); Ch. Claymore's Autumn MacGregor, one group I.

Group II and others

Am./Can. Ch. Rockaplenty's Real McCoy, one II; Ch. Warlock's Windjammer, one II, seven others; Ch. Rockaplenty's Sooner Victory, one II, six others; Ch. Castleglen's Happy Chips (Ch. MacAlder Mr. Chips x Ch. Calderwood Castle), Whorton, two II; Am./Can. Ch. Blossomaire Believe It or Not, two II, two III; Ch. Speedwell Buck Rogers (Ch. Afternod Yank of Rockaplenty x Kris Too-Too), H. Shelly, one II, two IV; Maxsohn's Scottish Bullet (from the classes) one II, (A. White); Ch. Boldbrook's Yankie Clipper, one II.

Group III and others

Ch. Warlock's Calypso Dancer, one III; Ch. Rockaplenty's Country Redlegs, Perkins, one III; Ch. Don-D's Gillian (B), Selle, one III; Ch. Riverside Tarboo Rachel, Boothroyd, one III; Ch. Don-D's Citation (Ch. Afternod Yank of Rockaplenty x Ch. Don-D's Miss Mischief), Gelbaugh, one III; Can Ch. Clansmen Wee Gordie, Johnston, two III (Can.); Ch. Tri-Sett Chartreuse (B) (Am./Can. Ch. Bonnie Brae's Apple Brandy x Am./Can. Ch. Jadehill Ashran of Tri-Sett, Am./Can. CD), Gatchell, one III, one IV (Can.).

Group IV

Ch. O'Eire's Lord Blak Magic Jason, four; Ch. Afternod Gilian of Milestone (Dual Ch. Loch Adair Monarch x Afternod Gunhilde), B. & J.L. Walter, one; Ch. McGehee's The Piper, one; Am./Can. Ch. Rockaplenty's Pride and Joy, one.

126

1981

How strange! Not one Gordon went Best In Show this year, and only four managed to place first in the group. Ch. Ben-Wen's Benjy McDee began winding down his long career with a Best Opposite Sex at the Combined Setter Specialty, and his fifth Best of Breed at the Mid Atlantic Specialty.

Am./Can. Ch. MacAlder Mr. Chips was named *Top Sire, All Breeds,* with a total of 20 champions in 1980. Chips has been top Gordon sire for 1979, 1980 and 1981, an impressive record in anybody's language.

Ch. Afternod Yank of Rockaplenty, CD, died at age of 11 after a life in which he did everything right. A winner of groups and Bests in Show at an early age, he was also a trained hunter and Mr. Whitney Clark's favorite companion dog. His first litters indicated that he was a prepotent sire which has been proven by his record of 83 champions (as of Sept. 1982), and to top it off he won his CD with ease, handled and trained by Mary Ann Alston. When your first Gordon is a dog like that, what can you do for encores?

Registrations were exactly one more than 1980, for a total of 1,171 and the breed stood at #66 on the American Kennel Club scale. It is most encouraging to find that the Gordon Setter is not being undermined by a wild spurt in population.

Icy conditions caused many fender benders the morning of the Combined Setter Specialty as vans and cars slid out of control down the steep Motel driveway in White Plains. Everybody made it, however, and the entry was 99. Best of Breed to Ch. Rockaplenty's Salute to Erik, the bitch who had been doing nice winning all the previous year. She also went Best Opposite the next day at the Garden, with Best of Breed to Ch. Gentry's Beauregard (Boyer) in an entry of 18.

Far West Combined Setter Specialty had 71 dogs. Am./Can. Rockaplenty's Nomad (Cohen) took the Breed; Ch. Loch Loin's Ebisu Ginger, CD, Best Bitch.

One hundred thirty-seven Gordons gathered in Springfield, Ohio, the largest entry of Gordons in the US in breed history. A sprightly Veteran dog, Ch. Don-Dee's Citation (Ch. Afternod Yank of Rockaplenty, CD, x Ch. Don-Dee's Miss Mischief) handled by his owner, Jerry Gelbaugh, took the breed. He was nine years old, and his condition was a tribute to the loving care he had always had. Ch. Rockaplenty's Salute to Erik won another big one, going Best Opposite.

At Mid Atlantic (Penn Ridge show in N.J.) where Benjy won his *fifth* in a row Best of Breed at this show, Best Opposite went to Ch. Samson's Sequel To Sassy (Ch. Rockaplenty's Hang 'Em High x Ch. Samson's Sweet Sassy for Alan), Haberman, in an entry of 53.

Paumanauk Gordon Setter Club Specialty had 23 with the Breed

TOP Picture: **Best of Breed at the North Country Specialty, Minneapolis, June 1981, Ch. Godiva G**
Gaylee, owner-handled by Debra Lee. Judge Warren Brewbaker. Club President Drieke Van Giffi
presenting trophy. *Olso*

BELOW: **Godiva also won the Brood Bitch class at the same show. A remarkable picture.** *Olso*

going to Ch. Claymore's Autumn MacGregor, and Best Opposite to Ch. Gordon Hill Zephyr (Ch. MacNeal of Ellicott x Gordon Hill Xcitation), DeSilver and Clement. Sadly, MacGregor was stolen not long after.

Tartan Gordon Setter Club had a good entry of 53. Mary Whorton's Ch. Castleglen's Happy Chips won the breed. Fieldstone's Halleluiah came from the classes to go Best Opposite. Owned by Alston and Boyd, she was sired by Ch. Rockaplenty's Hang 'Em High x Ch. Rockaplenty's Gaelic Ribbons.

In Minnesota at the North Country Specialty in an entry of 43 the Best of Breed went to a bitch, Ch. Greenglen's Godiva Go Gaylee (Ch. Greenglen's Up N Atem x Ch. Inwood Greenglen), Debbie Lee, with the Best male being Ch. Heatherhill's Battlestar (Ch. Ben-Wen's Benjy McDee x Am./Can. Ch. O'Hillock's Divine Sarah), Walter.

The Pacific Region, held at San Rafael, California, found Ch. Norcoaster's MacManus topping an entry of 42. Best Opposite to Ch. Chawanakee's Star Chaser (Ch. Norcoaster's MacManus x Ch. Lipe's Princess Anna), Mattox.

Fifty-four dogs were at the Northwest Regional in Washington State. Ch. Sutherland Saber, CD (Ch. Sutherland Talisman x Sutherland Dunnideer Waltz), Crittenden & Schepper, another Veteran dog doing his thing, won the breed while Ch. Sutherland Jessica, owned by the Hustons, was BOS. She was sired by Ch. Sutherland MacDuff x Ch. Sutherland Damask Rose.

The Great Lakes Regional Gordon Setter Club Specialty held in Wheaton, Illinois, had a big entry of 35 in Sweeps, 95 in classes. Yet another handsome Veteran went Best of Breed, this time Am./Can. Ch. Rockaplenty's Hang 'Em High (Dr. Carden) and Ch. Rockaplenty's Salute to Erik had another nice Best Opposite Sex.

Group Placements

Ch. Speedwell's Buck Rogers, one I; four II, two III and six IV; Ch. Claymore's Autumn MacGregor, one I; two II, two III, one IV; Ch. Rockaplenty's Salute to Erik, one I; one II, two IV; Ch. Enniscroft Jeffrey McGirr, one I, one II, one IV; Ch. Boldbrook's Minnesota Fats, two II, one III; Ch. Castleglen's Happy Chips, CD, one II, one IV; Ch. Ben-Wen's Benjy McDee, one II, one IV; Ch. Don-D's Gillian, one II; Dual Ch. Shadowmere Ebony Shane, CD; two III; Ch. Balcone's MacDuff of Glnshild (Ch. Boldbrook's Minnesota Fats x Anneke Meghan O'Balcones), Radziewicz, one II; Ch. Rockaplenty's Country Redlegs, two IV.

Others with single fourth place wins were: Ch. Gentry's Beauregard; Ch. Scottland's CB Supersport (Janzen); Ch. Riverside Tarboo Rachel; Am./Can. Ch. McMac's Hawkeye of Cameron; Ch. Chaparral Ace's High, CD, and Ch. Greenglen's Godiva Go Gaylee.

Ch. Chaparral Ace's High, CD, handler-owner-breeder, Linda Sanders.

130

Pacific Regional Specialty, Best of Breed Ch. Norcoaster's MacManus, handler-owner C. Grimm, Judge F.S. Cartwright.   *Jayne Langdon*

Ch. Kendelee Alleluia Jubilation going Best of Breed, GSCA Specialty, 5/81. Judge, Dick Webb. Multiple Breed and Specialty winner, untimely deceased.

1982 (to Nov. 1)

The Midwest Specialty held at Springfield, Ohio was a week later this year on May 15th. This meant that the weather was warmer and more stable. It was a wonderful show with a huge entry of 292, the largest Gordon Specialty ever held in the U.S. George Pugh was drafted to take the overload in addition to his Obedience classes but even then they had to run two rings at once for part of the time. Even the most ardent ringside observers were tired at the end of this long day. Many lovely dogs were lost in the crowd. Overall quality was excellent and quite uniform.

Though we had proudly thought this might be the biggest Gordon Specialty in the world, we soon learned that we had a ways to go. The Gordon Specialty in England had an entry of *420* made up of 212 individuals. *One* judge, Mrs. Ethel Short (Shoredale Kennels), handled the whole thing!

In September the American Kennel Club released some astonishing figures on changes since 1971. All good.

It was ten years ago in 1971 that the AKC reached its all-time high in registrations and they find an overall drop (in ten years) of over 8% in individual registrations, 10% in litter registrations. Gordon Setters peaked in 1976 at 1,383 and by 1981 registered 1,171. The AKC is pleased with this drop feeling that it represents a decline in activity of what can be lumped together as "undesirables." Evidence of this is startling *increase* of 50% in dogs competing in licensed events. The number of champions and other titles has grown nearly 46%. The number of all breed shows has doubled, specialty shows grew 100%; obedience trials and tracking grew by nearly 90%. An average of 166 new trials and shows have been added each year for the past ten years!

More use being made of fewer dogs sounds ideal, especially for the dogs.

Statistics for the year 1982 show that total registrations both of individual dogs and litters with the American Kennel Club were up slightly. The AKC also states that only half those dogs eligible for registration are actually registered. Gordon Setters slipped from 66th place to 69th, with total individual registrations of 1,082, while our total of 258 litters dropped us from 69th to 73rd place in this ranking.

This sounds serious until you remember that Gordon Setter numbers vary only slightly while other breeds surge and fade much more often.

All Gordon Setter Club Specialties for the year 1982 showed larger entries than ever before.

Twenty-eight Gordons placed in the Sporting Group during 1982, though none was selected for a BIS. Many of these dogs are young newcomers, and have promising futures. We can look forward to continuing success for the Gordon Setter.

132

Ch. Castleglen's Happy Chips, CD, with owner-handler Mary Whorton, a group and GSCA award winner. Judge W. Brewbaker. *Martin Booth*

Ch. Pandora's Magdelene of Buteo with owner-handler Susan Kilby.

Ch. Touchstone Yankee Patriot with owner-handler Camilla Anderson. Judge Mrs. Tipton awarding BB at MidWest Specialty, May 15, 1982. Kay Monaghan center, Jim Thacker, Show chairman, right.

Ch. Tri-Sett Duchess of Ashran, CD, with owner-handler Karen Gatchell. Judge Mrs. Tipton awarding BOS at MidWest Specialty, May 15, 1982.

134

Combined Setter Specialty, White Plains Civic Arena, was blessed with fine weather and a mammoth building where No Smoking signs were enforced. The entry of 96 was well divided. Best of Breed went to a California dog, Ch. Kendelee Alleluia Jubilation, owned by Al Cunningham. Sad to relate, this young dog died of cancer about six months later. BOS to Ch. Pandora's Magdelene of Buteo (Ch. Ironwood's Solar Eclipse x Ch. Rockaplenty's Pandora's Box), owned and bred by Susan Kilby. This bitch won the Sweepstakes at this show in 1980.

Westminster had a small entry of 17. Ch. Black Anvil Amiable Gent (Ch. Afternod Bondorhil Eveready x Gordon Hill Starloch), Pharr, took the breed and Pandora's Magdelene of Buteo was again BOS.

Far West Combined Setter Specialty, held in Southern California, had an entry of 66. Best of Breed to Kendelee Alleluia Jubilation and Best Opposite to Ch. MacAlder Unforgettable Star (Can./Am. Ch. Rockaplenty's Hang Em High x Ch. MacAlder Lara), Standish.

Midwest Specialty at Springfield, Ohio, 192 dogs and 292 entries. Best of Breed: Ch. Touchstone Yankee Patriot (Ch. Afternod Yank of Rockaplenty, CD, x Ch. Rockaplenty's Elspeth of Ayr, CD), owner-handled by Camilla Anderson. Best Opposite, also owner-handled, went to Am./Can. Ch. Tri-Sett Duchess of Ashran, CD (Am./Can. Ch. Bonnie Brae's Apple Brandy x Am./Can./Bda. Ch. Jadehill Ashran of Tri-Sett), Karen Gatchell.

Southern California GSCA Specialty Show, held at a lovely park just outside of the Rose Bowl. Entries were 102 from 72 dogs. A bitch owned by Mrs. Elizabeth Clark and Mary Ann Alston won Best of Breed at her first Specialty, Ch. Rockaplenty Run For The Roses (Ch. Rockaplenty's Inherit The Wind x Ch. Rockaplenty's Sassafras), born December 1, 1979. We'll be hearing more from her.

Best Opposite to that consistent winner, Kendelee Alleluia Jubilation, Cunningham.

Tartan Gordon Setter Club (Connecticut), 71 in regular classes, 12 in non-regular, 29 in Sweeps, and 13 Absentees. It rained all day. Best of Breed to a handsome Veteran dog, Ch. Gordon Hill Run For Daylight, Perrelli, winner of this Specialty some years back. Best Opposite to Susan Kilby and her Ch. Pandora's Magdelene of Buteo.

North Country, in Minneapolis in June. Eighty-one entries from 59 dogs. Best of Breed and group II to a very young male, Ch. Jennifer Farm's Edition DeLux (Ch. Blossomaire Believe It Or Not x Ch. Jennifer Farm's Decision), owner-handler Sheryl Martin. Best Opposite to the lovely Veteran Bitch, winner of many previous Specialty spots, Ch. Inwood Greenglen, CD, nine years old, proud owner, Alyce Westphal.

Northwest GSCA Specialty, Vancouver, Washington. Sixteen Sweeps, 63 in the classes. Best of Breed to yet another worthy Veteran, this one Ch. Sutherland Saber (Ch. Sutherland Talisman x Ch. Sutherland

Ch. Sutherland Saber, co-owner-handler Randy Schepper. Judge Neil Weinstein awarding BB, Northwest Specialty of the GSCA, Vancouver, Wash. 1982. *Lindemaier*

Ch. Jennifer Farms Edition De Lux, owner-handler Sheryl Martin, Judge Roy Ayers. At age of 26 months, this dog has won 15 BB, two group II, and one Specialty. *Shelwyn*

Dunnideer Waltz), Crittenden and Schepper, eight years old. BOS to Ch. Rockaplenty Run For The Roses, Clark/Alston.

Greeley, Colorado Gordon Setter Club Specialty. Forty-two entries. This show, known for its perfect weather and great post-show parties, was won by that up-and-coming young lady, Rockaplenty Run For The Roses. Best Opposite to Ch. Fauconnier's Extra Xtra (Ch. Chaparral Able Bodied x Coke-A-Mo), Baldwin.

September 19th, the Mid-Atlantic Specialty was held at Macungie, Pa. with the Lehigh Valley Kennel Club show, part of a three-day weekend. The show grounds are really nice, and perhaps the Gordon Setter Club show may become a fixture there. The entry was good, 22 Sweepstakes, and 72 in the classes.

Tomar's Brawbridge Intuition (Ch. Ironwood's Solar Eclipse x Ch. Tomar's Reflection of Beauty), R. Mellis & A. Boyd, won the Sweepstakes and Best of Winners. In May he won Sweeps in Ohio, Reserve dog at Tartan, all this before he turned 18 months old. Best of Breed to Ch. Applecross Black Demon (Ch. Hickory Smoke Macer MacNee x Ch. Windrock's Balcary's Jezebel), D. Fish, and BOS to a perennial winner, the fine bitch, Ch. Rockaplenty's Sooner Victory, L. Ragano.

September 19th, Pacific Region Gordon Setter Specialty had 115 entries made up of 75 individual dogs. Best of Breed to Dual Ch. Shadowmere Ebony Shane, CD, from the Veteran's Class. This is the first Dual to win a GSCA Specialty. (One other Dual Champion, Windy Hill's Lucky Chance, won a Specialty but he was not yet a Field Champion when he did it.) BOS went to the two-year-old class bitch Stonehenge Lass O'Camelot (Ch. Sutherland Falstaff x Am./Mex. Ch. Sutherland Delilah), Cunningham.

October 16th, Great Lakes Specialty Show and Obedience Trial, Wheaton, Ill. had ten Obedience entries, 24 in Sweeps and 67 in breed classes. Best of Breed was captured by the bitch, Ch. Rockaplenty's Sooner Victory, handled by Loree Ragano, co-owner with Dianne Avery and Dr. Fulger. BOS was a frequent Midwest winner, Ch. O'Eire's Lord Blak Magic Jason (Ashburn/B. Koch).

The catalog from this show reported the deaths of two noted Gordons: Am./Can. Ch. Johnston's Highland Storm (Carden) died in 1981 "full of years," 13 of them, and Ch. MacAlder Unanimous Decision (T. Popham) only four years of age.

Group Placements for 1982

Ch. Rockaplenty Run For The Roses (Alston & Clark), two group I, two group II, five group III, five group IV.

Ch. Bordalyn's Fieldstone Momento (D) (Ch. Torrance of Ellicott x Ch. Kris' Keepsake of Fieldstone), Goodson & Gelbaugh, one group I.

Ch. Riverside Tarboo Rachel (Idlenot's Northglen Rexford x Ch.

Ch. Gordon Hill Run For Daylight, owner, Perrelli. Best of Breed, Tartan GSC, 1982.

Ch. Rockaplenty Run For The Roses, handler, Marilyn Title. Owners, Mrs. E. Clark and Mrs. Mary Ann Alston. Judge Mrs. Ann Stevenson awarding BB at the Colorado GSCA Specialty, the second Specialty win for this team. *Cott/Francis*

Ch. Ironwood's Banneret winning group II.

Ch. Afternod Yank of Rockaplenty, CD 1969-1981, shown going group first enroute to BIS at the Trumbull County KC following his win at the Warren, Ohio GSCA Specialty. Handler, George Alston.

Riverside Tarboo Magic Mist), Boothroyd, one group II, two group III, two group IV.

Ch. Kendelee Alleluia Jubilation (Cunningham), one group II, two group III.

Ch. Jennifer Farm's Edition De Lux (D) (Martin), three group II.

Ch. Fauconnier's Extra Xtra (Baldwin), two group III.

Ch. Rockaplenty's Country Redlegs (Perkins), one group II, one group IV.

Ch. Ironwood's Banneret (D) (Ch. MacMurphy's Make Mine Scotch x Ch. Rockaplenty's Salute to Erik), Curtis, one group II, one group IV.

Ch. Stilmeadows The Devil U Say (D) (Ch. Stilmeadows Kaliber x Stilmeadows Eolande Desmona), Gidday, two group III, one group IV.

Ch. Dunvegan's Little Bit of Luck (D) (Ch. Gentry's Beauregard x Stawen's Loch Ness Monster), Boyer, one group II.

Ch. Blackthorn's Kymry's Amanda Lee (Ch. Don-D's Citation x Kymry's Abigail of Blackthorn), Spialek, one group II.

Ch. Greenglen's Gabrielle (Westphal), one group II.

Ch. Boldbrook Minnesota Fats (D) (Collins), one group II.

Ch. Dunvegan's Brian McNair (D) (Ch. Holly Creek Elvis x Sevshun's Cinder MacDuff), J.L. Foulk & F. Boyer, one group II.

Am./Can. Ch. Tri-Sett Duchess of Ashran, CD (Gatchell & Marson), two group III.

Ch. Castleglen's Happy Chips, CD (D), Whorton, one group III.

Ch. O'Eire's Lord Blak Magic Jason (D), Ashburn & Koch, two group IV.

One group Four placement to the following:

Ch. LTK's Time Lord (Ch. Tomar's Mighty MacTavish x Ch. MacMarlen's Braw Clan Ballad), Oneppo/Kurzawa.

Ch. MacMurphy's Make Mine Scotch (D) (Ch. Ironwood Solar Eclipse x Ch. Rockaplenty's Blackberry), Andrews.

Ch. Sevshun's Shasta MacKay (B) (Ch. MacNeal of Ellicott x Ch. Sevshun's Tracy MacKnight), B. Snyder.

Ch. MacAlder Best for Shojin (D) (Ch. MacAlder's Mr. Chips x Ch. MacAlder Penelope), Fronczak.

Ch. Gordon Hill Zephyr (B) (Ch. MacNeal of Ellicott x Gordon Hill Xcitation), DeSilver and Clement.

Am./Can. Ch. Sporting Time (D) (Bo-Cham's Sports Challenge x Am./Venezuelan Ch. Sangerfield Posie), Chambers and Itzenplitz.

Ch. Black Anvil Amiable Gent (Ch. Afternod Bondorhil Eveready x Gordon Hill Starloch), Pharr.

Ch. Kadan Lane's Bebhin (B) (Ch. Stilmeadows Flim Flam Man x Stilmeadows Jenny Leigh), L. & G. Faenzi.

140

Ch. Fauconnier's Extra Xtra (Baldwin). Best Opposite Sex, Colorado Specialty August 1982. Judge Ann Stevenson. *Cott/Francis*

Ch. Applecross Black Demon, handler Bob Jagger. Shown going BW in 1980 at Combined Setter Specialty under Anna Katherine Nicholas. Demon went Best of Breed September 1982 at the Mid-Atlantic GSCA Specialty under Warren Brewbaker. (Shown awarding trophy, Lou Layendecker, CSS show chairman).

141

Ch. Rockaplenty's Sooner Victory, Loree Ragano, co-owner-handler. BOS at Mid-Atlantic Specialty under Judge Brewbaker. October 16, 1982. She was Best of Breed at the Great Lakes Specialty show, judge L. Auslander. *John Ashbey*

Dual Ch. Shadowmere Ebony Shane, CD (J. & B. Cooper). Best of Breed at the Pacific Region GSCA Specialty, September 1982. This photo of Shane was taken at a show in 1981 where he won the breed under judge E. W. Tipton. *Rich Bergman*

Ch. McMac's Hawkeye of Cameron (Watson).

Ch. MacTyke's Best Bet Maggie (Ch. MacAlder's Unanimous
Decision x Ch. Fieldstone Speedwell Foxy), M. & R.L. Rodriguez.

Ch. Enniscroft Jeffrey McGirr, Gidday.

Leading New Kennels

1970-1982

Don Wilson	GAIRLOCH	WA
Karen Gatchell	TRI-SETT	ME
Jenien Ferguson	FERGUSON	OR
Gunda Abajian	LEDGEWOOD	NY
Jack and Katherine Jones	QUAILWOOD	AL
Don and Dottie Selle	DON-D	NY
Rudy and Nancy Zak	FLINTLOK	IL
David and Carol Green	ROSSDHU	CA
Nina Tenaglia	TARBABY	OH
Dick and Nancy Carleton	INDIANHEAD	OH
Robert Christianson	KRIS'	SD
Jane and Bob Friedman	MARKHAM	NY
Mr. and Mrs. Harry Watson, Nancy Watson	McMAC	PA
Darlene Wedeman	DARON	AZ
Kitty Pharr	BLACKADER	SC
Chuck Palm	DUNSMUIR	CA
Vincent Rivellese	BRIARCLIFFE	NY

1972-1982

Linda Sanderson	HIROLIN	MN
Dawn Ferguson	WARCHANT	Australia
Krishna Harris	INDIGO	B.C. Can.
Tom and Louise Mowbray	PINEGLEN	NC
Mrs. Gretchen Scott	SCOTTLAND	IN
Ann Boyd	TOMAR	VA
Dr. Carden	BENSEANTI	IL
Camilla Anderson	TOUCHSTONE	IN
Naomi Ware	AGARU	WI
Mr. and Mrs. Daniel Miller	STAWEN	VA
Pierre Brun	LOCH LOIN	OR
Charles Robinson	CREEK FARM	MI
C. and M. Collins	CC's	TX
Richard and Pat Alpert	SPEEDWELL	NJ

Ralph Del Buono	MAC BICK	NJ
Linda Sanders	CHAPARRAL	NV
Vernon and Shirley Yates	JENNIFER FARMS	MO
Mellisa White, Gerald and Helena Curtis	IRONWOOD	OH
Patricia Ann Helseth	KINGDOM	FL
Roy and Kathleen Mattox	CHAWANAKEE	CA
Elizabeth Schuster	GLENWOOD	PA
Keith and Caryl Jordan	HEDGESTONE	Ont. Can.
Jim and Janice Stomp	CLANSMEN	Al. Can.
Ollie, Geri, Kerry and Karl Reimer	ALISTAIR	MN
Bob and Joan Chambers	BO-CHAM	CO
Dan and Karen Arterberry	KA-DAN LANE	IL
Lynn and Kevin Shreve	RIVENDELL	NY
Carol Srnka	HIGH BRASS	NY
D. and K. Thomas	CASTLEGLEN	WI
Joan Abijian Schultz	SEVSHUN	NY
Jim and Alyce Westphal	GREENGLEN	MN
Fred Engler	NICKNEVEN	KS
Chuck and Janet Zepf	ZEPHYR	CA
Natalie Haberman	SAMSON	MA
Dale Fish	APPLECROSS	PA
Denise Dunham	SAVOY	IL
Pat Kennedy	EBONWOOD	IL
Tom Olson (with C. Stephenson)	MACALDER	SD
Nancy Thompson	CYNEBEARNE	CA
W. and D. Klumb	BYDAND	WI
Laura Silverstein	HALCYON	MA
Paul Pinna	DePINNA	NY
Bernice Haimson	FARMSTEAD	PA
C. Zirolli	BRAXFIELD	CT
Francis Perelli	BLACK ANVIL	CT
Mary Ann Alston	FIELDSTONE	MD
Barry Goodman	RIVERMIST	MD
Roberta Pringle	BALARRAN	CA
Janice Main	ENNISCROFT	OR
Ellen Bruck	KENDELEE	CA
Betty McGehee	McGEHEE's	CA
Jack and Barbara Cooper	SHADOWMERE	CA
Gerry and Shirlee Roberts	ROBALEE	CA
Nikki Maounis	BRAN LINN	CA
Lisa Vinyard	TIMBERSHINE	CA

Susan Arata	HARVEST GOLD	CA
Leslie Simon	CEARMAID	OH
Doug and Debbie Lee	GAYLEE	MI
Chuck and Gail Boyd	ABLEAIM	NC
Rob and Nina Stegeman	SARABANDE	MO
Kay McGuire	WILDWIND	TX
Loree Ragano	HEAVENLY	IL
Mrs. Billy Jo York		TX
Al Cunningham	STONEHENGE	CA
Lesley Andrews	McMURPHY	TN
Dan Greenleaf	FARMHOLME	NH
Kristen Rugg	MACMARLEN	DE
Nancy Large	RAVENWOOD'S	VT
James Thacker	DUNBAR	OH
Virginia Kick	ROYALDELL	MI
Jerry Gelbaugh,	FIREBRAND	TN
David Bouhl	"	IL
Stephen and Debbie Weber	HOWFF	OH
Ed and Lee Fronczak	SHOJIN	MI
Drieke Van Giffin	MACRAE	MN
Darcy Faas	UPLAND	MI
Susan Pontius	UPLORD	MT
Dean and Jane Matteson	MCERIN	CA
Holly and Barbara Manson	DOGGONE	WI
Susan Kilby	BUTEO	VA
Julia Ouska	TEMMOKU	CO
Richard Quaco	McQ	CO
Julie Burgard	FAUCONNIERS	WY
Archie and Mary Vomanchka	WHITMAN	WI
John Myles	INVERNESS	WA
Dr. Charlene Kickbush	BRAMBLEBUSH	CA
Charles and Penny Parsons	PENCHRIS	OR
Lynn Palmiter	ELYSIAN	WA
Teresa Popham	MACTYKE	MI
J.M. Pickell	O'MERLENE	IN
T. Camphausen	GLEN AYR	IL
D. Avery and B. Levi	WYTTSEND	MI
D. and L. Cline	THUNDER ROAD	MI
L. Walker	SUNAPEE	MI
V. Kick	ROYALDELL	MI
R. Zoll	HOLLY CREEK	VA

4

Gordon Setters
in the United Kingdom

Text and Photos provided by
Mrs. Mildred Adams, Chichester, England

A SHORT EXPLANATION is necessary to make it quite clear to readers exactly how U.K. Champions and Show Champions are made, so that they may be evaluated against other Gordons who have achieved this status through different methods in other countries.

Our Kennel Club issues Certificates for the best of both sexes at its championship shows. These are given irrespective of the numbers of dogs entered. Very strict instructions are given to the judge to withhold the award if he does not consider the exhibit worthy to become a Show Champion, and as opinions differ somewhat it will be seen that yesterday's Sh. Ch. may not be even placed today.

The proud title of Champion can only be achieved by winning a certificate at a recognized Field Trial or Working Gundog Trial *after* the dog has won at least one CC on the bench.

Unfortunately Champions are rather few and far between at the present time, especially in England. In Scotland with its moors well populated by game birds it is easier for Gordon owners to train their dogs, attend trials North of the Border, and "qualify" their Gordons than for those of us living in the "built up" South.

To become a Show Champion a dog has to win three challenge certificates under three different judges, two of which must be won when

Manchester Championship Show 1963. Left, M. Adams with Salters Heslops Bruce, Dog Champion and Best of Breed. Mrs. Gwen Broadley, judge.

1965 West of England Ladies Kennel Society Champion Show. Left: Miss D. Sivewright with Sh. Ch. Salter's Pacemaker, winner of Best Gun Dog. Center: judge Mrs. M. Lyndesay Smith; Mr. George Knight with Sh. Ch. Salter's Black Tulip of Calbrie, Best of Sex. *C. M. Cooke & Son*

the dog is over 12 months old, and no proof of working ability is necessary.

During the last twenty years the breed has increased numerically at quite an alarming rate, and some indiscriminate breeding has resulted in loss of type and substance.

Speaking as someone who has had the breed in a small way for fifty years, I would say that the general picture is one of very mixed quality; overall soundness has improved, though one misses some of the grand animals of the pre-1960 years.

We aim at real Gordons, and do not care for the very long "Irish Setter" heads, light bone, or gay tails. During the early 70's tails and tail carriage deteriorated and the true really stiff, short tail carried horizontally was almost non-existent.

Perhaps newcomers to the breed had got so used to seeing long, weak, rope-like tails, or the assertive type, carried like a hound, that they forgot what setter tails should be like. The setter tail should lash from side to side as he trots up the ring, or moves up to game in the field. This is a beautiful and characteristic sight, sadly lacking these days.

We rate beautiful, dark coloured eyes very highly. Colour is most important, and a bright, clear rich tan is essential, but it must be restricted to the correct positions as decreed by our standard.

We do not care for the tan extending beyond its permitted limits as is sometimes seen. Some people feel that a great many of our present day Gordons have lost a certain characteristic ruggedness essential to breed type.

Practically all Gordons are handled in the ring by their owners and the professional handler is almost unknown in this breed.

This may well account for the rather uneven skill seen in the handling and presentation of the exhibits; but dog handling is a hobby and a sport here, and not always taken as seriously as it might be.

A brief survey of the status of Gordon Setters in the United Kingdom for the year 1981 finds that registrations stood at 529. Eight Show Champions were made, and one Champion (qualified in the field). The largest entry at any championship show was 176 at the British Gordon Setter Club's Championship show under the judge, Mrs. S. Robinson Tye. Show Champion Carek Bronze Clansman was the top winning Gordon for the year, and twice won the Gundog Group.

The following are some of our most notable Gordon Setters. I have tried to view the breed objectively in this country, and tried to see just where we appear to be heading. It has not been easy to make this selection, but it would be quite impossible to mention all the good dogs individually.

The good dog Ch. Claytex Squire of Ambridge, winner of eight CCs, was practically unbeaten in the early 60's. He was owned by Miss Walton, and was one of the very few Gordons who was handled by a "pro." He was by Sh. Ch. Fearless of Ardagh x Shoredale Melody (Ch. Dandy of

Westerdale x Ch. Shoredale Morannedd Gainsome). He was a true setter with a beautiful outline, good body and couplings, sound strong quarters, perhaps a little more quality in head would have improved him, and a darker eye would have given a kinder expression. Having said that, he was a Gordon hard to beat.

At Cruft's show in 1961 an American lady, Mrs. Ruth Woade, living temporarily in U.K., exhibited her American Champion Heslop's Burnvale Dash by Ch. Matson's Robin x Heslop's Luscious Pixie, and won a Reserve Best of Sex. Dash was a wonderfully sound, medium sized dog, with an excellent body, very deep brisket and a really superb, short stiff tail, correctly carried. Unfortunately he was rather straight in the stifle, and he did pass this on to the majority of the one litter he sired in this country, this was to Sh. Ch. Susanna of Dendy. Quite three-quarters of the show Gordons here today trace back to this dog, either through Sh. Ch. Salters Pacemaker or his sister Salters Scotch Rose. The latter was never shown. Dash, although partly an outcross for our stock, did go back to many of our best dogs of the 1930's, several of which were sold to U.S.A. immediately before the second World War.

Pacemaker (mentioned above) was sold as a puppy to Miss Dorothy Sivewright and won 11 CCs and was Reserve Best Gundog at the West of England Ladies Kennel Association 1965 Championship Show. This group win was very unusual at this time as Gordons never seemed to do well in mixed breed classes or groups. Pacemaker was an excellent sire of honest medium sized animals of good type. He sired Sh. Ch. Kingsworthy Ragged Robin and his litter sister Sh. Ch. Kingsworthy Travellers Joy.

Now we come to two quite outstanding dogs who have had a marked influence on the breed in this country.

Sh. Ch. Marlplace Adam Richmond (by Sh. Ch. Yodel of the Speygrounds x Speygrounds Myra). Winner of 4 CCs and Best In Show at Windsor Gundog Show of 1966. Owned by Dr. J. Jackson-Richmond, this strikingly handsome dog, very reminiscent of the "Bydand" strain, was probably best of all the Speygrounds. A big dog with wonderful bone, a perfect mover, lovely head and expression and superb colour. He produced Sh. Ch. Salter's Adam Gordon and Sh. Ch. Heidi of Honeymaker.

Adam Gordon turned out to be one of the most outstanding dogs of the late 60's and early 70's, and winner of 11 CCs.

He was a beautiful Gordon with a most attractive temperament, his faults were few, his virtues many. A wonderfully compact dog with great depth of brisket, lovely neck and shoulder, a short, straight tail beautifully carried, his colour was good and his feathering and coat correct. He excelled in head, having the gentle wise look only seen with the correct dark eye. He was owned by Mrs. Louise Jackson-Richmond. There is no doubt that he would have won more than 11 CCs but, owing to family commitments, his owner was away in Australia for a year in 1969, and

Gordon was placed in boarding kennels and not exhibited during this period. He was the sire of Sh. Chs. Sikh of Boyers, Rum of Ardkeen, Rowancrag Tamerisk, Haighthorne Gay Gordon, Burnbeck Solo, Great Scot of Beaconsfield and the CC winners Rowancrag Topaz, Rowancrag Tarquin and Burnbeck Symphony.

The Cairlie Kennel is a small but long established one, with a wonderful breeding record. From a very few litters bred, Mrs. M. M. C. Rowe has retained a very high standard with her stock. During the last twenty years Sh. Ch. Yeoman of Cairlie, Vanity, Unity and Xella have won between them 25 CC and 27 Reserve Best in Sex, not counting the wins of Cairlie Cannie Lass and Cairlie Dixie Rene.

Yeoman (Uiane of Braeriac x Sh. Ch. Vanity of Cairlie) was an extremely good stud dog, excelling in temperament and colour. He was a great laster, at nine years of age he being able to win his last CC under Mrs. Judy de Casembroot who said his action was lovely to watch and an object lesson to the younger brigade. He sired Sh. Ch. Zest of Cairlie, Cannie Lass, and Tess of Everard.

Cannie Lass (out of Alnitak of Dulnan), was a bitch of excellent type, a real eye catcher with all the good "Cairlie" points. She won four CC and four Reserve Best of Sex. As a puppy she was Best Puppy All Breeds at a big two day Open Show.

Mr. and Mrs. R. Wombey of the Rowancrag Kennels are well known both here and overseas. Their first litter from two Sh. Ch. Haze Jan and Flicka of Fanfair produced Sh. Ch. Rowancrag Shadrach, winner of four CCs. As a sire with limited opportunities he excelled himself. He sired Ch. Swanley Strathspey, Sh. Ch. Belsud Black Admiral, Sh. Ch. Rowancrag Lively Lady, all out of Warfield Gypsy Moth. The fourth Sh. Ch., Haar Bencruachan, was a valuable purchase by the Wombeys. He won four CCs and was always praised for his movement and great strength. He sired two Show Champions, Oddington Clarsach of Gaelsett and Shelwell Fantasy.

The combination of the blood of Salter's Adam Gordon and Haar Bencruachan has produced many of the best Gordons and it is quite difficult to find a pedigree without one or both of these fine dogs. Shadrach's litter sister, Rowancrag Shuna, is the dam of two Show Champions, Rowancrag Tamarisk and Astera.

It was with particular sorrow that British Gordon Setter owners learned of the death of Mrs. Audrey Bromley early in the 70's. The famous Calbrie Kennel had been winning the top awards since the early 30's but with failing health she realized that she could not actively continue to breed and show her dogs, so very wisely she transferred her prefix to Mr. and Mrs. George Knight who had already had some modest wins with their own Gordons. The star of the Calbries at this time was Sh. Ch. Salters Black Tulip of Calbrie, bred by the writer, who won 11 CC and 18 Bests of Breed. She was by Sh. Ch. Salters Blakke Shadow of Calbrie out of Salters Scotch

Rose. Shadow was a litter brother to Ch. Blackgown of Calbrie who, besides getting CCs, also won at Field Trials. Black Tulip's son, Black Duke of Calbrie, carried on the Calbrie tradition, was a great sire and a beautiful Gordon with the perfect temperament which he handed down to his puppies to a marked degree.

The purchase of Sh. Ch. Tess of Everard put Miss Carol Laurie on the road to success with her Carorae Gordons. Tess was a good stylish bitch of lovely conformation and was Best of Breed at Cruft's in 1975. To date, none of the Caroraes have surpassed Sh. Ch. Wayfarer of Carorae (William of Everard, brother of Tess, out of Flora of the Haar. Winner of 13 CCs, eight Bests of Breed, six Reserve Best of Sex, he was Best in Show at an Open Show and Reserve in the Gundog Group at the 1976 Ladies Kennel Association Show at Olympia, London.

The gift of the beautiful young bitch, Susanna of Dendy (Ch. Officer of Cairlie x Sh. Ch. Gemma of Dendy), gave the small Salters Kennel a great fillip. Renowned for her soundness and lovely movement, Susanna soon got her three CCs and became a Show Champion. Mated to Am. Ch. Heslop's Burnvale Dash, a good litter resulted from which Salters Scotch Rose was retained. When later Rose was mated to Sh. Ch. Marlplace Adam Richmond, she produced the noted Sh. Ch. Salters Adam Gordon and Salters Rosalind, exported to Italy. Mated a second time to Sh. Ch. Salters Blakke Shadow of Calbrie, Scotch Rose produced Sh. Chs. Salters Black Tulip of Calbrie and Salters Heslops Bruce, who was retained. He sired Benjamin Ben of Glenrinnes, CC winner, and is in the foundation stock of the well known Emben Kennel.

Sh. Ch. Caerlanrig Adonis and his litter sister Sh. Ch. Cuprea Penny Black, by Black Duke of Calbrie, caused quite a sensation in the early 1970's. Penny won two CCs while still a puppy, a rare feat in a late maturing breed like the Gordon; altogether she went on to win 11 CCs, eight Bests of Breed, and Best In Show at the Gordon Setter Association Championship Show in 1973. She was always described in glowing terms, the only criticism being that she was usually rather short of coat and feathering. Very sadly she died at the age of three years of acute distention, which has claimed several of our best setters of all three varieties.

Her beautiful brother Adonis ("Brodie" to his friends) is still with us at the time of writing. He belonged to Mrs. Beckett who was unable through ill health to handle him herself in the show ring, and in consequence he had several different people handling him. He won 12 CCs while in this ownership. At the death of his owner he went to the well known kennels of Mr. and Mrs. Coupe, where he went from strength to strength, always in perfect condition. He won another 13 CCs, bringing his total to 25, and was many times Best of Breed. He had the most beautiful temperament and knew when he was being admired. At Crufts, 1979, Judy de Casembroot said, "Every inch a champion, the kind of dog one always remembers. His head and expression are a real blueprint for the breed."

151

Ch. Swanley Strathspey with Mr. and Mrs. G. Allan and week-old pup which became Ch. Swanley Strathfinella. 1977.

Ch. Swanley Strathspey w. 1971.

152

Sh. Ch. Marlplace Adam Richmond. *Fall*

Sh. Ch. Salter's Adam Gordon. *Fall*

The top kennel in Scotland is without doubt the Swanley Kennel of Mrs. Jeannette Allan. It has been established for many years and has always had its sights fixed on the ideal for the breed, i.e., the dual purpose Gordon Setter, able to win the show ring and work in the hottest competitions at field trials. This she has achieved to a remarkable degree. Though we still wait for our first Dual Champion in the breed, one cannot help feeling it will eventually come from this kennel.

The purchase of a beautiful puppy bred in 1972 by Mrs. Grimes (better known for her excellent Flatcoated Retrievers) gave Mrs. Allan the foundation bitch of her dreams, brilliant on the bench, in the field and as a brood bitch as well. Ch. Swanley Strathspey (Sh. Ch. Rowancrag Shadrach x Warfield Gipsy Moth), born 1971, was the winner of five CCs. Among her show wins were Blackpool, Darlington BOB, Crufts, and Manchester BOB. In the field she won two Certificates of Merit, a 2nd in Novice and a 3rd in Open. Very sadly she died at the early age of eight but not before she had produced really outstanding stock as the following will show.

Ch. Swanley Strathbeg (by Skean Dhu of Finegand) was born in 1975 and won 21 CCs under 21 different judges. He also had eight Reserve Best of Sex, two Best in Show awards. His early death at six years old was a tremendous blow both to his owner and to the whole Gordon Setter breed in this country.

Ch. Swanley Strathfinella (same breeding as above, later litter) was born in 1977. This mating of Strathspey to Skean Dhu has produced other CC winners as well. In France Swanley Strathtay is a great worker and his title of "French Field Trials Shooting Stakes Champion" seems very near. In Switzerland Swanley Strathblane is a good winner, as well as Swanley Strathbonne. Certainly this breeding *must* make a big mark on the breed.

The Drumwood Kennel of Mr. and Mrs. Atkinson in Kincardineshire, Scotland, has some excellent stock. Among several first class Gordons two stand out. One is Sh. Ch. Great Scot of Beaconsfield (Sh. Ch. Salters Adam Gordon x Tigh Orian Jean, going back to the Calbrie strain), 1973-1978. Scot was owned in partnership with Mrs. C. W. Savege. He was the youngest Sh. Ch. in the history of the breed, finishing at 22 months. His wins include Manchester, 1975, Gordon Setter Association Show 1975 and Birmingham City 1975.

The second is Sh. Ch. Drumwood Eriboll (Ch. Swanley Strathbeg x Drumwood Bertha, by Great Scot). His record so far is BOB at Leeds, 1980 and 1981; Scottish Kennel Club Show, 1981; and a CC at the National Gundog Show, 1981; three Reserve Best of Sex and Cup for Best Colour at the Gordon Setter Association Show, 1981.

Mr. and Mrs. David Reader commenced their Gordon activities by the purchase of a puppy from Mrs. Joan Smith of the Oddington Kennel. This foundation bitch became Sh. Ch. Oddington Clarsach of Gaelsett (Sh.

154

Sh. Ch. Caerlanrig Adonis. *Anne Roslin-Williams*

Sh. Ch. Great Scot of Beaconsfield w. 1973.

Ch. Haar Bencruachan x Pibroch of Finegand). Mated to Burnbeck Moss Royal (Sh. Ch. Salters Adam Gordon) she produced an outstanding litter which included Sh. Chs. Galesett Zephyr, Storm, and Gaelsett Breeze. Very few litters have been bred lately due largely to the ill health of Mrs. Reader, but their interest and enthusiasm for the breed continue.

Mention must be made here of an outstanding bitch owned by Mr. and Miss Fox, Sh. Ch. Deerswood Rosalind (Sh. Ch. Rum of Ardkeen x Haze Rebecca). Born in 1972, she is the winner of ten CCs, and ten Reserve Best of Sex.

Boyers Kennel: Mr. and Miss Jane Osborn have one of the smallest yet one of the most successful kennels, starting with Ch. Sikh of Boyers (Sh. Ch. Salters Adam Gordon z Borderland Quicke), 1972. She soon became a full champion qualifying in the field. She won seven CCs and two Reserve Best of Sex.

Her daughter, Sh. Ch. Boyers Serb, 1975, by Sh. Ch. Belsud Black Admiral (litter brother to Swanley Strathspey), won six CCs and 11 Reserve Best of Sex.

Her granddaughter, Sh. Ch. Boyers Switha, 1978, by Sh. Ch. Longlane Duncan (by Haighthorne Henry) was the winner of three CCs.

Her great grandson, Boyers Seil (Ft. Ch. Spinningloch Raven of Crafnant), has had many bench wins as a puppy including Best Puppy In Breed, Gundog Breeds Association of Scotland and at National Gundog Show. He also had the great distinction of being Best Puppy in Show at the latter.

Emben Kennel: When Mrs. Annette Millin started in the breed, she had real beginners luck! Her first Gordon, Benjamin Ben of Glenrinnes (Sh. Ch. Salters Heslop's Bruce x Skerryvore Carousel of Glenrinnes), put her on the first rung of the ladder of success in the breed. He won one CC but did not live to a great age.

Her next purchase was a bitch puppy who became Sh. Ch. Shelwell Fantasy (Sh. Ch. Haar Bencruachan x Dunlan Charm) who won four CCs. Her great worth as a brood bitch is shown by the following: her sons Sh. Ch. Emben Rowanvar, winner of five CCs, Best of Breed at Crufts, 1981, and Sh. Ch. Emben Traboyach, winner of three CCs. If Mrs. Millin goes on as she has begun, she will own one of the strongest kennels in the breed in a few years' time.

Mrs. S. Woodland's Winterwood Kennel, although not established very long, certainly looks like making itself felt in the breed. In 1975 she bred an excellent litter by Burnbeck Herb of Grace (Sh. Ch. Haar Bencruachan) x Setterthwaite Seana (Sh. Ch. Yeoman of Cairlie). From this litter came the notable Sh. Ch. Winterwood Righ, winner of three CCs. Very wisely Mrs. Woodland repeated this mating the following year which includes: Sh. Ch. Winterwood Moonbeam, three CCs, two Reserve Best of Sex; Winterwood Moonshine, five Reserve Best of Sex; Winterwood

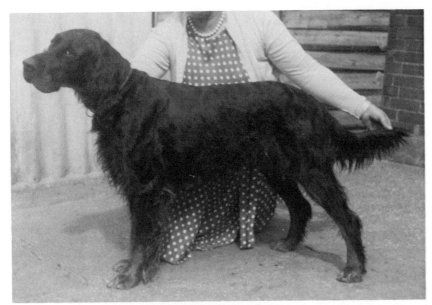

Sh. Ch. Haar Bencruachan.

Stunning group "of Cairlie" show champions. Left to right: Yeoman (7CC); Vanity (4CC); Unity (9CC) and Xella (5CC). 1968.

Moonshade, dam of Sh. Ch. Dudmoor Mylton of Lourdace; Winterwood Cloud, dam of Winterwood Thundercloud, one CC; Winterwood Jet, a big winner.

Two really outstanding dogs are housed at the Moonglade Kennel owned by Mr. and Mrs. C. J. Roberts: Sh. Chs. Inkersall Oberon of Moonglade and his sister, Inkersall Ophelia of Moonglade, whelped in 1977 (Sh. Ch. Wayfarer of Carorae x Inkersall Dawn). Oberon won four CC; BOB at Bath, Birmingham National, Setter and Pointer Club, 1981; four Reserve Best of Sex. He is always perfectly presented and beautifully handled by his owners. He has a lovely head with a gentle expression. This dog has great presence and cannot be overlooked in any company.

His lovely sister Ophelia is a big winner. In spite of having a litter in 1979 she has gained many awards. She won her CCs at Darlington, Setter and Pointer Club 1981, Ladies Kennel Association 1981, and Reserve Best of Sex seven times in 1980 and 1981.

The Rossend Kennel is a small one, but it houses excellent Gordons owned by Mrs. Margo C. S. Howe at Alloa in Scotland. The pride of the place must go to the really beautiful bitch, Sh. Ch. Carek Silver Dawn of Rossend, born 1977, bred by Mrs. Y. Horrocks, (by Sh. Ch. Gaelsett Storm x Cuprea Black Velvet). She has five CC and Best of Breed at Windsor, Driffield and Scottish Kennel Club Championship shows in 1980 and 1981. Also BOB at five other shows and winner of three Reserve Best of Sex in 1980 and 1981. At Tay Valley Open Show she was in the last three for Best in Show.

Now we come to one of the greatest winning Gordon dogs of them all: Sh. Ch. Carek Bronze Clansman, born 1978, owned by Mrs. Maureen Hart, bred by Mrs. Y. Horrocks, by Carek Red Admiral (Burnbeck Herb of Grace) x Sh. Ch. Carek Blue Angel (Sh. Ch. Caerlanrig Adonis). He has won 19 CCs, numerous Bests of Breed, was winner of the Gundog Group at Ladies Kennel Association Show, and also has seven Reserve Best of Sex during the 1980 and 1981 season, making him the top winning Gordon for both years. He is the darling of the ringside in variety classes, beloved of all-rounders and group judges, and it is easy to see why. His perfect presentation and handling make him a real eye-catcher. His lovely rich tan and blue-black gleaming coat, with his obvious delight in giving of his best before a large audience, is a lovely sight.

Mrs. J. Leney's Hichinbrook Kennel is one of our newest exhibitors but she has come right to the front with her excellent bitch, Sh. Ch. Salfran Starlight of Hichinbrook, born 1975 (Shelwell Fresco x Mischa of Kinfayre). With five CCs and two BOB in 1981 (at Leicester, and Setter and Pointer Ch. Club show), she has proved that she is a top class show bitch. Her first litter is of the highest quality and contains several first prize winners.

158

Sh. Ch. Inkersall Ophelia of Moonglade w. 1977, with Mrs. Elaine Roberts.

Working Gordons

It is much to be regretted that more people are not able to work their Gordons in the field. Nevertheless we have a few kennels with inmates of the highest standard and the premier position must be given to the famous Crafnant Kennel of Mr. George Burgess. He will be remembered for having the nearest thing to a Dual Champion in this breed. His famous Ft. Ch. Rowney of Crafnant was also a winner of one CC and Reserve Best of Sex six times. Rowney was born in 1950 and through the years following, Mr. Burgess was a keen and consistent winner at trials.

Next came Crafnant Teal, born 1967, bred by T. J. Conlon in Ireland. (FT. Ch. Joker of Cromlix x Templelogue Lady, Coolwinna strain). Run only twice, he won a first at the English Setter Club Trials, July 1970, held at Alston, Cumberland, and a second in All Aged Stake the following day.

FT. Ch. Crafnant Ruff, born 1970, bred by Mr. Conlon, same as Teal. His wins were: first prize All Aged Stakes, English Setter Club Trials, Alston, Cumberland, September 1972; first prize, Kennel Club Trials, Sutton Scotney, Hampshire, April, 1974; first prize, Open Irish and Gordon Trials, Sharp, Westmoreland; winner of numerous seconds and thirds during the 1970's.

FT. Ch. Index Dipper of Crafnant, born 1971, breeder, Dr. M. B. Thompson. By Crafnant Teal x Borderland Uppish (bred from Borderland show stock). Exported to Mr. Rolf, Aune, Norway, 1976. Dipper's wins in this country are as follows:

The Southern and Western Counties Field Trial Society Pointer and Setter Section, held at Sutton Scotney, Hampshire, April 1973.

First prize, Novice; third prize, All Aged.

English Setter Club Field Trial, Tisbury, Wiltshire, April 1973.

First prize, Novice; fourth prize, All Aged.

English Setter Club Field Trial, April 1974, second prize, All Age.

Southern and Western Counties Field Trial Society Pointer and Setter Section, Sutton Scotney, Hampshire, April 1974, second prize All Aged Stake.

The English Setter Club Field Trial, Alston, Cumberland, July 1974, second All Aged Stake.

Irish Setter Association England The Pointer and Setter Club Field Trial Meeting, Shap, Westmorland, July 1974; Reserve in the Irish and Gordon Open Stake.

The Yorkshire Gundog Club Field Trials, Newbiggin Moors, July 1974, Reserve and Certificate of Merit.

International Gundog League Pointer and Setter Society Field Trials, Blanchland, Northumberland, July 1974, fourth prize All Aged Stake.

Sh. Ch. Carek Silver Dawn
of Rossend w. 1977.

Field Trial Champions Index Dipper of Crafnant and Crafnant Ruff,
with owner-trainer G. J. Burgess (c. 1975).

The Scottish Field Trials Association Pointers and Setters, Skerriffmuir, Dunklane, August 1974, First Prize, Champion stake. The dog was only two years and eight months old at this time. The entries consisted of 14 Irish Setters, ten Pointers, four English Setters and two Gordons, all winners at previous trials.

International Gundog League Pointer and Setter Society Field Trials, Sept. 1974, second prize.

FT. Ch. Spinningloch Raven of Crafnant, born in 1978. Breeder, Mrs. P. Wood. Wins to his credit:

Open Gordon Stake, first Chatsworth, Derbyshire 1980.

All Aged Stake, first English Setter Club, Stetchworth 1982.

All Aged Stake, first International Gundog League, Blanchland and several seconds and thirds.

A most enthusiastic owner is Miss Brenda Partridge, with her Clitters Kennel, Dartmoor, Devon. Although she has quite a large measure of show blood in some of her Gordons, it is the working side that interests her the most. She is the breeder of Clitters Black Game of Crafnant, born 1976 (Crafnant Teal x Nighean NaCreae of Finegard), who usually gives a good account of himself when run in trials.

One of the newer working kennels belongs to Dr. M. B. Thompson of the Invercassley prefix. He has had much success in his breeding plans with the introduction of Norwegian blood. He has imported two FT. Chs. The first died before he could make his mark on the breed; the second, Ulvatnets Truls III (Jotun's Kim x Jervfjellets Sussy) is now established in several kennels' breeding stock. Invercassley Jock Scott has been a consistent winner in the past three years with a number of placements in All Age Stakes on Grouse. He is owned and trained by R. F. Truman.

Mrs. Barbara Swinden, Freebirch, has produced two winners, Freebirch Viner (owned by R. F. Truman), and FT. Ch. Freebirch Vincent who won the Pointer and Setter Championship Stakes for Great Britain in August of 1981. This was a real thrill for all Gordon breeders everywhere, as the competition was stiff, and no Gordon had won anything like this for a number of years.

The interest in Field Trials has greatly increased recently and the outlook for working Gordons has not appeared so bright for many years.

Copy of British Gordon Setter Standard in Chapter 5.

Sh. Ch. Carek Bronze Clansman w. 1978 with owner Mrs. Maureen Hart and Judge Joe Bradon. *Mitchell*

Invercassley Dusty Miller, owner Dr. M. B. Thompson. This photo of the border area between England/Scotland shows clearly the unique terrain. *Thompson.*

Mrs. Dawn Ferguson of Marchant Kennels, Australia. *Setters, Inc., Spring 1982 edition.*

Ch. Dalbeattie of Glencraig (w. 1961) shown at 11 years of age.

5

The Gordon Setter in Australia and New Zealand

Information for this chapter and most of the photos were supplied by Mrs. Dawn Ferguson, New South Wales.

GORDON SETTERS were first reported in Australia in 1865 when two were imported from what was said to be the best kennels in Great Britain. Exhibited at the Melbourne show for the first time, one was refused an award because of excessive white!

Later, five Gordons were imported from England to Victoria where they were bred and used for shooting, early in the century. At that time history records one being taken overland to the north by an explorer about 1904.

Up to the 1920's Mr. Hadden deserves much credit for his early importation of the "Heather" dogs and his consistent breeding of sound stock. The dogs he produced were all forerunners of today's Gordons.

Late in the 1920's the Tabilk Kennels carried on the breed, to be followed by Araniw and Wanalta kennels in Victoria, where birds are plentiful and hunting popular.

Meanwhile, in New South Wales (some 500 miles north), the Argyle Kennels, owned by George Edwards, bred some fine Gordons which were prominent in non-slip retrieving trials. Gordons, however, became a status symbol rather than a common dog. George Edwards refused to release puppies indiscriminately and kept close guard on his dogs. When he died, he requested that his last expected litter be destroyed as well as his kennel records. Although quite a few dozen Gordons still lived (mainly as pets) in NSW few were shown at that time. But, surprisingly, 16 were exhibited in 1947 at Sydney Royal Show. In Victoria, where hunting was popular, the Gordon was still being bred continually for shooting.

After a decline in Gordon population during the 50's, in 1965 Julie Dickinson imported two Gordon bitches (one in whelp) from New Zealand to Sydney, NSW. The ensuing litter started a revival of interest in the breed and four of the pups grew to be show champions and foundation stock for other kennels—Warchant and Jochem initially.

The steady growth of the breed both in America and Great Britain encouraged interest world wide. In Australia Gordons started to be bred and exhibited more frequently. The stock in NSW had an opportunity to be used with good, sound working dogs in Victoria. One of the dogs of Argyle descent was used in NSW also.

Then, in Victoria, Fieldpride Kennels and later Triseter began to emerge as strong kennels of the breed, while in NSW, Warchant surged with some outstanding young stock.

During the 1970's Mrs. Gilbert imported Ch. Ellerspark Black Rufus of Jaywick from England. He was used by Dooenbrae Kennels over a Warchant bitch and produced a nice litter in NSW.

In Queensland, Mosset Kennels started to breed and show, thus spreading interest in the breed in the north.

In New Zealand, Bruce and Sylvia Robson imported a bitch and a dog from Cuprea Kennels in England and based their kennel on this stock, now crossed with Ch. Sutherland Hallmark.

Further British imports were Neidpath McLeigh brought in by Glen Frazer (New Zealand) and used only a few times. Later Robyn Jones and Esther Joseph (Victoria) imported Rhovanion Royal Emissary, also limited in use.   (Stiff quarantine rules make the importation both expen sive and hard on the dogs).

In 1975 the first American champion was brought in by Mr. Graeme Lack of Melbourne. This is American, Australian and New Zealand Champion Sutherland Hallmark (Am. Ch. Sutherland MacDuff x Am. Ch. Sutherland Sybil). Hallmark has also obtained a Field Trial qualifying certificate.

At the present time there is a Setter Club in NSW serving all three breeds: Gordon Setter Clubs in Queensland; South Australia; New Zealand and, most recently, New South Wales. The Gordon Setter Club of Victoria, one of the older ones, is probably the largest with an active membership of over 100.

There are also Gun Dog Societies and Clubs for all the Sporting Group.

166

Am. Aust. and New Zealand Ch. Sutherland Hallmark.

Ch. Warchant Little Wonder in 1980. *Pearce*

As each state conducts its own Kennel or Canine Control, it is hard to estimate the total annual number of registrations and champions in the country. Private sources advise that in Victoria from 1976-1980, 315 Gordons were registered and twenty show champions and three CD's were made. The top producing bitch is Ch. Fieldpride Blue Carli (Ch. Lederle Rebel Scot x Fieldspride Contessa) owned by Esther Joseph. Her record is eleven champions. The all-time top producer is Ch. Sutherland Hallmark with an estimated 60 champions; many more will finish.

In New South Wales, from 1976-1980, three hundred registrations were recorded, while 16 show champions and two CDs were completed.

 Top Producers include: Ch. Warchant Magestic Scot (12 Ch.) and Ch. Warchant Drummer Boy (16 Ch.), both sired by Ch. Lederle Magestic Scot x Aust. Ch. Lorroy Scot Robin.

Ch. Lederle Magestic Scot, born in 1965, sired by K.C.C. Ch. Tabilk Chieftain x Araniw Lady Beatrix, was the sire of ten champions.

Aust. Ch. Lorroy Scot Robin produced eight champions from her only litter. Other top producers are: Ch. Warchant Scottish Lass, eight champions; Ch. Bagpiper Thistledown, five champions; and Jochem Lady Elinor, four champions; and Aust. Ch. Warchant Little Wonder, four show champions, one CD.

The greatest number of Gordons are and always have been concentrated in Victoria. The Gordon Setter Show in Victoria had an entry of 74 in 1978 which went up to 84 in 1980. The recent Gordon Setter Club Show in NSW had 53 entries.

In all breed shows and at Royal Shows entries run between 20 and 80. At small suburban and country shows, there are sometimes only a few.

The oppressive heat of the Australian sun is not kind to our Gordons. Perhaps this is one reason why the dogs in the cooler southern states have better coats and are bred in greater numbers.

There are several types of grass seeds here which imbed into the coat, penetrate the skin sometimes, and travel internally. Australians must be aware of this hazard as well as the prevalence of snake bite which kills quite a few working Gordons.

Kennel Profiles

(Dates refer to the kennel)

Lorroy (1965-   ) Julie Dickinson, Parks, NSW; producer of 6 champions 1976-1980.

Julie began with two bitches from New Zealand, one of which was Ch. Worthy Downs Black Poppy. Bred to the New Zealand dog, Dalbeattie of

Ch. Worthy Downs Black Poppy with Julie Dickinson.

Ch. Lorroy Scot Legend.

Glencraig, she produced four nice champions all carrying the Lorroy prefix: Scot Legend, Scot Bonnie Mary, Scot Robin, and Scot Tartan.

It is interesting to learn that Dalbeattie was imported to Australia at age of eleven after a lifetime of hunting. Properly conditioned and trained, he completed his show champimnship in 1972!

Ch. Lorroy Scot Legend was one of the first Gordons to be shown extensively and to do much winning. His record of 21 Bests of Breed, 12 group or "in show" awards was a record at that time. Lorroy-bred Gordons are to be found back of much of the current stock.

Being shown by Julie at this time is Ch. Lorroy Scot Leughan (Ch. Ellerspark Black Rufus of Jaywick x Ch. Lorroy Scot Lorina) a breeding which doubles up on Dalbeattie.

Warchant (1965-   ) Mrs. Dawn Ferguson, Taren Point NSW; since 1976 over 36 show champions, 7 CD's and two UD's.

This very active kennel began with Ch. Lorroy Scot Robin. Bred to Ch. Lederle Magestic Scot, Robin produced the first Warchant litter. Eight of the 13 puppies became champions and many of them went as foundation stock for newer kennels.

The outstanding dog from this litter was Ch. Warchant Drummer Boy (born 1967) who set a new record for show wins. He was the first Gordon to gain a Best Exhibit In Show, all-breeds; also Best of Breed at four Sydney Royals, Challenge and BOB at Melbourne, Brisbane and Adelaide Royals. As mentioned before, he became a Top Producer with 16 champions in Australia, two in New Zealand, one in South Africa, 4 CD holders, 2 with CDX and one with UD.

His litter brother, Ch. Warchant Magestic Scot, also had a most successful show career and sired eleven show champions. Among his get are Warchant Tapestry, first UD Gordon and Ch. Warchant Dandy, UD.

From Warchant Whimsical, CD, mated to Ch. Lederle Rebel Scot, came the famous Int. Ch. Dooenbrae Myola Lass (1970), dam of six champions. She was taken to Great Britain in the mid-70's where she quickly became an English show champion. Her best known son is Ch. Dooenbrae Glen Scotia (Glade Kennels in South Australia).

A litter by Ch. Sutherland Hallmark x Ch. Warchant Heather produced Best in Show winner, Ch. Piperhill Eilan Angus. Another Hallmark litter, this one from Ch. Warchant Little Wonder, gave Mrs. Ferguson the outstanding bitch, Ch. Warchant Crest, first Gordon to win Best in Show at the Setter Club of NSW Specialty. Crest was Setter of the Year in 1980 in NSW and has over 25 Best of Breeds. Her sister, Ch. Warchant Little Wonder, Setter of the Year in 1981 was twice Best Opposite in Show at the Victoria GSC show; a multi-award winner, and dam of six champions to date.

170

**Ch. Warchant Crest (center) at Setter Club of NSW 1981.
Best Gordon in Show, best Australian-bred in Show.**

Ch. Piperhill Eilan Skye (Hallmark x Ch. Warchant Heather) has been a prolific winner. Three years running she has won the Challenge at the Royal National, plus many bests of breed and in group awards.

Two current youngsters from Warchant are most exciting, each with six consecutive "in group" wins and Challenges: Warchant Kintyre (NSW) and Warchant Bijou (Queensland).

(Mrs. Ferguson is well known for her intimate knowledge of pedigrees and her excellent analyses of the breed in articles and remarkably effective sketches)—*Author's note*

Merrowlea Kennels (1968-   ) Mrs. C. Rethers, Turramuna, Sydney; ten champions.

Christine Rethers started with Ch. Warchant Piper, CD, in 1968 and then added Ch. Warchant Scottish Lass. Currently being campaigned are Ch. Merrowlea Maximus and Ch. Merrowlea Moray Lass.

Braegordon (1973-   ) Neil and Jenny Perrett, Weston, NSW; five champions since 1976.

Ch. Braegordon Bacchus (Ch. Warchant Kerribilli x Jochem Lady Elinor) was Setter of the year in 1979 in NSW. Littermates are Ch. Braegordon Lass, New Zealand Ch. Braegordon Seumas and Braegordon Wildfire.

Lass, when bred to Ch. Sutherland Hallmark, produced two winning males. Ch. Braegordon Abner went Best of Breed, Spring Fair 1977 at age of ten months, while his brother Adam was Best of Breed at Brisbane Royal in 1978.

Triseter (1973-   ) Esther Joseph, Melbourne, Australia.

Foundation bitch for this well established kennel is the lovely Ch. Fieldpride Blu Carli (Ch. Lederle Rebel Scot x Fieldpride Countess), the dam of eleven champions from three litters.

Bred to Ch. Sutherland Hallmark, Carli produced Ch. Triseter Black Ash, Ch. T. Abba Annwen and Ch. T. Aiden. Annwen was the top Gordon Setter bitch in Victoria for 1979 and 1980. Currently being shown is the successful Ch. Triseter Black Heath. Foundation stock for many other kennels has come from this reliable kennel.

Gooree (1975-   ) Margaret Carrick, Croydon, NSW; six champions since 1976.

With the outstanding winner, Ch. Warchant Drummer Boy, as foundation stud, and the fine bitch, Ch. Jochem Austral Lady (Drummer

Aust. Ch. Fieldpride Blue Carli.

Aust. and New Zealand Ch. Rainbird Glen Marni.

173

Boy x Ch. Lorroy Scot Tartan), as her foundation bitch, this kennel has had much success. Currently starring is the lovely bitch, Ch. Parwana Morag (Drummer Boy x Ch. Dooenbrae Glen Turret) with 15 "in group" awards, ten "in show," including ACT Gundog Society Best In Show.

Morag's daughter, Gooree Tay Elgin, sired by Ch. Gooree Ben Hall, recently won Best Exhibit at the Northern Gundog Championship Show and Best in Group and Best Intermediate at Liverpool and District.

Willochra (1976-　　) David and Liz Hazeldine, Yellingbo, Victoria

Ch. Bagpiper Thistledown (Ch. Warchant Drummer Boy x Ch. Dooenbrae Bonnie Lass) is the dam of Champions Willochra Glen Monarch, Willochra Summer Rover, Willochra Tamarisk and Willochra Royal Amy. From their Willochra Bonnie Skye, bred to Ch. Rainbird Glen Blair, they have Ch. Willochra MacKellor.

Current winners include Ch. Gunproud Bridey Mine (Ch. Dooenbrae Glen Scotia, sire) who won Best Opposite in Show in 1980 at the Gordon Setter Club of Victoria championship show. Another successful young bitch (sired by Summer Rover) is Willochra Shona Mine who completed her title in 1981.

Rainbird (1976-　　) Mrs. Helen Dempsey, Warragul, Victoria

This is home to the winning Aust. and N.Z. Ch. Rainbird Glen Marni (Ch. Triseter Black Ash x Ch. Glade Mulloben Killean). Among her many good wins, she was Best of Breed at the Melbourne Royal in 1979, and has "in group" awards.

Also at home are two successful brothers, Ch. Rainbird Glen Blair, sire of three champions for Willochra, and Ch. Rainbird Glen Stuart, CD (Ch. Sutherland Hallmark x Ch. Glade Mulloben Killean).

Glenquayle (1978-　　) Kay C. Murphy, Wandin Nth, Australia

This young kennel is doing very well with their Ch. Triseter Black Arran (a Hallmark son) and the nice bitch, Ch. Balmaghie Border Charm (Black Arran x Kirkside Alice). Their young male, Glenquayle Ebony Mylor (Ch. Wyngarde Highland Lad x Border Charm), is starting what is expected to be a satisfying show career.

Rokeena (1975-　　) Robyn Jones, Diggers Rest, Victoria

A very active kennel owned by an intensely interested breeder. Firstly involved in the import of Rhovanion Royal Emissary with Esther Joseph, Robyn is now planning an American import. Rokeena Reflections and Ch. Rokeena White Heather have been impressive young winners and have done well for the breed.

174

Aust. Ch. Dooenbrae Glen Scotia.

Ch. Piperhill Eilan Skye, 1981.

South Australia has two main producers:

Glade (1971-   ) owned by Bob Lott, Longwood.

The star of this kennel is the famous Ch. Dooenbrae Glen Scotia (Ch. Warchant Magestic Scot x Int. Ch. Dooenbrae Myola Lass). Considered to be probably the most successful show Gordon in Australia, he has had many bests in show, breed wins and groups, including those at Melbourne Royal in 1977 and Adelaide Royal in 1978. He is also an excellent producer.

The bitch, Ch. Daneson Glade Mull O'oe (Ch. Warchant Drummer Boy x Warchant Will O'the Wisp), bred to Ch. Sutherland Hallmark, has produced a trio of winners, all carrying the prefix Glade: Champions Mulguy the Boss, Mulguy the Chief and Mullamos Sprite. The Boss went Best in Show at the first Australian Gordon Setter Specialty and BOS at Adelaide Royal. The Chief got his Best in Show at the second Gordon Setter Club of Victoria Specialty show, and Sprite has had numerous "in group" and "in show" awards. This active kennel has made 22 champions in eight years.

Piperhill (1971-   ) Hans and Barb Groffer

Through their foundation bitch, Ch. Warchant Heather, the Groffers have bred some eight champions, and chalked up a long list of show awards both "in group" and "in show."

Ch. Piperhill Eilan Angus, sired by Ch. Sutherland Hallmark, has won many group and in show awards. Their highly successful bitch, Ch. Warchant Coronette, is recent challenge winner at three Interstate Royal Shows, and the dam of four champions, though she is only four years old.

In Queensland, some 500 miles to the north of Sydney, we have a much hotter climate where the dog world is less intensive than in the south.

Here is located the *Mosset Kennels,* owned by Mr. and Mrs. J. Mowbray.

This is perhaps the only kennel breeding over a long period of time, and they have accumulated a list of about ten champions. They have had a lot of satisfaction with their fine dog, Ch. Mosset Black Brutus, who has six Best in Group, 2 Reserve in Show, one Best in Show in Queensland, and numerous other awards.

In Tasmania a new kennel and perhaps the only one as yet is *Morseter,* established in 1979, owned by Michael and Cindy Williams in Windemere.

From their foundation bitch, Glade Spring Fantasy, bred to Aust. Ch. Dooenbrae Glen Scotia, the Williams had a fine litter, four of which had (by 1981) won 14 "in group" and "in show" awards and one Reserve exhibit in group. These youngsters are Morseter Famos MacDuff, Famos Benayre, Famos Kintore and Famos Skye. With a good start like this their luck is bound to continue.

6
The Gordon Setter
in Canada

*Contributed by Janice Stomp,
Bragg Creek, Alberta, Canada*

ALTHOUGH the Canadian Kennel Club is in charge of conformation, obedience and field trials, its records and files do not readily provide breed statistics upon request in the same way that the American Kennel Club does. No information on the number of individuals/breed registered per year is available, nor is any summary of titles earned by a breed provided. Breed fanciers can access this information by perusing offical C.K.C. results in past issues of *Dogs in Canada,* and in so doing, will gradually become aware of the status of the Gordon Setter in Canada. These show and trial records reveal that Gordon Setter entries have slowly increased over the past decade—indicating an overall rise in popularity. Approximately 150 Gordons have earned conformation titles over the past 10 years while close to 50 obedience titles were awarded to Gordons over the same period. However, the past decade has seen not one Gordon in Canada complete a field championship.

The "golden years" of Gordon field activity in Western Canada were the 1940's and 1950's when Jim Forbes' Glentanar Gordons of Saskatoon, Saskatchewan captured two dual championships. In recent years, Ontario has become a centre of Gordon field activity. Gordon Setter Club of Ontario members June and Bill Bradley, as well as Chris and Deb Loughran have encouraged and supported Gordon entries in local sporting dog field trials. As a result, in 1981 Gordons took 12 placings in Ontario

177

trials with Bradley's Blackhawk's Northern Gauge winning the Best Dog in Trial award, German Shorthaired Pointer Club of Ontario, May 9-10, Guelph, Ontario. Elsewhere in Canada, Gordon field trial activity has ebbed somewhat. Many field enthusiasts have pursued their hobby informally—enjoying their Gordons' ability as excellent personal hunting companions.

The Gordon Setter has proven himself as an adept and challenging obedience competitor as well.

The following is a list of some Gordon obedience title holders over the past decade, noting their highest degree and honours awarded:

Sangerfield Sports Penny, CD
Ch. Grianan Kennet MacEwan, CD
Breadalbane Victoria Banner, CDX
Ch. Kris' Gentle Gus, CD
Am. & Can. Ch. Jock the Scot of Karolly (Am. UD), Can. CDX
Glenappin Eriskay Wisteria, CD
Am. & Can. Ch. MacAlder Merry of Clansmen, CD
*Am. & Can. Ch. Inwood Meadow Rue (Am. UD), Can. CDX
Meghan McKay of Berridale, CD
McMac's Radar of Zedelbren, CD
Bradmar's Devilsome Duchess, CD
Hedgestone's Blue Will-O-Wisp, CD
Ch. Kennetkaird Chantilly, CD
*Ch. Cuprea Black Lady, CDX
Peer's Angel's Wings at Dawn, CD
Aarondale's C.C. Aaremus, CD
Stilmeadows Viscount, CD
Our Alladin of Heather's Lass, CD
Scottland's All About Abby, CD
Sungold's Burnished Ebony, CD
Am. Ch. Tri-Sett Black Bart of Robilee, CD
Sungolds Northern Light, CD
Bright Bracken, CD
Blackthorn's Lady Diana, CD
Alistair Meadow Melody, UD
*Ch. Clansmen Jasper, CDX
Clansmen Copperbottom, CD

*Indicates dogs have won High Score in Trial

The Top Obedience Gordons in Canada over the past five years are as follows:

1977 Am. Can. Ch. Inwood Meadows Rue (Am. UD), Can. CDX
1978 Ch. Cuprea Black Lady, CDX (Johnston)

178

Can. & Am. Ch. Kil-Mur-EE's Seonaid O'Grianan (B).
DNH Photographics, Ltd.

Can. Field Trial and Bench Champion Vagabond Jean of Glentanar shown after completing the second part of the Amateur Stake, Sept. 6, 1954.

1979 Alistair Meadow Melody, CDX (Hofer)
1980 Alistair Meadow Melody, UD (Hofer)
1981 Alistair Meadow Melody, UD (Hofer)

The Gordon Setter is not among the most populous breeds in Canada. Booster and Specialty shows held across our vast and thinly populated country are likely to draw the highest entry of Gordons in conformation competition. So it is that the largest Gordon entry to date in Canada was at the August 30, 1980 Ottawa Valley All Setter Association, when 18 Gordon entries were judged by Mr. George Pugh. Running a close second would be the November 29, 1981 Gordon Setter Booster held by the Gordon Setter Club of British Columbia with 17 Gordons entered under Dr. Chas. Lunn.

Based on official C.K.C. show results, each year *Dogs in Canada* awards "Top Three in Breed" placings. The point system is based on one point for each dog defeated, Best of Breed and better. The following is a list of the Top Three Gordons and their points earned over the past 10 years in Canada:

1972 Am. Ch. Briar Patch's Rob Roy (63)
  Ch. Kil-Mur-EE's Seonaid O'Grianan (59)
  Grianan Victoria Balfour (45)

1973 Ch. Robingreen Alistair (86)
  Ch. Grianan Kennet MacEwan, CD (73)
  Heathero's Autumn Schroeder (72)

1974 Am. & Can. Ch. Kil-MUR-EE's Seonaid O'Grianan (312)
  Am. & Can. Ch. Johnston's Highland Storm (161)
  Am. & Can. Ch. Daron Make Mine Scotch (153)

1975 Am. & Can. Ch. Johnson's Highland Storm (324)
  Ch. Cuprea Black Queen (97)
  Am. Ch. MacNeal of Ellicott (63)

1976 Am. & Can. Ch. Rockaplenty's Hang 'Em High (144)
  Ch. MacAlder Midnite Piper (127)
  Am. & Can. Ch. MacAlder Mr. Chips (106)

1977 Ch. Gordon Hill Very Special (129)
  Am. & Can. Ch. Blackthorn's Laird Aaron (124)
  Ch. Clansmen Colourgard (111)

1978 Am. & Can. Ch. Rockaplenty's Pride 'n Joy (277)
  Am. Ch. McMac's George (238)
  Ch. Boldbrook's Yankie Junior (136)

1979 Am. & Can. Ch. Clansmen Colourgard (793)
  Am. & Can. Ch. Rockaplenty's Pride 'n Joy (769)
  Ch. Cobblerwood Midnight Cowboy (173)

Can. & Am. Ch. Gillian of Grianan with Patti Grant, judge Len Carey.

Rich Bergman

Am. & Can. Ch. Indigo's Jasmine with owner-breeder-handler, Krishna Harris. *Hodges*

1980 Am. & Can. Ch. Clansmen Colourgard (2590)
     Am. & Can. Ch. McMac's Hawkeye of Cameron (419)
     Am. & Can. Ch. Rockaplenty's Pride 'n Joy (348) ·

1981 Am. & Can. Ch. Clansmen Colourgard (556)
     Ch. Woodbine's Diablo of Bludawns (126)
     Am. & Can. Ch. Rockaplenty's Country Redlegs (77)

Top Winning Gordon for 1980, Am. & Can. Ch. Clansmen Colourgard, won an All-Breed Best in Show that year, and his point total of 2,590 points earned him the placing of #8 Sporting Dog in Canada for 1980.

Listed below are breeders and breed fanciers, who through their interest in, and love for Gordons have made significant contributions to the breed in Canada over the past years. These contributions have been in the areas of show, field and obedience.

Bocking, Thomas and Margaret: Grianan Reg'd.

Mrs. Bocking's involvement with the Gordon breed spans 20 years and during that time Grianan Gordons have earned many awards and honours. The Bockings have produced 15 title holders to date. Grianan stock has offered a sound foundation upon which other breed fanciers could base their breeding programs, and over the many years, Margaret Bocking has supported generously every facet of breed activity. From 1974 to 1977, she served as a Director of the G.S.C.A., and from 1977 to 1979 was president of the Ottawa Valley All Setter Association.

The first Gordon to join the Bocking household was Can. Ch. Hickory Smoke Tay Brodie, CD (Am. Ch. Sangerfield Index x Am. & Can. Ch. Hickory Harvest) bred by M. Mitchell and Joyce Ruess. From her first litter by Windrock Skye McQueen came two outstanding bitches: Ch. Grianan Morag McTay and Grianan Rachel McTay.

Shown in the early 70's when Gordon entries were few, Morag became a "trail-blazer" for the breed—taking several Group placings and winning a Best Canadian Bred in Group. Overall, Morag produced seven champion offspring, and in 1975 was named a Brood Bitch of the Year by the G.S.C.A. Two of these pups went on to become Group-placing Gordons. Can. Ch. Grianan Kennet MacEwan, CD (Ch. Hickory Smoke Black Ebony x Morag), owned by Susan (Gilmour) Pontius, won Group II at the 1973 Crocus K.C., Manitoba, and Mrs. Bocking's own lovely Am. & Can. Ch. Grianan Victoria Balfour (Ch. George Gordon Sangerfield x Morag) took Group III in Weyburn, Sask. May 1972. Victoria Balfour went on to become # 3 Top Winning Gordon in Canada for 1972. Ch. Gillian of Grianan, out of Victoria Balfour by Am. Ch. Sports Index, was R.W.B. at the 1978 Combined Setter Specialty in New York, and went on to finish her American and Canadian championships in fine style.

Morag's litter sister, Grianan Rachel McTay, was bred to Am. Ch. Loch Adair Nabob's Flip in 1969, and produced among others the outstanding bitch, Am. & Can. Ch. Kil-Mur-EE's Seonaid O' Grianan. "Shona" won Best in Breed at the 1972 Ottawa Valley All Setter Association Booster and finished 1972 as #2 Top Winning Gordon Setter over kennel-mate Victoria Balfour, who was in 3rd place. That year saw Mrs. Bocking place two Gordon bitches among the Top Three Gordons in the country. In June of 1974 Shona won Group First at the Kawartha K.C. as well as Best of Breed at the Manitoba All Setter Association Specialty, Winnipeg, Manitoba, in October of that year to finish '74 as the Top Winning Gordon Setter in Canada.

Campbell, Lynne and Dave: Glenappin Reg'd.

The Campbell's involvement with Gordon Setters dates back to the late 60's. A. and J. Ruess' Hickory Smoke bloodline made up some of Glenappin's earliest stock with the likes of Ch. Hickory Smoke Glenappin Pypr and Hickory Smoke Glenna McQueen. Am. & Can. Ch. Fichtental's Brigadoon, sired by Ch. Hickory Smoke Neil Cameron, did considerable winning for them in the early 70's. In later years they were fortunate in acquiring two lovely bitches from Gentry Farms and throughout the years have handled more than a few "black-and-tans" to show championships. Their promotion of the breed did not end at the bench, however, and the Campbells have also been active over the years in obedience trials and local field associations.

Fanning, Tony: Cuprea Kennel

No longer active in Gordons, Fanning moved to Canada from England in the early '70's, bringing with him several Gordons of his noted Cuprea line including Can. Ch. Cuprea Black Lady (Deerswood Raven x Cuprea Penny Black) who won a Group III at the 1975 Lethbridge K.C. show. A number of his Canadian-bred Gordons have earned championship titles, and one bitch, Ch. Cuprea Black Lady, CDX, owned and handled by Johnstons, became Top Obedience Gordon in Canada in 1978.

Forbes, Jim: Glentanar

As a boy of 12 in Scotland, Jim Forbes became proud owner of his first Gordon and began a life-long love affair with the breed. After moving to Canada and acquiring mostly American-bred foundation stock, he began breeding Gordons under the Glentanar name in Saskatoon, Saskatchewan. Having worked with gamekeepers and dog trainers in the old country,

Forbes had a keen appreciation of bird sense in the Gordon Setter, and field ability became for him a "must" in any dogs he promoted. He preferred his Setters fast and on the small side in order to be competitive at trials with the other Setters and speedy Pointers. In the late 40's and early 50's Forbes accomplished the astonishing feat of finishing two home-bred Gordon bitches to C.K.C.-recognized dual championships. The fact that these two were mother and daughter simply added lustre to this sterling accomplishment.

Although her field championship was earned in accordance with C.K.C. regulations, Ch. Glentanar Birdie was not recognized by the American breed club as a dual champion. Nevertheless, Birdie can be regarded as the first dual champion Gordon in North America. Bred to Loch Ridge Major Rogue in 1947, Birdie whelped the bitch who was to become the lovely Can. Dual Ch. Vagabond Jean of Glentanar. Jean, handled by Forbes, went on to win her field championship in 1954 and her show championship in 1955 at the age of eight! Forbes' emphasis on dual purpose Gordons is evidenced by his decision to breed Jean back to the Dual Ch. Gunbar Dare Devil, CD. In recent years, the Forbes have continued their long association with the breed. Their two latest Gordons afford them much pleasure as personal hunting dogs and beloved companions.

Harris, Tony and Krishna: Indigo Reg'd.

Harris' love affair with Gordons began with the lovely foundation bitch, Can. Ch. Sangerfield Veronica (Am. Ch. Sangerfield Sports Don x Am. Ch. Sangerfield Rrenamere Tansy), whelped in 1974. With three litters to her credit, "Nica" has proven her quality as a producer. To date, her offspring have earned nine titles—eight Conformation champions (four American, four Canadian) as well as one CD obedience titlist. In addition, several others of her pups are both U.S. and Canadian pointed.

Perhaps one of the best known of the Indigo Gordons is Am. & Can. Ch. Indigo's Jasmine, whelped November 1976 (Ch. Sangerfield Sports Index x Can. Ch. Sangerfield Veronica). Jasmine won championship points as a puppy in both the U.S. and Canada. As a seven-month puppy in Canadian competition, she took a two-point win and a Best Puppy in Sporting Group, while at eight months, judge John Lawreck awarded Jasmine W.B. for four points at the G.S.C.A. Greeley, Colorado, Booster in 1977. With a Breed and Group IV win at the Gordon Setter Club of B.C. Booster 1980, she became the Top Winning Gordon Bitch in Canada, and #5 Gordon in Canada overall.

Another of Nica's fine offspring is Am. & Can. Ch. Indigo High Times (sired by Am. & Can. Ch. MacAlder Mr. Chips) who distinguished himself by finishing his Canadian Championship at 12 months of age with a five-

Can. & Am. Ch. Rockaplenty's Pride and Joy. Sandy Gunn with trophy, judge George Pugh.
Pierre Wibaut

185

point Breed win over Specials at the 1979 Gordon Setter Club of B.C. Booster. His American championship he completed at 20 months with a Breed win over Specials from the classes.

Tony and Krishna, founding members of the Gordon Setter Club of B.C., continue to support the breed through club participation and expect to remain actively involved in breeding and exhibiting fine Gordon Setters in years to come.

Johnston, Jim and Eleanor: Scotchguard Reg'd.

Although not having bred Gordons up to this point, the Johnstons have been staunch supporters of the breed for over seven years. Their first Gordon, Can. Ch. Cuprea Black Lady, CDX, became Top Obedience Gordon in Canada for 1978, and en route to that honour, had earned a coveted High Score in Trial. Am. & Can. Ch. Clansmen Wee Gordie (Am. & Can. Ch. MacAlder Mr. Chips x Am. & Can. Ch. MacAlder Lona) was campaigned to many Group placings in Canadian shows. Capably handled by owner Jim Johnston, Am. & Can. Ch. Clansmen Witchcraft (Am. & Can. Ch. Norcoaster's MacManus x Am. & Can. Ch. MacAlder Lona) completed her Canadian show championship against strong competition at only 11 months of age, winning a Best Puppy in Sporting Group en route to her title. Their Can. Ch. Darley's Miss Scotchguard, CD (Am. & Can. Ch. MacAlder Mr. Chips x Can. Ch. Clansmen Cara Mia), after finishing her conformation championship, completed her obedience CD in fine style and continues training toward her CDX.

Jordan, Caryl and Keith: Hedgestone Reg'd.

Although owners and exhibitors of Gordons prior to 1975, it was Jordan's acquisition in that year of their future foundation bitch, Can. Ch. Scottland's Liberty Belle (Am. & Can. Ch. Johnston's Highland Storm x Am. Ch. Vagabond Lark of Rockaplenty, CD) that marked their beginning as Gordon breeders.

Twice bred to the famous Top Producer Am. Ch. Afternod Yank of Rockaplenty, CD, Liberty Belle produced two Canadian champion offspring. One of these, Can. Ch. Hedgestone's Dynasty, co-owned with R. Seabrook, is major pointed in the U.S., having gone Best of Winners at the 1981 G.S.C.A. Midwest Specialty in Ohio.

In 1978 the Jordans were fortunate in acquiring Am. & Can. Ch. Rockaplenty's Pride 'n Joy (Am. Ch. Afternod Yank of Rockaplenty, CD, x Am. Ch. Rockaplenty's Pit-a-Pat), then nearly three years of age. By year's end, "PJ" had accumulated enough points to make him Top Winning Gordon Setter in Canada for 1978, and the following year, his point total placed him #2 Top winning Gordon in Canada, 1979. 1980 saw

186

PJ win Best of Breed at Mad River Valley K.C., Ohio, and on to a Group IV. That year as well, George Pugh judged him Best in Breed at the Ottawa Valley All Setter Association Specialty. Throughout his show career with the Jordans PJ has earned 17 Group placings—among them two Group Firsts, as well as uncounted Breed wins.

Twice Jordans bred Pride 'n Joy to Liberty Belle and from these two litters produced four more Gordon titlists with several others pointed in Canada and the U.S. Their own lovely bitch from this breeding, Am. & Can. Ch. Hedgestone's Flying Colours, finished almost entirely from the puppy classes going on to win her American championship before two years of age with a five-point Best of Winners at Mad River Valley K.C., Ohio. She became a Specialty winner in September 1981 when Judge H. Martin put her to the Breed at the Ottawa Valley All Setter Association Specialty. In 1982 Flying Colours was bred to Can. Ch. Scottland's de Droit, co-owned by Jordans with his breeder Gretchen Scott. Sired by Am. & Can. Ch. Rockaplenty's Hang 'Em High and out of Am. & Can. Ch. Scottland's American Spirit, de Droit won both his U.S. majors from the puppy class. Through their program of selective line-breeding, Caryl and Keith Jordan hope to produce both consistency in quality and type over the years to come.

Pontius, John and Susan: Uplord Kennels

Susan Pontius, formerly Gilmour, actively exhibited and promoted Gordons in Manitoba and Saskatchewan throughout the 70's under the kennel name Kennetkaird. Her Can. Ch. Grianan Kennet MacEwan, CD (Ch. Hickory Smoke Black Ebony x Ch. Grianan Morag McTay) finished his Canadian championship at an early age with a Best Canadian Bred Puppy in Group. In June '73 Kennet won Group II at the Crocus K.C. show to finish that year as #2 Top Winning Gordon in Canada. Following his early death, Susan acquired Gordons of Stilmeadows and Rockaplenty lines—notably Group-placing Am. & Can. Ch. Rockaplenty's Gunsmoke. Now Mrs. John Pontius, Susan resides in the U.S. where she and her husband John breed Gordons carrying the Uplord kennel prefix. Worthy of mention is their lovely Ch. Uplord Black Fantasy—Canadian Specialty Breed winner at under one year of age!

Scholz, Oscar F.: Fichtental (Perm. Reg'd.)

No longer very active in the Gordon breed, Mr. Scholz's association with Gordons dates back to the mid '60's. Three champion offspring resulted from his litter by Ch. Hickory Smoke Neil Cameron x Ch. Windrock's Aberdare Kyle. Am. & Can. Ch. Fichtental's Brigadoon, CD, shown in the U.S. and Canada during the period 1971-73, took nearly 25 Breed wins, while litter sisters, Ch. Fichtental's Bonnie and Ch. Fichtental's

Black Princess, both finished in Canada—with Black Princess winning a Group III in August of 1970.

Stomps, Jim and Janice: Clansmen Reg'd.

Although owners of a Gordon previous to 1973, their acquisition in '73 of the puppy who was to become Am. & Can. Ch. MacAlder Merry of Clansmen, CD (Am. & Can. Ch. Rogheath Ben MacDhui x Ch. MacAlder Dede) marked the beginning of the Stomps' serious involvement with the Gordon breed.

Finishing in Canada at 11 months of age with a Specialty BOS over champion bitches, "Birdie" went on to become a Booster Breed winner, and was judged Best in Breed by Wm. Trotter at the 1981 Tri-Setter Club of Alberta Specialty. Her Canadian CD obedience title was won in consecutive legs at a three-show weekend, and she earned her American championship title with four majors and points to spare—taking BOS from the classes at the G.S.C.A. Des Moines, Iowa Booster '74 and finishing later with a Breed over Specials.

Bred first to Am. Ch. Sangerfield Sports Index, Birdie produced two Canadian champions—among them Ch. Clansmen Jasper, CDX. Jasper, a High Score in Trial winner owned/handled by Thuens, Regina, went on to become 2nd Top Obedience Gordon in Canada for 1981. Also from the Sports Index litter came Am. Ch. Clansmen Merriment of Savoy, Am. CDX, handled by owner Denise Dunham to her Dog World obedience award.

Birdie's litter by kennelmate Am. & Can. Ch. Clansmen Colourgard produced Am. & Can. Ch. Clansmen Honourgard—B.W. for five points at the 1982 Mad River Valley K.C., as well as Breed over Specials for a four-point major 1982 Richland, Washington. Honourgard's litter brother, Clansmen Copperbottom, CD, brings titles earned by Birdie's offspring to ten.

Am. & Can. Ch. MacAlder Lona (Am. & Can. Ch. Rogheath Ben MacDhui x MacAlder Beauty) joined the Setters at Clansmen in 1975—aged two years. Lona finished quickly in Canada, winning Breeds and a Group IV from the classes. Like Birdie, Lona went on to become a Booster Breed winner as well as Best of Breed at 1977 Tri-Setter Club of Alberta Specialty under Harold Schlintz, and B.O.S. to her son, Colourgard, at the 1979 Northern Alberta Setter Association Specialty under judge Roy Jerome. Lona barnstormed her way to her American championship title winning four majors in four consecutive shows—among them BW and BOS over Specials for five points at both the G.S.C.A. Waukesha Specialty and West Bend, Wisconsin shows, July 1975.

Bred first to Am. & Can. Ch. MacAlder Mr. Chips, Lona produced a litter of four pups—all of whom won both American and Canadian

Can. & Am. Ch. MacAlder Lona.
Don Hodges

Can. & Am. Ch. Blackthorn's Laird Aaron.

championships. Son Am. & Can. Ch. Clansmen Wee Gordie (Johnston) went on to win nearly 10 Canadian Group placings while litter sister, Am. & Can. Ch. Clansmen Ms. Tiffany, became a Canadian Specialty Breed winner under Ted Eldredge at the 1980 N.A.S.A. Specialty. Perhaps best known of her offspring by Mr. Chips is Am. & Can. Ch. Clansmen Colourgard. Finished in Canada at one year of age with a Specialty BW, Best in Sweepstakes, as well as a Best Puppy in Group, by one and a half years of age, "Mike" had won his first Group placing—a Group II. At year's end, while still under age 2, Colourgard had earned enough points to place him #3 Top Winning Gordon in Canada for 1977. Colourgard earned his American championship in fine style—with BW at the 1977 G.S.C.A. Booster, Greeley, Colorado, several Breed wins over Specials, including his Group II from the Open class at Walla, Walla, Washington 1978.

Colourgard's sterling record in Canadian show rings includes three Booster Bests of Breed and four Specialty Bests of Breed. From his 102 Canadian breed wins, he went on to 37 Group placings—among them six Group I's. In February 1980, by winning Best in Show at the all-breed Alberta Kennel Club Diamond Jubilee Show (at nearly 1200, the largest entry ever in Canada) Colourguard joined the ranks of the select few BIS Gordons. In so doing, he also became the only Canadian-bred BIS Gordon ever, as well as the only known breeder/owner/handled BIS Gordon in breed history. Mike became the #1 Top Winning Gordon in Canada for 1979, 1980 and 1981, as well as #8 Top Sporting Dog in Canada for 1980— the first Gordon ever to place among Canada's Top Ten Sporting Dogs. With very limited showing stateside, he won nine Breeds and two Group placings in 11 times shown. To date, Colourgard has sired three American show champions, two Canadian titlists and has others pointed in both countries.

The Stomps' Lona produced one other litter and from that, sired by Am. & Can. Ch. Norcoaster's MacManus, came several more champion offspring. Among them is major-pointed Clansmen Black Bond (Grimm)—Best in Sweepstakes, as well as BW at the 1980 G.S.C.A. Southern California Specialty. Two litter sisters, Am. & Can. Ch. Clansmen Sun-Yak Ebony (Sunderland) and Am. & Can. Ch. Clansmen Witchcraft (Matteson/Stomp) finished in fine style in both Canada and the U.S.—with Witchcraft taking BW for five points at the 1982 G.S.C.A. Far West Specialty, California. As a puppy in Canada, handled by then co-owner Johnstons, she had taken BW over American Specials up in the classes, and with her Best Puppy in Group, Northwinds K.C. '79, finished her Canadian show championship at under one year of age.

From Lona's two litters have come 12 earned titles, with others pointed. Among her offspring are two Best Puppy in Group winners, Booster and Specialty Breed winners, Multi-Group winners, and of course, a Best in Show son. The G.S.C.A. twice recognized her worth as a Top

Producer when in both 1977 and 1979, she was named a G.S.C.A. Brood Bitch Award winner.

With 10 years and over 20 earned titles behind them, Jim and Janice Stomp look forward to many more years of supporting the Gordon breed—through membership in various breed clubs, breeding and exhibiting their "black-and-tans."

Thomson, John and Cherri: Blackloch Reg'd.

Their serious involvement with the Gordon breed began when Am. & Can. Ch. Blackthorn's Laird Aaron (Am. & Can. Ch. Rogheath Ben MacDhui x Can. Ch. Madrona Vetern Lady) joined their household. Aaron finished in Canada by 12 months of age and in the U.S. by 2½ years—going on to win 57 Bests of Breed, one Group III, one Specialty Best of Breed and a Booster Best of Breed. In 1977, Aaron was campaigned to finish the year as Canada's #2 Top Winning Gordon Setter—#1 Canadian bred/owned. To date, Aaron has sired four title holders, among them Ch. Blackloch Lochinvar (Aaron x Ch. Feathercroft Christmas Carol) who in 1981, was awarded Puppy of the Year by the Gordon Setter Club of B.C. Litter sister, Ch. Blooma Tara, was awarded, in 1980, Best of Opposite Sex to Top Gordon by the G.S. Club of B.C. Thomson's lovely bitch, Can. Ch. Feathercroft Christmas Carol (Am. Ch. Torrance of Ellicott x Can. Ch. Highcountry Moonwind) also produced the 1980 G.S. Club of B.C. Puppy of the Year, in Can. Ch. Blackloch's Bold Design, sired by Am. & Can. Ch. Norcoaster's MacManus. As Gordon breeders over the years, the Thomsons have produced six title holders with others pointed.

Their support for the breed goes beyond exhibiting and breeding, for John and Cherri were instrumental in getting the fledgling Gordon Setter Club of B.C. off the ground. Through a limited program of selective breeding, and continuing club involvement and support, the Thomsons intend to remain active in the breed for many years to come.

Watt, Ron and Cheri: Highcountry Reg'd.

No longer as active in breeding and exhibiting Gordons, during the 70's the Watts were strong promoters of the dual potential Gordon. Gordons bred and owned by Highcountry first had to prove their worth in the field prior to conformation competition. To that end, they imported several good bitches from overseas and actively bred for strong field ability. One of their bitches, English import, Ch. Inkersall Black Beauty, was bred to Dual Ch. St. Andrew's Gaelic Brogue, CD, with hopes of producing capable and intelligent all-round setters.

Various clubs across Canada associated with Gordons, and their location:

Gordon Setter Club of B.C.
c/o 7905 - 127 Street
Surrey, B.C. V3W 4E7

Town & Country Setter Fancier, Inc.
c/o Sec: 23 Bonnydoon Place
Winnipeg, Manitoba R2K 3L5

Gordon Setter Club of Ontario
c/o 707 Beech Street
Whitby, Ontario L1N 3B6

Northern Alberta Setter Association
c/o Sec: R.R. #2
New Sarepta, Alberta T0B 3M0

Ottawa Valley All Setter Association
c/o Sec: 194 Booth Street
Ottawa, Ontario K1R 7J4

Tri-Setter Club of Alberta
c/o Treas: 12116 Lake Waterton Way S.E.
Calgary, Alberta T2J 2M4

Controlling and recording all registration, show and trial results is the:

Canadian Kennel Club
2150 Bloor Street West
Toronto, Ontario M6S 4V7

As well as supporting their local or regional clubs, a large number of Canadians hold membership in the Gordon Setter Club of America. Over the past ten years, two Canadians have served as Directors on the G.S.C.A. Board of Governors. Mrs. Margaret Bocking, Osgoode, Ontario was elected a Director from 1974 to 1977, while from 1979 to 1981 Mr. Sandy Gunn of Carlsbad Springs, Ontario ably served on the Board. Their years spent serving the breed's interest, as well as the rising level of support and participation across the country, ensure the welfare of the Gordon Setter in Canada.

7

The Modern Gordon Setter in Other Countries

Norway

Unique hunting conditions in Norway contribute to developing a unique type of Gordon Setter. Showing the breed is not a well supported effort. The emphasis is entirely on hunting ability, combined as far as possible with good looks.

As described by Godfrey Gompertz, field trial grounds were formidable at a trial he attended in Kongsvoll in the Dovre Mountains, some seventy miles southwest of Trondheim. The day began with an hour's climb over rocks, streams and mud to reach the trial grounds. The thick cover was dwarf birch and willow about the same height as heather. There were many mountain streams and areas of marshlands a foot or more under water. The game was entirely ptarmigan in their white plumage.

To qualify, a dog needed to run a total of an hour and a half.

The dogs were rangy and medium size, fit and lean with tremendously powerful hindquarters. Gordons are especially prized for their exceptional intelligence and ability to maintain close contact with their masters and to know instinctively what is required of them. This trial was open to Pointers and all Setters. Only one Gordon was entered.

At the trial, the dogs were allowed to range widely, running and leaping over rocks and scrub at full speed and splashing through the water. As a rule they worked from four to six hundred yards away. Very little direction was given them by their handlers—there was no whistling and

"The Ptarmigan Hill," etching by Sir Edwin H. Landseer (1802-1873). Gordons and Ptarmigan (lower left). Perhaps similar to conditions described in Norway by Mr. Gompertz.

194

The Post House: Kongsvoll Fjeldstue, near location of trial.

The Gordon Setter Bovi—a good performer but not a winner at this trial.

signaling. The dogs seemed to know what was required of them and to need no instruction.

The breed is supported by an active club which, in 1976, had over 500 members.

France

The French have been enthusiastic Gordon Setter owners ever since the 1800's, prizing the breed for its hunting ability. In spite of several devastating wars, bloodlines have been maintained through thick and thin.

Show qualities are appreciated but working ability is an absolute MUST. Thus we find the breed in the 80's to be excellent field dogs, strong, well marked, but lacking entirely the prodigious coats which have been developed on American Gordons. Retrieving on land and in water is regarded as vital.

The lovely prints of Gordons by French artists portray the dog sloshing around with ducks in mouth, something startlingly different for most American owners who feel the breed is strictly an upland game bird hunter.

Gordon Setter enthusiast, Jaques Bliard, gives us this interesting information on field trialing in France:

"Each year about 12 to 15 Field Trials are organized in the spring in which Gordon Setters may be entered, and just about as many in the fall. In the spring only partridges are looked for, but in the fall points count with pheasants, partridges and woodcocks. The Gordon Setter Club sponsors one Field Trial only for Gordon Setters in the spring and two in the fall. In the spring and in summer (before the hunting season starts) one Interclub Field Trial with the Irish Setter Club where both breeds compete against one another is held. Otherwise, all other Field Trials are "open" to all British breeds, i.e. Pointers and three Setters. Field Trials are also organized for the German Shorthairs, Wirehairs, Brittanies, French Shorthairs, French Spaniels, etc., but they are all competing together in what we call the "Continental breeds' and *these never meet the British breeds.* (Emphasis, the author's.)

"Obedience trials do not exist in France.

"Our rules are such that no more than two dogs of the same sex can be champion each year, thus no more than four in total. We never have four champions each year. This is for the National Championship. The International Championship is different. There is NO limit.

"All gun dogs must have one Field Trial placement in order to be awarded the title of Show Champion, either National or International. In 1981 there were three National show champions, three International show champions, and five Field Trial champions."

Mr. Bliard gives us some surprising statistics. More Gordons are

Painting by Leon Danchin (early 1900's). Gordons then and now are used for retrieving on land and in water.

Ne'mo du Chas des Jeubes (w. 1977), owner Jacqueline Rizet.

Fld. Ch. and Int. Show Ch. Tosca de la Haie Castelayne, 1975. Owner, Jaques Bliard.

registered in France than in Great Britain; in fact, the number more closely approaches that of America. Figures for 1978, '79 and '80 are 1003, 867 and 827. Yet total all breed registrations for a year in France are no more than one month for the United States.

Show entries are small. Only 68 shows had Gordon entries in 1980, and the largest number at any show in 1981 was 99 at a Championship show.

Probably the biggest surprise is the size of the membership of their club, Reunion des Amateurs du Setters Gordon, founded in 1922, which now boasts a total of 1200 members.

Czechoslovakia (CSSR)

In the years 1976-1980, 80 to 120 young Gordon Setters were tested and registered each year. All breed totals were 10,000 to 12,000 yearly.

Twenty to thirty Gordon Setters take part in shows, yearly. The most Gordons entered at any show is three.

Six Gordons were awarded Champion title between 1976-1980.

Gordon Setters in the CSSR are considered hunting dogs and are obliged to demonstrate their ability to hunt in order to earn the title of Champion.

There is an active Gordon Setter Club with a big membership of 750, including 120 breeders.

National Field Trials take place in Bohemia, Moravia, and Slovakia. International Trials are run under FCI granting the title of CACIT. These trials are open to the three Setters and English Pointers.

Obligatory obedience tests are part of hunting trials and the same for all Setters.

Currently the leading Gordon Setter is International Champion Arow Zarici deń CS, having won CACIT in three states and competed in all trials taking place with best results.

Italy

The Gordon Setter has long been popular with Italian hunters. In April 1982, the Societa Italiana Setters (for all Setters) held their *Centenary* Championship Show in Verona. Registrations for Gordons were 381 in 1979 and 398 in 1980. All breed registrations are not too far behind those in France, thus equalling about one month's total in the United States.

Two Championship Dog Shows for all breeds are held each year. There were no Italian Gordon Setter Champions in 1978 or 1979.

Gordons must demonstrate in trials the ability to hunt in order to earn the title of Italian Champion.

Many Field Trials are open to all breeds but also there are trials reserved to one breed or several breeds.

In 1983 an Italian Gordon Setter Club was established.

Obedience work is unknown in Italy.

The Italian Gordon resembles the French Gordon. It is a working dog, strong and well built, with only a medium length coat.

Prominent breeders are: A. Scamazzo, G. Spadoni, and A. Salvadori.

Germany

The new Gordon Setter Club of Germany was formed in August 1981 and by 1982 it had 112 members. Its President, Christa Heyde, has kindly provided current information on the breed.

In order to be allowed to breed their dogs (in addition to the necessary qualification in a show), all Gordon Setter Club members now are obliged to enter them in a field trial where the dog must perform successfully.

In the spring the trials comprise only work in the field, single or in couples. In autumn the trials include field work, work in the water and retrieving of feathered and furred game.

The new club is organizing what in the US is referred to as "shoot-to-kill trials," including retrieving.

There is a large number of trials arranged by the Gun-Dog Association which require all types of work. A dog is supposed to perform for game shooting and stalking; for example, retrieving a fox, blood trailing, etc. A great number of Gordon people take part in these trials.

It is NOT required to show hunting ability in order to obtain a National show title, but it is for the International Championship.

Registration figures are not maintained except for puppies. In 1980, 24 litters and 188 puppies were recorded. The largest number of Gordons at any one show was 15.

This newly formed club anticipates much more activity in the breed now that they can have their own field trials and shows and come out from under the shadows cast by the other breeds in the old Pointer and Setter Club.

Prominent kennels of today

vom Teutoburger Wald	vom Ottenstein
of Tartan	von Eixelberg
von Helory	von der Hatzburg
Ebony	vom Zabelstein
Black Devillss	of Grevaon

List of German Champions since 1976

International Show Champion
Barbara's Champion
Astella von der Hatzburg
Assur Ebony
Aster Ebony

Early (1895) print of Gordon with Fox, something they are still required to handle in Germany.

Am. & German Ch. Gordon Hill Wilscot Lektor shown with owner Frau Waldtraut Venz of W. Germany.

The Gordon Setter made a Postage Stamp in Italy.

Kaledoniens Blossom (Salters Ilex x Vermeille des Aulnes (owner, B. Muller) (late 1970's).

Ch. Boy IV (c. 1976) owned by Mr. and Mrs. Alexai Kamernitsky.

Weltsieger (World Champion)
    Carol von Helory

Europasieger (European Champion)
    Gordon Hill Wilscott Lektor
        (also an American show Ch.)
    Asurka of Tartan

Bundessieger (Best of the Year
in Germany at the special show)
    Gordon Hill Wilscott Lektor
    Shelwell Aylwen
    Aika vom Siebengebirge
    Astella von der Hatzburg
    Galina vom Hopfengarten

VDH-Sieger (German Champion)
    Anatol McNulty
    Carlo of Tartan
    Arras von der Donnerburg
    Shelwell Aylwen
    Astella von der Hatzburg
    Galina vom Hopfengarten
    Agi von der Donnerburg

Deutscher Prufungs-Champion
(German Trialer Champion):
    Werygood d'Flumilly

Sweden

Therese Wikstrom, Gordon Setter Club of America member residing in Lidingo, Sweden, has provided information on Gordons in her country. Registrations per year were 86 in 1980, but dropped to 40 in 1981. The number of all breeds registered during those two years were 57,318 in 1980, and 56,848 in 1981.

The Swedish Kennel Club organizes all championship shows which total between 10 and 14 each year. Usually no more than one or two Gordons appear at these shows except for the Stockholm show where as many as ten may be entered.

No Gordon Setter is known to have been awarded a championship during the years 1976-1980. The reason, Mrs. Wikstrom feels, is that Swedish field trials are very difficult, and all sporting dogs have to qualify in field trials to become a champion.

There is a breed club "Svenska Gordon Setter Ringen," with approximately 90 members.

Anita and Anders Aslund are currently the most prominent Gordon Setter breeders, concentrating mostly on field trials.

203

8

The Breed Standards

In America

The Gordon Setter has had six standards in America beginning with the description by Stonehenge in the 1870's, which served to guide judges both in Great Britain and America, given here in its entirety.

"He is a long, low setter, his gallop noiseless, and he is remarkably quick in his turn, from the power of his shoulders and loin, and length of neck, and general muscular development. A trifle heavier in the head, a trifle shorter in his stern, rather deeper in his "brisket", more boney and muscular than the English Setter, with a remarkably gay carriage and temperament, "always busy"—he is quite the beau ideal of a sportsman's favorite."

This outline was replaced when the Gordon Setter Clubs in Great Britain and America produced standards almost simultaneously in 1891. Oddly, no effort was made to synthesize the two. The British standard has had only minor changes in its wording under "General Impression," and often has been copied. The American form has gone through four quite different revisions, and is used only in the United States.

The 1891 American version provided a good description of the dog. It laid down where the tan should be and discouraged the appearance of white. It called for a Gordon to "look the thorough workman all over and . . . absolutely be without lumber." A "Value of Points" gave 45 to the body and legs; 25 went to head, ears and neck; coat and color accounted for 16; the tail got eight, and so did symmetry.

The decline of the breed and disappearance of the American Gordon

Setter Club by the early 1900's apparently led to the disuse of this standard.

The next version we find in *The Complete Dog Book* by Dr. William A. Bruette, published in 1925. This was the forerunner of the American Kennel Club standard books. Since there was no active breed club, one can assume Dr. Bruette and committee prepared a Gordon Standard as best they could. It is brief and non-specific.

In part it says, "In general appearance the Gordon differs from his English cousin, in that he is heavier all over, showing strength rather than speed in his makeup. His skull is broad between the ears, slightly rounded, with well developed occiput. Muzzle well carried out to a well developed nose, showing no snipiness or pinched appearance."

The rest of this short standard is devoted to describing the exact location and color of the tan markings.

Once Charles Inglee and his friends had reorganized the Gordon Setter Club of America, they wrote a new standard that was accepted by the American Kennel Club in 1929. This is moderately long, but most noteworthy for its shift in emphasis from heaviness as noted by Dr. Bruette to "A stylish rather racy built, medium size, muscular dog of clean setter type, usual length of legs . . . strong, fairly short back and short tail, fine head . . . clear colors and straight or wavy coat." (That comment about *usual length of legs* is puzzling, and rather amusing, isn't it?—*Author)*

Once again considerable space is devoted to the matter of the size and location of the tan markings. No scale of points was given, but size was stated as 22 to 25 inches for males, 21 to 24 inches for females, shoulder height. No weight limits were suggested.

This standard worked fine until late in the 1930's when the importation of larger stock from Great Britain brought about a change in conformation from the typical Inglehurst dog to one that was an attractive combination of the two types.

By 1945 the club officers felt a need to revise the standard and go back to the earlier emphasis on "strength rather than speed" in order to bring it into conformity with the dogs that were being bred in America at that time.

The opening paragraph was changed again, this time to read, "A good sized sturdily-built dog, well muscled with plenty of bone and substance, but active, upstanding and stylish, appearing capable of doing a full day's work in the field. . . A dog that suggests strength and stamina rather than extreme speed."

Size was changed upwards for both males and females, a generous two inches. For the first time weights were mentioned: males 55 to 75 pounds, females 45 to 65 pounds. The committee added the sentence, "As a guide, the greater heights and weights are to be preferred. . ."

This certainly encouraged the development of a larger strain. The steady increase in the breed as show dogs, plus the success of some really big dogs (big even by today's standards) put extra attention on size.

This 1945 Standard included a scale of points. It differs from our current version in that it allotted 25 points to head, neck, ears and eyes, nothing to temperament, 12 to size, general appearance and action. Other points were similar.

The 1962 revision, which is current, was long in the making. Everybody made suggestions and it was a task to winnow out the final phraseology.

It is rather long winded and in some areas needs pruning and revision, but basically it has served us well. It did increase top weight limits five pounds, but nothing was done to heights.

This draws attention to the fact that dogs get bigger because they are better fed and more free from diseases which hamper growth. This trend is apparent in the human race as well, especially in prosperous countries.

A discussion of the Gordon Setter standard will appear in the chapter **Blueprint of the Standard.**

GORDON SETTER CLUB OF AMERICA
Standard and Description of The Gordon Setter

General Impression: The Gordon Setter is a good sized, sturdily built, black and tan dog, well muscled, with plenty of bone and substance, but active, upstanding and stylish, appearing capable of doing a full day's work in the field. He has a strong, rather short back, with well-sprung ribs and a short tail. The head is fairly heavy and finely chiseled. His bearing is intelligent, noble, and dignified, showing no signs of shyness or viciousness. Clear colors and straight or slightly waved coat are correct. He suggests strength and stamina rather than extreme speed. Symmetry and quality are most essential. A dog well-balanced in all points is preferable to one with outstanding good qualities and defects. A smooth, free movement, with high head carriage, is typical.

Size: Shoulder height for males, 24 to 27 inches. For females, 23 to 26 inches.

Weight: Males, 55 to 80 pounds; females, 45 to 70 pounds. Animals that appear to be over or under the prescribed weight limits are to be judged on the basis of conformation and condition. Extremely thin or fat dogs should be discouraged on the basis that under or overweight hampers the true working ability of the Gordon Setter. The weight-to-height ratio makes him heavier than other Setters.

The Head: The head is deep, rather than broad, with plenty of brain room; a nicely rounded good sized skull, broadest between the ears. The head should have a clearly indicated stop. Below and above the eyes should be lean, and the cheek as narrow as the leanness of the head allows. The

206

muzzle is fairly long and not pointed, either as seen from above or from the side. The flews should not be pendulous. The nose should be broad, with open nostrils and black in color. The muzzle is the same length as the skull from occiput to stop and the top of the muzzle is parallel to the line of the skull extended. The lip line from the nose to the flews shows a sharp, well defined, square contour.

The Eyes: Of fair size, neither too deep-set, or too bulging, dark brown, bright and wise. The shape is oval rather than round. The lids should be tight.

The Ears: Set low on the head approximately on line with the eye, fairly large and thin, well folded and carried close to the head.

The Teeth: The teeth should be strong and white, and preferably should meet in front in a "scissors" bite, with the upper incisors slightly forward of the lower incisors. A level bite is not to be considered a fault. Pitted teeth from distemper or allied infections should not be penalized.

The Neck: Long, lean, arched to the head, and without throatiness.

The Shoulders: Should be fine at the points, and laying well back, giving a moderately sloping topline. The tops of the shoulder blades should be close together. When viewed from behind the neck appears to fit into the shoulders in smooth, flat, lines that gradually widen from neck to shoulder.

The Chest: Deep and not too broad in front; the ribs well-sprung, leaving plenty of lung room. The chest should reach to the elbows. A pronounced forechest should be in evidence.

The Body: The body should be short from shoulder to hips, and the distance from the forechest to the back of the thigh should approximately equal the height from the ground to the withers. The loins should be short and broad and not arched. The croup is nearly flat, with only a slight slope to the tailhead.

The Forequarters: The legs should be big-boned, straight and not bowed, with elbows free and not turned in or out. The angle formed by the shoulder blade and upper arm bone should be approximately 90° when the dog is standing so that the foreleg is perpendicular to the ground. The pasterns should be straight.

The Hindquarters: The hind legs from hip to hock should be long, flat and muscular; from hock to heel, short and strong. The stifle and hock joints are well bent and not turned either in or out. When the dog is standing with the hock perpendicular to the ground the thigh bone should hang downward parallel to an imaginary line drawn upward from the hock.

The Feet: The feet should be formed by close knit, well-arched toes with plenty of hair between; with full toe pads and deep heel cushions. Feet should not be turned in or out. Feet should be cat-like in shape.

The Tail: Short and should not reach below the hocks, carried horizontal or nearly so; thick at the root and finishing in a fine point. The feather which starts near the root of the tail should be slightly waved or straight, having triangular appearance, growing shorter uniformly toward the end. The placement of the tail is important for correct carriage. If the croup is nearly flat, the tail must emerge nearly on the same plane as the croup to allow for horizontal carriage. When the angle of the tail bends too sharply at the first coccygeal bone, the tail will be carried too gaily or will droop. The tail placement should be judged in its relationship to the structure of the croup.

Temperament: The Gordon Setter should be alert, gay, interested, and aggressive. He should be fearless and willing, intelligent and capable. He should be loyal and affectionate, and strong-minded enough to stand the rigors of training.

Gait: The action of the Gordon Setter is a bold, strong, driving, free-swinging gait. The head is carried up and the tail "flags" constantly while the dog is in motion. When viewed from the front the forefeet move up and down in straight lines so that the shoulder, elbow and pastern joints are approximately in line with each other. When viewed from the rear, the hock, stifle and hip joints are approximately in line. Thus the dog moves in a straight pattern forward without throwing the feet in or out. When viewed from the side the forefeet are seen to lift up and reach forward to compensate for the driving hindquarters. The hindquarters reach well forward and stretch far back, enabling the stride to be long and the drive powerful. The overall appearance of the moving dog is one of smooth-flowing, well-balanced rhythm, in which the action is pleasing to the eye, effortless, economical and harmonious.

The Coat: Should be soft and shining, straight or slightly waved, but not curly, with long hair on ears, under stomach and on chest, on back of the fore and hind legs, and on the tail.

Color and Markings: Black with tan markings, either of rich chestnut or mahogany color. Black pencilling is allowed on the toes. The borderline between black and tan colors should be clearly defined. There should not be any tan hairs mixed in the black. The tan markings should be located as follows: (1) Two clear spots over the eyes and not over three-quarters of an inch in diameter; (2) On the sides of the muzzle. The tan should not reach to the top of the muzzle, but resembles a stripe around the end of the muzzle from one side to the other; (3) On the throat; (4) Two large clear spots on the chest; (5) On the inside of the hind legs showing down the front of the stifle and broadening out to the outside of the hind legs from the hock to the toes. It must not completely eliminate the black on the back of the hind legs; (6) On the forelegs from the carpus, or a little above, downward to the toes; (7) Around the vent; (8) A white spot on the chest is allowed, but the smaller the better. Predominantly tan, red or buff dogs which do not have the typical pattern of markings of a Gordon Setter are ineligible for showing and undesirable for breeding.

Scale of points in judging Gordon Setters: While not a part of the official breed standard, may be helpful in placing proper emphasis upon qualities desired in the physical make-up of the breed.

Head and Neck (incl. Ears & Eyes) 10	Coat 8
Body 15	Color and Markings 5
Shoulders, forelegs, forefeet ..10	Temperament 10
Hind Legs and feet 10	Size, General Appearance ...15
Tail 5	Gait 12

Total Points — 100

The Standard in the United Kingdom
as issued by The Kennel Club

General appearance: A stylish dog, built on galloping lines, having a thoroughbred appearance consistent with its build which can be compared to a weight carrying hunter. Must have symmetrical conformation throughout, showing true balance. Strong fairly short and level back. Shortish tail. Head fairly long, clearly lined and with intelligent expression, clear colours and long flat coat.

Head and skull: Head deep rather than broad, but definitely broader than the muzzle showing brain room. Skull slightly rounded and broadest between the ears. The head should have a clearly indicated stop and length from stop to occiput should be slightly longer than from stop to nose. Below and above the eyes should be lean and the cheeks as narrow as the leanness of the head allows. The muzzle should be fairly long with almost parallel lines and not pointed, as seen from the side or from above. The flews not pendulous but with clearly indicated lips. Nose big and broad, with open nostrils and black in colour. The muzzle should not be quite as deep as its length.

Eyes: Of fair size, not too deep nor too prominent but sufficiently under the brows to show a keen and intelligent expression. Dark brown and bright.

Ears: Set low on head and lying close to it, of medium size and thin.

Mouth: Must be even and not under or overshot.

Neck: Long, lean and arched to the head without any throatiness.

Forequarters: Shoulders should be long and sloped well back; with flat bone and fairly close at the withers; should not be loaded, i.e. too thick, which interferes with the liberty of movement. Elbows well let down and showing well under the body, which gives freedom of action. Forelegs big flat boned and straight with strong upright pastern, well feathered.

Body: Of moderate length, deep in brisket, with ribs well sprung. Deep in back ribs, i.e. well-ribbed up. Loins wide and slightly arched. Chest not too broad.

Hindquarters: Hindlegs from hip to hock should be long, broad and muscular; hock to heel short and strong, stifles well bent; hocks straight, not inclined either in or out. Pelvis should tend to be horizontal, i.e. opposite of goose rump.

Feet: Oval, with close knit, well arched toes, with plenty of hair between. Full toe pads and deep heel cushions.

Tail: Fairly short, straight or slightly scimitar shaped and should not reach below the hocks. Carried horizontal or below line of the back. Thick at the root tapering to a fine point. The feather or flag which starts near the root should be long and straight, and growing shorter uniformly to the point.

Coat: On the head and front legs and tips of ears should be short and fine, but on all other parts of the body and legs it ought to be of moderate length, fairly flat and free as possible from curl and wave. The feather on the upper portion of the ears should be long and silky, on the back of the hindlegs long and fine; a fair amount on the belly forming a nice fringe which may extend on chest and throat. All feathering to be as flat and straight as possible.

Colour: Deep shining coal black, with no sign of rustiness, with tan markings of a rich chestnut red, i.e., colour of a ripe horsechestnut as taken from the shell. Tan should be lustrous. Black pencilling allowed on the toes and also a black streak under jaw. Tan Markings: two clear spots over the eyes not over three-quarters of an inch in diameter. On the sides of the muzzle, the tan should not reach above the base of the nose, resembling a stripe around the end of the muzzle from one side to the other. On the throat: two large, clear spots on the chest. On the inside of the hindlegs and inside the thighs showing down the front of stifle and broadening out to the outside of the hind legs from the hocks to the toes. It must, however, not completely eliminate the black on the back of the hind legs. On the forelegs, up to the elbows behind, and on the knees or a little above, in front. Around the vent. A white spot on the chest is allowed but the smaller the better.

210

Weight and size: As a guide to size, shoulder height for males 26 inches and weight 65 pounds. Females, 24½ inches and weight about 56 lbs. in show condition.

Faults: General impression: unintelligent appearance; the bloodhound type with heavy and big head and ears and clumsy body; the collie type with pointed muzzle and curved tail. The head: pointed, snipy, down or upturned muzzle, too small or large mouth. The eyes: too light in colour, too deep set or too prominent. The ears: set too high, or unusually broad and heavy. The neck: thick and short. Shoulders and backs: irregularly formed. The chest: too broad. The legs and feet: crooked legs. Out-turned elbows. The toes scattered, flat footed. The tail: too long, badly carried or hooked at the end. The coat: curly, like wool, not shining. The colour: yellow, or straw-coloured tan, or without clearly defined lines between the different colours. White feet. Too much white on the chest. In the black there should be no tan hairs.

The Canadian Kennel Club Standard

General Appearance: A good-sized, sturdily built dog, well muscled, with plenty of bone and substance, but active, upstanding and stylish, appearing capable of doing a full day's work in the field. Strong, rather short back, well-sprung ribs and short tail, a fairly heavy head, finely chiselled, intelligent, noble and dignified expression, showing no signs of shyness; clear colours and straight or slightly waved coat. A dog that suggests strength and stamina rather than extreme speed.

Symmetry and quality are most essential. A dog well balanced in all points is preferable to one with outstanding good qualities and defects.

Size: Shoulder height for males, 24-27 in. (61-69 cm); for females, 23-26 in. (58-66 cm). Weight—males, 55-75 lb. (25-34 kg); females, 45-65 lb. (20-29 kg).

As a guide the greater heights and weights are to be preferred provided that character and quality are also combined. Dogs over and under these heights and weights are to be discouraged.

Coat and Colour: Coat should be soft and shining, resembling silk, straight or slightly waved—the latter preferred—but not curly, with long hair on ears, under stomach, on chest, and on back of the fore and hind legs to the feet. Deep, shining coal-black with tan markings, either of rich chestnut or mahogany red colour. The tan should be shining and not dull, yellowish or straw colour and not mixed with black hairs. Black pencilling allowed on toes. The borderlines between black and tan colours should be clearly defined. There should not be any tan hairs mixed in the black.

Tan markings:
a) Two clear spots over the eyes not over ¾ inch (2 cm) in diameter.
b) On the sides of the muzzle, the tan should not reach above the base of nose, resembling a stripe around the end of the muzzle from one side to the other.
c) On the throat.
d) Two large, clear spots on the chest.
e) On the inside of the hind legs and inside of thighs showing down the front of the stifle and broadening out to the outside of the hind legs from the hock to the toes. It must, however, not completely eliminate the black on the back of hind legs.
f) On the forelegs from the knees or a little above downward to the toes.
g) Around the vent.

A white spot on the chest is allowed, but the smaller the better.

Head: Deep rather than broad, with plenty of brain room, nicely rounded good-sized skull, broadest between the ears. The head should have a clearly indicated stop. Below and above the eyes should be lean and the cheek as narrow as the leanness of the head allows. The *muzzle* fairly long with almost parallel lines and not pointed either as seen from above or from the side. The flews not pendulous but with clearly indicated lips. The *nose* big, broad with open nostrils and of black colour. *Eyes* of fair size, neither too deep set nor too bulging, dark brown, bright and wise. *Ears* set low on the head, fairly large and thin.

Neck: Long, lean, arched to the head and without throatiness.

Forequarters: Shoulders should be fine at the points, deep and sloping well back, giving a moderately sloping topline. Forelegs big-boned, straight, not bowed either in or out, with elbows free, well let down and not inclined either in or out.

Body: Chest deep and not too broad in front; the ribs well sprung, leaving plenty of lung room.

Hindquarters: The hind legs from hip to hock should be long, flat, and muscular, from hock to heel short and strong. The stifle and hock joints well bent, and not inclined either in or out. Both fore and hind feet should have close knit, well-arched toes with plenty of hair between with full toe pads and deep heel cushions.

Tail: Short and should not reach below the hocks, carried horizontal or nearly so, thick at the root and finishing in a fine point. The feather, which starts near the root of the tail, should be slightly waved or straight and have a three-square appearance growing shorter uniformly toward the end.

Gait: A smooth free movement with high head carriage.

212

Faults:

1. General Impression—Unintelligent appearance. The Bloodhound type with heavy and big head and ears and clumsy body, as well as the Collie type with its pointed muzzle and curved tail, or showing any signs of shyness.
2. Head—Houndy, pointed, snipey, drooping or upturned muzzle, too small or large mouth.
3. Eyes—Too light in colour, too deep-set, or too prominent.
4. Ears—Set too high or unusually broad or heavy.
5. Neck—Thick and short.
6. Shoulders and Back—Irregularly formed.
7. Chest—Too broad.
8. Legs and Feet—Crooked legs. Out-turned elbows. The toes scattered, flat-footed.
9. Tail—Too long, badly carried or hooked at the end.
10. Coat—Curly like wool, not shining.
11. Colour—Yellow or straw coloured tan or without clearly defined lines between the different colours. White feet. Too much white on the chest. In the black there must be no tan hairs which can appear often around the eyes.

HEAD fairly heavy, finely chiseled; deep rather than broad; high carriage; nicely rounded; good size, broadest between ears

APPEARANCE: Good-sized; sturdily built; well muscled; plenty of bone and substance; stylish; free moving; close-coupled

EYES fair size; neither deep-set nor bulging; bright; dark brown; oval; lids tight; lean below and above

EARS low-set; fairly large, thin; well-folded; carried close to head; on line with eye

STOP clearly defined

NECK long, lean, arched; not throaty

NOSE: Broad, black; nostrils open

SHOULDERS: Top of blades close together; well-laid back; moderately sloping; 90° angle formed by shoulder blade and upper arm; fine at points; smooth

MUZZLE same length as skull from occiput to stop; top parallel to extended skull line; lip line from nose to flews sharp, well-defined, square, not pendulous; cheeks narrow; teeth strong, white, scissors bite preferred, level not faulted

BACK strong; rather short. Loins short, broad, not arched; croup nearly flat

TAIL short; carried horizontally; should not reach below hocks; feather slightly waved or straight; triangular appearing, growing uniformly shorter toward end; thick at root; fine point; set on nearly same plane as croup

THIGHS long, flat; muscular

STIFLES well-bent; turn neither in or out

HOCK to Heel: Short, strong; turned neither in nor out; well-bent

COAT straight or slightly wavy (not curly); soft, silky; feathering

CHEST deep; not too broad; should reach to elbows; pronounced forechest

RIBS well-sprung

ELBOWS free, well-let-down

COLOR: Clear; black with tan markings of rich chestnut or mahogany; color lines clearly detailed. Predominantly tan, red or buff colors without typical pattern markings of B/T are ineligible for showing

FORELEGS big boned, straight; pasterns straight

FEET close-knit; turning neither in nor out; well-arched toes; catlike; full pads; heel cushions deep

SIZE: Height, males, 24-27"; females, 23-26". Weight, males, 55-80 lbs; females, 45-70 lbs; over or under prescribed weight limits to be judged on condition and conformation. Weight-to-height ratio makes Gordon heavier than other setters

GORDON SETTER standard visualization, modeled by CH. BLAKEEN SAEGRYTE, owned by Geo. W. Thompson. Selected by the Gordon Setter Club of America as its ideal of the breed.

9

The Blueprint of the Gordon Setter Standard

THE MOST UNDERSTANDABLE DISCUSSION of the Gordon Setter standard has to be based on full appreciation of the basic structural differences among the three setters as well as the unique hunting style of each.

All too often we find articles on How to Trim *the* Setter—as though all three could be handled the same. Statues are made, one shape of dog, three colors. Anatomical drawings are presented, lectures on movement are delivered far and wide on the basis that one Setter is just like the other in build.

Not so! No less an authority than Mrs. Bede Maxwell puts it in a nutshell. In her splendid book, *The Truth About Sporting Dogs,* she says, "The English is basically a Spaniel, the Irish is basically a scent hound. The Gordon partakes of both groupings."

The *General Impression* paragraph in the Gordon standard emphasizes many of the more obvious differences between him and his cousins. By referring to him as ". . . good sized, sturdily built . . . well muscled, with plenty of bone and substance . . ." the picture is drawn which sets him apart. Further comments such as, "He has a strong, rather short back, with well-sprung ribs, and a short tail. The head is fairly heavy . . ." add to the visual differences. Finally, by stressing that "He suggests strength and stamina rather than extreme speed" it becomes obvious that we are aiming at a Setter that is quite different from the smaller English and the more racy Irish. This is confirmed by the weight and height requirements.

While all Setter heads have the same basic outlines, the Gordon has more stop; a larger, rounder skull; more square, blocky look; and seen from the front, the muzzle is broader and blends into the skull without bulging cheeks. This is what is meant by the following: ". . . The cheek as narrow as the leanness of the head allows." All this talk of "lean" does not imply narrow heads.

Standards for the English and Irish want the eyes to be dark brown and mild or soft in expression; the Gordon asks for dark brown, and bright and wise expression. We can go on to say that the expression of the eyes is also piercing and keen. As a breed they look into people's faces and eyes most intently. More than the other Setters, Gordons are apt to have loose lids or rolled lids, though the standard makes no comment on these serious faults. Both conditions can cause endless trouble to a hunting dog and can lead to loss of vision.

Ears set low and well back are desired by the other two Setters while the Gordon ear needs only to be set on the head about on a level with the eye. They are to be large and thin, well folded and carried close to the head. This position, plus the heavy coat on the ears, protects both the ear and the ear canal, so necessary in a hunting dog. Gordons use their ears much more than the other Setters, too. Because of their mobility the ears offer a good reading on what the dog is thinking about.

Desirable shoulder assembly will be stronger in the Gordon in order to be compatible with the heavier bone and more weight. The blades will be wider and laid back more than is customary with the Irish and English.

Our standard requires a forechest, created by the sternum. This is all part of the deep, well sprung ribcage which is called for. This gives a heavier appearance to the front and with this build the Gordon must move wider than do the other two Setters.

The Gordon back is to be short from shoulder to hip and the distance from the forechest to back of thigh should approximately equal the height from the ground to the withers. If everything else is right the dog will have the appearance of being short bodied and strong. But straight shoulder, shallow chest, and weak rears can give the illusion of length even though the measurements still may be equal.

Another point of difference is the croup which in the Gordon is supposed to be nearly flat, with loins short and broad, and not arched, with slight slope to tailhead. English are to have loins strong and slightly arched. Hipbones should be wide apart and without too sudden a drop to the root of the tail. Only the Irish Setter is to have a top line which slopes slightly downward, yet he should not have a sharp drop at the croup.

When discussing the hindquarters, the Gordon and English standards settle for having them "well bent." The Irish standard speaks of hind legs well angulated at stifle and hock joint.

Feet differ widely. The English Setter foot is strong, close knit, covered with thick short hair. The Irish foot is small, very firm, toes close and well arched. The Gordon standard requires close-knit, well-arched toes with plenty of hair between; with full toe pads and deep heel cushions, cat-like in shape. It should say BIG cat, for the breed does have big feet to match their heavy bone and to help carry their weight. The phrase "plenty of hair" is certainly true. Left untrimmed the hair will obscure the toenails and over the pads, not altogether a blessing as this can cause trouble and inconvenience if the feet are not constantly checked for wads of mud and burrs, etc.

This is as good a place as any to point out that most puppies are born with good feet. During periods of rapid growth, teething, severe illness or stress, the feet can go flat. Poor nutrition, bad kennel surface and lack of exercise, can worsen the problems. If checked immediately and corrections made the feet can be restored to their proper condition. One thing often overlooked is keeping the nails moderately short. Some dogs never need a trim, others must be done every few weeks.

When it comes to describing gait the English Setter standard asks for an easy, free graceful movement. The Irish standard goes into a bit more detail. "Seen from the front or rear the forelegs, as well as the hind legs below the hock joint, move perpendicularly to the ground, with some tendency toward a single track as speed increases."

The Gordon standard goes into considerable detail both as to the gait seen going and coming, and from the side. What is wanted is a long, smooth stride, with the head up, tail flagging. The tail, by the way, should be carried horizontally. Describing gait as seen from the front or rear is a matter of semantics. The Gordon standard talks about the forefeet moving up and down in straight lines so that the shoulder, elbow and pastern joints are approximately in line. When viewed from the rear the hock, stifle, and hip joints are approximately in line.

It should be pointed out that a small dog is much better at this than a large dog who, because of his height, must tend towards a single track to keep his balance when gaiting.

The hackney gait is not wanted, and sickle hocks will create gait problems. Both hamper a hunting dog and cause lack of endurance.

Mrs. Maxwell has some revealing comments to make which apply to Gordons as well as the English, about which she was writing in her previously mentioned book. She states, ". . . the forehands (of English Setters and Gordons) should have considerable flexibility. The (early) 'setting dogge' had to lift and drop his body continually between his shoulders. The requisite flexibility is a long term inheritance of the breed . . .

"A judge may accept a slight degree of looseness in an English (and Gordon) that he should not tolerate in an Irish. The Irish, of different work habit, never need depress and elevate himself between his gazehound

217

angulated shoulder assemblage."

Mrs. Maxwell continues, ". . . in a confined ring space, . . . the ultimate assessment of a dog's worth cannot be made solely on the basis of what he does with his back legs, especially.

"Hung up, as many are on a gallows lead, dogs cannot find their proper center of gravity and legs can sprawl every which way in consequence.

She concludes by saying, ". . . if a dog is built right it can move right—under reasonable conditions, which, alas, too many show rings do not provide."

Another commentator states that the Gordon Setter is the most solidly structured of the three Setters. His action is lower to the ground and (the body) may have some tendency to twist as he goes ahead. He is not a straight out runner, but more of a questor and this is why he may often appear to be loosely structured when he is not.

Coat and Markings are dealt with fairly carefully but since this standard was approved in 1962 both factors have taken on added importance and deserve attention.

The coat is correctly described as soft and shining, straight or slightly waved, but not curly, with long hair on ears, under stomach and on chest, on *back* of the front and hind legs, and on tail. Limitations are only implied as to the amount of coat, since at that time, the Gordon was not an especially long coated dog. Dense coat, yes, but heavy feathering, rarely. The use of the dog for hunting also implies restrictions to enable him to appear "capable of doing a full day's work in the field."

The rapidly growing popularity of the Gordons as a show dog has encouraged the breeding for coat, and now he is often seen with an extraordinary amount of feathering.

Confusion exists over the markings. The standard describes the uppermost limit of the amount of tan desired but this is not stated. Therefore it is too often assumed that *less* amount of tan is negative. Regrettably the breed carries a recessive factor for solid red puppies, and breeding only from correctly marked dogs or more surely from those with an excessive amount of tan, the possibility of getting red puppies is ever present. The Gordon with lesser amounts of tan does have a place in a breeding program, as it can help control this problem. A breeder may lose thousands of dollars producing litters with red pups which take the place of saleable black and tans.

White markings are another matter which deserves comment. First, it must be remembered that the early Gordons were often tricolored, and the white gene cannot ever be completely eliminated. Spots of white often appear on the chest of pups and more often than not they diminish to a few white hairs. Pups may be born with white toenails and white hairs on the toes but these grow out as well. Same for the white hair found in the tail and the long hair on the back of the thighs; it grows out. There is no known reason for this phenomenon. Color changes on pups, as well. Those born with brilliant tan markings often turn darker and more moderate, while the pups with little tan will surely develop more. When a Gordon reaches the age of eight or nine years his tan will often diminish both on the muzzle and on the feet.

FAULTY CONFORMATION

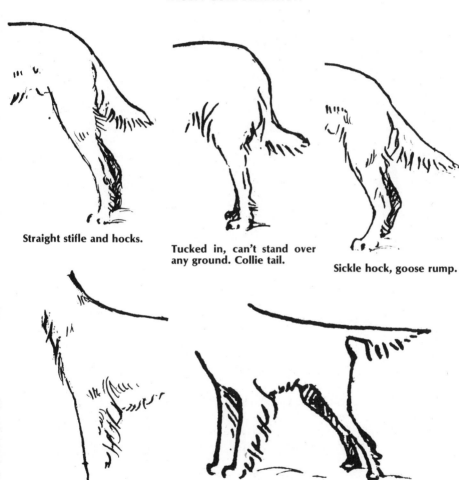

Straight stifle and hocks.

Tucked in, can't stand over any ground. Collie tail.

Sickle hock, goose rump.

Upright shoulders show elbows too far forward— neck held at wrong angle.

Undeveloped hindquarters and Chow hocks.

Drawings by the late Mrs. Kitty Gray, owner of the well-known Ch. Bydand Coronach, and reproduced courtesy of the Gordon Setter Association of Great Britain.

FRONTS

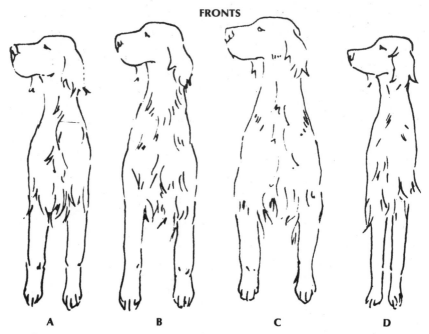

A   B   C   D

A is the correct Gordon Setter Front. B may be acceptable with a mature, solid dog. C is too wide and coarse. D is narrow, pinched and generally weedy.

REAR MOVEMENT

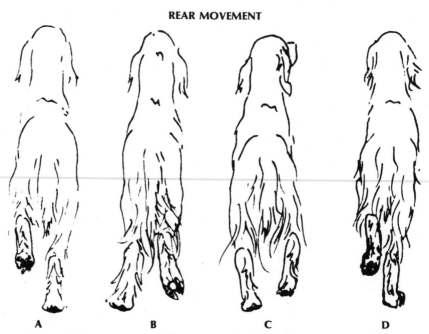

A   B   C   D

A shows correct rear movement for the Gordon Setter. B is "cow-hocked" and C is "bandy-legged." D is "bow-legged." B and D are both common faults with D being harder to see in heavily coated dogs unless one is specifically looking for it. A dog with a correct rear will tend to "line tread" or converge as speed increases, but that is not the same as the faulty gaits shown in B, C, and D.

Commentary and Sketches
by Dawn Ferguson

CORRECT CONFORMATION

Drawings by the late Mrs. Kitty Gray, owner of the well-known Ch. Bydand Coronach, and reproduced courtesy of the Gordon Setter Association of Great Britain.

Elbows well back.

Correct angulation.

Material on this page is adapted from comments by Roy Jerome, sketches by Nedra Jerome which appeared in 1971 in THE WORLD OF SETTERS.

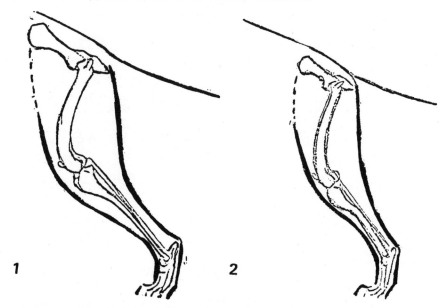

Figure 1 "...width of thigh is governed by length of hipbone. This can vary up to 1½ inches in dogs of the same size and sex. ...shorter hocks equal stamina, longer hocks equal speed." **Figure 2** "Shorter hip bones affect entire assembly."

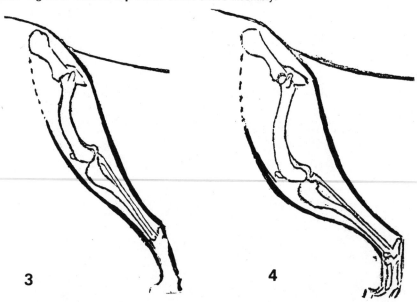

Figure 3 "...steep hipbone placement leads to poor stifle angulation, a high rear and often a poor topline." **Figure 4** "Steep hipbone but good angulation contributes to a low tailset, and predisposes the dog to travel at a gallop and break out of a trot at a relatively low speed. But it is possible to have a steep hip and a high tailset."

In this photo the parallel planes of the skull and muzzle are clearly seen. Back skull is well rounded. Earset is level with the outside corner of the eye. Muzzle is nicely squared, there is no loose skin on the throat. Skull and muzzle are of equal length.

This striking photo illustrates Mrs. Maxwell's comments regarding the need for flexibility of shoulder assembly.

10

Picking a Gordon Setter Puppy

THE BUYER of a puppy is always at the mercy of the seller. Given a relatively rare breed such as the Gordon Setter, the situation is compounded because quite often the buyer has never seen a representative adult specimen. Libraries offer little help other than the official publication of the American Kennel Club. But it is surprising how many people will choose a Gordon from this book alone.

And then the search begins for a breeder with puppies to sell. More often than not, no pups are available locally. Dog magazines and the parent club provide names of kennels and the determined buyer must resort to letters, phone calls, perhaps a long drive. As is often the case with other products, the flamboyant ads are not always from the best kennels. If the prospective buyer can get a reference from a satisfied customer, this is valuable.

Buyers have to take the word of the breeder. If dealing by mail photos of parents and pups are usually available and should be promptly returned if this is requested. If the litter is near enough to visit, an appointment should be made with the kennel. It is not fair to drop in at odd hours. Seeing the parents of the pups will make the decision much easier. Furthermore, a reliable breeder willingly provides the buyer with all health records, AKC papers, pedigree, and feeding schedules. Some unconditionally guarantee puppies, which should be in writing.

Ideally the litter should be whelped and raised in the home rather than in a kennel. Nothing takes the place of the extra care and association with people which is given a litter tucked away in a corner of the kitchen or a spare bedroom.

Life's sweetest moment! Mark Sorby with six-week-old puppy.

As a buyer, be prepared to satisfy the breeder concerning the care you will give the puppy. A fenced yard, well trained children, plenty of time to work with the pup are all essentials. Gordons grow to be big, energetic dogs and no one should buy a gentle little pup without realizing that it won't stay that way for very long.

No one should buy *any* young pup if it is to be left alone all day, day after day, or if it will be forced to live in the shadow of an adult dog without constant supervision.

Pediatricians now say that children should not be given a dog until they are at least four or five years old because younger children may provoke the family pet with hugs, pulls or tail-twisting.

A conscientious breeder is quite willing to bring down the wrath of a prospective customer by refusing to sell a pup if, in his heart, he is not happy with the setup.

Fortunately, the breed is quite well protected from exploitation by puppy mills and pet shops because the standards of Gordon breeders are high. They seldom have many dogs, it is not an easy breed to sell except to a limited, discriminating segment of society. To be safe it is best to avoid kennels which have a number of other breeds of puppies and where care appears to be minimal. Never buy an unhealthy pup, no matter how sorry you feel for it or how much you want a Gordon.

Prices for a good pup may be more than expected but a buyer should be aware of the amount of care that goes into a litter. Matings are planned after much study and because of the rarity of the breed, hundreds of dollars go into stud fees and costs of shipping the bitch to be bred. Prices on shots, wormings and food for puppies have skyrocketed, as well.

Only experience can impart a knowledge of how a Gordon pup should look at various ages so it is best to buy from someone who has had a few successful litters. Watching them from birth to the day they are sold gives the breeder intimate knowledge of the temperament and the physical qualities of each pup.

A visitor's normal reaction on seeing his first litter of Gordons is to gasp, "Why, they all look exactly alike! How can you tell them apart?"

No problem—to the breeder.

If the buyer has a specified purpose in mind for his pup—obedience, show, hunting or pet—he should be honest and make his wishes clear to the breeder. Trying to get a show dog at pet price usually backfires, the buyer gets just what he paid for. Puppies inherit their dispositions and talents from their parents.

Many problems can arise if the buyer wishes to take his pup at 49 days of age, considered by some dog psychologists as being the optimum day for a pup to go to his new home. Actually, this is not practical.

1. Airlines require that a pup be 12 weeks old.
2. At this age pups are not always fully weaned and wormed.

3. Distemper and Parvo shots may not have had time to develop the pup's maximum resistance.
4. Pups may not have had enough outdoor freedom to develop self assurance.
5. Big changes in looks and temperament are just beginning, making selection of a pup more uncertain.
6. AKC registration papers may not have been processed—(this is not a speedy procedure).

Remember, only puppy mills dispose of their pups when four or five weeks of age.

When eight weeks old, puppies can be evaluated against the breed standard. This gives a scale of points which serves to keep things in perspective. This procedure is primarily important to those purchasing a potential show or breeding prospect.

A puppy head should be large and already showing the square look which is a feature of the adult Gordon head. The muzzle is short but usually matches the length of the skull. The end of the muzzle should be squared off and deep. Puppy necks are strong and not especially long. There may be some loose skin under the chin called throatiness, but given the large head and the normal, loose skin all over the pup, this may well lessen as the pup grows up.

Overall, the body of the pup looks about as long as it is high at the shoulder.

Colouring of the eyes is not yet what it will be at maturity but one can detect those that will be lighter than is desirable in a show or breeding prospect. The chest should be deep, down to the elbow, and well developed in front, which is called forechest. Puppies whose front legs are extremely close together seldom develop a proper build as an adult.

The points of the shoulder blades (at the withers or base of neck) should not have a depression between them. Correct build means a smooth roundness from shoulder to shoulder.

The puppy's back should be relatively flat; the spine should not be prominent as this is often a sign of poor nutrition. Tails ought to be short and thick and they are often carried high. This must be a matter of balance for as the puppy grows he gradually carries his tail more level with his back, which is correct.

The boning of an eight week old pup should be heavy with big feet and thick pads. The bigger the boning the bigger the adult. Thin, splayed feet sometimes indicate poor nutrition or lack of exercise.

Puppies should trot straight, not sideways, and feet should point ahead, neither turning in nor out.

Seldom does one find a poor bite in a pup of this age. Not until the second set of teeth grow in can you tell much about the bite.

The size and weight of young pups is dependent on how big the litter was. Small litters are often much heavier than those with many pups but after they have been weaned, differences diminish.

Size is inherited and knowing the parents will give you an accurate idea of the potential size to which the pup will grow. Bitches are nearly always smaller than males, a factor which exists in adults of the breed as well. At four months a pup that is perfectly balanced is likely to be small as an adult.

Pups grow in spurts, one week the body will look long, the next week it might be that the rump is too high. So it goes, often until the dog is 18 months of age.

Heads change progressively as well. The muzzle and skull become longer and narrower; the skull may seem flat or sloped at a year and slowly it will develop the proper planes and be more rounded from ear to ear and much more handsome.

If the Gordon pup is properly nourished and exercised it will grow to its full potential. Since Gordons vary in size, ranging from the small field trial type to the larger show dog, giving weights and heights for pups at specific ages is not practical. The breed standard is generous in its size limitations so virtually every Gordon can fit in.

Puppies seem to grow out of their awkwardness for a brief time when they are six months old, so this is a good time to evaluate them once again. Nine months is another good age to give them a close look, especially the teeth. Now is the time when the first signs of the undershot jaw may be found.

Until the dog is 18 months old he will change many times and the bite may correct.

Gordons are not fully mature until four years of age. They stay in their prime for many years as is attested to by the fact that many Specialties are won by dogs from the Veteran Classes.

Confusion exists on the matter of color and markings. These are of importance only if the dog is destined for show or breeding.

Let's take the matter of white spots on the chest or a few white hairs on the toes or in the tail feathers.

All of these diminish as the pup grows. White in Gordons is as old as the breed itself and does not always imply hanky-panky in the breeding.

Pups may be born with very restricted tan markings. In almost all cases more tan develops as the dog grows. If, on the other hand, they are born with more tan than permitted by our standard this will often moderate as the pup matures.

In choosing a show prospect, however, first consideration should be given the overall quality of the puppy and one with medium coloring is the best bet. It is also the most useful type for breeding.

The tan should be a rich tan or dark mahogany in preference to the light straw shades which never darken and are considered a fault in an adult show dog.

228

All this information sounds as though puppy picking was a real challenge, but it is surprising to find that when viewing a litter the best pups stick right out of the crowd, whether you know the breed or not. The best choice is the pup that is a happy medium among his littermates.

Following are photos of two fine young Gordons, a bitch and a dog, as they went from puppyhood to maturity. There are no great changes, as is clearly seen, except for added size and coat. Faults that are apparent in a puppy won't go away, nor will they suddenly develop virtues they never had.

These photos also serve to show the noticeable difference between the sexes at maturity. These are not obvious at an early age but, as mentioned before, adult Gordon males are nearly always larger, more strongly built and heavier coated than the bitches.

Indigo Solitaire (B) at 8 weeks, owner, Krishna Harris.

Solitaire at six months of age.

Solitaire when a little over a year of age. Winners Bitch, shown by breeder-owner. *Hodges*

MacAlder Best for Shojin (Ed and Dee Fronczak) at six months of age, best of winners at his first show under Ed. Stevenson. *Martin Booth*

At one year, MacAlder Best For Shojin, Winners Dog for five points under Anne Clark, Pam Shaar handling. *Martin Booth*

At two years, MacAlder Best For Shojin, a champion with group Iv, judge E. W. Tipton.
Martin Booth

Introduction to the Grooming Chapter

Just as the three Setters appear at first glance to be the same dog in different colors, so it is easy to assume that the same trimming instructions can be applied to all three. Of course, neither premise is correct.

To begin with, only in America are Gordon Setters trimmed extensively.

Our Standard states, "The Gordon Setter is . . . a black and tan dog . . . appearing capable of doing a full day's work in the field."

There are no stated limits to the amount of coat, either way, and our suggested scale of points allows a meager 8 points for this factor. Obviously, too much coat is a handicap for a field dog, while a short, strong coat is a plus.

The well supported efforts of the Gordon Setter Club of America to maintain the dual purposes of the breed are most successful. We should see coats continuing to be serviceable rather than spectacular. The future of the breed depends on that.

Because the Gordon comes in several different coat textures the Trimming Guide is confined to a basic pattern which can be modified to suit the individual dog.

Why does the Gordon coat vary so? Mrs. Mildred Adams comments on this in her enlightening monograph, *The Story Of The Gordon Setter,* published by the Gordon Setter Association, (1967).

"Whether we like it or not," Mrs. Adams says, "it is absolutely certain that there have been several different crosses in the breed, and from them it is likely we get the different types of coat."

She refers to dogs from the Duke of Gordon's kennels which were wavy coated; dogs from Mr. Coke's kennels which were curly—"the more curly the coat, the better the dog," was Coke's motto. A possible cross to the solid black Welsh Setter would bring in curls as well.

Mrs. Adams says that opinion has it that a black pointer may have contributed to the make-up of the modern Gordon. This would account for the sleek, short coats which appear now and then. "Houndy" looking Gordons show up occasionally which also reflects a possible cross in the past and introduces a different coat texture. Nor can we altogether forget the much debated Collie cross made by the Duke of Gordon which certainly would affect coat type.

Mrs. Adams concludes by saying, "It was said . . . that in a litter there may be smooth, wavy coated and flat, all pure blood." Even today few litters have identical coats and markings.

With this background in mind, let us look at three examples of the coat textures which appear today, as handled for show.

1. *Short:* With a smooth, gleaming coat like this the dog need be tidied up more than actually trimmed. Hair at the top of ears, down the sides of the neck where the two growth patterns meet and under the ear, can be thinned either with shears or a coarse blade to make the ears lie close to the head and low set. What long hair there is on the toes should be snipped back to give the foot a well arched look. Hair on the back of the hocks should be evened up but not clipped close as it adds to the appearance of bone and substance.

There is increasing reluctance to remove whiskers and eyebrows. These are important assets to a hunting dog and people are claiming that it is very painful to the dog to have them cut. Goodness knows, we have had more struggles over whisker cutting than anything else and have abandoned the effort. (Done in the first place supposedly to reveal the contours of the muzzle, it is impossible to see why a few black hairs make that much difference.)

2. *Curly:* The hair is coarse in texture and very dense, and usually there is an undercoat. Much hand work goes into smoothing down these coats, aided by frequent bathing and blanketing. Overall clipping is seldom the answer as it is terribly obvious and judges penalize it. Worse, clipping destroys the natural lay of the coat and its valuable texture. Dogs with this coat make wonderful cold weather hunters and often are eager retrievers from water. Once the coat is conditioned and smoothed down, the effect is a gleaming, rippling surface that is most attractive.

3. *Ideal:* Trimming guidelines are stated with such a dog in mind. This coat is nice for show and with the loss of a feather or two, it serves well for the hunter.

4. Only in America do we find what judges refer to as the Cocker Spaniel or Afghan coat on Gordons. Every breeder gets a dog like this now and then, though the genetics are not clear. Where did it come from??

At first it seems a gift from heaven but as time goes by and one struggles with the problems of such coats, it becomes a burden. For the pet owner or hunting man it is a serious nuisance and often leads to disposing of the dog.

Grooming such an over-coated dog is a never-ending program, impossible to write out. Each dog has a different texture of coat. Some are soft and fluffy; most have a tendency to be fuzzy and snarl at the drop of a pin brush. A damp climate or being caught in the rain is aggravation.

Such coats are a new departure for the breed and it is becoming apparent that there is such a thing as having too much coat even on a show dog. Spectacular as it may be to see feathers almost to the ground on a Gordon, judges are hesitant to place such deviations.

Short

Curly

Ideal

235

11

How to Groom
The Gordon Setter

Text by Fred J. Itzenplitz
Illustrations by Ronald Andrews

IF YOUR GORDON is to be shown he will require trimming. The following procedures keep the necessary equipment simple. At the shows you may hear many suggestions (offered freely) on how your trimming job can be improved but you will not win or lose with the removal of a few hairs here and there. It is the general outline that counts.

You can start to accustom your show puppy to the noise and the feel of clippers as early as two or three months of age. It is helpful to have assistance until the pup learns to stand willingly, as they all do eventually. It is not safe to use the tie bar on the grooming table until you have confidence that your pup will not jump off and hang himself. Never leave him alone on the table even for a short period. Talk to him and encourage him while you apply the clippers; if he panics or fights hold him on the table until he relaxes. Be gentle, but do not scold, have your assistant rub the pup's belly which seems to have a soothing effect.

Nail clipping must be started early and not confined to preparations for showing but to be a continuing process. Clip each nail not forgetting the dewclaws; little and often is the best rule. Short nails are a must for the development of tight, high knuckled feet and for maintaining them. Washing is another early-in-life procedure that should not be confined only to show time. Even if your dog is used in the field he will not pick up as many burrs if his coat is clean and free of dead hair. For a good texture and

236

sheen the coat must be kept clean. Do not skimp on the shampoo. Use a good quality black shampoo made for dogs and use it often. After washing, while the coat is still damp, fasten a wide turkish towel over the dog's body using blanket pins to secure it under the neck, chest, loin and tail. Several hours later when you remove the towel you will have a smooth, shiny dog.

Plan to trim several weeks before the show date. With a dog that has not been trimmed for some time plan on two trims, a rough trim and then a final trim several days later. Do not attempt to trim the day before a show unless it is an emergency. It takes a few days for the pattern to soften and blend after the dog has been clippered.

The basic equipment is: an Oster Animal Clipper, model No. A-5, and blades for same numbered 5, 7, 8½, 10, possibly a 15; two pair of shears, a thinning double edge and a barber straight, sharp point; two Resco combs, medium and coarse; and a Millers Forge Safety nail clippers. When you purchase the Oster A-5, be sure to get a supply of Kool-Lube and use it often while trimming. Also, you might want to have on hand Kwik-Stop just in case you clip a nail a bit too much. This will stanch the bleeding.

The Gordon is trimmed for show to bring out its best points and to reveal the quality beneath all that hair. It should resemble the animal described in the Standard of the Breed. Extreme examples to point out what is meant are: if your dog has a large head and a small body, trim the head closely and leave more hair on the body. If the reverse is true, leave the hair on the head and trim the body. Remember Gordons are a hunting dog and should look the part even after they have been trimmed.

Planning must be a deliberate prelude to trimming. The first step is to study the untrimmed dog to foresee the shape of what is to come and how to achieve it.

First, keep in mind the General Impression as put forth by the standard:

> The Gordon Setter is a good sized, sturdily built, black and tan
> dog, well muscled, with plenty of bone and substance . . . He
> suggests strength and stamina rather than extreme speed.

We will proceed and I will quote from the standard, then explain how to trim your dog so that a judge may easily see how well this dog conforms.

> The head is deep, rather than broad, with plenty of brain room;
> a nicely rounded good sized skull, broadest between the ears.
> The head should have a clearly indicated stop. Below and above
> the eyes should be lean, and the cheek as narrow as the leanness
> of the head allows.

With the #10 blade on your clipper take off only the long whiskers on the muzzle and eyebrows. Trim under the chin and ears (Panel I). Trim the cheeks and the outer side of ears one third of the way from the top. Clip with the grain of the hair (Panel II).

The muzzle is the same length as the skull from occiput to stop and the top of the muzzle is parallel to the line of the skull extended.

Lay the #10 blade aside and take the effective #8½. Trim the sides and back of the skull in order to show the occiput and suggest "neck arched to the head" (Panel III). Use care when doing the top of the skull so that the result is a plane parallel with the top of the muzzle. Often this is important to a knowledgeable judge.

The Chest: Deep and not too broad in front; the ribs well-sprung, leaving plenty of lung room. The chest should reach the elbow. A pronounced forechest is in evidence.

Continue with the #8½ blade. Trim the front of the neck and below the ears. With the #5 or #7 blade, blend this area into the feathers on the forechest to a point that can be located by placing your hands on the shoulder blades (Panel IV). Blend the feathers on the side of the forechest to the shoulder and elbows. The feathered area remaining will be somewhat triangular in shape.

The Neck: Long, lean, arched to the head and without throatiness.
The Shoulders: Should be fine at the points (withers) and lying well back, giving a moderately sloping topline. The tops of the shoulder blades should be close together. When viewed from behind, the neck appears to fit into the shoulders in smooth, flat lines that gradually widen from neck to shoulder.

It is essential that the neck and shoulders blend together appearing to be all of a piece. This is a critical moment. Using the 8½ or 7—(#5 is for the faint-hearted, keeping in mind that it is difficult to put hair back again)— place the clippers at the base of the skull. Following the growth of the hair bring them back in continuous sweep in a slanting line down the sides of the neck across the shoulder blades. This must be a straight line. Avoid pushing in with the clippers where the neck joins the body (Panels V and VI).

Use the clippers sparingly on the top of the neck and never on the withers where thinning shears can be used to clean up any roughness. Over trimming of the withers will result in a poor top line when the dog is moving. Step back several times as you trim to check your work from a distance (Panel VII).

The Body: The body should be short from shoulder to hips and the distance from the forechest to the back of the thigh should approximately equal the height from the ground to the withers.

238

Panel I

Panel II

Panel III

239

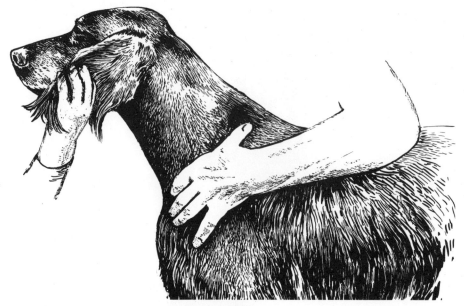

Panel IV

Panel V

Panel VI

240

Panel VII

The loins should be short and broad and not arched. The croup is nearly flat, with only a slight slope to the tailhead.

Using the thinning shears tidy up the ribcage, loin and sides of the hindlegs. Some Gordons grow profuse hair on the outside of the legs in the stifle and hock joint area. This hair is disfiguring, making the dog look bowlegged, it should be removed.

Thin hair over the loin, blending into the croup (Panel VIII). Thin hair on the back of hind legs from base of croup down about four inches so that this area on the legs and around the vent is perpendicular (Panel IX). Remove rough hair on the sides of the ribcage about two-thirds of the way down. When viewed from above, this hair on the lower third of the ribcage should not be visible as it gives the impression that the chest ends at that point. View your dog from the same angles as the judge will in the show ring.

The hindlegs from hip to hock should be long, flat and muscular; from hock to heel, short and strong. The feet should be formed by close knit, well-arched toes with plenty of hair between; with full toe pads and deep heel cushions. Feet should be cat-like in shape.

Using straight sharp-pointed shears, trim the bottoms of the feet leaving the hair just even with the pads. With the dog standing with his feet flat on the table, trim excess hair. Working with the shears at a slight angle, remove the hair between the nails, but not from between the toes (Panel X). Comb down the hair on the hock, and with shears perpendicular, make a nicely rounded (from side to side) shape to the hock. It is unfortunate that hocks are trimmed too close, even clippered in some instances. This makes the bone look weak and spindly (Panel XI).

The Tail: Short and should not reach below the hocks, carried horizontal or nearly so; thick at the root and finishing in a fine point. The feather which starts near the root of the tail should be slightly waved or straight, having triangular appearance, growing shorter uniformly toward the end.

While holding the tail horizontal, comb hair straight down. Cut hair off the end almost to the tip of the bone. Even up feathers on a slanting line to give the triangular shape. Remove the feathers on the underside of the tail for about two inches from the vent so that there is a definite break between the feathering on the back of the legs and the feathers on the tail (Panel XII). If there is excess bushiness on top of the tail, I would suggest a thorough combing after a bath before resorting to thinning shears.

The trim job is now completed. You will find it easier to do the sensitive area around the muzzle, eyes and ears before the dog becomes

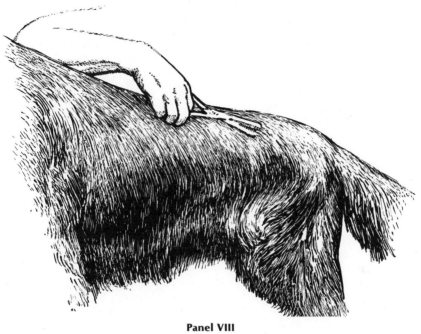

Panel VIII

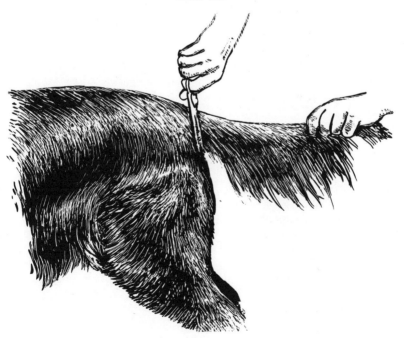

Panel IX

243

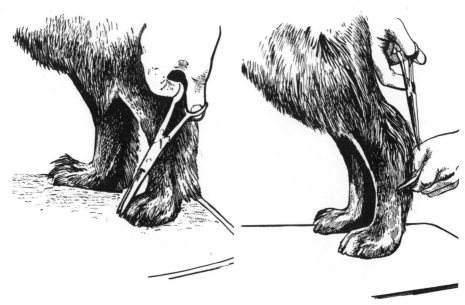

Panel X   **Panel XI**

Panel XII

244

restless. It is just as important where hair is left *on* as where it is trimmed *off*. Leave hair on top of the neck, withers, middle of the back and croup, with just enough thinning to blend neck, shoulders, back, loin and tail in a smooth line (Panel XIII).

Avoid excessive trimming on top of ears as a "spaniel expression" is not desired. Your Gordon should have more the expression of a Scottish gentleman counting his change.

It is best to proceed with each step on one side, then go to the other side of the dog to be sure you get a balanced effect. When finished let the dog run around the yard, then set him up in show position to see if you missed anything. The more clearly you have perceived the Standard and Description, the better your chance of success.

If you have bathed the dog a day or two before the show, then dampen his coat and apply a turkish towel as you would after a bath and leave this on as you drive to the show. Remove towel just before entering the ring. There should be no additional grooming necessary under pressure of "show time" except a quick going over with brush and comb.

With luck your judge will be familiar with the Standard and your trim job will help you go home with a winner that day.

Oh! It is such a *short* drive home after winning.

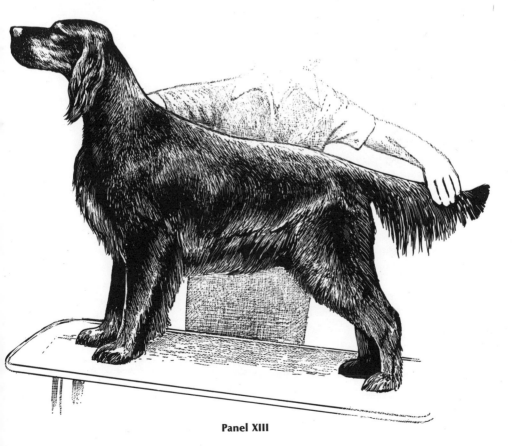

Panel XIII

12

How to Show
a Gordon Setter

CHOICE OF A SHOW LEAD for a Gordon Setter depends on the size and strength of the dog and handler. A martingale nylon lead is excellent and comes in many weights and lengths. The color should be black. This type of lead gives the handler good control because it will stay up under the dog's ears and there is little danger that it will loosen and permit the dog to escape.

Some handlers prefer a lightweight but very strong chain choke, quite long, on a narrow leather or nylon lead.

When you are gaiting the dog, bunch up the excess lead in your left hand. It works well to extend your left arm straight out to the side. Position the lead well up under the dog's ears. This style does three things: it gives you good balance when running; it keeps the dog away from you so that it can't trip you, and it gives the judge a clear view of the movement of the dog.

Gordons should be gaited on a lead held just tight enough so that the dog is aware of being controlled and keeps its head up. If the lead is allowed to sag down the neck, control is lost and the dog may wander and weave while moving. (This is the instinctive questing gait of all bird dogs.)

On the other hand, if the lead is kept too taut the dog may gag and cough, stopping in his tracks to do so. Every dog is different and each has its own reaction to show leads. It may take several tries and much practice before you hit just the right combination for your dog.

Because Gordons are dignified, big dogs, they must be moved at their own best speed, which is *not* fast. If forced, they may lower their heads and fight the lead all the way around the ring.

Look who's showing a Gordon Setter! (Providence R.I. show 1952). Marsha Hall, now Marsha H. Brown, then an outstanding Junior Handler of her own Stone Gable English Setters. Gordon not identified.

Moving them too fast also results in their tossing legs around. Often, they break stride and gallop or leap in the air. Gordons are not spaniels, it is inappropriate to show them in spaniel style. Here again, it is a matter of trial and error to find the right speed for your dog. Once you find it stick with it, no matter what anybody else in the ring is doing.

The three Setters are posed much the same, allowing for their differences in structure. Since the Gordon is a square dog with moderate angulation, the hindquarters are not to be stretched to excess, or spread to try to create something that isn't there. The back of the hocks should be vertical; the stance of the dog very nearly that he adopts on his own when he stops at attention.

A real No-No is attempting to force angulation and sloping topline by holding the head high by the show lead (which shoves the ears up and forward, spoiling the look of the head) while clutching the tail at its base, pushing it forward and down at the same time. Held in this position the tail is limp and droops over the hand like a wilted plant. Usually the back feet are too far out for the hocks to be vertical and the dog appears to be all out of balance. Quite aside from the way it looks, this must be uncomfortable for the dog since Gordon tails are seldom placed so they can be elevated like this without pain. Judges should insist that the dog be shown with the tail in the proper position, that is, level with the back.

Baiting a Gordon is a matter of personal choice. It is useful for keeping some dogs in good spirits, but most Gordons do just as well without. In fact, they may totally ignore bait while they are in the ring.

If the dog is trained at home to gait towards a judge (as when being moved individually) with the expectation of receiving a tidbit while standing for that final checking, he will do this in the ring, bait or no bait. More often than not baiting has the undesirable side effect of causing the dog to elevate his ears in anticipation, thus spoiling the true Setter expression the judge wants to see.

It goes without saying that all dogs should be well trained at home so that they behave in the ring. No one can win with a dog that is dragging every whichway, charging at the other entries, or backing away from the judge.

Keep training sessions hort, and do not take away all the bounce and play. Every dog is a bit subdued by being at a show. If perfect at home, he may be dull in the ring.

Handling classes put on by many show-giving clubs offer an ideal environment to train both handler and dog.

One last word of caution: don't be surprised if, after many shows in a short time, your Gordon loses his enthusiasm for the whole thing. A few weeks of R & R should bring him back on top.

Newcomers to dog shows are often astounded to find that there are surprisingly strict Codes of Ethics and Dress Codes. While the atmosphere

Many handlers find using this style in gaiting to be successful.

No frills posing is best for Gordon Setters. Handler, however, is dressed too informally for show.

249

at shows is relaxed, anybody can wear almost anything—*unless* he or she is going to step into the ring.

If the weather is not unbearably hot, men find it expedient to dress in a conservative fashion—slacks with harmonious sports jacket, shirt and tie. Even in extreme heat, a tailored shirt and slacks is about as informal as one should get. No jeans, T-shirts, chopped off shorts or sandals for the handler!

Women should avoid slacks or jeans unless the weather is windy and extremely cold. One should select clothes that are flexible so that it is no problem to run, twist, bend and reach. A wrap skirt with a tailored short sleeved shirt is ideal, especially since the blouse can be changed during the day to maintain the neat and clean appearance that is so important.

Shoes must be comfortable, low heeled and *safe*. Color is not important. Safety is the big item because there is a constant risk of slipping on wet grass (early mornings), muddy patches, or on extremely dry short grass (late afternoon). Fortunately there are now many choices beyond the sneaker.

Do not wear bracelets, long necklaces, or carry pockets loaded with jingling change and keys.

Good manners are essential. Pay attention to the judge, don't banter and talk to him, and keep your conversation with ringsiders or other handlers to a minimum. Do what the judge tells you to do without any sign of resentment. Accept whatever ribbon he gives you with a polite "Thank you." Be on time at ringside. Don't crowd or run up on your competitors. The looks and behavior of a handler play a definite part in his success.

One of the most helpful books on the market is Howell's *Guide to Successful Dog Showing* in which Jane and Bob Forsyth go through a list of Do's and Don'ts illustrated with beautifully clear and precise photos of them taken by Evelyn Shafer. This book will serve to amplify the various points brought up in the preceding chapter.

13

Special Care of
the Gordon Setter

WHEN ONE ACCEPTS the responsibility of owning a Gordon the most important matter to face is being ready to provide the best possible dog food and plenty of it. Coat texture, color, weight of dog, animation, endurance, productivity and good disposition all depend on correct nutrition. It is not enough to provide just an adequate, maintenance diet. Gordons need more *good* food than do other breeds of their size.

At the present time there are only two or three brands of food which should be considered. They are expensive and sometimes hard to get but the rewards make it worth the effort. Try to find one with minimum or no soy bean content. The dogs will eat better but not as much; coats will be a good glossy black; the risks of digestive problems, skin irritations, runny eyes and lifeless coat are minimized. Puppies grow stronger without skeletal problems.

For every dollar you spend on good food you save on vet bills.

Other than needing excellent nutrition the Gordon is an easy dog to care for, with very few health problems. It is just as happy in an unheated as heated kennel, always assuming that a comfortable dog house is provided. Rain or snow doesn't slow the Gordon up because the breed develops a dense undercoat in cold climates, making it surprisingly waterproof.

The Gordon Setter population has long been confined to the cool Northeast section of the U.S. and, of course, it was developed in a cool, stormy climate in Great Britain. In these areas they grow far more heavy

251

coats than do the other two Setters. An untrimmed Gordon in full winter coat is unrecognizable. Ears are blanketed in curls; a thick ruff around the neck develops; feet look twice as big as normal with hair on top and the bottom. Even the tail is encased in dense coat which extends well beyond the tip to protect it from freezing. Many Gordons grow topknots several inches long. The whole effect is to make him look not unlike a miniature musk ox!

As the population of the United States moves South and Southwest, and to California, Gordons are going along. More and more of them are now located in areas where this ability to withstand rotten weather is not required. For those dogs the need is to keep cool, not warm. Nature is helpful and no such output of coat occurs in warm climates. Gordons really do not like heat and find the combination of high temperatures and humidity hard to take. For them extra care must be taken.

Air conditioning seems like the quick and easy answer but studies prove that kennels equipped only with shade, insulation, good cross ventilation and fans are far healthier. Sun, dry air, parasites, internal and external, spell disaster to black coats. During the oppressive days the dogs should be kept quiet and inside except for early morning or evening. Some handle this by letting the dogs stay out all night. Every effort must be made to prevent the development of allergies which stem from fleas, ticks, fly bites and worms.

In any climate, the type of kennel run best suited to the Gordon is one which has a surface that keeps the nails worn down, the pads hard and thick, and the toes strong. Cement in any climate has its drawbacks. In winter, it becomes icy and dangerously slippery, impossible to clean. In the heat it may become too warm to walk on, and runs made of cement will hold the heat for hours after the sun goes down.

Gravel or dirt runs are the best even though it is difficult to keep them looking pristine. The advantages are that they can be replaced *in toto* as frequently as need be. Furthermore, they can be deodorized more successfully and by using a flame thrower, brine mixture and fertilizer Borax they can be kept as free from parasites and odor as any surface. Dogs will be dogs and dig holes, make paths. This isn't serious; consider it their hobby.

In any climate, runs must be made wide enough to prevent these tail waggers from banging their tail tips on the fence which will break them open. Six feet is none too wide. Runs also should be of sufficient length so that the dogs can move freely. A length of 25 feet is good, more is better. It has been determined that dogs get much more exercise in a long narrow run than they do in a square one.

The black coat of the Gordon is durable and does not break easily. Of course, field work and feathering are incompatible as with any hunting breed but in the normal course of events this coat is not easily damaged nor is it given to matting badly except at shedding time or if it gets caked with mud.

If the Gordon is hunted, it is imperative to check him closely after every day afield. Burrs, twigs, weed seeds can cause havoc. Eyes should be rinsed out with a mild solution of salt water. Check to see that there is nothing lodged in the eye. Ears must be checked, burrs removed, and the ear canal looked at to be sure nothing has gotten in it. Feet should be cleaned up with burrs and twigs removed from between the toes and pads. Broken toenails are not uncommon and should be taken care of by your veterinarian. Check over the whole body to be sure no burrs and twigs are wound up in the hair of the armpits and the groin.

With good care your hunting pal can go out day after day and give you the best performance he's capable of.

14

The Character of
the Gordon Setter

IT IS A MISTAKE to assume that the differences between the three Setters consist only of size and color.

The basic good nature, love of outdoors, fondness for people rather than other dogs, are there in each. But further acquaintance will reveal some rather sharp contrasts in temperament which may affect your opinion of the breed as a pet for you.

As each Setter evolved over the years, it achieved increasing suitability for the special hunting conditions under which it was expected to work and for the temperament of the people of the land.

Irish Setters are often referred to as rollicking, carefree, high spirited.

The English Setter brings forth comments such as mild, loving, gentlemanly and quiet.

The Gordon impresses people as aloof and not partial to strangers. Young dogs are considered boisterous and a bit tough to handle.

The rugged country and life in Scotland led to a strong bodied, determined dog of seemingly boundless energy.

Each breed, sporting or otherwise, has its own sphere of special aptitude and intelligence. Dogs work from their own brains not solely from what is taught them.

A good hunting Gordon works with its owner—in fact, guides him, and is quite confident that he knows what's best. This does not necessarily flatter the owner, especially when it turns out to be true!

254

This ten week old pup personifies the alert, intelligent Gordon expression. With her ears pricked, she is calmly watching every move of the photographer. *Shafer*

One must be prepared to be outsmarted more than a few times by his Gordon. They are discreet about it and do not gloat, but they sure can catch you flatfooted.

Gordons develop a devotion to one or two people which is so intense that to break this tie is to weaken the confidence of the dog. Passed from owner to owner, a Gordon becomes less and less interested in anyone and more and more intent on doing what he wants to do. Older dogs make slower adjustments. Often this is accompanied by a personality reversal. The shy dog becomes a wild extrovert, or the brave dog becomes a spook.

Because of their involvement with their owners, Gordons are jealous and protective. For this reason it is not always successful to try to have two house dogs. These black Setters are not above fighting and the female is just as peppery as the male.

They are protective and careful with children. Many stories exist of Gordons rescuing a child from danger as one would expect a Collie or Shepherd to perform. However, they must not be teased or dragged around endlessly. Their patience grows thin and they will learn to avoid contact with the children rather than seeking them out willingly.

Many Gordons are great "talkers." This seems to run in families. They can develop quite a vocabulary with various tones to express pleasure at seeing the food dish approaching; needing a drink; greeting the family; or warning of strangers. Constant, gentle wagging of the tail seems to be part of their style, as well.

Members of this breed do not demand constant attention though they do like to be where their family is. It is quite possible to have contented Gordons that are kennel dogs, especially if it is a one breed kennel. What they don't experience, they don't miss. So it is better not to give them a taste of being a house pet unless one can keep it up. If the dog is to be shown or field trained, it will look forward to these activities far more eagerly than does a lazy house pet.

Hunting dogs are often kept as house dogs but this requires that the owner devote adequate time to keeping the dog in good condition. A kennel dog, on the other hand, fares a bit better if he is given a large yard and comfortable sleeping quarters. He gets used to being out in all weather and gives himself needed exercise.

But, NO dog does well in a kennel or as a house pet unless proper care is given on a daily basis.

There is some question as to how successful it is to send a Gordon to a professional show handler or field trainer. Show handlers always face the problem of homesick dogs, and they have many artful ways of helping such animals through this difficult time. Field trainers, on the other hand, have no time to spare babying a dog and, as a result, the Gordon may come home from his allotted two or three month stay in poor condition, hardly trained.

Boarding a Gordon can be a disaster. Pick the kennel with care. Start

Full of life and eager to retrieve, Ch. Chapparal Able Bodied. *Linda Sanders.*

Irresistible photo of Barry Sunderland and Ch. Rural Rhythm (1954-55). The dog's eyes are nearly closed and her attitude is one of polite resignation.

257

the dog off with a stay of a day or two and make sure it is not caged or exercised with any other dogs. Try not to leave a pet more than two weeks. For some reason this seems to be the limit of the dog's faith; beyond this time he may give up hope that his owners will return. Gordons may lose weight dramatically under such circumstances.

Prospective purchasers of Gordons always want to know if they are easy to train. Yes they are, very easy. They housebreak readily, like to ride in cars, quickly learn to walk nicely on a leash. There is no reason for harsh treatment. In fact, it only worsens the problem as it does with any breed.

An important aspect of the breed is how they fare as stud dogs and brood bitches. The Gordon, being a dog of natural build, has few problems reproducing itself.

If a male is destined to be a stud dog, for best results he should be handled as such from puppyhood. He should have the company of bitches so that he knows such things exist. He should not be constantly disciplined if he attempts to mate with every dog in sight. Be gentle about it and just remove the object of his affections. He will soon outgrow the worst of this.

By rights this future stud dog should not share a run. Snapped at and rebuffed by adult bitches, he'll never have the courage of his convictions as a grown dog.

If, at a year of age he appears to be of good quality, it is helpful if this dog can be bred to a sensible, experienced bitch. Not only does this give him invaluable training, it gives the owner an equally important clue as to what kind of puppy his dog sires.

A stud dog must learn to accept help from its owner. Bitches, even kennel mates, must be muzzled at time of mating. One bad experience can ruin a promising producer. Well trained stud dogs are a prized possession.

Sometimes dogs are not considered for breeding until they are well on in years. If they have been house pets, it is better to forget it. They are just not properly trained for this and often fail to comprehend what is expected of them. There must be other dogs just as good, waiting in the wings.

As brood bitches, Gordons score well. They produce litters ranging from five to ten, seldom more. The size of the litter seems to be an inherited factor.

Problems with whelping do not plague the breed and one seldom encounters a bitch who cannot feed all her pups. Gordons are good, sensible mothers. Rarely do they want to leave their pups until they are six or seven weeks old, and even then the mother often prefers to check on them at will rather than being removed entirely.

These mothers mean business. Once, when we were novices, we followed the advice in a book and removed the dam when the pups were six weeks old. She had other ideas. First she tore her way out of the kennel. Then she ripped the screen door off the back porch. When she could not get through the master door, she went under the house and crawled over to the

All time top Gordon Setter show winner, Ben-Wen's Benjy McDee, shown at his retirement party with owner Mrs. Marie Annello and his proud breeder, George Bennett. After four years in the show ring, Benjy is now a loving pet full time.

puppy room. We found her vigorously chewing on the floorboards under the pups. Never again did we try to make this decision for any of our bitches.)

And what about the puppies? Not too big when born, they grow steadily though not fast. Congenital defects are at a minimum.

They are as clean as they are allowed to be and by encouraging this quality from the very first these pups will grow to be instinctively clean adults. Sadly, the reverse is equally true. Pups raised in a dirty environment seem to lose their standards and never regain them as adults.

One last comment: keeping one dog as a house pet is preferable to keeping two or more. Unfortunately the dogs become so interdependent that the role of the owner is quite secondary. If these dogs are to be shown or field trained, more than likely they will spend all their time looking for each other when separated, making it impossible to do much with them. Furthermore, two dogs will think up mischievous things to do and two dogs will run away whereas one will never leave home.

What kind of person will be happy with a Gordon Setter? First of all, someone who is active and likes the outdoors. The grooming and exercising of the dog should be a pleasure. The cost of feeding such a big dog the best possible food should not be any problem. A person with patience and an interest in developing the latent ability of his dog will find a Gordon Setter truly rewarding.

Good Reading from Howell Book House

Joy of Breeding Your Own Show Dog	Seranne
Collins Guide to Dog Nutrition	Collins
Dog Care and Training for Boys and Girls	Saunders
Dog Owner's Home Veterinary Handbook	Carlson and Giffin
Dog Psychology	Whitney
How Puppies Are Born	Prine
The New Complete Junior Showmanship Handbook	Brown and Mason
Why Does Your Dog Do That?	Bergman

How it all begins—with a birdy puppy, like Duncan McChips. *Linda Sanders*

Ch. Timberdoodle Dan of Avalon, UDT (c. 1945), gundog par excellence.

15

The Gordon Setter
as a Hunting Dog

WALTER HUTCHINSON, in his *Dog Encyclopedia* (1872), covered in four sentences the whole gamut of Gordon Setter breeding:

> *"Happy is the country which evolved the Black-and-Tan or Gordon Setter. The Gordon is to be found in practically every country in the world, owned always by the discriminating sportsman who prefers to walk up his game and to whom a good working Setter is 90 percent of the day's enjoyment.*
>
> *"The best advice to breeders is to stick to type, color and dual qualities, and last but not least, expression. In retaining the breed's dual qualities soundness is assured."*

He makes it sound easy, doesn't he?

Certainly nothing brings joy to a Gordon Setter more than a few hours hunting with his master, no matter how informal or unsuccessful it may be.

A novice owner has to begin with the proper attitude: that when it comes to basics, the dog instinctively knows much more about what he should be doing afield than his owner does. Training for hunting is best done by giving the dog every opportunity to contact game and work various types of terrain, and to learn to accept the gun.

The breed is gifted with exceptional keenness of nose. For this reason, even as pups they are not inspired to dash off in all directions, but prefer to

262

So your dog won't hunt woodcock? Try a Gordon Setter. Arthur Itzenplitz with Old Don (early 1940's).

stay in close, concentrating on the new scents. Only as they age and develop knowledge do they swing out at a distance.

It is essential to teach a pup to "heel," "whoa" or "stay," and to come when called. For this a whistle is far more effective than shouting because the sound carries better. If the dog is a house pet, rapport develops rapidly, making training easier.

All pointing breeds use their heads as well as their noses to find game. Experience is the best teacher. Gordons willingly work any type of upland game, and many are useful duck dogs.

Severe punishment in the course of training is never successful with any breed. Setters are notoriously "soft" and must be handled accordingly. Of the three, the Gordon is the least likely to accept abuse without protest. Beyond a certain point he will stand up for himself, and this can develop into a confrontation which destroys whatever bond may have existed between owner and dog. The Gordon will neither forget nor forgive, and further attempts at training under such circumstances may meet with implacable resistance from the dog.

A word of caution to the novice trainer: Beware of the electronic training collar! Incorrectly used it can permanently ruin a dog for hunting. Most Gordons do not need one.

Not as many Gordon Setter owners want to get into Field Trialing as we would like to see. They like the idea of an outing now and then with kindred souls but beyond that the incentive is lacking. The expense and time involved in readying a dog for trialing effectively curbs enthusiasm.

For these people the answer may be the newest development by the Gordon Setter Club of America, Inc., the Working Certificate. After 25 years of discussion, a set of rules has been developed which require a decent performance in the field without necessitating years of hard training. Good personal gun dogs are what the Gordon Setter Club has in mind. Tests are given at certain club trials around the country, open to all.

Chances are that, once the dog is qualified for a Working Certificate, more owners will be tempted to try advanced training, perhaps even to have a go at the ultimate glory, a Dual Championship for their Gordon.

Training for field trials is beyond the novice and requires professional help. It is best to ask a pro to train *you* to train your dog. It sometimes works to leave all the training of the dog to a professional, but much of the pleasure and companionship is lost this way. It is not uncommon for a Gordon to fail to work for anyone other than his trainer, even his owner, so bear this in mind when you make your plans.

Howell Book House has an excellent book for do-it-yourselfers written by Chuck Goodall, a famous trainer, called *How to Train Your Own Gun Dog*.

A beautiful example of cooperation and varying styles. 1977 photo by John Ansley (Tomarcan Kennels) of his Dual Ch. MacGeowl's MacDougal.

Tom Olson at right with Ch. MacAlder Lara after a successful Opening Day pheasant hunt in South Dakota. Tom says of Lara, "she has an incredible nose and is a very intense hunter. She is 27" and weighs 85 pounds. It is a joy to watch her muscle her way through dense cover." Lara is also a Top Producer.

16

The Gordon Setter
as a Field Trial Dog

In 1981 THERE WERE 26 field trials sponsored by various Gordon Setter Clubs from coast to coast and in Hawaii. Participation by club members is not as extensive as could be wished. One big problem is the disparity between the professional (or dedicated) field trialers and the once-a-year-at-the-local-trial participants with hunting dogs. Additionally discouraging, all but a few of the trials are open to other pointing breeds, with only a class or two just for Gordons.

Some experts question the wisdom of attempting to force different breeds into a competitive situation when the basic style of each is unique. On the other hand, it is argued that the trials serve to keep alive the reputation of the Gordon as a hunting dog.

The history of field trials held by the Gordon Setter Club of America goes back to the late 1800's.

This first breed club attempted two trials, one in 1893 and again in 1894. Support was poor and so were the performances, so no further attempts were made.

When the GSCA was reestablished in 1924 a strong effort was launched to promote trials. Large cash prizes were offered, yet trials never caught on. After a few years the club abandoned its efforts. (At that time the American Kennel Club did not handle field trials or offer field trial championships.)

Oddly enough, interest in field trials among the club membership was good and during the next 15 years Gordons ran successfully at many inter-breed Gun Club trials located along the east coast from New Jersey into

Svane's June's Baby (very rare photo) circa mid-1930's.

Legendary Fld. Ch. Page's Shuriridge Liz (Jack Page). This painting was done by James Lockhart for a special series titled "American Sporting Dog Greats" published in 1955 by *Sports Afield.*

267

The first Dual Champion in breed history, Loch Ridge Saegryte's Tibby, owned by George Penterman, 1952.

View of the grounds at the Clarksville, Md. trial site.

Interesting photo of a training session with Sheila Lehan handling her Springset Toma-
hawk while Fld. Ch. Danny Boy O'Boy honors. They were getting ready for the GSCA
field trial held Nov. 27, 1977 at San Miguel, Ca. Photo by Steven C. LaMarine.

268

New England. A few members in California became quite active, as well.

Of importance are two Gordon Setters, mother and daughter, who ran so well that memories of them have never faded. Being the first Gordons to appear in competition in many, many years, they faced a highly critical audience, and passed the tests with class.

Dr. A. P. Evans, whose kennel name was SVANE, began his breeding program with Inglehurst dogs. His first winner, from his first litter, was Svane June, born in 1922. Her pedigree is of interest:

Stylish Ben (English import)

Sire: Ch. Governor Edwards

Am. & Can. Ch. Trampus Shannon

Bulrush Tam O'Shanter

Dam: Inglehurst Lady
(later, Svane Lady)

Bulrush Judy

June made history. Her career had begun to take off when she was five years old and she just got better as she got older, ending her career with three Firsts in All Age Stakes during 1929-1930.

Her daughter, Svane June's Baby (1929-1944), sired by Don IV, a son of Ch. Inglehurst Joker, was also a late developer. She was still competing when she was eight and she lived to be fifteen. Her record of 16 wins against 300 competitors was impressive for any breed at that time.

The blood of these two bitches still flows in certain American lines.

As it was with the show scene, just as things were looking good for the Gordon Setter the sudden plunge into World War II by the United States ended the momentum.

Not until 1949 were efforts to revive field trials successful. The first one was a Gordons—only affair held in New Jersey. The committee was made up of George Penterman (Shuriridge), Larry Hills, owner of Mace's Old Bessie, Jake Poisker (Windy Hill), and Miriam Steyer Mincieli (Milestone).

Goodness knows there was nothing professional about this first trial. No one was quite sure what to do or where to go. The young dogs chased each other madly; the birds they found just as madly. Several dignified, well trained gun dogs with their dignified and kindly owners proceeded to show us how it should be done. The weather was hot and sticky. But, everyone had such a splendid time that plans were promptly made for the next trial.

In a matter of three years the club was running successful, well managed trials. The Gordons were adequately trained (except for the puppies); support was excellent; and we were receiving good publicity. By then the Field Trial Committee had evolved into a close knit group comprised of George and Jane Penterman (Trial Secretary), Bill and Marge Platt, Fred and Ollie Richardson, Jake Poisker, Vincent Wilcox.

269

Later on they were joined by Jack and Dottie Page, Nathan and Sally Putchat with son Bruce, and Bill Chinnick.

Gordon trials were opened to other Pointing breeds, at first just Setters, and in turn, those breed clubs invited Gordons to participate in their trials. This meant that Spring and Fall the avid field trialer could look forward to as many as 12 trials each season, two per weekend, within easy driving distance. Most were held in Pennsylvania, New Jersey, New York and Connecticut.

Inevitably, changes came towards the end of the 1950's when it was necessary to cut back the number of Gordon Setter Club trials. Financial woes, plus lack of breed support and loss of our committee members to other pursuits left no choice. Remaining were the Pennsylvania Regional, the New England Regional, and the trials of the Tartan Gordon Setter Club in New England.

From 1952 to 1959, however, there were four Dual Champions made, and five additional Field Champions, impressive figures for such a numerically small breed.

From 1963 to 1969 many new faces and new dogs appeared at our trials, mostly owner handled, as they had been in the past.

Seven Field Championships were won, all by different owners.

Three important Dual Championships were completed. These dogs contributed much by their subsequent use as breeding stock.

From 1970 to 1982, 23 Field Champions have been made, and in addition, ten Dual championships were won. (These will be dealt with in detail under Kennel Profiles).

Field trials began in California in 1968. Run under different rules from Eastern trials, they require shoot-to-kill, and few handlers ride. The trials grounds are vast open spaces compared to the tight Eastern courses.

In 1976 trials were begun in Illinois under the aegis of the Mid-America Gordon Setter Field Trial Club. Most recently, the Gordon Setter Club of Hawaii was formed in 1978, and now runs two trials per year. Members boast (with justice) that they have the best climate and the most spectacular field trial grounds in the world. Don't plan on taking your dog, however! There is a 120 day quarantine for dogs coming from the United States.

Norm Sorby (Springset) has provided me with some very interesting statistics on the growth of Gordon Setter Trials in the past five years:

In 1976 there was a total of 135 entries for the year.

In 1981, the total had grown to 863, made up of 677 American Kennel Club entries, and 186 American Field entries.

There were 79 AKC trials, and 43 American Field trials represented, with a total of 242 placements by Gordon Setters; 192 of these were at AKC trials.

The breakdown on the number of Gordons in each class is really

Alec Laurence with one of his dual purpose Gordons, Ch. Ravenscroft Jean's Debutante, 1955.

Winners of All Age Stake, 1954 Gordon Setter Club Spring trial, 1954. From left: First place—Fld. Ch. Page's Shuriridge Liz (Page); 2nd—Fld. Ch. Ebony Sultan with George Penterman; 3rd—Judge Palmer with Jean Look. *Shafer*

Show Champion Springset Sanday Piper on a beautiful intense point. (Sorby)

The breed's latest Dual Champion, Shadowmere Scylla Savoy (B). Trainer-handler Jim Basham, left: one owner, Jim Thacker, with trophy, 1981.

interesting: 209 Puppies, 214 Derbies, 313 Gun Dog, 84 Shooting Dog, and 43 All Age.

A closer look should be taken at the careers of individuals whose efforts have brought success to Gordon Setter trials.

Alec Laurence (1926-1981) Rhythm, (California)
(Please remember that dates given are for the life of the kennel.)

Never one to put himself forward, Alec nonetheless had a great deal to do with the survival and development of the Gordon on the West Coast. His friends remember him with affection and speak of how helpful he had always been to other Gordon breeders, and his efforts to promote Gordons.

Alec's association with field setters goes back to his early boyhood. In 1941 he purchased a Gordon from the field-show kennel of Dr. Rixford, also a Californian. During the next 20 years he was active as an exhibitor; always hunted his dogs extensively; and bred upwards of 200 pups that were placed in the Bay area.

During the 50's Alec served on the Board of Directors of the Gordon Setter Club of America.

Dogs he bred or owned, which can be found in today's pedigrees, were Chs. Rippling Rhythm, Rural Rhythm, Ravenscroft Jean's Debutante; also Sun-Yak Medicine Man, Lad's MacTavish, Springset Storm Huntress, Fld. Ch. Danny Boy O'Boy.

About 1961 Alec began his own gardening business which reduced the time he had for his dogs. Also, he had a tragic loss of many of them by poison while on a hunting trip in northern California. Hence his activities, though not his interest, were curtailed.

He and his wife Gladys moved to Hawaii about 1973, taking with them his Gordon interests. Thus it is that Jim Hustace, now a Director of the Gordon Setter Club of America, became a Gordon field trial enthusiast.

After Alec's death in 1981, the Gordon Setter Field Trial Club of Northern California named a major stake the Alec V. Laurence Memorial Classic, as a tribute to his considerable contribution to the breed.

George and Jane Penterman (1945-1960) Shuriridge, (New Jersey)

This popular couple deserve the credit for establishing Field Trials for Gordon Setters. George spent many hours learning to train and then training his first two Gordon Setters, and was rewarded by achieving the history-making first Dual Champion, Loch Ridge Saegryte's Tibby, always a consistent performer and winner. She gained her Field Championship in 1952. Her kennel mate, Ebony Sultan, also show bred, became the third Field Champion in 1955. In between the two, a pup of theirs became the *second* Field Champion, the famous Page's Shuriridge Liz. Quite a story. Tibby won her show title in 1955 at the age of eight.

The Pentermans had one more outstanding Field Champion, considered one of the best ever, in Shuriridge Hummingbird. Born in 1956, she won her title in 1959 and died shortly thereafter.

George was active in the Gordon Setter Club and served as President during 1955 and 1956. By the 60's business commitments made it imperative that dog activities take a second place, and the Pentermans regretfully cut back.

Willard (Bill) and Marjorie Platt (1946-1970) Gunbar, (Illinois)

One of the better pups that ran during the first GSCA Field Trial was Kipling, a son of Tibby and Sultan. Always a great contender at trials, Kip never quite completed his Field championship, but he did succeed in getting his owners thoroughly involved. The Platts like dog shows and bred for dual purpose Gordons with much success.

By 1956 they had become established in Illinois and had organized the first field trials for Gordons ever held in that area. Soon they had their first Dual Ch., Gunbar Dare Devil. When he earned his CD he became the first Gordon to have all three titles. Platts' efforts in the world of show dogs were equally successful, as their homebred Ch. Gunbar's Flapper became the first Gordon bitch to win Best in Show since the days of Charles T. Inglee in the '20's.

Their Ch. Scotch Burr of Gunbar racked up an enviable record of Bests of Breed and group placements, as did their Ch. Windy Hills Ablaze of Gunbar.

Bill served as President of the Gordon Setter Club of America for 1958 and 1959, and from 1960 to 1963 he was club Delegate to the AKC.

By 1970 pressure of business commitments forced a severe curtailment of kennel activities for these two valued fanciers.

John (Jack) O. Page (1949-   ) Page's, (Connecticut)

Page's Shuriridge Liz, Jack's second Gordon, remains the most successful Field Trial winner in the history of the breed. Jack says of her that she was a once-in-a-lifetime dog for him, too. She began winning as a yearling in 1951 and her career of consistent performances lasted until 1959 with a lifetime total of over 100 placements. 76 of these were at American Field registered trials, which means that she competed against other pointing breeds.

Liz produced Fld. Ch. Page's Flash MacBess. Fld. Ch. Jock MacBess sired Fld. Ch. Page's Daisy MacBess from a Liz daughter. Daisy gave them Page's Jake, the youngest Gordon ever to win his field title (age 2).

Ch. Page's MacDonegal II (Page's MacDonegal x Mace's Old Bessie) is well known through his sons Afternod Hedemac and Ch. Afternod Hickory, back of present day Gordons.

Liz, bred to MacDonegal II, produced another winner, Ch. Page's Captain MacGregor, sire of many champions in the 1950's.

The Gordon Setter Club of America has benefited from Jack's long career as an officer. He served on the Board in 1957, 1960, then from 1971 until he became Vice President, followed by the Presidency in 1980.

Also active in the Tartan Gordon Setter Club, Jack served continuously in one capacity or another since its inception: terms as Vice President, Field Trial Chairman, President, Editor of *Tartan Tidings,* among others.

When the American Kennel Club established its Pointing Breed Field Trial Rules Advisory Committee, Jack represented the Gordon Setter Club in 1969 and 1974.

Using the kennel name of Page's, Mrs. Dorothy Whitney, formerly Mrs. Page, utilizes the same basic stock to produce her show dogs. She, too, has had a long involvement with the Tartan Gordon Setter Club.

Their combined efforts to maintain the dual aspect of the breed have been essential in keeping the breed going during bad times and good in the New England area.

Nathan Putchat (1955-1965) Chance's, (Pennsylvania)

In 1955 Mr. Putchat, wife Sally, and son Bruce joined the Field Trial ranks with their show Champion Windy Hill's Lucky Chance, then slightly over one year of age. The dog was campaigned extensively in the field and proved to be a flashy worker. In 1957 "Cloud," as he was known, won the Gordon Setter Club Specialty show, then went into serious field training and won his Field Championship in 1959.

His lifetime record of 60 Field Trial wins, 38 of which were in all-breed competition was notable, but his record as a sire is even more so. Of the ten champions he sired, all have proved to be influential producers. Among them are:

1). On the West Coast, Dual Ch. Chance's National Velvet, CD, was also a Canadian show champion, and the dam of five show champions carrying the Heathero kennel name of her owner, Jean Althaus Metzler. Jean also owned a litter sister, which became American and Canadian Ch. Chance's Lucky Lady.

2). In New England, Al Rost's Dual Ch. Glascott's Scottish Majesty produced five show champions. Among them was the Best in Show dog, Am. & Can. Gerdon's Ambrose Hobkirk, Am. & Can. CD (Salter).

3). A litter brother of National Velvet was show champion Bonnie's Mac's Macgeowls, CD (Blasser). He sired six show champions, two Dual champions, both of which became top producers.

a). One was Dual Ch. MacGeowls MacDougal which became the foundation stud for the Tomarcan Kennels of John Ansley. One of

MacDougal's daughters, Ch. Stumpy Acres Kadon Katie, is the dam of two well known current producers, Ch. Rockaplenty's Miss Kitty and Ch. Rockaplenty's Gunsmoke.

b). The other was Dual Ch. Glenraven Autumn Smoke, trained and owned by Eric Backman. Smoke sired ten show champions, among them Ch. Afternod Penny, Ch. Agaru Smokey Souchong, Ch. Page's M'Lord Royal Scot, Ch. Wilscot Black Granite.

The greatest winning Gordon Setter of his time, and the first to win Best in Show repeatedly, was a double grandson of Lucky Chance—you all know of him, Ch. Legend of Gael, CD (Ann Tessler Rich and Mrs. Cheever Porter).

The Putchat family were active participants in all Gordon Setter Club events, and could always be found helping out at shows and trials. Nathan served on the Board and became club President in 1959.

All this came to an end when poor health forced Nathan to greatly curtail his activities. Today, son Bruce is a busy Veterinarian at the family home in Pennsylvania.

Sam and Katherine (Kit) Christine (1950-   ) Hacasak, (Pennsylvania)

In the late 1950's the Christines built a striking modern home and kennel on a large acreage in rural Pennsylvania where they have plenty of room to train their dogs. In keeping with their kennel name of Hacasak, they use Indian tribe names for all their Gordons.

Sam and Kit have always been involved both in showing and field training their dogs.

They chose Windy Hill dogs for their basic stock, with emphasis on the Lucky Chance line and they have stayed with it. To date they have made ten show champions, two Dual Chs. One of their first champions was Windy Hill's Honey B, a foundation bitch. Other familiar names included Ch. Buddy D. of HanMar, Best of Breed, Combined Setter Specialty, 1965; Ch. Hacasak Sioux's Chance, BOS at the 1967 Combined Setter Specialty.

Christines purchased Gordon Hill Lollipop and completed both her field and show titles by 1974.

Their second Dual Champion is Hacasak Jenka's Lowako, CD. His sire, Ch. Hacasak Comanche, is a direct descendant of Lucky Chance. The dam, Jotun's Jenka, was imported from Norway.

One of the better known show dogs and producers of the 1970's was Am. & Can. Ch. Johnston's Highland Storm (Carden). His sire was Hacasak Ecorce, his dam Hacasak Chickasaw, both tracing back to Ch. Hacasak Sioux's Chance.

For many years Sam has been active in the numerous Pointer and Setter field trial clubs of their region, serving on Boards of Governors, as Secretary, American Field reporter, and trial judge.

276

Fld. Ch. MacGeowls Braird, youngest female Field Trial Champion. Gun dog of the year (GSCA Awards), 1969, 1970. Dr. Joel Morris, owner-trainer.

Dual Ch. Hacasak's Lowako, CD (Christine) finishing his show championship under Don Sandberg, 1975.

For the Gordon Setter Club of America he has been a Director, Vice President, and President in 1970 and 1971.

The Christines took over the management of the GSCA Pennsylvania Regional Field Trial and built it into the most important such event in the East. Kit has served as Secretary since 1959 (except for the years 1965-69).

In 1964 Sam and Kit represented the GSCA on the AKC Pointing Breed Field Trial Rules Advisory Committee. She also has handled the taxing jobs of Field Trial chairman and Field Trial Awards Chairman for ten years, retiring in 1981.

Careful planning over the years have given the Gordons of Hacasak a well deserved position of prominence for their superior dual purpose qualities. Fortunately the Christines are actively continuing this breeding program.

Dr. Joel and Barbara Morris (1960-   ) Belmor Farm, Somerville, Va.

In the early 60's the Morrises became converts to Gordon Setters and soon found field trials to their liking. Their first Field Champion was MacGeowl's Braird, born in February 1967. She finished her title in October of 1969, the youngest bitch to do so. In doing so she established new standards in earning points towards the Gun Dog of The Year Award (GSCA).

Belmor is an outstanding example of a small kennel which has developed practical gun dogs that are competitive with other pointing breeds in field trials.

Though limiting themselves to one litter per year, the Morrises have seen their dogs win Gordon Setter Club of America National Field Trial Awards in 15 of the past 16 years. Many of these dogs have placed consistently in American Field trials.

The success of Belmor Gordons has brought welcome publicity to the breed through TV, *Gun Dog Magazine, Hunting Dog Magazine, American Field, AKC Gazette, N.Y. Times, The Gordon Setter: History and Character* by Godfrey Gompertz and Goodall's *How To Train Your Own Gun Dog.*

Five Field Trial Champions, two Amateur Field Champions have resulted from this careful breeding-training program: MacGeowl's Braird, Belmor's Pretty Missy, Belmor's Knight, Belmor's Allspice Ginger and Belmor's Pretty Belle.

Seeing the need for a Gordon Setter Club field trial south of the Mason-Dixon line, Joel and Barbara established a two day fixture held twice a year at Clarksville, Md.

Dr. Morris' well illustrated reviews of field trial activities are a feature of the two most recent Gordon Setter Club Yearbook-Reviews.

Barbara Morris served as GSCA Secretary during 1972 and 1973. In

1979 Dr. Morris was appointed GSCA representative to the AKC Field Trial Rules Advisory Committee.

The first Dual Champion in California set all kinds of records. St. Andrew Gaelic Brogue (Bechler) won his show championship at the age of one year; his CD in three shows; and his Field Trial championship in eight starts—all this by the time he was three and a half years old!

Proving that it was no fluke, he sired a pup named Springset Duncan MacDuff who chopped six months off his sire's performance by finishing both titles when only three years old, PLUS winning an Amateur Field Championship. Bruce Birdwell owned and handled this precocious dog.

Norm and Sue Sorby (1961-   ) Springset, (California)

Sue Sorby purchased her first Gordon when she was seventeen from Alec Laurence (Springset MacDuff, sired by Sun-Yak Medicine Man x Ch. Princess Barbara). Subsequently, when she and Norm turned their thoughts to raising the breed, they again went to Alec and got their foundation bitch, Springset Breeze, CD (Am. & Mex. Ch. Windy Hill's MacGregor x Smoke Signal).

Later they purchased Fld. & Amtr. Fld. Ch. Danny Boy O'Boy and Springset Storm Huntress from Alec. These littermates were sired by Lad Bannockburn x Stormalong Rhythm. Working within these bloodlines ever since, the Sorbys have concentrated on breeding dogs that would excel in the field and at trials.

Their record of wins on the West Coast is impressive. Norm says that 91% of the Gordon entries at field trials are Springset bred or derivative and that they win 58% of the time. In addition, Norm has had a hand in training nearly every Gordon running.

This program has been highly rewarding. During the past 12 years they have bred and trained seven Field champions (including the Dual Ch. Springset Duncan MacDuff). Three of the seven have gained their Amateur Field Championships as well.

In addition to the Dual Champion, the Sorbys have bred five show champions, the most recent finishing in July, 1982. Ch. Springset Yesterday's Dream (B) was sired by Ch. Springset Sanday Piper x Springset Valkyrie Pebertrae.

Springset Gordons have invaded Hawaii with great success under the guidance of GSCA Director, Jim Hustace. Proving adaptable to the unusual terrain, Jim's dogs have walked off with numerous American Field trial placements, including a major one hour open stake won by Springset Kahua Viper (Springset Speeding Bullet x Springset Flying Cloud).

The Sorbys devote their full time to the dogs, raising numerous litters each year, training their own and other people's Gordons for trials and hunting. They think nothing of driving half way across the country with a

The outstanding winner, Fld. Ch. and Amtr. Fld. Ch. Springset Lady Bug, CD, displaying her "Hardware."

vanload of a dozen or more Gordons to support breed field trials. A hectic life, but surely a worthwhile one.

Jack and Barbara Cooper (1973-   ) Shadowmere, (California)

In ten short years the Coopers have had more success with their Gordons than many people have in a lifetime—success, I should add, almost entirely of their own making.

Number one was Springset Lady Bug (Springset Cascade Thunder x Springset Storm Huntress) who began winning at field trials as a puppy in 1974 and concluded by being awarded the GSCA Gun Dog of the Year Award for 1976, 1977, and 1978, with a total of over 80 placements. She completed her career with Amateur and Field championships and a CD.

Number two was Shadowmere Ebony Shane (1974), sired by Ch. Sunburst Ebony Tartan Lad x Mairi Windrock McLean. Field trained as a puppy, he switched careers and became a show dog long enough to finish his championship, then went back to complete his Field championship and earn a CD in 1979-80. He returned to the show ring to garner over 20 Bests of Breed and two group placements, unique for a Dual Champion. In 1982, Shane was Best of Breed at the Pacific Region Specialty from the Veteran's Class.

On top of *that*, Lady Bug, bred to Ch. MacNeal of Ellicott, is the dam of the newest breed Dual Champion and Amtr. Fld. Ch., Shadowmere Scylla Savoy, Gun Dog of the year 1981 for the GSCA. "Corey," co-owned by Bruce Elliott, Barbara Burgess and Jim Thacker, was bred to Ebony Shane in early 1982 and produced a litter which will probably make more history.

For 1981 and 1982 Jack Cooper has served as President of the Gordon Setter Club of America, a job which he sometimes thinks may be even harder than training field dogs!

Field and Dual Champions of Record

(NOTE: In this table where sex is known, D indicates dog, B indicates bitch)

Name of Dog	Owner	Made First Championship
D.C. Loch Ridge Saegryte's Tibby (Ch. Blakeen Talisman x Ch. Blakeen Saegryte)	G. Penterman	1952
Page's Shuriridge Liz	J. Page	1953
D.C. Vagabond Jean of Glentanar (Loch Ridge Major Rogue x Glentanar Birdie)	J. Forbes	1954
Ebony Sultan	G. Penterman	1955
Manheim Pat (D)	J. Weist	1955
Page's Jock MacBess	T. Page	1956
D.C. Windy Hill's Lucky Chance (Ch. Fast's Falcon of Windy Hill x Windy Hill's Double Scotch)	N. Putchat	1955
D.C. Gunbar's Dare Devil, CD (D) (Kipling x Ch. Topsy of Windy Hill)	W. Platt	1955
Shuriridge Humming Bird (B)	G. Penterman	1959
Denida's Bonnie Velvet (B)	S. Gaydos	1963
Glascott's Something Special (B)	R. Healy	1963
Page's Johnny Walker	P. Glass	1964
Page's Daisy MacBess	R. Hyslop	1965

Name	Owner	Year
D.C. MacGeowl's MacDougal (Ch. Bonnie's Macs MacGeowls, CD x MacGeowl's Miss Misty)	J. Ansley	1967
D.C. Glascott's Scottish Majesty (Dual Ch. Windy Hill's Lucky Chance x Breadalbane Copper Coin)	A. Rost	1967
Page's Flash MacBess (D)	H. Czekanski	1967
D.C. Glenraven Autumn Smoke (D) (Ch. Bonnie's Macs MacGeowls x Ch. Gerdon's Bridget Motherwell)	E. Backman	1968
Page's Jake	J. Page	1969
MacGeowl's Braird (B)	J. Morris	1969
D.C. St. Andrew Gaelic Brogue, CD (Ch. Wildfire Black Watch x Ch. St. Andrew's Bonnie Par)	K. Bechler	1967
D.C. Chance's National Velvet, CD (Dual Ch. Windy Hill's Lucky Chance x Fld. Ch. Denida's Bonnie Velvet)	J. Metzler	1965
Page's Andrew of Elmhurst	J. Page	1971
Page's Dinan Rogue	T.K. Rydgren	1972
Page's Janie of Cascades	J. Page	1972
D.C. & Amtr. Fld. Ch. Springset Duncan MacDuff (Dual Ch. St. Andrew Gaelic Brogue, CD x Springset Cascade Showers)	B. Birdwell	1972
D.C. Gordon Hill Lollipop (Ch. Yorkley Hawk of Gunbar x Ch. Gordon Hill Holly, CD)	S.W. Christine, Jr.	1973
D.C. Loch Adair Monarch (Ch. Afternod Gallant x Loch Adair Diana of Redchico)	L. Smith	1967

283

Name	Owner	Year
D.C. Wymore's Sean MacCumhal, CD (Ch. Braun MacCumhal of Brookview x Sangerfield Bonnie)	R. Young	1971
D.C. Hacasak Jenka's Lowako, CD (Ch. Hacasak Comanche x Jotun's Jenka)	S.W. & K. Christine	1975
Springset Kilsythe Circe (B)	T. Griffin	1977
D.C. Ben-Wen's Scottee MacDuff (D) (Lochaber Shawnee Macqueen x Ben Wen's Ginger Snap)	W. Donato	1973
Fld. & Amtr. Fld. Ch. Springset Lady Bug, CD	J. & B. Cooper	1976
Fld. & Amtr. Fld. Ch. Danny Boy O'Boy	N. Sorby	1978
Amtr. Fld. Ch. Belmor's All Spice Ginger (B)	D'Amico	1979
D.C. Shadowmere Ebony Shane, CD (Ch. Sunburst Ebony Tartan Lad x Mairi Windrock McLean	J. & B. Cooper	1977
Springset Little Black Fox (D)	Sorby/Hebein	1979
Springset Charger	T. Griffin	1980
Fld. & Amtr. Fld. Ch. Springset Crusader	S.T. Morrison	1980
D.C. Shadowmere Scylla Savoy (B) (Am./Can./Bda. Ch. MacNeal of Ellicott x Fld. and Amtr. Fld. Ch. Springset Lady Bug, CD	Elliott/Burgess Thacker	1981
Fld. & Amtr. Fld. Ch. Belmor's Knight	A. Sumner	1981
Belmor's Pretty Missy	J. Morris	1981
Springset Tomahawk	Lehan/Sorby	1981
Belmor's Pretty Mister	J. Morris	1981

Name of Dog	Sex	Birth Date	Name of Owners	First Title	Second Title
Loch Ridge Saegryte's Tibby	F	1947	George Penterman	1952 Field	1955 Show
Vagabond Jean of Glentanar (Can.)	F	1947	James Forbes (Can.)	1954 Field	1955 Show
Windy Hill's Lucky Chance	M	1954	Nathan Putchat	1955 Show	1959 Field
Gunbar Dare Devil, CD	M	1952	Willard Platt	1955 Show	1959 Field
Glascott's Scottish Majesty	F	1960	Al and Edna Rost	1962 Show	1967 Field
St. Andrew Gaelic Brogue, CD	M	1966	Keith Bechler	1967 Show	1970 Field
MacGeoul's MacDougal	M	1964	John Ansley	1967 Field	1970 Show
Chance's National Velvet, CD	F	1963	R. Althaus and J. Metzler	1965 Show	1971 Field
Glenraven Autumn Smoke	M	1965	Eric Bachman	1968 Field	1971 Show
Springset Duncan MacDuff	M	1970	Bruce Birdwell	1972 Field 1973 Am. Field	1973 Show
Gordon Hill Lollipop	F	1964	Sam W. Christine, Jr.	1973 Field	1974 Show
Loch Adair Monarch	M	1966	Leonard Smith	1967 Show	1974 Field
Wymore's Sean MacCumhal, CD	M	1968	Ron Young	1971 Show 1971 CD	1975 Field
Hacasak Jenka's Lowako, CD	M	1969	S.W. and K. Christine	1975 Field 1979 CD	1975 Show
Ben-Wen's Scottee MacDuff	M	1970	William Donato	1973 Show	1976 Field
Shadowmere Ebony Shane, CD	M	1974	Jack and Barbara Cooper	1977 Show 1980 CD	1979 Field
Shadowmere Scylla Savoy	F	1977	Bruce Elliott, Barbara Burgess, James Thacker	1981	1982 Show, Amtr. Fld.

Field Trials For Gordon Setters

AKC Licensed — Gordon Setter Club Member Club Allentown, PA —
three per year
Clarksville, MD — two per year
Yaphank, L.I., NY — three per year
Winemac, IN — one per year
Des Plaines, IL — one per year
California — three per year with three separate committees and chairmen
— locations and date vary

AKC Sanctioned — GCSA Member Club

Mansfield, GA — two per year

AKC Licensed — Licensed Club

Tartan Gordon Setter Club — Enfield, CT — two per year
Paumanauk Gordon Setter Club — Yaphank, L.I., NY — two per year

AKC Sanctioned — Sanctioned Club

Gordon Setter Club of Hawaii — Honolulu, HI — two per year

Field Trials Run under Rules of THE AMERICAN FIELD

Mid-America Gordon Setter Field Trial Club — one per year
    Gordon Setter Shooting Dog Championship and Derby Classic
Mid-Atlantic Gordon Setter Field Trial Club — two per year
Gordon Setter Field Trial Club of Northern California — two per year—
    Alec Laurence Memorial Shooting Dog Classic (for Gordons)
Gordon Setter Club of Hawaii — two per year
As of 1982, this club will run AKC recognized trials.

17

The Gordon Setter
in Obedience

IN ITS INFANCY Obedience work was classified under Field Trials by the American Kennel Club. This was in 1933. The three degrees (CD, CDX and UDT) were established with Tracking included in the UD title. Instead of being called *Trials,* these exercises were referred to as *Tests,* and as an activity for the general public they caught on rather slowly. Nobody was slower to espouse this innovation than the Gordon Setter fraternity.

In 1936 the AKC established a separate department for Obedience and while routines are much the same today, down through the years various exercises have been modified or transposed and scoring systems revised.

The meteoric career of a Cleveland, Ohio, Gordon Setter owned by George Dixon, Ch. Timberdoodle Dan of Avalon (1938) was a high point for Gordon Setters, even to this day. Always handled by his owner, Dan easily completed his show championship and in 1941 Dan won his UDT. This made him the first Gordon to win both titles, and in addition, it made a Gordon Setter one of the first breeds to win both titles. By 1982, *no* other Gordon had won a UDT title.

Dan, a versatile and talented gun dog, was entered in Retriever water trials and won! After this, Setters were excluded from these trials.

When activities involving dogs began after the War, one of the first CD Gordons recorded was in 1946—Barnage Highland Chloe, owned by J. D. Rogers.

Ch. Timberdoodle Dan of Avalon. First advanced degree holder in US, first and only UDT (as of 1982). Owner-trainer, George Dixon (c. 1941).

Ch. Sangerfield Sports Penny, Am. Can. CD, Am. T. First Gordon bitch to win Tracking Degree (1973). The second T degree in breed history. Ken and Joan Wohlpart, owners-trainers.

Kirkaldy's Iowa Summer. First Gordon bitch to win UD. Owner-trainer, Linda Sanders (1975).

The next year Muriel Clement started a trend for her Gordon Hill Kennels by putting a CD on her first Gordon, Ch. Heslop's Burnvale Bonnie. This was the start of a chain of Obedience titles on Gordon Hill dogs continuing up to the present.

The same year another novice breeder, Mrs. Vincent Wilcox, took her first show champion foundation bitch, Ch. Wilson's Corrie, to her CD, a first for this kennel as well.

In 1948 there was a grand total of three CDs earned, including the first one on the west coast. This was Idolizin' Ida, handled by Ann Laurence, daughter of the well known Gordon breeder, Alec Laurence.

For the next 22 years an average of four CDs were earned each year. By 1970 things improved somewhat and by 1978, 38 were recorded. The total for 1981 is an impressive 36, while for the first six months of 1982 there were 24 CDs and 3 CDX, showing increased activity.

From the first, however, advanced work seemed to be avoided. Perhaps this is not so surprising. Obedience work as it came out of World War II was based on coercion. Usually taught by former K-9 Corps. trainers, they used the same rigorous methods. There was an excuse for this in training War dogs. Lives were at stake, not just points towards a title. Only certain working breeds were used, those which could accept the necessarily tough routine and who could learn exceptionally fast.

When these instructors began working with a civilian group of pet owners they soon realized their methods were too drastic.

Slowly a new approach became recognized, not as sissy stuff but as a legitimate tool for all breeds. Motivation to please, encouragement and rewards, proved far more successful with the dogs and more enjoyable for the owners. Trainers have turned into professionals, holding schools and seminars for aspiring owners. As a result, more and more owners dare to venture past the relatively calm and gentle CD routine to the more demanding advance work.

Once considered a tool solely for remedying personality problems in dogs, Obedience has gradually emerged as a sport where intelligent, well behaved dogs can excel. It is welcomed as one more field of activity open to any purebred dog, show quality or not. Intense, competitive trialing appeals to a few participants but Obedience is more widely acknowledged as an outlet for dog and owner to have fun, do well and enjoy friends.

Let it be said, however, (and your author speaks from dismal experience) that a poor teacher is worse than none. Put another way, a good Obedience book is better than an inept instructor.

Much training can be done alone (with a book) if no good training classes are available. The fun of being with others is a big part of Obedience work, no question, also there is the stimulus to make the most of your lessons. But the harm done by a goofy trainer is something that cannot be undone and could ruin your dog.

Scenes from the first obedience trials held with the Gordon Setter Club Specialty in Ohio, 197
The Long Sit is breaking up as curiosity gets the better of some contestants. . . .

Only three stalwarts are left . . . .

Exercise over! All very humorous to the spectators. Of the 17 entries, three qualified. Family re
unions are demoralizing, obviously.

Participation in this sport by Gordon Setter owners has grown steadily and this can be attributed to the fact that there are more and better trainers, and more and better dogs.

Not until 1958 did a second CDX Gordon appear (see chart). After another dry spell, we find one in 1964 and one each in 1969, 1970 and 1971. The second UD title was not won until 1972. That year there were also four CDX. The first Tracking Degree was won in 1973 since its separation from the UD title of the 1940's.

By 1976 on a percentage-of-registration basis the breed was ahead of Irish Setters, Springers, Shorthairs, Brittanys, Dobermans and Poodles!

Of all the titles, Tracking is the least sought after, perhaps because there are limited opportunities to take tests. Gordons really like to track and do it instinctively when hunting, locating their "lost" owners this way. As of 1982 only seven "T" degrees have been won.

Obedience buffs in the know claim that the best time to train a Gordon for Tracking is before any other form of training is instituted. The idea is that the heeling exercises, or in the case of a field dog, the strong emphasis on looking for birds by upper air scent, not foot trailing, inhibits the freedom a dog needs to enjoy tracking.

The institution by the American Kennel Club of an Obedience title Championship is encouraging continued involvement of dogs with their titles. Possibly the Gordon is not the best for this high powered competition but it is challenging to have the title there to aim at.

Howell Book House publishes many books on Obedience covering every phase:

Complete Book of Dog Obedience	Saunders
Dog Training for Kids	Benjamin
Go Find! Training Your Dog To Track	Davis
Koehler Method of Dog Training	Koehler
Koehler Method of Open Obedience	Koehler
Koehler Method of Utility Dog Training	Koehler
Novice, Open & Utility Courses	Saunders
Guide to Successful Dog Training	Pearsall
Training Your Dog to Win Obedience Titles	Morsell
Training Your Dog, the Step-by-Step Manual	Volhard and Fisher

Gordon Setter
Advanced Obedience Title Holders

1941	Ch. Timberdoodle Dan of Avalon (D) Dixon	UDT
1958	Blarneystone's Black Beauty (B) McGlenn	CDX
1964	Afternod Zealot (D) VanderVliet	CDX

Bob Zak with Ch. Idlenot's Lady Guinevere, CD (1973), owner-trainer. Excellent photo showing the amount of effort involved on the part of the dog.

Karl Reimer, owner-trainer, with Am. Can. Ch. Inwood Meadow Rue (B), Am. UD, Can. CDX. First Am. *show champion* to win a UD.

Tomarcan Devon's Joy Ruffles, CDX-T (1977), shown with Sami Simons. Owner-trainer, Martha Kuhn. This photo also shows the strength involved by the dog.

The number one Gordon Setter in obedience since 1980 is Alistair Meadow Melody (F) 2/77. She is the first Gordon to hold UD degrees in US and Canada, plus a Can. OTCH. She is a member of a winning Scent Hurdle Race Team that is undefeated in US and Can. and a member of an award winning parade unit since 1979. Her dam is a record holder as well: Am. Can. Ch. Inwood Meadow Rue, UD, Can. CDX, is the first show champion UD bitch.

Melody won her titles with excellent scores:
   Am. CD — 3 shows — average 194
   Can. CD — 3 shows — average 196
   Am. CDX — 4 shows — average 193
   Can. CDX — 3 shows — average 194
   Am. UD — 8 shows — average 190
   Can. UD & Can. OTCH — 5 shows — average 190.
Owner-trainer, Jan Hofer, White Bear Lake, Minn.

Rockaplenty's Zetland Codger, shown as a young pup in training for his Tracking Degree. He won this at age of 7½ months, the youngest ever. Owner-trainer, Bruce Stiftel (1981).

293

1970	Maze's Autumn Harvest (B) Zebrowski	CDX
1971	Blackwatch Hickory Heather (B) Summers	CDX
1972	Ch. Sutherland Ullapool Piper (B) Green	CDX
	Viking Hill's Kimberwicke (B) Kronheim	CDX
	Steelawae Wildfire Weesmokee (D) Steele	UD
1973	Ch. Sangerfield Sports Penny (B) K. & J. Wohlpart	Am. & Can. CD,T
	Ch. Briarpatch Criss Cross (D) Ogilvie	UD
1975	Kirkaldy's Iowa Summer (B) Sanders	UD
	Am. & Can. Ch. Jock The Scot of Karolly (D) O. Reimer	Can. CDX, Am. UD
	Ch. Oak Ridge Magic Marker (B) Herschler	CDX
	Galadriel Lady of Lothlorien (B) Yund	UD
	Briarpatch's Black Sambo (D) Ferguson	CDX
	Camelot's Highland Piper (D) Barker	CDX
	Hickory Smoke Sanda MacInnes (B) Summers	CDX
	Wilscot Mithrandir (D) Israel	CDX
1977	Pacesetter Jakob of Savoy (D) Dunham	UD
	Petty's Scottish Samantha (B) Wright	CDX
	Tomarcan Devon's Joy Ruffle (B) Kuhn	CDX,T
	Am. & Can. Ch. Inwood Meadow Rue (B) K. Reimer	Can. CDX, Am. UD
	Rockaplenty's Through The Rye (B) Clark / Rodenhauser	CDX
1978	Ch. Bluemeco's Gaelic Gillian (B) Van Giffen	Am. & Can. CDX
	MacMarlen's Abecedarian (B) Everett	CDX
	Ch. Rockaplenty's Tarragon Vee (B) Stringham	CDX
	Howling Banshee 'N Earnest (B) M. & T. Earnest	CDX
	Ch. Braemar's Ballater of Savoy (D) Dunham	UD
	Bydand Wildfire (B) R. & G. Larson	CDX
	Highland's Gaelic Gideon (D) Davis	UD
	Ch. Linden Vegas MacDuff (D) Sanders	UD
	Ch. Newkirk's Black Bart (D) Staatz	UD
	Ch. Ferguson's Birnam Wood Heather (B) Bates	CDX,T
1979	Stilmeadow's Royal Rosalyn (B) Wright	CDX
	Ch. Berridale's Scottish Gynn (B) Gear	CDX
	Our Alladin of Heather's Lass (D) Austin	CDX
1980	Sevshun's April MacBride (B) Pond/Schultz	CDX
	Ch. Sangerfield Black Dawn (B) Mowbray	CDX,T
	Alistair Meadow Melody (B) Hofer	Am. & Can. UD Can.OTCH.

Ch. Chapparal Ace's High (Mathies/Sanders). Highest Scoring Dog In Trial at the GSCA Pacific Specialty, San Rafael, Ca. 9/13/1980. Handler-owner, Linda Sanders.

	Ch. Clansman Merriment of Savoy (B) Dunham	CDX
	Birnam Wood Runaway Sam (D) Bates	CD,T
	Casey Brodie of Oliphant (D) Wheeler	CDX
	Ch. Briarpatch Ovation (D) DeLamerens	CDX
1981	Gordon Hill Rob Roy MacGregor (D) Lesiow	CDX
	Ch. Tarbaby's Cuss of Cabin Creek (B) Kuhn	CD,T
	Ch. Blackader's Blaze (D) W. & D. Ladkau	CDX
	Bonnie's Black Tartan (B) Crownsberry	UD
1981	Atascosa Pathfinder (D) Kenny	CDX
	Steve's Gift of Love (D) J. & S. Bristow	UD
	Rockaplenty's Zetland Codger (D) Stiftel	T
	Tri-Sett Daydream Shadow (B) J. Thomas	CDX
	Am. & Can. Ch. Scottland's C.B. Lark's Angel (B) K. McGuire	CDX
	Standishes Black Magic (D) Standish	CDX
1982	Ch. Black Anvil Amy of Gordon Hill (B) E. Gordon and M. Clement	CDX
	Am. & Can. Ch. Rockaplenty's Real McCoy C. Robinson	CDX
	Ch. Stilmeadows Xceptional Lady (B) L. Simon	CDX
	Am. & Can. Ch. Scottland's Martha Custis B. Craft	CDX

18

The Gordon Setter Club of America, Inc.

THE GORDON SETTER has always had staunch supporters though its popularity has fluctuated considerably.

Though the population of Gordons in the United States during the late 1800's was small, a breed club was formed, and it became a charter member of the newly-established American Kennel Club.

The membership was active: it wrote the first American standard for the breed, held a couple of field trials, and supported various shows. Reorganized in 1892, this club continued until about 1908.

For the next 15 years the breed population dropped to a handful, and no club represented the Gordon Setter.

But, starting in 1924 when Mr. Inglee began his restoration of the breed, a club was formed. The membership lost no time writing a new standard and by-laws. Field trials were instituted, and by the late 1930's the breed was having considerable success both at trials and at bench shows. World War II stopped this momentum, as it did for the dog game in general.

From 1940-1945 club activities were limited but the GSCA Annual Meeting was held each year at the Westminster Show, war or no war. The breed column in the *American Kennel Gazette,* begun in the 20's, was the strong thread which held the dwindling membership together. William Cary Duncan, a playwright, produced a column full of humor, news and enthusiasm for the Gordon. A man of many talents, Mr. Duncan had

Group of officers and committee members at the home of Dave Cook for the Summer Board Meeting, 1974. Back row, left: Gerry Windus, Dick Corcoran, Charles Levy, Bill Miller, Dr. Willis Kittleman, Tom Bocking. Left, second row: Bill Schultz and below him, Dave Cook. Seated, top row: Jack Page, Katherine Jones, Ellie Cook, Kay Miller. Front row: Phyllis Lawreck, Margaret Bocking, Fred Itzenplitz.

1954 Parent Club officers at the Spring field trial. Every one with an entry! Left: John T. (Jake) Poisker (then Club President, currently Honorary Member; Jane Penterman, Field Trial Sec'y.; Jean Look, club Sec'y.; Marion Wilcox, Treas.; Margot Bradbury, Newsletter Editor; John O. (Jack) Page, Director; and kneeling, Harold Sydney, Vice-President; George Penterman, Field Trial chairman.   *Shafer*

written a score of Broadway musicals between 1911 and 1929. Her served as a Director of the American Kennel Club in 1927 and he faithfully turned out a column until his death in 1941.

Highlights of the War Years, 1940-1945

1940: The Annual GSCA Specialty was held at North Westchester show with 24 Gordons. In September the first club yearbook ever was distributed. Dated 1939, made up of 50 pages, it covered the breed in the United States from colonial days.

1941: Charles T. Inglee (Inglehurst Kennels) died in April. He is considered to have been the savior of the breed in America.

1942: The effects of the War were being felt. For the year, only 179 Gordon Setter show entries were made. Yearly registration dropped to 212. Breed standing was 40th place (higher than we have ever been since!) and the bank balance of the club was $357.22.

1944: Statistics were published which revealed that of the 45 dog shows held between May and September, only 12 had a Gordon entry and the largest number at any show was seven.

By the end of 1945 dog activities had made an astonishing resurgence, while 250 Gordons were registered that year.

The Gordon Setter standard was revised, primarily to increase the size and weight limitations.

Highlights, 1946-1960

In 1946 the club held two Specialties, both in the east. One had 47 entries, the other 48—surprising, considering how few Gordons there were at this time.

By 1947 activity had surged, the club had 57 members, and Miriam Steyer Mincieli (Milestone Kennels) was Club Secretary. She instituted a monthly club newsletter which became the backbone of the Gordon Setter Club and has continued all these years with only a few months missing.

Annual Awards were renewed in 1948, and the beautiful 1½ oz. sterling silver medallion given to champions owned by club members was a treasure. In 1979, because of the enormous expense involved, this was discontinued and a smaller bronze medal with a new design replaced it.

The first Club sponsored Field Trial since the 1930's was held in the fall of 1949 and was an instant hit. Since then trials have been held without interruption, and now a total of 26 per year are scheduled.

Membership grew to the point where having elections only by those present at the Annual Meeting in February was deemed not to be representative. A new system of mail balloting was put into effect in 1955.

The first Combined Setter Specialty, the brain child of Dr. Wolfgang

Casper, took place in February of 1960, the day before Westminster. There was an entry of 60 English Setters, 40 Gordons and 85 Irish.

1960-1982

1962: The breed standard was revised once again, making it more detailed and dealing with the subject of solid red Gordons, long a sore subject. The Club had 237 members, and breed registrations for the year were 274.

1963: A second modest-sized yearbook was published in soft cover. It reviewed briefly the years from 1940 to 1960.

In 1964 the club became incorporated, and its constitution was revised.

Ralph Mace (Mace's) club member for many years, was found murdered. His involvement with the breed dated back to the early 1900's and in his heyday he had upwards of 300 Gordons at once. He left the club a large collection of color slides and albums of photos of his dogs, but because he died without heirs, and the lawyers could not have cared less about boxes of old pictures, it took considerable effort by Pete Campbell, Club Director, to rescue them.

Working Certificates were proposed for the first time in 1966. This idea caused lively controversy and not until 1981 was a format developed that got tentative approval.

A third yearbook, covering 1960 to 1966 was published, this one hard cover and more comprehensive with almost 100 pages.

The membership ate up this yearbook so a fourth edition, for 1966-1969, expanded to 175 pages and costing $3.50, was printed.

The fifth edition, expanded to 250 pages, covered 1970-72, and the sixth and most elaborate edition appeared in 1979, covering 1973-1977. Much of this lovely book presented photos in color making it quite the most beautiful Gordon Setter book ever printed. This climaxed the series created by Jean Look, George Pugh, Anita Lustenberger and Fred Itzenplitz. Many members contributed key articles to each edition covering the various aspects of GSCA activity.

During the 1970's regional specialties proliferated, supported by groups which remained under the wing of the parent club. Soon there were three in California; one each in Washington State, Ohio, Illinois, Pennsylvania, New York and Georgia. By 1981 Colorado and Minnesota had joined the ranks, and the GSC of Michigan was holding qualifying shows.

In 1974 the Board of Directors of the club began a delightful tradition of holding a summer weekend work session at an officer's home. The first was held at then-President Dave Cook's beautiful farm in central New York. This event has moved around the country and most recently was held in California.

300

Louise and George Pugh, honored guests at the dinner following the 1982 GSCA Specialty in Ohio. With them Dave Cook, and Jack Jones, far right, both former club Presidents.

Muriel Clement, current AKC Delegate, who has devoted her efforts as a club member since 1945 to being supportive of both the Gordon Setter Club of America and the TarTan Gordon Setter Club. She has served almost continuously in some official capacity to the ultimate benefit of both clubs.

Gordon Setter Club of America President, 1981 and 1982, Jack Cooper (Calif.), addressing the dinner group in Ohio, 1982.

RULES FOR THE GORDON SETTER CLUB OF AMERICA ANNUAL FIELD TRIAL AWARDS

The Gordon Setter Club of America, Inc., will annually make the following awards for field trials:

Gun Dog of the Year - for points earned in AKC gun dog, limited gun dog, amateur gun dog, all age, limited all age, and amateur all age stakes, and their American Field and Amateur Field Trial Club of America equivalents.

Derby Dog of the Year - for points earned in derby stakes only.

Puppy Dog of the Year - for points earned in puppy stakes only.

To receive an award, the dog must be owned or co-owned by a GSCA member, and only those points earned while a member shall count.

The awards are made for points earned on a calendar year basis, January 1 through December 31.

Only trials licensed or sanctioned by the AKC or the Amateur Field Trial Clubs of America (American Field) shall count toward the awards. Results from the National Shoot to Retrieve Association and the National Bird Hunters Association sanctioned trials do not count.

Application for Awards

To earn an award, application must be made on the form provided on the back of this sheet. All information requested must be provided. The burden of proof for the awards shall be on the person submitting the application. The person applying shall list the issue of the AKC Gazette or American Field and the page number on which the results appear.

In the event that results do not appear in these publications, a letter from the field trial secretary certifying the results must be included in the application. The issue and page number on which the advertisement for the trial (American Field) appeared must be included.

Calculating Points

Points are calculated in the following manner for all stakes:

          First Place   - 5 points multiplied by the number of dogs defeated
          Second Place - 3 points multiplied by the number of dogs defeated
          Third Place   - 2 points multiplied by the number of dogs defeated
          Fourth Place - 1 point multiplied by the number of dogs defeated

Extra credit is given for the degree of difficulty of the stake. Multiply the result from above by the following factors:

Gordon Setter Only (AKC or AF)	1.0
Setters Only, or more than two breeds restricted from entry	1.5
Restricted Breed, one or two breeds restricted	2.0
AKC all breed stakes	2.5
American Field all breed stakes	3.0

Credit is also given for the length of the stake, under the following guidelines. Multiply the results from above by the factors below:

One hour or more all breed stake	2.0
One hour or more Gordon Only or Setter Only stake	1.5

Complete the form on the reverse side and return by March 15 to the Field Trial Awards Chairman:

          James S. Thacker
          125 Moore Drive
          Franklin, OH 45005

302

APPLICATION FOR GSCA FIELD TRIAL AWARD FOR 19____

Circle one: Gun Dog   Derby   Puppy

Name of dog _____ Date of birth _____

AKC # _____ FDSB # _____ Name of owner _____

Sire _____ Dam _____

Breeder _____

Host Club	Date	Stake	Sanc. Body	Breeds	Place-ment	No. of entry	Points	Results Published	AUDIT

Abbreviations: GD – Gun Dog   G – Gordon
               AA – All Age   S – Setters
               Op – Open   R – Restricted
               Am – Amateur   A – All Breed

I certify that the reported results are accurate to
the best of my knowledge.

Signed _____

Address _____

Date _____   _____

303

AWARDS

The Gordon Setter Club of America, Inc., provides several Awards in recognition of various accomplishments by Gordon Setters owned or co-owned by club members in good standing. Only titles granted by the American Kennel Club or the Canadian Kennel Club may be used in claiming an award.

Annual Awards are based on the calendar year, January 1 through December 31. Deadline for applications for each year's Annual Awards is March 15 of the following year.

Club medals and Certificates of Achievement may be applied for at any time after a Certificate of Title has been received, and must be applied for within one year after publication of a title.

Awards will be presented at GSCA spring Specialty shows, to be announced.

The owner or co-owner is responsible for making application for any award. An application form,* with instructions, is on the back of this sheet.

CLUB MEDALS and CERTIFICATES OF ACHIEVEMENT

A Club Medal is awarded for the attainment of each of the following titles:
CHAMPION, FIELD CHAMPION, AMATEUR FIELD CHAMPION, UTILITY DOG, and TRACKING DOG.

A Certificate of Achievement is awarded for the attainment of each of the following titles:
DUAL CHAMPION, COMPANION DOG, COMPANION DOG EXCELLENT, and UTILITY DOG, TRACKING.

A Certificate of Achievement is awarded to any Gordon Setter which wins BEST IN SHOW, where the show is open to all breeds.

A Certificate is also awarded to any Gordon which is granted a Champion title, Field or Show, from both AKC and CKC.

ANNUAL AWARDS

Bench Show

BENCH GORDON OF THE YEAR. Awarded on a Calendar Year basis, to the Gordon Setter accumulating the highest number of points from Group and Best in Show placements, using the "Phillips System."

BEST OF OPPOSITE SEX TO BENCH GORDON OF THE YEAR. Determined in the same manner, and for the same time span, as Bench Gordon of the Year.

BEST OF BREED FOR THE YEAR. Awarded to the Gordon which has placed over the largest number of Gordons in point shows during the year.

BEST OF OPPOSITE SEX TO BEST OF BREED FOR THE YEAR. Determined in the same manner as the Best of Breed for the year.

Field Trial

GUN DOG OF THE YEAR. Awarded to the Gordon which has accumulated the highest number of points, according to a schedule available with the application for the Award, for placements in Gun Dog and All Age stakes.

DERBY OF THE YEAR. Awarded to the Gordon which has accumulated the highest number of points for placements in Derby stakes, according to a schedule available with the award application.

PUPPY OF THE YEAR. Awarded to the Gordon which has accumulated the highest number of points for placements in Puppy stakes, according to a schedule available with the award application.

Obedience

HIGH SCORING NOVICE OBEDIENCE DOG OF THE YEAR. Awarded to the Gordon which has the highest average for its first three qualifying scores in either Novice A or Novice B obedience trial classes.

HIGH SCORING ADVANCED OBEDIENCE DOG OF THE YEAR. Awarded to the Gordon which accumulates the highest number of points, using the "Shuman System," while competing in Open or Utility obedience trial classes.

Other Awards

STUD DOG OF THE YEAR. Awarded to the Gordon Setter Dog which has sired the largest number of Champions to finish during the year. Both Field and Show titles, granted by either AKC or CKC, to be used.

BROOD BITCH OF THE YEAR. Awarded to the Gordon Setter Bitch which has produced the largest number of Champions to finish during the year. Both Field and Show titles, granted by either AKC or CKC, to be used.

JUNIOR SHOWMAN OF THE YEAR. (Note: This is the only Award for personal accomplishment offered by the Club. Awarded to the club member who has accumulated the highest number of points, while showing a Gordon in Junior Showmanship competition, according to the schedule given on the reverse of this sheet.
(Applicants for this Award should keep complete records of their placements and the number competing in each class in which they have shown during the year, and submit these records on the application form.)

Exception: Please use the attached special form for Field Trial Awards. If the Field Trial Award form is missing, request another from the Awards Chairman or the Field Trial Awards chairman (addresses on the back of this sheet.)

304

GORDON SETTER CLUB OF AMERICA - AWARD APPLICATION

Please use this form to apply for all GSCA Awards.* Applications for Obedience Annual Awards and Certificates of Achievement should be sent to the Obedience chairman; all other applications* to the Awards Committee Chairman. (Request additional forms from these chairmen, or use photocopies.)

Applicants for Club Medals and Certificates of Achievement for titles received need not fill out the form in detail, but should include the AKC or CKC publication data, and/or a photocopy of the title certificate.

Award Applied for _____ Calendar Year _____

Dog's Name _____ Sex _____ AKC No. _____

Owner's Name _____ Breeder _____

Owner's Address _____

		BENCH						OBEDIENCE/JR. SHOWMANSHIP				AKC	
Date	Location	BOB	BOS	Group Place	BIS	Number Defeated		Class	Score or Placement	Number Defeated		Gazette Month	Page

Date joined GSCA _____ SIGNED _____ Date _____

Point Schedule for Junior Showmanship Award:
  1st Place - 4 points, multiplied by number of competitors defeated in the class.
  2nd Place - 3 points,   "   "   "   "   "   "   "   "   "
  3rd Place - 2 points,   "   "   "   "   "   "   "   "   "
  4th Place - 1 point,   "   "   "   "   "   "   "   "   "

Awards Committee

  Chairman - Mary Whorton, Rt 1, Box 179, Colvin Circle, Gadsden, AL 35901; ph 205-442-6493.
  Field Trial Awards - Jim Thacker, 125 Moore Drive, Franklin, OH 45005; ph 513-746-0022.
  Obedience Awards - Louise Mowbray, Rt 3, Box 207, Advance, NC 27006; ph 919-998-2264.

*Exception: Please use the attached special form for Field Trial Awards, and return it to the Field Trial Awards chairman. If the form is missing, request one from the Awards Chairman or the Field Trial Awards chairman.

In 1975 the breed and the club lost one of its most active and hardworking member-breeders. Mrs. Vincent Wilcox, known more familiarly as Marion, died in September. Vincent had preceded her in death in 1953. Their Afternod strain had become widely known.

Gordon Setter registrations had been climbing all through the 70's and reached a peak of 1383 in 1976, while club membership rose to over 800 in 1982.

The prestigious Mid-West Specialty set a new record, with an entry of 292, in the spring of 1982.

Health problems beset the dog world. Parvo, finally identified as a new virus, made inroads on the dog population starting in 1978 and in spite of recently developed shots, it is still with us in 1982.

A Committee on Genetic Defects was created within the club to help the membership better deal with the more recent problems.

The club attempts to place unwanted Gordons through appeals made via the Newsletter. As yet no specific facilities have been established to take charge of this effort largely because each breeder tries to care for his own "take-backs" and not too many Gordons find their way to pounds or S.P.C.A.'s.

Annual Awards, which had been created in the early years of the club, have gone through many changes, most of them required by the American Kennel Club. Today, Certificates of Merit are awarded to the nine top dogs. These awards are open only to club members for the year covered and applications must be made by the owners of the contestants.

These awards cover:

Best of Breed Gordon Setter of the Year
Best of Opposite Sex to Best of Breed Gordon Setter of the Year
Bench Gordon Setter of the Year
Best of Opposite Sex to Bench Gordon Setter of the Year
Gordon Setter Gun Dog of the Year
Gordon Setter Derby of the Year
Gordon Setter Puppy (Field Trial) of the Year
Highest Scoring Novice Obedience Gordon Setter of the Year
Highest Scoring Advanced Obedience Gordon Setter of the Year
Junior Showman of the Year

Membership in the Gordon Setter Club is open to all. Applicants need to be sponsored by two active members.

History Highlights
Gordon Setter Club of America, Inc.

Officers

YEAR(S)	PRESIDENT	SECRETARY	TREASURER
1924-25	Frank Burke	Charles Inglee	Hugh MacLaughlin
1926-1929	Donald Fordyce	Charles Inglee	Hugh MacLaughlin
1930-37	Charles Inglee	Hugh MacLaughlin	Dr. A.P. Evans
1938-43	H. MacLaughlin	Donald Fordyce	Dr. A.P. Evans
1944	Charles Allison	George Thompson	(Sec'y-Treas)
1945-46	James M. Mitchell	George Thompson	(Sec'y-Treas)
1947-48	George E. Heslop	Miriam Steyer	(Sec'y-Treas)
1949-50	George Thompson	Virginia Fischer	Joseph Fischer
1951-52	Vincent Wilcox	Virginia Fischer (1951)	Joseph Fischer
1953-54	John Poisker	Jean Look (also 1952)	Marion Wilcox
1955 (3 mo.)	William Dillon	Dorothy Poisker	Marion Wilcox
1955-56	George Penterman	Dorothy Poisker	Marion Wilcox
1957	Nathan Putchat	Margot Bradbury	Marion Wilcox
1958	Willard Platt	Margot Bradbury	John P. Campbell
1959	Willard Platt	Muriel Clement	John P. Campbell
1960-61	Richard Wilcox	Muriel Clement	John P. Campbell
1962-63	John P. Campbell	Muriel Clement	Jean S. Look
1964-65	John Lawreck	Betty Scott	Jean S. Look
1965-66	George S. Pugh	Anita Lustenberger	Jean S. Look
1968-69	David B. Cook	Anita Lustenberger	Jean S. Look
1970	Sam Christine, Jr.	Cheryl Dunham	Jean S. Look
1971	Sam Christine, Jr.	Joyce Ruess	Jean S. Look
1972	William Dwelly	Barbara Morris	Jean S. Look
1973	William Dwelly	Barbara Morris	Phyllis Lawreck
1974	David B. Cook	Kay Monaghan	Phyllis Lawreck
1975	David B. Cook	Kay Miller	Phyllis Lawreck
1976-77	Jack Jones	Nancy Zak	David B. Cook
1978-79	William Schultz	Louise Mowbray	David B. Cook
1980	John O. Page	Jean Lacy	Donald Selle
1981-82	Jack Cooper	Jean Lacy	Donald Selle

Delegates to the American Kennel Club

1924-41	Charles T. Inglee
1941-51	Donald Fordyce
1952-53	Vincent Wilcox, Jr.
1953-55	Joseph Fischer
1956-59	Hugh MacLaughlin
1960-63	Willard Platt
1964-71	John Lawreck
1972-74	George Pugh
1975-	Muriel Clement

Honorary Members

*Cornelius McGlynn
*Hugh MacLaughlin
Miriam Steyer Mincieli

*Amy Reid Knox
John and *Dorothy Poisker
George and Luise Pugh

Mrs. Edna E. Girardot	Jean Sanger Look
*George and Myrtle Heslop	Steve Gaydos
*George Thompson	John O. Page

*Deceased.

Locations of Specialty Shows

Combined Setter Specialty	New York	February
Far West Specialty	California	February
Mid-West Specialty	Ohio	May
Southern California Specialty	California	June
North Country Specialty	Minnesota	June
Northwest Specialty	Washington	July
Mid-Atlantic Specialty	Pennsylvania	August (September)
Northern California Specialty	California	September
Colorado Specialty	Colorado	August
Chicago Specialty	Illinois	October

Member Clubs

Miami Valley Gordon Setter Club — host-Specialty (May) (Ohio)
North Country Gordon Setter Club — host-Specialty (June) (Minnesota)
Gordon Highlanders — host-Specialty (October) (Chicago)

Licensed Specialty Clubs

Tartan Gordon Setter Club — Specialty (Connecticut) (June)
Booster (Maine) (October)
Booster (Massachusetts) (November)
Paumanauk Gordon Setter Club Specialty — Long Island (September)

Boosters

Gordon Setter Club in Michigan — Michigan (March)
Magnolia Gordon Setter Club — Georgia (April)

(Field Trials are listed in chapter 16)

TarTan Gordon Setter Club

This club, the oldest independent, was founded in 1955 by Gordon Setter fanciers in New England and has continually emphasized an "all-around" Gordon.

Spring and Fall field trials with some stakes for Gordons only are held each year and they have stimulated most area breeders and club members to consider field aptitude when planning breedings.

Jack Page, breeder of so many Field Trial champions of the 50's, 60's and 70's, has spurred interested members to assist in conducting Field Days and Clinics.

In the early 1980's several young women club members, notably Pam McLean Backman and Susan DeSilver, have earned many field trial wins.

Obedience has been encouraged by Annual Awards and obedience demonstrations. In the last decade Dorothy Page Whitney has held a series of classes each spring at her home. Gordons in New England have been increasingly successful in advanced obedience competition.

Interest of members in show competition has been focused by the Annual Specialty, plus supported entries at additional shows.

Yearly matches have been held since the late 1950's when they were first held at the homes of Harold Sydney and Muriel Clement in Rhode Island.

Later these well attended social events took place in Connecticut at the homes of Marion Wilcox, Pete and Kay Campbell (Breadalbane), the Chevaliers, or Muriel Clement (now living in that state).

These "Fun Day" events (held in June) have been expanded to include a picnic and full program of field, obedience and show handling clinics taking place at the time-honored field trial grounds, Pelton's Pasture, north of Hartford, Connecticut.

The five present charter members—Carol Chevalier, Muriel Clement, Jack Page, Edith West and Dottie Page Whitney—bear witness to the accomplishments of their many, many fellow members through the years, especially of Marion Wilcox who was such a sparkplug of interest in Gordon Setters for over thirty years, both in New England and the entire U.S.A.

TarTan's other services include a frequent newsletter now named *The Tartan Tidings* initiated in 1955 by Ken Lasher. Susan DeSilver is currently its producer. Tom Isaac has developed a breed Rescue Service, a most important club effort.

Annual Awards are given at a February Annual Dinner and there are several other meetings held at field trials, matches or shows. The many enthusiastic members of the TarTan Gordon Setter Club continue to foster the breeding of Gordon Setters with "Brains, Beauty and Bird Sense."

(The above information was provided by Muriel Clement.)

19

Leading Sires and Dams of the 1950s to 1980s

Compiled by Anita Lustenberger

FOR MANY YEARS Anita's hobby has been keeping records on Gordon Setter title winners. How fortunate we are that she was willing to put it all together for this book!

Anita has been an active member of the Gordon Setter Club of America since 1952, serving as Secretary 1965-1970 and Director 1970-1973. Her kennel name is Joyous.

She earned her MS in Genetic Counseling at Sarah Lawrence and has worked in Laboratory Cytogenetics, Genetic Counseling, birth defects clinics and epidemiological research.

It requires thousands of hours of painstaking effort to compile the champion progeny for the breed's leading producers.

To qualify for entry herein, the minimum champions produced was set at 10 for sires and 6 for dams. The champion progeny listed are up to date as of the 1982 issue of *Pure-bred Dogs—The American Kennel Gazette.* The reader may extend this compilation by adding new champions as produced by the listed dogs. Reference to later issues of the *Gazette,* published monthly by the American Kennel Club, will extend and amplify this listing as long as the official AKC magazine publishes the names of new champions. These continuing studies can be a pleasurable, creative and rewarding activity.

The wise breeder will remember that sheer numbers of champions produced are not necessarily the only criteria for considering a sire or dam a "great" producer. Frequency of matings, outstanding show records, accessibility to certain sires and dams, and other factors have a bearing on the records. A sire or dam may produce several champions from only one litter and never produce another champion; or it may "nick" successfully with one mate and not others. Even repeat matings of the same sire and dam may not duplicate the high quality of progeny born of the first mating; genetic influences may vary from mating to mating of the same parents. The quality of champions, preferably from more than one mate, is the best measure of a stud or dam.

The reader is strongly advised to temper his statistical study with a sound knowledge of breeding principles, good judgment and the fruits of his own experience.

As an author, editor and publisher, I am painfully aware of the occasional error that inevitably creeps into any such complex compilation as follows. While every effort has been made to insure accuracy, the publisher will welcome notice of errors, providing, however, that the correction has been verified by the AKC. The publisher hereby absolves the compiler, Anita Lustenberger, of any errors which may appear. As a geneticist she is a paragon of meticulosity.

—ELSWORTH HOWELL

Wm. P. Gilbert

CH. AFTERNOD ADVOCATE

AKC No. SA 273335-6-65   Whelped 23 April, 1964   Dog
          Owner: R. Noren, WI.   Breeder: G. Windus, NY.

```
                                                    Ch. Lancer of Serlway
                    Ch. EEG's Scotia Nodrog Rettes  Ch. Larrabee's Avalon Beauty
          Ch. Afternod Buchanan                     Loch Ridge Major Rogue
                    Ch. Wilson's Corrie, CD          Loch Ridge Victoria
Ch. Afternod Drambuie                               Ch. Gregorach Fast
                    Ch. Fast's Falcon of Windy Hill Heslop's Burnvale Janet
          Ch. Afternod Sue                          Ch. Scotia Nod's Duncan, CD
                    Afternod Ember of Gordon Hill   Ch. Heslop's Burnvale Bonnie,CD

                                                    Ch. Great Scot of Blakeen
                    Heslop's Burnvale Scot          Heslop's Burnvale Maid
          Ch. Matson's Robin                        Ch. Heslop's Courageous
                    Ch. Heslop's Burnvale Jean      Ch. Heslop's Burnvale Duchess
Ch. Meghan Maguire                                  Ch. Heslop's Courageous
                    Ch. Heslop's Burnvale Laird     Ch. Heslop's Burnvale Duchess
          Fletcher's Scotch Lorelei                 O'Field's Ready Response
                    Kitty Lightfoot                 Heslop's Burnvale Edie
```

Sire of 19 Champions: Out of:

Ch. Idlenot's Colby II   ⎤
                              ⎥   Ch. Idlenot's Satin Doll, CD
Ch. Idlenot's Jobling   ⎦

Ch. Idlenot's Windy Bairn   Idlenot's Shady Lady

Ch. Idlenot's Louisa   ⎤
Ch. Idlenot's Lady Guinevere, CD ⎥   Ebony Lady
Ch. Idlenot's Chinook   ⎦

Ch. Idlenot's Sparky   ⎤
                              ⎥   Ch. MacAlder Dora of Seneca Hill
Ch. Sean of Seneca Hill   ⎦

Ch. Afternod Hecate   Ch. Afternod Kippa

Ch. Bootleg's Anisette
Ch. Afternod Vagabond Rogheath
Ch. Sunbrust Arapahoe, CD
Ch. Sunbrust Cheyenne Autumn]
Ch. Wildfire Manua of Piets
Ch. Idlenot's Black Thistle
Ch. Idlenot's Lille]
Ch. MacAlder Feather
Ch. MacAlder Flame
Ch. MacAlder Ingenue of Chris]

Ch. MacAlder Accent
Afternod Victoria II

HiLaway Dardinella

Ch. Wildfire Willow

Scottland's Deed

MacAlder Beauty

CH. AFTERNOD ALDER

AKC NO. SA 42856-7-63　　　　Whelped 16 April, 1960　　　　Bitch
　Owner: M. Wilcox & C. Stephenson　　　Breeder: Paine

```
                    Ch. EEG's Scotia Nodrog Rettes   Ch. Lancer of Serlway
        Ch. Afternod Buchanan                        Ch. Larrabee's Avalon Beauty
                    Ch. Wilson's Corrie, CD          Loch Ridge Major Rogue
Ch. Afternod Drambuie                                Loch Ridge Victoria
                    Ch. Fast's Falcon of Windy Hill  Ch. Gregorach Fast
        Ch. Afternod Sue                             Heslop's Burnvale Janet
                    Afternod Ember of Gordon Hill    Ch. Scotia Nod's Duncan, CD
                                                     Ch. Heslop's Burnvale Bonnie,CD


                    Ch. Page's MacDonegal II         Page's MacDonegal, CD
        Afternod  Hedemac                            Mace's Old Bessie
                    Afternod Hedera                  Ch. Heslop's Burnvale Piper
Afternod Kalmia                                      Afternod Benbecula
                    Ch. Fast's Falcon of Windy Hill  Ch. Gregorach Fast
        Ch. Afternod Sue                             Heslop's Burnvale Janet
                    Afternod Ember of Gordon Hill    Ch. Scotia Nod's Duncan, CD
                                                     Ch. Heslop's Burnvale Bonnie, CD
```

CH. AFTERNOD ALDER

Dam of 6 Champions: Sired by:

Ch. Afternod Ian Langsam
Ch. Afternod Ivy III
Ch. Afternod Scot of Blackbay, CD
Ch. Afternod Simon   Afternod Fidemac
Ch. Afternod MacAlder Tyr
Can. & US Ch. Afternod Sybilla

CH. AFTERNOD AMBER

AKC No. SA 136538-7-64   Whelped 11 February, 1962   Bitch
Owner: M. Wilcox   Breeder: D. Chevalier

	Ch. EEG's Scotia Nodrog Rettes	Ch. Lancer of Serlway
Ch. Afternod Buchanan		Ch. Larrabee's Avalon Beauty
	Ch. Wilson's Corrie, CD	Loch Ridge Major Rogue
Ch. Afternod Drambuie		Loch Ridge Victoria
	Ch. Fast's Falcon of Windy Hill	Ch. Gregorach Fast
Ch. Afternod Sue		Heslop's Burnvale Janet
	Afternod Ember of Gordon Hill	Ch. Scotia Nod's Duncan, CD
		Ch. Heslop's Burnvale Bonnie, CD

	Ch. Page's MacDonegal II·	Page's MacDonegal, CD
Afternod Hedemac		Mace's Old Bessie
	Afternod Hedera	Ch. Heslop's Burnvale Piper
Ch. Afternod Kate		Afternod Benbecula
	Ch. Fast's Falcon of Windy Hill	Ch. Gregorach Fast
Ch. Afternod Sue		Heslop's Burnvale Janet
	Afternod Ember of Gordon Hill	Ch. Scotia Nod's Duncan, CD
		Ch. Heslop's Burnvale Bonnie, CD

Dam of 6 Champions: Sired by:

Ch. Afternod Karma
Ch. Afternod Kyle of Sutherland
Ch. Afternod Kate II   Ch. Afternod Callant
Ch. Afternod Maud MacKenzie
Ch. Afternod Oliver   Afternod Fidemac
Ch. Afternod Bramble   Afternod Profile of Sark

AFTERNOD BABBIE OF ABERFOYLE

AKC No. SA379184-7-67   Whelped 5 January, 1966   Bitch
     Owner: C. Stephenson   Breeder: W. Chavkin

                                        Ch. EEG's Scotia Nodrog Rettes
          Ch. Afternod Buchanan   Ch. Wilson's Corrie, CD
     Ch. Afternod Drambuie   Ch. Fast's Falcon of Windy Hill
          Ch. Afternod Sue   Afternod Ember of Gordon Hill
Ch. Afternod Callant   Ch. Page's MacDonegal II
          Ch. Afternod Hickory   Afternod Hedera
     Ch. Afternod Woodbine   Ch. Afternod Buchanan
          Ch. Afternod Elgin II   Afternod Ember of Gordon Hill

                                        Page's MacDonegal, CD
          Ch. Page's MacDonegal II   Mace's Old Bessie
     Ch. Afternod Hickory   Ch. Heslop's Burnvale Piper
          Afternod Hedera   Afternod Benbecula
Ch. Afternod Wishbone   Ch. EEG's Scotia Nodrog Rettes
          Ch. Afternod Buchanan   Ch. Wilson's Corrie, CD
     Ch. Afternod Elgin II   Ch. Scotia Nod's Duncan, CD
          Afternod Ember of Gordon Hill Ch. Heslop's Burnvale Bonnie, CD

     Dam of 7 Champions: Sired by:

     Ch. MacAlder Blaze

     Ch. Highlander's MacAlder Brutus

     Ch. MacAlder Collin

     Ch. MacAlder Casey, CD   Ch. Afternod MacAlder Tyr

     Ch. MacAlder Cairn of Goldenrod

     Ch. MacAlder HiLines Cassandra, CD

     Ch. Gordon Hill Tyrelle MacAlder

CH. AFTERNOD CALLANT

AKC No. SA 149901-8-64   Whelped 12 March, 1962   Dog
        Owner: Edith West   Breeder: M. Wilcox

                    Ch. EEG's Scotia Nodrog Rettes   Ch. Lancer of Serlway
        Ch. Afternod Buchanan   Ch. Larrabee's Avalon Beauty
                    Ch. Wilson's Corrie, CD   Loch Ridge Major Rogue
Ch. Afternod Drambuie   Loch Ridge Victoria
                    Ch. Fast's Falcon of Windy Hill   Ch. Gregorach Fast
        Ch. Afternod Sue   Heslop's Burnvale Janet
                    Afternod Ember of Gordon Hill   Ch. Scotia Nod's Duncan, CD
                                                      Ch. Heslop's Burnvale Bonnie, CD

                    Ch. Page's MacDonegal II   Page's MacDonegal, CD
        Ch. Afternod Hickory   Mace's Old Bessie
                    Afternod Hedera   Ch. Heslop's Burnvale Piper
Ch. Afternod Woodbine   Afternod Benbecula
                    Ch. Afternod Buchanan   Ch. EEG's Scotia Nodrog Rettes
        Ch. Afternod Elgin II   Ch. Wilson's Corrie, CD
                    Afternod Ember of Gordon Hill   Ch. Scotia Nod's Duncan, CD
                                                      Ch. Heslop's Burnvale Bonnie, CD

CH. AFTERNOD CALLANT

Sire of 19 Champions: Out of:

Ch. Afternod Bran of Aberfoyle   Ch. Afternod Wishbone

Ch. HiLaways Gregory C Squared   Ch. HiLaways Calopin

Ch. Afternod Maud MacKenzie ⎤
Ch. Afternod Karma   │
                            │   Ch. Afternod Amber
Ch. Afternod Kyle of Sutherland │
Ch. Afternod Kate II   ⎦

Field Ch. Page's Andrew of Elmhurst   Ch. Afternod Gwen Adair

Ch. Stilmeadow's Aragant Alex ⎤
Ch. Stilmeadow's Aragant Alfie │
                               │   Can. & US Ch. Afternod Sybilla
Ch. Stilmeadow's Aragant Angie │
Ch. Stilmeadow's Aragant Aaron ⎦

Ch. Loch Adair Laird   ⎤
Ch. Loch Adair Meg of Sutherland │
Ch. Loch Adair MerriMac   │
Ch. Loch Adair My Jo of Redchico │
                              │   Loch Adair Diana of Redchico
Dual Ch. Loch Adair Monarch   │
Ch. Loch Adair Teo of Thornyburn │
Ch. Wee Jock Adair   │
Ch. Wee Laurie Adair   ⎦

CH. AFTERNOD DRAMBUIE

AKC No. S675528-10-59   Whelped 1 May, 1954   Dog
     Owner: M. Wilcox   Breeder: E. West

	Ch. Lancer of Serlway	Ch. Downside Bonnie of Serlway
Ch. EEG's Scotia Nodrog Rettes		Ch. Valiant Nutmeg of Serlway
Ch. Larrabee's Avalon Beauty		Ch. Larrabee's Pietro
Ch. Afternod Buchanan		Dochfour Beauty
Loch Ridge Major Rogue		Ch. Black Rogue of Serlway
Ch. Wilson's Corrie, CD		Ch. Rita of Avalon, CD
Ch. Loch Ridge Victoria		Ch. Black Rogue of Serlway
		Ch. Rita of Avalon, CD

	Ch. Gregorach Fast	Ch. Ginger
Ch. Fast's Falcon of Windy Hill		Stylish Madame
Heslop's Burnvale Janet		Ch. Heslop's Courageous
Ch. Afternod Sue		Ch. Heslop's Burnvale Duchess
Ch. Scotia Nod's Duncan, CD		Ch. EEG's Scotia Nodrog Rettes
Afternod Ember of Gordon Hill		Ch. Wilson's Corrie, CD
Ch. Heslop's Burnvale Bonnie. CD		Ch. Heslop's Courageous
		Ch. Heslop's Burnvale Duchess

<u>Sire of 21 Champions:</u>   <u>Out of:</u>

Ch. Afternod Angus of Rogheath	
Ch. Afternod Aberdeen	Ch. Afternod Ivy III
Ch. Afternod Angus of Aberfoyle	
Ch. Afternod Abbie of Aberfoyle	Ch. Afternod Wishbone
Ch. Afternod Clove	
Ch. Afternod Curry	Allspice of Redchico
Ch. Afternod Redchico Cutty Sark	
Ch. Gordon Hill Bydand Bonnie	Gordon Hill Happy Chum
Ch. Afternod Cutty Sark	
Ch. Afternod Callant	Ch. Afternod Woodbine
Ch. Afternod Caramel	
Ch. Afternod Advocate	Ch. Meghan Maguire
Ch. Afternod Alder	Afternod Kalmia
Ch. Afternod Amber	Ch. Afternod Kate
Ch. Afternod Anagram	
Ch. Afternod Gallant Adair	
Ch. Afternod Gwen Adair	Loch Adair Diana of Redchico
Ch. Meadow Ridge Ghillie Adair	
Ch. Wee Geordie Adair	
Ch. HiLaway's Calopin	
Ch. HiLaway's Catriona, CD	Gay Bonnie Glascott

AFTERNOD FIDEMAC

AKC No. SA 26283-5-61   Whelped 13, September, 1959   Dog
      Owner: M. Wilcox   Breeder: C. Parsons

                                       Page's MacDonegal, CD
           Ch. Page's MacDonegal II   Mace's Old Bessie
      Afternod Hedemac   Ch. Heslop's Burnvale Piper
           Afternod Hedera   Afternod Benbecula
ternod Sumac   Ch. Gregorach Fast
           Ch. Fast's Falcon of Windy Hill Heslop's Burnvale Janet
      Ch. Afternod Sue   Ch. Scotia Nod's Duncan, CD
           Afternod Ember of Gordon Hill Ch. Heslop's Burnvale Bonnie, CD

                                       Braw Lad of Dendy
           Ch. Great Scot of Blakeen   Juliet of Ardale
      Ch. Milestone Monarch   Ch. Black Rogue of Serlway
           Loch Ridge Reckless Lady   Ch. Blakeen Saegryte
. Afternod Fidelia   Ch. Black Rogue of Serlway
           Loch Ridge Major Rogue   Ch. Rita of Avalon, CD
      Ch. Wilson's Corrie, CD   Ch. Black Rogue of Serlway
           Ch. Loch Ridge Victoria   Ch. Rita of Avalon, CD

                         AFTERNOD FIDEMAC

Sire of 29 Champions: Out of:

Ch. Afternod Ian Langsam   ⎤
Ch. Afternod MacAlder Tyr   │
Ch. Afternod Ivy III   │
Ch. Afternod Simon   │   Ch. Afternod Alder
Ch. Afternod Scot of Blackbay, CD │
Can. & US Ch. Afternod Sybilla   ⎦

Ch. Afternod Asset of Ballantrae ⎤
Ch. Lochinvar's Merry MacDuff   │   Loch Adair Kimberley
Ch. Afternod Adair of Ballantrae ⎦

Ch. Afternod Ripple   Ch. Afternod Caramel

Ch. Wildfire Windfall   ⎤
Ch. Wildfire Wendy   │
Ch. Wildfire Willow   │
Ch. Wildfire Black Watch   │
Ch. Wildfire Tara   │   Ch. Afternod Woodbine
Ch. Wildfire Highland Lancer   │
Ch. Wildfire Heather   │
Ch. Afternod Greenbank Aladdin   ⎦

Ch. Afternod Kippa   Ch. Afternod Ingin of Mapleknoll

Ch. Loch Adair Peer of Sutherland, CD
Ch. Loch Adair Pilot
Ch. Loch Adair Neil
Can. Ch. Loch Adair Nabob's Flip

    Ch. Wee Laurie Adair

Ch. HiLaway's Burl Ives
Ch. HiLaway's Burgundy Babe

    Glascott's Gordon Hill Imp

Ch. Just Another MacGregor   Bonnie Cricket MacGregor

Ch. Afternod Oliver   Ch. Afternod Amber

Ch. Afternod Octavia III   Afternod Ember IV

Ch. Afternod Firth of Clyde   GerDon's Beryl Clydebank

CH. AFTERNOD KYLE OF SUTHERLAND

AKC No. SA 472971-11-68   Whelped 5 March, 1967   Do
Owner: J. Lawrence   Breeder: M. Wilcox

Ch. Afternod Buchanan	Ch. EEG's Scotia Nodrog Rettes
Ch. Afternod Drambuie	Ch. Wilson's Corrie, CD
Ch. Afternod Sue	Ch. Fast's Falcon of Windy Hill
Ch. Afternod Callant	Afternod Ember of Gordon Hill
Ch. Afternod Hickory	Ch. Page's MacDonegal II
Ch. Afternod Woodbine	Afternod Hedera
Ch. Afternod Elgin II	Ch. Afternod Buchanan
	Afternod Ember of Gordon Hill
Ch. Afternod Buchanan	Ch. EEG's Scotia Nodrog Rettes
Ch. Afternod Drambuie	Ch. Wilson's Corrie, CD
Ch. Afternod Sue	Ch. Fast's Falcon of Windy Hill
Ch. Afternod Amber	Afternod Ember of Gordon Hill
Afternod Hedemac	Page's MacDonegal II
Ch. Afternod Kate	Afternod Hedera
Ch. Afternod Sue	Ch. Fast's Falcon of Windy Hill
	Afternod Ember of Gordon Hill

Sire of 11 Champions: Out of:

Ch MacAlder Duke of Goldenrod
Ch. MacAlder Dede   MacAlder Beauty
Ch. MacAlder Dora of Seneca Hill

Ch. Sutherland Sybil   Ch. Afternod Woodbine

Ch. Dunnideer Dana
Ch. Dunnideer Dugan, CD   Ch. Sutherland Dunnideer Walt
Ch. Dunnideer Dendragon
Ch. Sutherland Squaredance

Ch. Sutherland Pavane
Ch. Sutherland Pathfinder   Ch. Sutherland Xenia
Ch. Sutherland Pan of LochLoin

CH. AFTERNOD MACALDER TYR

AKC No. SA 201050-2-67   Whelped 3 May, 1963   Dog
      Owner: C. Stephenson   Breeder: C. Stephenson & M. Wilcox

                    Afternod Hedemac
          Afternod Sumac
                    Ch. Afternod Sue
Afternod Fidemac
                    Ch. Milestone Monarch
          Ch. Afternod Fidelia
                    Ch. Wilson's Corrie,CD

                    Ch. Afternod Buchanan
          Ch. Afternod Drambuie
                    Ch. Afternod Sue
Ch. Afternod Alder
                    Afternod Hedemac
          Afternod Kalmia
                    Ch. Afternod Sue

Ch. Page's MacDonegal II
Afternod Hedera
Ch. Fast's Falcon of Windy Hill
Afternod Ember of Gordon Hill
Ch. Great Scot of Blakeen
Loch Ridge Reckless Lady
Loch Ridge Major Rogue
Loch Ridge Victoria

Ch. EEG's Scotia Nodrog Rettes
Ch. Wilson's Corrie, CD
Ch. Fast's Falcon of Windy Hill
Afternod Ember of Gordon Hill
Ch. Page's MacDonegal II
Afternod Hedera
Ch. Fast's Falcon of Windy Hill
Afternod Ember of Gordon Hill

CH. AFTERNOD MACALDER TYR

Sire of 22 Champions: Out of:

Ch. Highlander MacAlder Brutus   ⎤
Ch. Gordon Hill Tyrelle MacAlder   ⎥
Ch. MacAlder Blaze   ⎥
Ch. MacAlder Cairn of Goldenrod   ⎥   Afternod Babbie of Aberfoyle
Can. & US Ch. MacAlder Collin   ⎥
Ch. MacAlder HiLine's Cassandra, CD   ⎥
Ch. MacAlder Casey, CD   ⎦

Ch. Galadriel Lady of Lothlorien, UD   Ch. MacAlder Feather
Ch. Quaco's Zachariah of Marakesh   Ch. Oakridge Marakesha

Ch. MacAlder Alcy of Rochaplenty   ⎤
Ch. MacAlder Amy LaMere   ⎥   Ch. Afternod Corrie of Teequinn
Ch. MacAlder Accent, CD   ⎦

Ch. MacAlder Hacasak Jasmine   Ch. Hacasak Pocohantas

Ch. MacAlder Esnix Tam O'Shanter   ⎤
Ch. Itoba Part of the Plan   ⎥   Heather's Bonnie Lass
Ch. Tyr's Royal Chestnut   ⎦

Ch. Tyrtaun's A-One Maggie   Shantuck Tauni Joy
Ch. Nellie Bly of Hast-View   Afternod Hast-View A'Rogheath
Ch. Afternod Ellen of Teequinn   Afternod Ginger
Ch. Sunburst Ebony Tartan Lad   Ch. Sunburst Cheyenne Autumn
Ch. Quailwood's Brae of Berridale   Ch. Rambling Rose of Quailwood
Ch. Killiedrum Charlie   Ch. Saturday Farm Killiedrum Eve

Ashbey

CAN.& US CH. AFTERNOD NIMROD NUGGETS

AKC No. SB 174495-9-74   Whelped 6 June, 1972   Dog
    Owner: Mitchell   Breeder: Graff & M. Wilcox

```
                                          Ch. Afternod Buchanan
            Ch. Afternod Drambuie         Ch. Afternod Sue
    Ch. Afternod Callant                  Ch. Afternod Hickory
            Ch. Afternod Woodbine         Ch. Afternod Elgin II
Ch. Wee Jock Adair, CD                    Ch. Page's MacDonegal II
            Ch. Afternod Hickory          Afternod Hedera
    Loch Adair Diana of Redchico          Ch. Loch Adair Blair
            Allspice of Redchico          Ch. Afternod Kate


            Afternod Fidemac              Afternod Sumac
    Ch. Afternod Simon                    Ch. Afternod Fidelia
            Ch. Afternod Alder            Ch. Afternod Drambuie
Ch. Afternod Wendee                       Afternod Kalmia
            Ch. Afternod Anagram          Ch. Afternod Drambuie
    Afternod Dee of Aberdeen              Loch Adair Diana of Redchico
            Afternod Nora Beinn Breagh    Ch. Afternod Drambuie
                                          Afternod Yew II
```

Sire of 10 Champions: Out of:
_____   _____

Ch. Viking Hill's Highland Jo   ⎤
Ch. Viking Hill's Piper   ⎥   Viking Hill's Lorna Doone
Ch. Viking Hill's Shondar   ⎦

Can. Ch. Dresden of Robingreen   Robingreen Bridget

Ch. Cameron's Colonel Teddy   ⎤
Can. Ch. Cameron's Dufftown Majesty ⎦   Ch. Viking Hill Lady Bea

Can. Ch. Aranmore's Bonnie Lassie ⎤
Can. Ch. Aranmore's Mr. Bo-Jangles ⎦   Can. Ch. Piper's Gentle Belle

Can. Ch. Candence of Robingreen   Can. Ch. Robingreen Annie Laurie

Can. Ch. Bonny Hunter Abbey   Can. Ch. Loch Adair Ulyssa

CH. AFTERNOD OCTAVIA III

AKC No. SA 596706-7-70   Whelped 3 July, 1968   Bitch
    Owner: Stahl   Breeder: Merrow & Wilcox

                                    Ch. Page's MacDonegal II
            Afternod Hedemac   Afternod Hedera
    Afternod Sumac   Ch. Fast's Falcon of Windy Hill
            Ch. Afternod Sue   Afternod Ember of Gordon Hill
Afternod Fidemac   Ch. Great Scot of Blakeen
            Ch. Milestone Monarch   Loch Ridge Reckless Lady
    Ch. Afternod Fidelia   Loch Ridge Major Rogue
            Ch. Wilson's Corrie,CD Loch Ridge Victoria

            Ch. Afternod Drambuie   Ch. Afternod Buchanan
    Ch. Afternod Callant   Ch. Afternod Sue
            Ch. Afternod Woodbine   Ch. Afternod Hickory
Afternod Ember IV   Ch. Afternod Elgin II
            Afternod Fidemac   Afternod Sumac
    Ch. Afternod Kippa   Ch. Afternod Fidelia
            Ch. Afternod Ingin of Mapleknoll Ch. Afternod Individualist
                                    Ch. Afternod Elgin II

Dam of 10 Champions: Sired by:

Ch. Oakridge Merrydown Mead   ⌉
Ch. Oakridge Mr. Mike of Shinfayne │
Ch. Oakridge Marakesha   │
Ch. Oakridge Magic Marker   │
Ch. Oakridge Timbershine, CD   │   Ch. Rogheath Ben MacDhui
Ch. Oakridge Trick Or Treat   │
Ch. Oakridge Tweed MacDhui   │
Ch. Oakridge Treebeard   │
Ch. Oakridge Tisha of Fianafail   ⌋
Ch. Daron Avatar Travis McGee   Ch. Daron Rebel With A Cause

CH. AFTERNOD RIPPLE

AKC No. SA 267298-2-67   Whelped 20 June, 1964   Bitch
      Owner: Fisher   Breeder: Recht & Wilcox

                    Afternod Hedemac   Ch. Page's MacDonegal II
          Afternod Sumac   Afternod Hedera
                    Ch. Afternod Sue   Ch. Fast's Falcon of Windy Hill
    Afternod Fidemac   Afternod Ember of Gordon Hill
                    Ch. Milestone Monarch   Ch. Great Scot of Blakeen
          Ch. Afternod Fidelia   Loch Ridge Reckless Lady
                    Ch. Wilson's Corrie, CD   Loch Ridge Major Rogue
                                              Loch Ridge Victoria

                    Ch. Afternod Buchanan   Ch. EEG's Scotia Nodrog Rettes
          Ch. Afternod Drambuie   Ch. Wilson's Corrie, CD
                    Ch. Afternod Sue   Ch. Fast's Falcon of Windy Hill
    Ch. Afternod Caramel   Afternod Ember of Gordon Hill
                    Ch. Afternod Hickory   Ch. Page's MacDonegal II
          Ch. Afternod Woodbine   Afternod Hedera
                    Ch. Afternod Elgin II   Ch. Afternod Buchanan
                                              Afternod Ember of Gordon Hill

Dam of 6 Champions: Sired by:

Ch. Afternod Heiress of Sark   Ch. Afternod Cutty Sark

Ch. Afternod Yauld MacKenzie   ⎤
                                    |
Ch. Afternod Yank of Rockaplenty |
                                    |
Ch. Loch Adair Ripple's Rumpus | Ch. Wee Jock Adair, CD
                                    |
Can. & US Ch. Loch Adir Dyce |
                                    |
Ch. Loch Adair Ripple's Regal Aire ⎦

Rich Bergman Studios

CH. AFTERNOD ROBENA OF ABERDEEN

AKC No. SA 20617-12-71   Whelped 4 August, 1968   Bitch
          Owner: Thomas   Breeder: Kugelmass & Wilcox

                                    Afternod Hedemac
            Afternod Sumac   Ch. Afternod Sue
      Afternod Fidemac   Ch. Milestone Monarch
            Ch. Afternod Fidelia   Ch. Wilson's Corrie, CD
Ch. Afternod Simon   Ch. Afternod Buchanan
            Ch. Afternod Drambuie   Ch. Afternod Sue
      Ch. Afternod Alder   Afternod Hedemac
            Afternod Kalmia   Ch. Afternod Sue

                                    Ch. EEG's Scotia Nodrog Rettes
            Ch. Afternod Buchanan   Ch. Wilson's Corrie,CD
      Ch. Afternod Drambuie   Ch. Fast's Falcon of Windy Hill
            Ch. Afternod Sue   Afternod Ember of Gordon Hill
Afternod Nora Beinn Bhreagh   Afternod Sumac
            Afternod Fidemac   Ch. Afternod Fidelia
      Afternod Yew II   Afternod Sumac
            Afternod Annie Laurie   Afternod Fancy Fraser

  Dam of 7 Champions: Sired by:

  Ch. Kiltklan's Robbie MacBean ⌉
  Ch. Kiltklan's McNish |
                                  | Ch. Rogheath Ben MacDhui
  Ch. Kiltklan Regina of Aberdeen|
  Ch. HiLite Delight of Kiltklan ⌋
  Ch. Kiltklan Black Jamie   ⌉
  Ch. Warwick's Haggis of Kiltklan| Ch. Afternod Yank of Rockaplenty
  Ch. Warwick's Timothy of Kiltklan⌋

AKC No. SA 282062-10-67   Whelped 11 July, 1964   Dog
     Owner: Kugelmass   Breeder: M. Wilcox

                    Afternod Hedemac   Ch. Page's MacDonegal II
              Afternod Sumac   Afternod Hedera
                    Ch. Afternod Sue   Ch. Fast's Falcon of Windy Hill
        Afternod Fidemac   Afternod Ember of Gordon Hill
                    Ch. Milestone Monarch   Ch. Great Scot of Blakeen
              Ch. Afternod Fidelia   Loch Ridge Reckless Lady
                    Ch. Wilson's Corrie,CD   Loch Ridge Major Rogue
                                               Loch Ridge Victoria

                    Ch. Afternod Buchanan   Ch. EEG's Scotia Nodrog Rettes
              Ch. Afternod Drambuie   Ch. Wilson's Corrie, CD
                    Ch. Afternod Sue   Ch. Fast's Falcon of Windy Hill
        Ch. Afternod Alder   Afternod Ember of Gordon Hill
                    Afternod Hedemac   Ch. Page's MacDonegal II
              Afternod Kalmia   Afternod Hedera
                    Ch. Afternod Sue   Ch. Fast's Falcon of Windy Hill
                                               Afternod Ember of Gordon Hill

                         CH. AFTERNOD SIMON

Sire of 14 Champions: Out of:

Ch. Afternod Robena of Aberdeen   Afternod Nora Beinn Bhreagh

Ch. Afternod Wendee   Afternod Dee of Aberdeen

Ch. Afternod Alexandra   Ch. Afternod Aberdeen

Ch. Afternod Sequel to Simon   Ch. Afternod Ember V

Ch. Afternod Quindina   ⎤
Can. & US Ch. Afternod Ace of Lochiel ⎦ Ch. Afternod Asset of Ballantrae

Ch. Afternod Bondorhil Eveready   Bondorhil Rosemary Adair

Ch. Loch Adair Titan of Tedmar   Ch. Wee Laurie Adair

Ch. Scothill's Goode Faithe   Birchwood's Gretna Green

Ch. Idlenot Moxie   Ch. Afternod Ellen McKenzie

Ch. Cheridan Blacksmoke   Loch Adair Jessica

Ch. Tallydoon Farm Fancy Alina   Tallydoon's Evening Star

Ch. Stilmeadow's Haughty Harrigan ⎤
Ch. Stilmeadow's Kaird Heritage   ⎦   Can. & US Ch. Stilmeadow's Elegant Erica

Jim Galbraith

CAN. & US CH. AFTERNOD SYBILLA

AKC No. SA 274723-1-67   Whelped 11 July, 1964   Bitch
        Owner: D. Gidday   Breeder: M. Wilcox

Afternod Hedemac
    Afternod Sumac
        Ch. Afternod Sue
Afternod Fidemac
        Ch. Milestone Monarch
    Ch. Afternod Fidelia
        Ch. Wilson's Corrie, CD

        Ch. Afternod Buchanan
    Ch. Afternod Dranpute
        Ch. Afternod Sue
Ch. Afternod Alder
        Afternod Hedemac
    Afternod Kalmia
        Ch. Afternod Sue

Ch. Page's MacDonegal II
Afternod Hedera
Ch. Fast's Falcon of Windy Hill
Afternod Ember of Gordon Hill
Ch. Great Scot of Blakeen
Loch Ridge Reckless Lady
Loch Ridge Major Rogue
Loch Ridge Victoria

Ch. EEG's Scotia Nodrog Rettes
Ch. Wilson's Corrie, CD
Ch. Fast's Falcon of Windy Hill
Afternod Ember of Gordon Hill
Ch. Page's MacDonegal II
Afternod Hedera
Ch. Fast's Falcon of Windy Hill
Afternod Ember of Gordon Hill

Dam of 11 Champions:

Ch. Stilmeadows Aragant Angie ⎤
Ch. Stilmeadows Aragant Alex |
Ch. Stilmeadows Aragant Alfie |
Ch. Stilmeadows Aragant Aaron ⎦

Ch. Stilmeadows Elgin   ⎤
Ch. Stilmeadowns Encore |
Ch. Stilmeadows Elegant Ephraim |
Ch. Stilmeadows Elegant Erica |
Ch. Stilmeadows Eolande Desmona ⎦

Ch. Stilmeadows Dara Dundrenan ⎤
Ch. Stilmeadows Dandy Dundrenan ⎦

Sired by:

Ch. Afternod Callant

Ch. Wee Jock Adair, CD

Afternod Pirate

CH. AFTERNOD WOODBINE

AKC No. SA 52078-6-62   Whelped 6 April, 1960   Bitch
     Owner: S. Freedman   Breeder: Greene & Wilcox

Page's MacDonegal, CD	Captain O'Field
Ch. Page's MacDonegal II	Susan Q Gayne
Mace's Old Bessie	Ch. Black Rogue of Serlway
Ch. Afternod Hickory	Blakeen Heather
Ch. Heslop's Burnvale Piper	Ch. Heslop's Courageous
Afternod Hedera	Ch. Heslop's Burnvale Duchess
Afternod Benbecula	Ch. EEG's Scotia Nodrog Rettes
	Ch. Wilson's Corrie, CD

Page's MacDonegal, CD
Ch. Page's MacDonegal II
Mace's Old Bessie
Ch. Afternod Hickory
Ch. Heslop's Burnvale Piper
Afternod Hedera
Afternod Benbecula

Captain O'Field
Susan Q Gayne
Ch. Black Rogue of Serlway
Blakeen Heather
Ch. Heslop's Courageous
Ch. Heslop's Burnvale Duchess
Ch. EEG's Scotia Nodrog Rettes
Ch. Wilson's Corrie, CD

Ch. EEG's Scotia Nodrog Rettes
Ch. Afternod Buchanan
Ch. Wilson's Corrie, CD
Ch. Afternod Elgin II
Ch. Scotia Nod's Duncan, CD
Afternod Ember of Gordon Hill
Ch. Heslop's Burnvale Bonnie, CD

Ch. Lancer of Serlway
Ch. Larrabee's Avalon Beauty
Loch Ridge Major Rogue
Ch. Loch Ridge Victoria
Ch. EEG's Scotia Nodrog Rettes
Ch. Wilson's Corrie, CD
Ch. Heslop's Courageous
Ch. Heslop's Burnvale Duchess

Dam of 12 Champions: Sired by:

Ch. Afternod Callant ⎤
Ch. Afternod Caramel   Ch. Afternod Drambuie
Ch. Afternod Cutty Sark ⎦

Ch. Sutherland Sybil   Afternod Kyle of Sutherland

Ch. Wildfire Windfall ⎤
Ch. Wildfire Black Watch
Ch. Wildfire Wendy
Ch. Wildfire Willow   Afternod Fidemac
Ch. Wildfire Highland Lancer
Ch. Wildfire Tara
Ch. Wildfire Heather
Ch. Afternod Greenbank Aladdin ⎦

CH. AFTERNOD YANK OF ROCKAPLENTY, CD

AKC No. SA 696635-2-72   Whelped 2 June 1969   Dog
Owner: Clark   Breeder: Fisher

		Ch. Afternod Buchanan
	Ch. Afternod Drambuie	Ch. Afternod Sue
	Ch. Afternod Callant	Ch. Afternod Hickory
	Ch. Afternod Woodbine	Ch. Afternod Elgin II
Ch. Wee Jock Adair, CD		Ch. Page's MacDonegal II
	Ch. Afternod Hickory	Afternod Hedera
	Loch Adair Diana of Redchico	Ch. Loch Adair Blair
	Allspice of Redchico	Ch. Afternod Kate

		Afternod Hedemac
	Afternod Sumac	Ch. Afternod Sue
	Afternod Fidemac	Ch. Milestone Monarch
	Ch. Afternod Fidelia	Ch. Wilson's Corrie, CD
Ch. Afternod Ripple		Ch. Afternod Buchanan
	Ch. Afternod Drambuie	Ch. Afternod Sue
	Ch. Afternod Caramel	Ch. Afternod Hickory
	Ch. Afternod Woodbine	Ch. Afternod Elgin II

Sire of 83 Champions: Out of:

Ch. Goldanne's TarTac Treasure

Ch. Cedarwood's Tarboo Brandy

Ch. Riverside's Tarboo Magic Mist

Ch. Riverside's Tarboo Ames

Can. & US Ch. Riverside's Tarboo Best A Mist   Ch. Ben Brogh Sister Margaret

Can. & US Ch. Riverside's Tarboo Miss Mandee

Ch. Riverside's Tarboo Mie Tie

Ch. Highland Bo Jock of Riverside

Ch. Rockaplenty's Hibiscus

Ch. Rockaplenty's Hang Em High

Ch. Rockaplenty's Honeybee

Ch. Rockaplenty's Mercury Morris

Ch. Rockaplenty's Mish Mash

Ch. Rockaplenty's Mountain Dew

Ch. Rockaplenty's Peaches N Cream

Ch. Rockaplenty's Pride N Joy

Ch. Rockaplenty's Pandora's Box, CD

Ch. Rockaplenty's Pillow Talk

Ch. Rockaplenty's Royall Holy Hell

Ch. Rockaplenty's Real McCoy, CD

Ch. Rockaplenty's Pit-A-Pat

Ch. Rockaplenty's Hot Stuff

Ch. Rockaplenty's Ice Storm

Can. Ch. Rockaplenty's Tarzan

Ch. Timbershine Lochiel Braenna

Rockaplenty's Vendetta

Ch. Rockaplenty's Move Em Out

Rockaplenty's Black Gold

Ch. Oakridge Tweed MacDhui

Can. & US Ch. McMac's Linwood's Misty

Ch. McMac's Amos
Ch. Princemoor's McMac Ebony Mist

Ch. McMac's Amazing Grace

Ch. McMac's September Morn

Can & US Ch. Donwood's Taaka

Ch. Donwood's Yankee Dandy

Kim's Missie

Ch. Glenwood's Damn Yankee, CD

Ch. Glenwood's Whistling Dixie

Ch. Glenwood's Heavenly Body

Ch. Kris' Keepsake of Fieldstone

Ch. Kris' Black Bart

Can. Ch. Kris' Gentle Gus, CD

Ch. MacAlder's Ingenue of Chris

Ch. Stilmeadows Salahie Garm

Ch. Stilmeadows Aragant Angie

Ch. Kennelot's Southern Comfort

Ch. Meghan's Shannon of Halmarque

Ch. MacGeowl's Allez Meghan

Ch. Speedwell's Buck Rogers

Ch. Speedwell Kris' High Jinx

Ch. Fieldstone Speedwell Foxy, CD

Kris' TooToo

Ch. Warlock's Windjammer

Can. & US Ch. Warlock's Calypso Dancer

Ch. Fieldstone Warlock Sweet Sue

Ch. Fieldstone Warlock Windsong

Ch. Kadon's Blue Tango of Warlock

Ch. Scottland's Esprit De Vie

Can. & US Ch. Scottland's American Spirit

Can. Ch. Hedgestone's Dynasty

Can. Ch. Hedgestone's Dash of Ginger

Can. Ch. Scottland's Liberty Belle

Ch. Warwick's Haggis of KiltKlan
Ch. KiltKlan Black Jamie   Ch. Afternod Robena of Aberdeen
Ch. Warwick's Timothy of KiltKlan

Ch. Touchstone Tory
Ch. Touchstone Yankee Patriot
Ch. Touchstone Yankee Heritage   Ch. Rockaplenty Elspeth of Ayr, C
Ch. Touchstone Yankee Fife 'N Drum

Ch. Rockaplenty's Abigail
Can. & US Ch. Rockaplenty's Gunsmoke   Ch. Stumpy Acres Kadon Katie
Ch. Stumpy Acres Blandwagin Kate
Ch. Stumpy Acres Blandwagin Al
Ch. Rockaplenty's Miss Kitty

Ch. Tarbaby's Candidate
Ch. Tarbaby's Color Guard
Ch. Tarbaby's Cockleburr Deacon   Ch. Tarbaby's Midnight Sapphire
Ch. Tarbaby's Cuss of Cabin Creek, CD, TD

Ch. Boldbrook's Minnesota Fats
Ch. Boldbrook's Road Runner
Ch. Boldbrook's Bwana, CD
Ch. Boldbrook of Candy Lane, CD   Ch. Rockaplenty's Band Wagon
Can. & US Ch. Boldbrook's Yankie Junior

Ch. Marakesh Echo
Ch. Quaco's Magic Negra Marakesh   Ch. Oakridge Marakesha

Can. & US Ch. Vagabond Lark of Rockaplenty, CD
Ch. Vagabond's Yes I Can   Ch. Rockaplenty's Rugged But Rite

Ch. DonD's Citation   Ch. DonD's Miss Mischief
Ch. DonD's Classic Example, CD

Ch. Rockaplenty's Cinnamon
Ch. Rockaplenty's Celebration, CD   Ch. Rockaplenty's Rack On
Ch. Rockaplenty's Kissing Cousin

Can & US Ch. Rockaplenty's Nomad
Ch. Rockaplenty's Country Redlegs   Ch. Rockaplenty's Bonanza

Ch. Rockaplenty's Country Roads, CD
Ch. Rockaplenty's Rambling Rose   Ch. Rockaplenty's Glory Bound
Ch. Rockaplenty's Through The Rye, CDX

Wm. P. Gilbert

CH. BEN BROGH SISTER MARGARET

AKC No. SA 848615-4-74   Whelped 20 July, 1970   Bitch
    Owner: Boothroyd   Breeder: Olsson

                                          Ch. Blake's Rogue of Windy Hill
              Windy Hill's Davey B   Windy Hill's Heidi of Shuriridge
      Ch. Buddy D of HanMar   Windy Hill's Butch
              Dixie Means   Lady Venue of Shiloh
  Ch. Hacasak Comanche   Ch. Fast's Falcon of Windy Hill
              Dual Ch. Windy Hill's Lucky Chance Windy Hill's Double Scotch
      Ch. Hacasak Sioux's Chance   Ch. Fast's Falcon of Windy Hill
              Ch. Windy Hill's Regina   Windy Hill's Radiance

                                          Afternod Sumac
              Afternod Fidemac   Ch. Afternod Fidelia
      Ch. Afternod MacAlder Tyr   Ch. Afternod Drambuie
              Ch. Afternod Alder   Afternod Kalmia
  MacAlder A'Shelli Ben Brogh   Ch. Afternod Drambuie
              Ch. Afternod Anagram   Loch Adair Diana of Redchico
      Ch. Afternod Corrie of Teequinn   Ch. Afternod Drambuie
              Afternod Ginger   Afternod Victoria II

Dam of 10 Champions: Sired by:

Ch. Goldanne's TarTac Treasure

Ch. Riversides Tarboo Magic Mist

Ch. Riversides Tarboo Ames

Can. & US Ch. Riversides Tarboo Best A Mist   Ch. Afternod Yank of Rockaplenty

Ch Riverside Tarboo Mie Tie

Ch. Highland Bo Jock of Riverside

Can. & US Ch. Riverside Tarboo Miss Mandee

Ch. Cedarwood's Tarboo Brandy

Ch. Temacar Dundee Maiden   Can. & US Ch. Johnston's Highland Storm

Ch. Riverside Tarboo Black Max

CH. BO-CHAM'S CRICKET OF CROMARTY

AKC No. SA 631184-11-72   Whelped 30 May, 1968   Bitch
        Owner: Chambers   Breeder: Smith & Clayton

                Ch. Sangerfield Index   Can. & US Ch. Sangerfield Jed
    Ch. George Gordon Sangerfield   Ch. Sangerfield Tracy
            Sangerfield Edie   Can. & US Ch. Sangerfield Smokey
Crestland's Duncan's Fancy   Ch. Sangerfield Tracy
            Ch. Blarney Stone's Banshire   Windy Hill's Weir of Kay
    Ch. Blarney Stone's Gael   Ch. Blarney Stone's Deluxe Baby
            Ch. Windy Hill's Claudia B   Ch. Blake's Rogue of Windy Hill
                                           Ch. Sycamore Lodge Sue

            Bud O'Field Brookview   Piper's Don O'Field
    Sangerfield's Blackwatch   Debonair Patty O'Field
            Sangerfield Nell   Pride of Dixey
Ch. Brookforest April Dancer   Sangerfield Fly
            Afternod Fidemac   Afternod Sumac
    Wildfire Tina Brookford   Ch. Afternod Fidelia
            Ch. Afternod Woodbine   Ch. Afternod Hickory
                                           Ch. Afternod Elgin II

Dam of 7 Champions: Sired by:

Ch. Bo-Cham's Arrogant Christopher ⎤
                                   │   Ch. Brookforest Black Bart
Ch. Bo-Cham's Ambassador   ⎦

Ch. Bo-Cham's Blackwatch Piper   ⎤
                                   │
Ch. Bo-Cham's Blackberry Brandy   │
                                   │
Ch. Bo-Cham's Boone Wynds   │   Ch. Sportin' Life
                                   │
Ch. Bo-Cham's Byline On Sports   │
                                   │
Ch. Bo-Cham's Butter Rum   ⎦

CH. BONNIE GAY OF RU-BERN

AKC No. SA 263330-6-66   Whelped 27 May, 1964   Bitch
         Owner: J. Look   Breeder: Betzold

                    Ch. Sangerfield Peter   Ch. Heslop's Burnvale Christopher
          Can. & US Ch. Sangerfield Jed   Sandy's Bess
                    Ch. Sangerfield Tillie   Judge Palmer
Ch. Sangerfield Index   Ch. Heslop's Burnvale Dawn
                    Look's Black Daniel   Ch. Heslop's Criss Cross
          Ch. Sangerfield Tracy   Dandy
                    Ch. Heslop's Burnvale Edie Ch. Heslop's Courageous
                                               Ch. Heslop's Burnvale Duchess

                    Roevalley Duke   Eng. Ch. Blaze of Westerdale
          Ch. Thurston's Stylish Angus   Eng. Ch. Angela of Gramerci
                    Osborne's Stylish Tammerlane II Heslop's Burnvale Scot
Ch. Alice of Achnacarry   Ch. Osborn's Stylish Tammerlane
          Can. & US Ch. Sangerfield Peter   Ch. Heslop's Burnvale Christopher
                    Sangerfield Sally   Sandy's Bess
                    Ch. Sangerfield Tillie   Judge Palmer
                                               Ch. Heslop's Burnvale Dawn

Dam of 8 Champions: Sired by:

Ch. RuBern's Sanderfield Dolly

Ch. RuBern's Sangerfield Dennis

Ch. RuBern's Callie Girl

Ch. RuBern's Gentle Lochiel   Ch. George Gordon Sangerfield

Ch. Spring Heather of RuBern

Ch. Sangerfield Prudent Susan

Can. & US Ch. Sangerfield Sir Clipsby Crew

Ch. Sangerfield Bonnie of RuBern   Can. & US Ch. Sporting Look

CAN. CH. & US DUAL CH. CHANCE'S NATIONAL VELVET, CD

AKC No. SA 212058-10-66   Whelped 2 July, 1963   Bitch
          Owner: Althaus   Breeder: Amos & Althaus

                    Ch. Gregorach Fast   Ch. Ginger
          Ch. Fast's Falcon of Windy Hill   Stylish Madame
                  Heslop's Burnvale Janet   Ch. Heslop's Courageous
Dual Ch. Windy Hill's Lucky Chance   Ch. Heslop's Burnvale Duchess
                  Flash's Craig of Windy Hill   Ch. Fast's Flash of Windy Hill
          Windy Hill's Double Scotch   Fast's Glory of Windy Hill
                  Ch. Sycamore Lodge Sue   Ch. Fast's Falcon of Windy Hill
                                                    Ravenall BonBon

                  Gabriel of Serlway   Ch. Brutus of Serlway
          Ch. Pell Mell's Bonnie Bruce   Lady Katherine of Perthshire
                  Ch. Pell Mell Penelope   O'Tail
Field Ch. Denida's Bonnie Velvet   Nelson's Heather Beauty
                  Ch. Heslop's Stylish Lad   Loch Ridge Vagabond King
          Ch. Calvert's Highland Queen   Ch. Highland Queen of Tweedvale
                  Mississippi Valley Jet   Bing of Parkwood
                                                    Lady of Cliffhaven

CAN. CH. & US DUAL CH. CHANCE'S NATIONAL VELVET, CD

Dam of 6 Champions: Sired by:

Can. & US Ch. Heathero's MacDonagal, CD ⎤

Ch. Heathero's Joyous Dawn   Ch. Mac's Casey of Camino

Ch. Heathero's Windsong   ⎦

Can. & US Ch. Heathero Amber Velvet   ⎤

Ch. Heathero Arran Ben Ayr   Ch. Wildfire Blackwatch

Ch. Heathero Aristocrat   ⎦

Patsy's Studio

CH. CRICKET OF MACALESTER

AKC No. SA 713279-3-72   Whelped 6 June, 1969   Bitch
Owner: Martin   Breeder: Stivers

Ch. Sangerfield Peter
Can. & US Ch. Sangerfield Jed
Ch. Sangerfield Tillie
Brookview Rebel of Blackmore
Bud O'Field Brookview
Hewitt's Dutchess
Sangerfield Nell

Ch. Heslop's Burnvale Christopher
Sandy's Bess
Judge Palmer
Ch. Heslop's Burnvale Dawn
Piper's Don O'Field
Debonair Patty O'Field
Pride of Dixey
Ch. Sangerfield Fly

Ch. Afternod Hickory
Ch. Afternod Wallace
Ch. Afternod Elgin II
Afternod Thistle II
Ch. Afternod Drambuie
Afternod Firethorn
Afternod Annie Laurie

Ch. Page's MacDonegal II
Afternod Hedera
Ch. Afternod Buchanan
Afternod Ember of Gordon Hill
Ch. Afternod Buchanan
Ch. Afternod Sue
Afternod Sumac
Afternod Fancy Fraser

<u>Dam of 7 Champions</u>:   <u>Sired by</u>:

Ch. Inwood Greenglen, CD

Can. & US Ch. Inwood Meadow Rue, UD   Ch. Rogheath Ben MacDhui

Ch. Inwood Wildflower

Can. & US Ch. Jock The Scot of Karolly, UD

Ch. Gorduk of Greycoach   Ch. Jock of Inwood

Ch. Alec of Greycoach

Ch. Inwood Kerrie On

Bill Francis

CH. DARON REBEL WITH A CAUSE

AKC No. SB 373264-5-75   Whelped 21 March, 1973   Dog
          Owner: Wedeman & Grant   Breeder: Wedeman & Solheim

	Ch. Afternod Drambuie	Ch. Afternod Buchanan
Ch. Afternod Anagram		Ch. Afternod Sue
	Loch Adair Diana of Redchico	Ch. Afternod Hickory
Can. & US Ch. Rogheath Ben MacDhui		Allspice of Redchico
	Afternod Fidemac	Afternod Sumac
Ch. Afternod Ivy III		Ch. Afternod Fidelia
	Ch. Afternod Alder	Ch. Afternod Drambuie
		Afternod Kalmia
	Ch. George Gordon Sangerfield	Ch. Sangerfield Index
Can. & US Ch. Sporting Look		Sangerfield Edie
	Ch. Sangerfield HiJinks	Ch. Sangerfield Index
Ch. Sangerfield Bonnie of RuBern		Sangerfield Judy
	Ch. Sangerfield Index	Can. & US Ch. Sangerfield Jed
Ch. Bonnie Gay of RuBern		Ch. Sangerfield Tracy
	Ch. Alice of Achnacarry	Ch. Thurston's Stylish Angus
		Sangerfield Sally

CH. DARON REBEL WITH A CAUSE

Sire of 13 Champions: Out of:

Ch. Don-D's Gillian
Ch. Don-D's Hal Holbrook
Ch. Don-D's Hello Dolly   Ch. Don-D's Miss Mischief
Can Ch. Don-D's Madadhdubh Hamon
Ch. McGehee's Molly Malone   MacAlder K Mary Queen of Scots
Ch. Chawanakee Rebel's Courage
Ch. Chawanakee Rip Roarin'   Sangerfield Scotch Snap
Ch. Chawanakee Determination
Ch. Timbershine Highland Rebel
Can. & US Ch. Timbershine's Piece A The Rock   Ch. Oakridge Tweed MacDhui
Ch. Daron Avatar Travis McGee   Ch. Afternod Octavia III
Can. Ch. Daron Pride O'Clyde   Daron Debutante
Ch: HiRolin's Shot In Flight   Ch. HiRolin's Sangerfield Fancy Me

CH. DON-D'S MISS MISCHIEF

AKC No. SA 775008-9-73   Whelped 26 November, 1969   Bitch
     Owner: Selle   Breeder: Selle

                  Ch. George Gordon Sangerfield   Ch. Sangerfield Index
        Can. & US Ch. Sporting Look   Sangerfield Edie
                  Ch. Sangerfield HiJinks   Ch. Sangerfield Index
Ch. Sportin' Life   Sangerfield Judy
                  Ch. Sangerfield Index   Can. & US Ch. Sangerfield Jed
        Ch. Terlo's Lady of Clan Cameron   Ch. Sangerfield Tracy
                  Ch. Terlo's Andrea   Ch. Denida's Bonnie Rebel, CD
                                                  Ch. Look's Carolina Redbird

                                                  Eng. Ch. Blaze of Westerdale
                  Roevalley Duke   Eng. Ch. Angela of Gramerci
        Can. & US Ch. CynDan's Mister MacTavish   Algonquin Bruce
                  Lady of Ancastle   Bede of Ancastle
Ch. Thurston's R Lady MacTavish   Roevalley Duke
        Ch. Donnie Brae Eric Knight   Ch. Fletcher's Scotch Belle
        Thurston's Stylish Pandora   Ch. Thurston's Scot
                  Thurston's Stylish Evelyn   Thurston's Stylish Astrid

                    CH. DON-D'S MISS MISCHIEF

Dam of 7 Champions: Sired by:

Ch. Don-D's Citation   ⎤
                                        │   Ch. Afternod Yank of Rockaplenty
Ch. Don-D's Classic Example   ⎦

Ch. Ivan Oglennon   Don-D's Mister Bojangles

Ch. Don-D's Gillian   ⎤
                                        │
Ch. Don-D's Hal Holbrooke   │
                                        │   Ch. Daron Rebel With A Cause
Ch. Don-D's Hello Dolly   │
                                        │
Can. Ch. Don-D's Madadhdubh Hamon   ⎦

Earl Graham

CH. DUCHESS OF WINDY HILLS

AKC No. SB 438101-6-75   Whelped 20 June, 1972   Bitch
       Owner: Dwelly   Breeder: Hopp

Ch. Bonnie's Macs MacGeowls, CD	Dual Ch. Windy Hill's Lucky Chance
Enterprise MacSanger Rake	Field Ch. Denida's Bonnie Velvet
Enterprise Sangerfield Gigi	Ch. George Gordon Sangerfield
Smoky of Windy Hills	Ch. Sangerfield Hi-Jinks
Killiedrum Jay of OakLynn	Can. & US Ch. Sangerfield Jed
Hudson's Sage Hill Scarlet	Borderland Taupie
RuBern's Miss Pepper	Ch. George Gordon Sangerfield
	Ch. Bonnie Gay of RuBern
	Ch. Afternod Callant
Ch. Afternod Kyle of Sutherland	Ch. Afternod Amber
MacAlder Duke of Golden Rod	Ch. Afternod MacAlder Tyr
MacAlder Beauty	Afternod Babbie of Aberfoyle
Smokey's Lady Penny	Afternod Fidemac
Ch. Afternod MacAlder Tyr	Ch. Afternod Alder
MacAlder Coco of Golden Rod	Ch. Afternod Callant
Afternod Babbie of Aberfoyle	Ch. Afternod Wishbone

CH. DUCHESS OF WINDY HILLS

<u>Dam of 6 Champions</u>:   <u>Sired by</u>:

Ch. Dandy Dirk of Berridale

Ch. Daalakis Bonnie Berridale

Ch. Caesar of Berridale

Ch. MacLinden of Berridale   Ch. Laird Duncan of Berridale

Ch. Kolumbo's Berridale Flasher

Ch. Highland Brooke of Berridale

Martin Booth

CH. FLINTLOK'S ROBIN MACNEAL

AKC No. SB 513728-7-76   Whelped 4 May, 1974   Bitch
            Owner: Zak   Breeder: Zak

                    Windy Hill's Davey B   Ch. Blake's Rogue of Windy Hill
            Hugh's Sir Gordie of Windy Hill   Windy Hill's Heidi of Shuriridge
                    Abbie of Ann an Charr   Ch. Star Farm Best Bet
        Can, Ber. & US Ch. MacNeal of Ellicott   Laurel Lane's Cindy Lou
                    Ch. Wee Geordie Adair   Ch. Afternod Drambuie
            Ch. Loch Adair Kate   Loch Adair Diana of Redchico
                    Ch. Afternod Curry   Ch. Afternod Drambuie
                                                   Allspice of Redchico

                    Ch. Afternod Drambuie   Ch. Afternod Buchanan
            Ch. Afternod Advocate   Ch. Afternod Sue
                    Ch. Meghan Maguire   Ch. Matson's Robin
        Ch. Idlenot's Lady Guinevere, CD   Fletcher's Scotch Lorelei
                    John's Gorde   Glenbel Drambuie
            Ebony Lady   Riverside's Merry
                    Kulhavy's Lady Gay Brookview   Bud O'Field Brookview
                                                   Sangerfield Nell

Dam of 6 Champions: Sired by:

Ch. Flintlok's Black Watch Piper, CD ⎤
Ch. Flintlok's Bouncing Bette   ⎥
Ch. Flintlok's Charlie Brown   ⎥
                                      ⎥   Ch. McMac's Return To Ravenscraig
Ch. Flintlok's Raven Bairn, CD   ⎥
Ch. Flintlok's Gloamin' Star   ⎥
Ch. Flintlok's Piper of River Glen   ⎦

CH. GLENRAVEN AMBUSH

AKC No. SA 355739-11-69   Whelped 28 September, 1965   Bitch
        Owner: Anderson   Breeder: Corbett

                    Ch. Fast's Falcon of Windy Hill   Ch. Gregorach Fast
            Dual Ch. Windy Hill's Lucky Chance   Heslop's Burnvale Janet
                    Windy Hill's Double Scotch   Flash's Craig of Windy Hill
    Ch. Bonnie's Macs MacGeowls, CD   Ch. Sycamore Lodge Sue
                    Ch. Pell Mell's Bonnie Bruce   Gabriel of Serlway
            Field Ch. Denida's Bonnie Velvet   Ch. Pell Mell Penelope
                    Ch. Calvert's Highland Queen   Ch. Heslop's Stylish Lad
                                                          Mississippi Valley Jet

                    Ch. Afternod Hickory   Ch. Page's MacDonegal II
            Ch. Afternod Wallace   Afternod Hedera
                    Ch. Afternod Elgin II   Ch. Afternod Buchanan
    Ch. GerDon's Bridget Motherwell   Afternod Ember of Gordon Hill
            Dual Ch. Windy Hill's Lucky Chance   Ch. Fast's Falcon of Windy Hill
    Dual Ch. Galscott's Scottish Majesty   Field Ch. Denida's Bonnie Velvet
            Breadalbane Copper Coin   Vagabond's Heir
                                                          Copper Penny of Dee

                    CH. GLENRAVEN AMBUSH

Dam of 6 Champions: Sired by:

Ch. Viking Hills Scotson   ⎤
Ch. Viking Hills Lady Tiffany   ⎟
Ch. Viking Hills Lady Bea   ⎟
Can. & US Ch. Viking Hills Tammi   ⎬   Can. & US Ch. Afternod Scot of Blackbay
Ch. Viking Hills Driftwood Dora   ⎟
Can. Ch. Kent of Viking Hill   ⎦

Steve Klein

CH. GEORGE GORDON SANGERFIELD

AKC No. SA 245697-8-65   Whelped 2 July, 1963   Dog
          Owner: J. Look, N.Y.   Breeder: J. Look, N.Y.

                    Ch. Sangerfield Peter   Ch. Heslop's Burnvale Christopher
          Can. & US Ch. Sangerfield Jed   Sandy's Bess
                    Ch. Sangerfield Tillie   Judge Palmer
Ch. Sangerfield Index   Ch. Heslop's Burnvale Dawn
                    Look's Black Daniel   Ch. Heslop's Criss Cross
          Ch. Sangerfield Tracy   Dandy
                    Ch. Heslop's Burnvale Edie   Ch. Heslop's Courageous
                                                   Ch. Heslop's Burnvale Duchess

                    Judge Palmer   Ch. Heslop's Courageous
          Can. & US Ch. Sangerfield Smokey   Tam O'Shanter
                    Holt's Dolly of Greymount   Ch. Heslop's Burnvale Christopher
Sangerfield Edie   Dandy Lou
                    Look's Black Daniel   Ch. Heslop's Criss Cross
          Ch. Sangerfield Tracy   Dandy
                    Ch. Heslop's Burnvale Edie   Ch. Heslop's Courageous
                                                   Ch. Heslop's Burnvale Duchess

Sire of 10 Champions: Out of:

Can. & US Ch. RuBern's Sangerfield Dolly ⎤
Ch. RuBern's Sangerfield Dennis   ⎥
Ch. RuBern's Callie Girl   ⎥
                                         ⎥   Ch. Bonnie Gay of RuBern
Ch. RuBern's Gentle Lochiel   ⎥
Ch. Spring Heather of RuBern   ⎥
Ch. Sangerfield Prudent Susan   ⎦

Can. & US Ch. Sportin' Look   Ch. Sangerfield HiJinks

Ch. Hickory Smoke Gilda Cameron   ⎤
                                         ⎥   Heslop's Hickory Huntress
Can Ch. Hickory Smoke Neil Cameron   ⎦

Can. Ch. Grianan Victoria Balfour   Can. Ch. Grianan Morag MacTay

CAN. CH. GRIANAN FANNY DE COURVOISIER

CKC No. EEB463   Whelped 12 March, 1973   Bitch
       Owner: Quesnel   Breeder: Bocking

                Ch. George Gordon Sangerfield   Ch. Sangerfield Index
      Can. & US Ch. Sporting Look   Sangerfield Edie
                Ch. Sangerfield HiJinks   Ch. Sangerfield Index
h. Sportin' Life   Sangerfield Judy
                Ch. Sangerfield Index   Can. & US Ch. Sangerfield Jed
      Ch. Terlo's Lady of Clan Cameron   Ch. Sangerfield Tracy
                Ch. Terlo's Andrea   Ch. Denida's Bonnie Rebel, CD
                                                  Ch. Look's Carolina Redbird

                Windrock's Wis scot Torgue   Ch. Afternod Drambuie
      Windrock's Skye MacQueen   Ch. Meghan Maguire
                Windrock's Highland Heather   Thane of Windrock
an. Ch. Grianan Morag MacTay   Dem's Torbolton Lass
                Ch. Sangerfield Index   Can. & US Ch. Sangerfield Jed
      Can. Ch. Hickory Smoke Tay Brodie, CD   Ch. Sangerfield Tracy
                Can. & US Ch. Hickory Harvest   Can. & US Ch. Hickory Smoke Wild 'N Wully, CD
                                                  Heslop's ShoField Misty

Dam of 6 Champions: Sired by:

Can. &US Ch. Fantan's Maxime de Courvoisier ⎤
                                            ⎥
Can. Ch. Fantan Tory of Penmarick   ⎬ Can. Ch. Deerswood Pintail
                                            ⎥
Can. Ch. Fantan Blue Boy of Burdale   ⎦

Can. Ch. Fantan Highland Drummer   ⎤
                                            ⎬ Sangerfield Trademark
Can. Ch. Fantan Trademark's Summer Storm   ⎦

Can. Ch. Loch Na Keal Banner Boy   Ch. Windrock's Braircliff Brandy

DUAL CH. GLENRAVEN AUTUMN SMOKE

AKC No. SA355169-12-69   Whelped 28 September, 1965   Dog
     Owner: E. Backman   Breeder: Corbett

```
                    Ch. Fast's Falcon of Windy Hill      Ch. Gregorach Fast
          Dual Ch. Windy Hill's Lucky Chance             Heslop's Burnvale Janet
                 Windy Hill's Double Scotch              Flash's Craig of Windy Hill
Ch. Bonnie's Macs MacGeowls, CD                          Ch. Sycamore Lodge Sue
                 Ch. Pell Mell's Bonnie Bruce            Gabriel of Serlway
          Field Ch. Denida's Bonnie Velvet               Ch. Pell Mell Penelope
                 Ch. Calvert's Highland Queen            Ch. Heslop's Stylish Lad
                                                         Mississippi Valley Jet


                 Ch. Afternod Hickory                    Ch. Page's MacDonegal II
          Ch. Afternod Wallace                           Afternod Hedera
                 Ch. Afternod Elgin II                   Ch. Afternod Buchanan
Ch. GerDon's Bridget Motherwell                          Afternod Ember of Gordon Hill
                 Dual Ch. Windy Hill's Lucky Chance      Ch. Fast's Falcon of Windy Hill
          Dual Ch. Glascott's Scottish Majesty           Field Ch. Denida's Bonnie Velvet
                 Breadalbane Copper Coin                  Vagabond's Heir
                                                         Copper Penny of Dee
```

Sire of 10 Champions:

Out of:

Ch. Afternod Penny ⎤
Ch. Afternod Pegeen of Dunans   ⎬   Ch. Afternod Ellen of Teequinn
Ch. Afternod Glen Carron Pibroch ⎦

Ch. Agaru Smokey Souchong   ⎤
Ch. Wilscot Black Granite   ⎬   Ch. Stilmeadows Fenella

Ch. Cedarwood Bold Scamp   Thistlewood's Amber Storm

Ch. Page's Meghan of Glomara, CD   Page's Cascade Drambuie

Ch. Page's M'Lord Royal Scot   Ch. Page's Bit-O-Liz Betsy

Ch. Loch Adair Vagabond   Ch. Wee Laurie Adair

Can. Ch. Loch Adair Ulyssa   Ch. Loch Adair Ripple's Regal Aire

CH. GORDON HILL TYRELLE MACALDER

AKC No. SA 502491-8-69   Whelped 24 April, 1967   Bitch
          Owner: M. Clement   Breeder: C. Stephenson

Afternod Sumac
Afternod Fidemac
    Ch. Afternod Fidelia
Ch. Afternod MacAlder Tyr
    Ch. Afternod Drambuie
Ch. Afternod Alder
    Afternod Kalmia

Afternod Hedemac
Ch. Afternod Sue
Ch. Milestone Monarch
Ch. Wilson's Corrie, CD
Ch. Afternod Buchanan
Ch. Afternod Sue
Afternod Hedemac
Ch. Afternod Sue

Ch. Afternod Drambuie
Ch. Afternod Callant
    Ch. Afternod Woodbine
Afternod Babbie of Aberfoyle
    Ch. Afternod Hickory
Ch. Afternod Wishbone
    Ch. Afternod Elgin II

Ch. Afternod Buchanan
Ch. Afternod Sue
Ch. Afternod Hickory
Ch. Afternod Elgin II
Ch. Page's MacDonegal II
Afternod Hedera
Ch. Afternod Buchanan
Afternod Ember of Gordon Hill

Dam of 6 Champions: Sired by:

Ch. Wilscot MacLaine of Lochbuie, CD

German Sieger & US Ch. Gordon Hill Wilscot Lektor ⎤ Ch. Sportin' Life

Ch. MacAlder Ebony of Seneca Hill   Ch. HiLaway's Burl Ives

Ch. Gordon Hill Run For Daylight   Hacasak Metacom

Ch. Gordon Hill Scaramouche   Ch. Wee Jock Adair, CD

Ch. Gordon Hill Pendragon   Gordon Hill Jock MacGregor

CAN. CH. GRIANAN MORAG MACTAY

AKC No. 702408   Whelped 13 July, 1967   Bitch
     Owner: Bocking, Ont.   Breeder: Bocking, Ont.

            Ch. Afternod Drambuie   Ch. Afternod Buchanan
     Windrock's Wainscot Torgue   Ch. Afternod Sue
            Ch. Meghan Maguire   Ch. Matson's Robin
     Windrock's Skye MacQueen   Fletcher's Scotch Lorelei
            Thane of Windrock   Can. & US Ch. Hickory Smoke
     Windrock's Highland Heather   Ch. Meghan Maguire   Wild 'N Wully, C
            Dem's Torbolton Lass   Milestone Princess
                                           Milestone Belle's Delilah

            Can. & US Ch. Sangerfield Jed Ch. Sangerfield Peter
     Ch. Sangerfield Index   Ch. Sangerfield Tillie
            Ch. Sangerfield Tracy   Look's Black Daniel
     Can. Ch. Hickory Smoke Tay Brodie, CD Ch. Heslop's Burnvale Edie
            Can. & US Ch. Hickory Smoke Wild 'N   Sergeant's Colorful Major, CD
     Can. & US Ch. Hickory Harvest   Wully,CD   Windy Hill's Zoe
            Heslop's ShoField Misty   Ch. Matson's Robin
                                            Fletcher's Scotch Lorelei

     Dam of 7 Champions: Sired by:

     Can. & US Ch. Grianan Victoria Balfour   Ch. George Gordon Sangerfield

     Can. Ch. Kennetkaird Kilts of Grianan   Can. Ch. Grianan Kennet MacEwan,

     Can. Ch. Grianan Kennet MacEwan, CD   Ch. Hickory Smoke Black Ebony

     Can. Ch. Grianan Fanny De Courvoisier ⌉

     Can. Ch. Grianan Felicity

     Can. Ch. Grianan Fellside Cutty Sark   Ch. Sportin' Life

     Can. Ch. Grianan Flint   ⌋

Steve Klein

CAN. & US CH. HICKORY HARVEST

No. 184694-8-66   Whelped 10 June, 1962   Bitch
     Owner: Mitchell   Breeder: Jobin & Heslop

Can. Ch. Glentanar's Color Sergeant   Glentanar's Black Mungo
Sergeant's Colorful Major   Can. Dual Ch. Vagabond Jean of Glentanar
     Queen of Lyn D'Or   Glentanar Tinker
, & US Ch. Hickory Smoke Wild 'N Wully, CD   Belle of Lyn D'Or
     Windy Hill's Rampart   Ch. Fast's Falcon of Windy Hill
Windy Hill's Zoe   Windy Hill's Radiance
     Windy Hill's Gillian B   Ch. Blake's Rogue of Windy Hill
                                       Fast's Glory of Windy Hill

                                       Ch. Great Scot of Blakeen
     Heslop's Burnvale Scot   Heslop's Burnvale Maid
Ch. Matson's Robin   Ch. Heslop's Courageous
     Ch. Heslop's Burnvale Jean   Ch. Heslop's Burnvale Duchess
lop's ShoField Misty   Ch. Heslop's Courageous
     Ch. Heslop's Burnvale Laird   Ch. Heslop's Burnvale Duchess
Fletcher's Scotch Lorelei   O'Field's Ready Response
     Kitty Lightfoot   Ch. Heslop's Burnvale Edie

am of 6 Champions: Sired by:

an. Ch. Hickory Smoke Dirk Brodie   ⎤
                                            |
an. Ch. Hickory Smoke Morag Brodie, CD |
                                            | Ch. Sangerfield Index
an. Ch. Hickory Smoke Bonnet Brodie |
                                            |
an. Ch. Hickory Smoke Tay Brodie, CD   ⎦

h. Hickory Smoke Black Douglas   Can. & US Ch. Hickory Smoke Wild N Wully, CD

h. Hickory Smoke Black Ebony   Ch. Legend of Gael, CD

CH. HI-LAWAY's CALOPIN

AKC No. SA 289780-12-67   Whelped: 17 April, 1964   Bitch
          Owner: J. Lawrence   Breeder: J. Hill

	Ch. Lancer of Serlway
Ch. EEG's Scotia Nodrog Rettes	Ch. Larrabee's Avalon Beauty
Ch. Afternod Buchanan	Loch Ridge Major Rogue
Ch. Wilson's Corrie, CD	Loch Ridge Victoria
Ch. Afternod Drambuie	Ch. Gregorach Fast
Ch. Fast's Falcon of Windy Hill	Heslop's Burnvale Janet
Ch. Afternod Sue	Ch. Scotia Nod's Duncan, CD
Afternod Ember of Gordon Hill	Ch. Heslop's Burnvale Bonnie,CD
	Piper's Don O'Field
Bud O'Field Brookview	Debonair Patty O'Field
Resthaven's Hill Artist	Windy Hill's Weir of Kay
Blarney Stone's Bonnie Belle	Ch. Blarney Stone's Deluxe Baby
Gay Bonnie Glascott	Gabriel of Serlway
Ch. Pell Mell's Bonnie Bruce	Ch. Pell Mell Penelope
Field Ch. Denida's Bonnie Velvet	Ch. Heslop's Stylish Lad
Ch. Calvert's Highland Queen	Mississippi Valley Jet

Dam of 8 Champions: Sired by:

Ch. HiLaway Gregory C Squared   Ch. Afternod Callant

Ch. Sutherland Zircon   ⎤
Ch. Sutherland Zark   ⎥   Ch. Afternod Cutty Sark
Ch. Sutherland Zinnia of Rixford, CD ⎦

Ch. Sutherland Dunnideer Waltz   ⎤
                                 ⎥   Ch. Afternod Anagram
Ch. Sutherland Warlock   ⎦

Ch. Sutherland Xenia   ⎤
                                 ⎥   Ch. Wee Jock Adair,CD
Ch. Sutherland Xenophanes, CD   ⎦

CH. IDLENOT'S LADY GUINEVERE, CD

AKC No. SA 798551-1-73   Whelped 19 May, 1970   Bitch
     Owner: Zak   Breeder: Noren

                 Ch. Afternod Buchanan   Ch. EEG's Scotia Nodrog Rettes
        Ch. Afternod Drambuie   Ch. Wilson's Corrie, CD
                 Ch. Afternod Sue   Ch. Fast's Falcon of Windy Hill
Ch. Afternod Advocate   Afternod Ember of Gordon Hill
                 Ch. Matson's Robin   Heslop's Burnvale Scot
        Ch. Meghan Maguire   Ch. Heslop's Burnvale Jean
                 Fletcher's Scotch Lorelei   Ch. Heslop's Burnvale Laird
                                                Kitty Lightfoot

                 Glenbel Drambuie   Dual Ch. Gunbar's Dare Devil, CD
        John's Gorde   Gunbar Highland Lassie
                 Riverside's Merry   Perk's Jack
Ebony Lady   Thurston's Stylish Dame
                 Bud O'Field Brookview   Piper's Don O'Field
        Kulhavy's Lady Gay Brookview   Debonair Patty O'Field
                 Sangerfield Nell   Pride of Dixey
                                                Ch. Sangerfield Fly

am of 9 Champions: Sired by:

h. O'Eires Lord Black Magic Jason ⎤
h. Flintlok's Beau O'Shamerin   ⎥   Ch. McMac's Return To Ravenscraig
h. Flintlok Jock of Tanaiste   ⎥
h. Flintlok Lady Liza of Teva   ⎦

h. Ka-Dan's Flintlok Frizzen, CD   ⎤
h. Flintlok's Robin MacNeal   ⎥
h. Flintlok's Muffin MacNeal   ⎥   Can.,Ber., & US Ch. MacNeal of Ellicott
h. Flintlok's Mister Peebles   ⎥
h. Portici's Shade O'Flintlok   ⎦

Lloyd Olson

CH. INWOOD GREENGLEN, CD

AKC No. SB 356217-4-76   Whelped 28 June, 1973   Bitch
          Owner: Westphal   Breeder: Martin

                                          Ch. Afternod Buchanan
                 Ch. Afternod Drambuie   Ch. Afternod Sue
          Ch. Afternod Anagram   Ch. Afternod Hickory
                 Loch Adair Diana of Redchico   Allspice of Redchico
Can. & US Ch. Rogheath Ben MacDhui   Afternod Sumac
                 Afternod Fidemac   Ch. Afternod Fidelia
          Ch. Afternod Ivy III   Ch. Afternod Drambuie
                 Ch. Afternod Alder   Afternod Kalmia

                                          Ch. Sangerfield Peter
                 Can. & US Ch. Sangerfield Jed   Ch. Sangerfield Tillie
          Brookview Rebel of Blackmore   Bud O'Field Brookview
                 Hewitt's Dutchess   Sangerfield Nell
Ch. Cricket of Macalester   Ch. Afternod Hickory
                 Ch. Afternod Wallace   Ch. Afternod Elgin II
          Afternod Thistle II   Ch. Afternod Drambuie
                 Afternod Firethorn   Afternod Annie Laurie

Dam of 8 Champions: Sired by:

Ch. Greenglen's Gold Nugget   ⎤
                                 ⎥   Can & US Ch. MacAlder Mr. Chips
Ch. Greenglen's Gold Dust   ⎦

Ch. Greenglen's Alistair Glory   ⎤

Ch. Greenglen's Dark Cavalier   ⎥

Ch. Greenglen's Gay Gambit   ⎥

Ch. Greenglen's Grenadier   ⎥   Ch. Greenglen's Up N Atem

Ch. Greenglen's Godiva Go Gaylee ⎥

Ch. Greenglen's Gabrielle   ⎦

Petrulis

CAN. & US CH. JENNIFER FARMS DECISION

AKC No. SB 808655-12-77   Whelped 12 June, 1975   Bitch
          Owner: Yates   Breeder: Meeks

                    Ch. Afternod Advocate   Ch. Afternod Drambuie
          Ch. Wildfire Manua of Picts   Ch. Meghan Maguire
                    Ch. Wildfire Willow   Afternod Fidemac
an. & US Ch. Jennifer Farms First Hoorah   Ch. Afternod Woodbine
                    Hacasak Piper's Hollow Kaka   Ch. Bonnie's Macs MacGeowls, CD
          Hacasak Janos' Okuwa   Hacasak Grand Ute
                    Hacasak Janos   Ch. Afternod MacAlder Tyr
                                                    Ch. Hacasak Pocohantas

                    Ch. Sangerfield Index   Can. & US Ch. Sangerfield Jed
          Ch. George Gordon Sangerfield   Ch. Sangerfield Tracy
                    Sangerfield Edie   Can. & US Ch. Sangerfield Smokey
usannah York   Ch. Sangerfield Tracy
                    Farman's Lucky Jack   Donnie Brae Eric Knight
          MacBeth Boo   Ch. Thurston's Stylish Fantasy
                    Farman's Stylish Princess II   Afternod Tweed
                                                    Farman's Stylish Princess

Dam of 7 Champions: Sired by:

Ch. Jennifer Frams Amulet

Ch. Jennifer Farms Azela Alpha, CD

Ch. Jennifer Farms Abner   Can. & US Ch. MacAlder Mr. Chips

Ch. Jennifer Farms Chips Ahoy

Ch. Jennifer Farms Edition DeLux   Can. & US Ch. Blossomaire Believe
                                                               It Or Not
Ch. Jennifer Farms Brigadoon
                                             Ch. Laird Duncan of Berridale
Ch. Jennifer Farms Music Man

Patsy's Studio

CH. JOCK OF INWOOD

AKC No. SA 579977-1-72   Whelped 8 April, 1968   Dog
          Owner: Martin   Breeder: Schultz

```
                    Afternod Fidemac          Afternod Sumac
          Ch. Wildfire Black Watch            Ch. Afternod Fidelia
                    Ch. Afternod Woodbine      Ch. Afternod Hickory
Heathero A'Highwayman                          Ch. Afternod Elgin II
                    Dual Ch. Windy Hill's Lucky Chance    Ch. Fast's Falcon of Windy
          Can. Ch.& US Dual Ch. Chance's National Velvet, CD  Windy Hill's Double Scotch
                    Field Ch. Denida's Bonnie Velvet         Ch. Pell Mell Bonnie Bruce
                                                            Ch. Calvert's Highland Quee
```

```
                    Afternod Fidemac          Afternod Sumac
          Afternod Rockingham                  Ch. Afternod Fidelia
                    Ch. Afternod Caramel        Ch. Afternod Drambuie
Proud Piper of Blackmore                        Ch. Afternod Woodbine
                    Bud O'Field Brookview        Piper's Don O'Field
          Hewitt's Dutchess                      Debonair Patty O'Field
                    Sangerfield Nell             Pride of Dixey
                                                Sangerfield Fly
```

<u>Sire of 12 Champions</u>:   <u>Out of</u>:

Ch. Greycoach Vis-A-Vis   ⎤
Ch. Greycoach Diligence   │   Ch. Inwood Windflower
Can. & US Ch. Greycoach Caleche   │
Can. & US Ch. Greycoach Brougham   ⎦

Ch. Alec of Greycoach   ⎤
Ch. Gorduk of Greycoach   │   Ch. Cricket of Macalester
Ch. Inwood Kerrie On   │
Can. & US Ch. Jock The Scot of Karolly, UD⎦

Ch. Jock's Tag-A-Long Gaily   Black Velvet O'Heathero

Ch. Alistair Brook of Gaylee   ⎤
Ch. Alistair Meadow Piper, CD   │   Can. & US Ch. Inwood Meadow Rue, UD
Ch. Alistair Meadow Vanguard   ⎦

CAN. & US CH. JOHNSTON'S HIGHLAND STORM

AKC No. SA 703221-272   Whelped 24 July, 1968   Dog
        Owner: Carden   Breeder: Gaines

                                    Windy Hill's Davey B
            Ch. Buddy D of HanMar   Dixie Means
        Ch. Hacasak Comanche
            Ch. Hacasak Sioux's Chance   Dual Ch. Windy Hill's Lucky Chance
Hacasak Ecorce   Ch. Windy Hill's Regina
            Afternod Fidemac   Afternod Sumac
        Afternod Rona II   Ch. Afternod Fidelia
            Ch. Afternod Caramel   Ch. Afternod Drambuie
                                        Ch. Afternod Woodbine

                                    Ch. Blake's Rogue of Windy Hill
            Windy Hill's Davey B   Windy Hill's Heidi of Shuriridge
        Ch. Buddy D of HanMar
            Dixie Means   Windy Hill's Butch
Hacasak Chickasaw   Lady Venus of Shiloh
            Dual Ch. Windy Hill's Lucky Chance Ch. Fast's Falcon of Windy Hill
                                       Field Ch. Denida's Bonnie Velvet
        Ch. Hacasak Sioux's Chance
            Ch. Windy Hill's Regina   Ch. Fast's Falcon of Windy Hill
                                        Windy Hill's Radiance

Sire of 15 Champions: Out of:

Ch. Misty Isle Kent of Braemar
                                    ] Braemar's Autumn Mist
Ch. Misty Isle Braemar's AnTeTula, CD

Ch. Temarcar Ambitious Aloysius   Temarcar Highland Heather

Ch. Riverside Tarboo Black Max
                                    ] Ch. Ben Brogh Sister Margaret
Ch. Temarcar Dundee Maiden

Ch. Hacasak Bithani
                                    ] Mistaree Kadon's April Magic
Ch. Hacasak Dogi

Can. & US Ch. Scottland's Eagle of Jayvanna

Can. & US Ch. Scottland's American Spirit

Can. & US Ch. Scottland's Great American

Can. Ch. Scottland's Liberty Belle
                                        Can. & US Ch. Vagabond
Ch. Scottland's American Patriot
                                            Lark of Rockaplenty,
Can. & US Ch. Scottland's Martha Custis, CD   CD

Ch. Scottland's Glacier Glory, CD

Ch. Scottland's Black Thorn Leigh

Lloyd Olson

CAN. & US CH. LAIRD DUNCAN OF BERRIDALE

AKC No. SB53644-6-75   Whelped 11 November, 1971   Dog
     Owner: W. Dwelly   Breeder: W. Dwelly

Ch. Afternod Drambuie	Ch. Afternod Buchanan
Ch. Afternod Anagram	Ch. Afternod Sue
Loch Adair Diana of Redchico	Ch. Afternod Hickory
Can. & US Ch. Rogheath Ben MacDhui	Allspice of Redchico
Afternod Fidemac	Afternod Sumac
Ch. Afternod Ivy III	Ch. Afternod Fidelia
Ch. Afternod Alder	Ch. Afternod Drambuie
	Afternod Kalmia

Windrock's Wainscot Torgue	Ch. Afternod Drambuie
Windrock's Skye MacQueen	Ch. Meghan Maguire
Windrock's Highland Heather	Thane of Windrock
Ch. Wee Bonnie Corrie Sue, CD	Dem's Torbolton Lass
Thane of Windrock	Can. & US Ch. Hickory Smoke's Wild 'N Wully,C▮
B. Bonnie Breigh	Ch. Meghan Maguire
Dhu's Heather Lass	Milestone Prince
	Monarch Belle's Delilah

<u>Sire of 16 Champions:</u>   <u>Out of:</u>

Ch. Highland Brooke of Berridale ⎤

Ch. Dandy Dirk of Berridale

Ch. Daalakis Bonnie of Berridale

Ch. Caesar of Berridale   Ch. Duchess of Windy Hills

Ch. MacLinden of Berridale

Ch. Kolumbo's Berridale Flasher ⎦

Can. & US Ch. Lochalsh Boyach of Berridale ⎤

Ch. Tara Gwenivere of Berridale

Ch. Wee Shannon of Berridale   Ch. Quailwood's Brae of Berridale

Ch. Berridale's Scottish Gynn, CDX

Can. & US Ch. Lindsey Jane of Berridale ⎦

Ch. Berridale's Tribute To Duncan ⎤

Can. Ch. Banbrae's Lady Sue O'Berridale ⎦   Lady Famebrose McDuff

Ch. MacAlder O'Cullen MacGregor   Ch. MacAlder Flame

Ch. Jennifer Farms Music Man ⎤

                           Ch. Jennifer Farms Decision

Ch. Jennifer Farms Brigadoon ⎦

E. Shafer

LOCH ADAIR DIANA OF REDCHICO

AKC No. SA 90221-4-63   Whelped 20 February, 1961   Bitch
      Owner: C. Chevalier   Breeder: D. Chevalier

                    Page's MacDonegal, CD   Captain O'Field
          Ch. Page's MacDonegal, II   Susan Q Gayne
          Mace's Old Bessie   Ch. Black Rogue of Serlway
Ch. Afternod Hickory   Blakeen Heather
          Ch. Heslop's Burnvale Piper   Ch. Heslop's Courageous
          Afternod Hedera   Ch. Heslop's Burnvale Duchess
                    Afternod Benbecula   Ch. EEG's Scotia Nodrog Rettes
                                                 Ch. Wilson's Corrie, CD

                    Ch. Halenred Robin Adair   Ch. Halenfred Scorched Gold
          Ch. Loch Adair Blair   Ch. Heslop's Burnvale Bonnie, CD
          Ch. Afternod Fidelia   Ch. Milestone Monarch
Allspice of Redchico   Ch. Wilson's Corrie, CD
          Afternod Hedemac   Ch. Page's MacDonegal II
          Ch. Afternod Kate   Afternod Hedera
                    Ch. Afternod Sue   Ch. Fast's Falcon of Windy Hill
                                                 Afternod Ember of Gordon Hill

   Dam of 13 Champions: Sired by:

   Ch. Afternod Anagram   ⌉
   Ch. Afternod Gallant Adair   │
   Ch. Afternod Gwen Adair   │   Ch. Afternod Drambuie
   Ch. Meadow Ridge Ghillie Adair   │
   Ch. Wee Geordie Adair   ⌋
   Ch. Loch Adair Laird   ⌉
   Ch. Loch Adair Meg of Sutherland, CD │
   Dual Ch. Loch Adair Monarch   │
   Ch. My Jo of Redchico   │
   Can. & US Ch. Loch Adair MerriMac │   Ch. Afternod Callant
   Ch. Loch Adair Teo of Thornyburn │
   Ch. Wee Jock Adair, CD   │
   Ch. Wee Laurie Adair   ⌋

Steve Klein

DUAL CH. LOCH ADAIR MONARCH

AKC No. SA 394364-5-68   Whelped 10 March, 1966   Dog
          Owner: Smith   Breeder: Chevalier

```
                              Ch. Afternod Buchanan      Ch. EEG's Scotia Nodrog Rettes
            Ch. Afternod Drambuie                        Ch. Wilson's Corrie, CD
                              Ch. Afternod Sue           Ch. Fast's Falcon of Windy Hill
Ch. Afternod Callant                                     Afternod Ember of ·Gordon Hill
                              Ch. Afternod Hickory       Ch. Page's MacDonegal II
            Ch. Afternod Woodbine                        Afternod Hedera
                              Ch. Afternod Elgin II      Ch. Afternod Buchanan
                                                         Afternod Ember of Gordon Hill

                              Ch. Page's MacDonegal II   Page's MacDonegal, CD
            Ch. Afternod Hickory                         Mace's Old Bessie
                              Afternod Hedera            Ch. Heslop's Burnvale Piper
Loch Adair Diana of Redchico                             Afternod Benbecula
                              Ch. Loch Adair Blair       Ch. Halenfred Robin Adair,CD
            Allspice of Redchico                         Ch. Afternod Fidelia
                              Ch. Afternod Kate          Afternod Hedemac
                                                         Ch. Afternod Sue
```

Sire of 15 Champions: Out of:

Ch. Afternod Gilian of Milestone   Afternod Gunhilde

Ch. Balarran Hoot Mon   Ch. Sutherland Balarran Vanity

Ch. Mygatt's Dugan   Page's Meghan Mygatt

Ch. MacLeod's Electra O'Chaparral, CD   Ch. Windrock's Kelly MacLeod

Can. &US Ch. Stilmeadows Jennifer   ⎤
                                          ⎬ Ch. Stilmeadows Aragant Angie
Can. & US Ch. Stilmeadows Jenny Leigh   ⎦

Ch. Sutherland Maid O'Siobahan   ⎤
Ch. Sutherland Mariah   ⎬ Ch. Sutherland Dunnideer Waltz
Ch. Sutherland MacDuff   ⎦

Can. & US Ch. Tri-Sett Black Bart of Robilee, CD Can. & US Ch. Jadehill Ashran of
                                                                      Tri-Sett, CD
Ch. Hunting Janet of Glenraden   ⎤
                                          ⎬ Loch Adair Valshiva
Ch. Lord Tye-Burr of Huntington   ⎦

Ch. Markham Crown Jewel   ⎤
                                          ⎬ Ch. Lady Jane of Markham
Ch. Markham Rhum Reuben   ⎦

Amat. Fld. Ch. Belmor's Allspice Ginger Belmor's Winged Victory

CH. LOCH ADAIR PEER OF SUTHERLAND, CD

AKC No. SA 620538-3-70 Whelped 6 September, 1968   Dog
Owner: J. Lawrence   Breeder: Chevalier

```
                                        Ch. Page's MacDonegal II
         Afternod Hedemac               Afternod Hedera
    Afternod Sumac                       Ch. Fast's Falcon of Windy Hill
            Ch. Afternod Sue            Afternod Ember of Gordon Hill
Afternod Fidemac                         Ch. Great Scot of Blakeen
            Ch. Milestone Monarch       Loch Ridge Reckless Lady
    Ch. Afternod Fidelia                Loch Ridge Major Rogue
            Ch. Wilson's Corrie, CD     Loch Ridge Victoria


            Ch. Afternod Drambuie       Ch. Afternod Buchanan
    Ch. Afternod Callant                Ch. Afternod Sue
            Ch. Afternod Woodbine       Ch. Afternod Hickory
Ch. Wee Laurie Adair                    Ch. Afternod Elgin II
            Ch. Afternod Hickory        Ch. Page's MacDonegal II
    Loch Adair Diana of Redchico        Afternod Hedera
            Allspice of Redchico        Ch. Loch Adair Blair
                                        Ch. Afternod Kate
```

Sire of 13 Champions: Out of:

Ch. Auld Sod's Bewitched   Ch. Kingswood Fannie of Faraday

Ch. Rossdhu Adriana

Ch. Rossdhu Christopher Sly   Ch. Sutherland Ullapool Piper, CDX

Ch. Sutherland Vanessa

Ch. Sutherland Vaillance Gilda

Ch. Sutherland Odds On   Ch. Afternod Karma

Ch. Sutherland Lass of Shambray

Ch. Sutherland Balarran Vanity

Ch. Sutherland Talisman

Can., Mex.& US Ch. Sutherland Tartan of Auld Sutherland Sybil
            Sod, CD
Ch. Sutherland Sweetbriar   St. Andrew Fiel Tabatha

Ch. Sutherland Daer of Dunsmuir   Ch. Sutherland Xenia
Ch. Sutherland Damask Rose

CH. MACALDER ALCY OF ROCKAPLENTY, CD

AKC No. SA 476553-10-69   Whelped 11 April, 1967   Bitch
Owner: Clark   Breeder: C. Stephenson

	Afternod Sumac	Afternod Hedemac
Afternod Fidemac		Ch. Afternod Sue
	Ch. Afternod Fidelia	Ch. Milestone Monarch
Ch. Afternod MacAlder Tyr		Ch. Wilson's Corrie, CD
	Ch. Afternod Drambuie	Ch. Afternod Buchanan
Ch. Afternod Alder		Ch. Afternod Sue
	Afternod Kalmia	Afternod Hedemac
		Ch. Afternod Sue
	Ch. Afternod Drambuie	Ch. Afternod Buchanan
Ch. Afternod Anagram		Ch. Afternod Sue
	Loch Adair Diana of Redchico	Ch. Afternod Hickory
Ch. Afternod Corrie of Teequinn		Allspice of Redchico
	Ch. Afternod Drambuie	Ch. Afternod Buchanan
Afternod Ginger		Ch. Afternod Sue
	Afternod Victoria II	Afternod Sumac
		Ch. Afternod Elgin II

Dam of 15 Champions: Sired by:

Ch. Rockaplenty's Pit-A-Pat

Ch. Rockaplenty's Black Jack

Ch. Rockaplenty's Move 'Em Out

Ch. Rockaplenty's Whangdoodle

Ch. Rockaplenty's Wheeler Dealer

Ch. Rockaplenty's Bill Bailey

Ch. Rockaplenty's Rack On

Ch. Rockaplenty's Razzledazzle

Ch. Rockaplenty's Rugged But Rite   Ch. Torrance of Ellicott

Ch. Rockaplenty's Blackberry, CD

Ch. Rockaplenty's Bonanza

Ch. Rockaplenty's Beau Brummell

Ch. Rockaplenty's Dandy Virgil

Ch. Rockaplenty's Glory Bound

Ch. Rockaplenty's Bandwagon

MACALDER BEAUTY

AKC No. SA 485088-2-69   Whelped 24 April, 1967   Bitch
Owner: C. Stephenson   Breeder: C. Stephenson

Afternod Sumac   Afternod Hedemac
Afternod Fidemac   Ch. Afternod Sue
    Ch. Afternod Fidelia   Ch. Milestone Monarch
Ch. Afternod MacAlder Tyr   Ch. Wilson's Corrie, CD
    Ch. Afternod Drambuie   Ch. Afternod Buchanan
Ch. Afternod Alder   Ch. Afternod Sue
    Afternod Kalmia   Afternod Hedemac
                                        Ch. Afternod Sue

        Ch. Afternod Drambuie   Ch. Afternod Buchanan
Ch. Afternod Callant   Ch. Afternod Sue
    Ch. Afternod Woodbine   Ch. Afternod Hickory
Afternod Babbie of Aberfoyle   Ch. Afternod Elgin II
    Ch. Afternod Hickory   Ch. Page's MacDonegal II
Ch. Afternod Wishbone   Afternod Hedera
    Ch. Afternod Elgin II   Ch. Afternod Buchanan
                                        Afternod Ember of Gordon Hill

Dam of 8 Champions: Sired by:

Ch. MacAlder Duke of Goldenrod ⎤
Ch. MacAlder Dede   ⎬   Ch. Afternod Kyle of Sutherland
Ch. MacAlder Dora of Seneca Hill ⎦
Ch. MacAlder Ingenue of Chris ⎤
Ch. MacAlder Flame   ⎬   Ch. Afternod Advocate
Ch. MacAlder Feather   ⎦
Ch. MacAlder Lara   ⎤
Can. & US Ch. MacAlder Lona   ⎦   Ch. Rogheath Ben MacDhui

CH. MACALDER DEDE

AKC No. SA 672665-3-72   Whelped 2 November, 1968   Bitch
    Owner: C. Stephenson   Breeder: C. Stephenson

                    Ch. Afternod Drambuie   Ch. Afternod Buchanan
        Ch. Afternod Callant   Ch. Afternod Sue
                    Ch. Afternod Woodbine   Ch. Afternod Hickory
Ch. Afternod Kyle of Sutherland   Ch. Afternod Elgin II
                    Ch. Afternod Drambuie   Ch. Afternod Buchanan
        Ch. Afternod Amber   Ch. Afternod Sue
                    Ch. Afternod Kate   Afternod Hedemac
                                                 Ch. Afternod Sue

                    Afternod Fidemac   Afternod Sumac
        Ch. Afternod MacAlder Tyr   Ch. Afternod Fidelia
                    Ch. Afternod Alder   Ch. Afternod Drambuie
MacAlder Beauty   Afternod Kalmia
                    Ch. Afternod Callant   Ch. Afternod Drambuie
        Afternod Babbie of Aberfoyle   Ch. Afternod Woodbine
                    Ch. Afternod Wishbone   Ch. Afternod Hickory
                                                 Ch. Afternod Elgin II

Dam of 7 Champions: Sired by:

Ch. MacAlder Kris Blaze   ⎤

Ch. MacAlder Kelley   │ Ch. MacAlder Blaze

Ch. MacAlder Keltic Trailblazer   ⎦

Ch. MacAlder Melody   ⎤

Can. & US Ch. MacAlder Mr. Chips   │

Can. & US Ch. MacAlder Merry of Clansmen, CD │ Can. & US Ch. Rogheath Ben MacDhui

Can. Ch. MacAlder Midnight Piper   ⎦

CH. MACALDER LARA

AKC No. SB 263950-5-76   Whelped 6 March, 1973   Bitch
        Owner: Olson   Breeder: Stephenson & Baker

Ch. Afternod Drambuie	Ch. Afternod Buchanan
Ch. Afternod Anagram	Ch. Afternod Sue
Loch Adair Diana of Redchico	Ch. Afternod Hickory
Can. & US Ch.Rogheath Ben MacDhui	Allspice of Redchico
Afternod Fidemac	Afternod Sumac
Ch. Afternod Ivy III	Ch. Afternod Fidelia
Ch. Afternod Alder	Ch. Afternod Drambuie
	Afternod Kalmia
Afternod Fidemac	Afternod Sumac
Ch. Afternod MacAlder Tyr	Ch. Afternod Fidelia
Ch. Afternod Alder	Ch. Afternod Drambuie
MacAlder Beauty	Afternod Kalmia
Ch. Afternod Callant	Ch. Afternod Drambuie
Afternod Babbie of Aberfoyle	Ch. Afternod Woodbine
Ch. Afternod Wishbone	Ch. Afternod Hickory
	Ch. Afternod Elgin II

<u>Dam of 8 Champions:</u>   <u>Sired by:</u>

Ch. MacAlder Tara   Can. & US Ch. MacAlder Mr. Chips

Ch. MacAlder Phoenix

Ch. MacAlder Penelope

Can. & US Ch. MacAlder Pride of Castle
                                      Hill, CD
Ch. MacAlder Unforgetable Star   Can. & US Ch. Rockaplenty Hang Em High

Ch. MacAlder Unforgetable Dream

Ch. MacAlder Unanimous Decision

Ch. MacAlder Up N'Coming

CAN. & US CH. MACALDER LONA

AKC No. SB 264113   Whelped 6 March, 1973   Bitch
          Owner: Breeder: Stephenson & Baker

                Ch. Afternod Drambuie   Ch. Afternod Buchanan
      Ch. Afternod Anagram   Ch. Afternod Sue
                Loch Adair Diana of Redchico Ch. Afternod Hickory
Can. & US Ch. Rogheath Ben MacDhui   Allspice of Redchico
                Afternod Fidemac   Afternod Sumac
      Ch. Afternod Ivy III   Ch. Afternod Fidelia
                Ch. Afternod Alder   Ch. Afternod Drambuie
                                             Afternod Kalmia

                Afternod Fidemac   Afternod Sumac
      Ch. Afternod MacAlder Tyr   Ch. Afternod Fidelia
                Ch. Afternod Alder   Ch. Afternod Drambuie
MacAlder Beauty   Afternod Kalmia
                Ch. Afternod Callant   Ch. Afternod Drambuie
      Afternod Babbie of Aberfoyle   Ch. Afternod Woodbine
                Ch. Afternod Wishbone   Ch. Afternod Hickory
                                             Ch. Afternod Elgin II

    Dam of 6 Champions: Sired by:

    Ch. Clansmen SunYak Ebony   ⎤
                                     ⎥   Ch. Norcoaster's MacManus
    Can & US Ch. Clansmen Witchcraft ⎦

    Can & US Ch. Clansmen Colourgard ⎤
    Can & US Ch. Clansmen Ms. Tiffany ⎥
                                     ⎥   Can & US Ch. MacAlder Mr. Chips
    Can.& US Ch. Clansmen MacAlder Cari ⎥
    Can & US Ch. Clansmen Wee Geordie ⎦

Carl Lindemaier

CAN. & US CH. MACALDER MR. CHIPS

AKC No. SB 347525-4-76   Whelped 17 June, 1973   Dog

Owner: C. Stephenson   Breeder: C. Stephenson

Ch. Afternod Drambuie	Ch. Afternod Buchanan
Ch. Afternod Anagram	Ch. Afternod Sue
Loch Adair Diana of Redchico	Ch. Afternod Hickory
Can. & US Ch. Rogheath Ben MacDhui	Allspice of Redchico
Afternod Fidemac	Afternod Sumac
Ch. Afternod Ivy III	Ch. Afternod Fidelia
Ch. Afternod Alder	Ch. Afternod Drambuie
	Afternod Kalmia
Ch. Afternod Callant	Ch. Afternod Drambuie
Ch. Afternod Kyle of Sutherland	Ch. Afternod Woodbine
Ch. Afternod Amber	Ch. Afternod Drambuie
Ch. MacAlder Dede	Ch. Afternod Kate
Ch. Afternod MacAlder Tyr	Afternod Fidemac
MacAlder Beauty	Ch. Afternod Alder
Afternod Babbie of Aberfoyle	Ch. Afternod Callant
	Ch. Afternod Wishbone

Sire of 64 Champions: Out of:

Can. & US Ch. Clansmen Colourgard   ⎤
Can. & US Ch. Clansmen Ms. Tiffany   ⎥
Can. & US Ch. Clansmen MacAlder Cari ⎥ Can. & US Ch. MacAlder Lona
Can. & US Ch. Clansmen Wee Geordie   ⎦

Ch. Braemar Ballater of Savoy, UD   ⎤
Ch. Braemar Brandy Booda   ⎥ Ch. Misty Isles Braemar's An Te Tula
Ch. Braemar Bewitching Josie   ⎦

Can. Ch. Rob Roy of Berridale   ⎤
Can. Ch. Gallant Mac of Berridale   ⎦ Ch. Highland Brooke of Berridale

Ch. Black Anvil Call Me Gypsy   ⎤
Can. & US Ch. Black Anvil Chips Ahoy, CD ⎦ Sevshun's Katy MacNab

Ch. Chaparral AuNatch O'Ral   ⎤
Ch. Chaparral Able Bodied   ⎥
Ch. Chaparral Ablaze Aglory, CD   ⎥ Ch. MacLeod's Electra O'Chaparral, CD
Ch. Chaparral Ace's High, CD   ⎥
Ch. Chaparral Amaretta   ⎥
Ch. Chaparral Affirmed   ⎦

Ch. Honeyglen Nu Buckwood Forest   Honey Glen's Buttons and Bows

Can. & US Ch. Castleglen's Happy Chips, CD ⎤ Ch. Calderwood Castle
Ch. Temacar Winsome Ruffles   ⎦

Ch. Heather Hill's Inverness   Ch. O'Hillock's Devine Sarah

Ch. Baejac's Aziz   ⎤
Ch. Baejac's Ace High Quail Ridge   ⎥
Ch. Baejac's Antoinete Bellringer   ⎥ Ch. MacAlder Nike Angel Baejac's
Ch. Baejac's Arabian Princess   ⎥
Ch. Baejac's A Woodsland Guardian   ⎦

Ch. Enniscroft Maggie McGirr   ⎤
Ch. Enniscroft Jason McGirr   ⎥
Ch. Enniscroft Jeffrey McGirr   ⎥ Ch. Sutherland Fandango
Ch. Enniscroft Wendy McGirr   ⎥
Ch. Enniscroft Jody McGirr   ⎦

Ch. Lodestar Kai Kasaan   Ch. MacAlder Nutmeg of Lodestar
Can. Ch. Darley's Miss Scotchguard   Can. Ch. Clansmen Cara Mia
Ch. Savoy's Just My Style   Ch. Clansmen Merriment of Savoy, CDX

Ch. Greenglen's Gold Dust   ⎤
Ch. Greenglen's Gold Nugget   ⎦ Ch. Inwood Greenglen, CD

Ch. Stilmeadows Winsome Vanessa

Ch. Stilmeadows Black Velvet   Can. & US Ch. Stilmeadows Kaird Heritage, CD

Can. & US Ch. Stilmeadows Darth Vader, CD

Ch. Zephyr's Artful Dodger

     Ch. Wee Shannon of Berridale

Can. Ch. Wyven Whispering Zephyr

Can. & US Ch. MacAlder Amber

Ch. MacAlder Aconnemara Wyland

Ch. MacAlder Astra of Quail Ridge   Ch. Siobahans Hope of Blackmagic

Ch. MacAlder Alcazar

Mex. Ch. MacAlder Aredhel Grendel

Ch. MacAlder Tara   Ch. MacAlder Lara

Ch. MacAlder Glory B

Ch. MacAlder Belle Starr   Ch. MacAlder Penelope

Can. & US Ch. MacAlder Best For Shojin

Can. & US Ch. Indigo High Times

Ch. Indigo Velvet of Inverness

     Can. Ch. Sangerfield Veronica

Can. Ch. Indigo Raven

Ch. Indigo Moonshine of Inverness, CD

Ch. Jennifer Farms Azela Alpha, CD

Ch. Jennifer Farms Chips Ahoy

Ch. Jennifer Farms Abner   Can. & US Ch. Jennifer Farms Decision

Ch. Jennifer Farms Alta

Ch. Jennifer Farms Amulet

Ch. Samson's McDuff of Ankor

     Ch. Mandy

Ch. Samson's Sweet Sassy for Alan

Ch. Valcar's Athena Chipia Sassia

     Ch. Fieldstone Sassy Ms. Yank

Ch. Valcar's Aphrodite Ms. Chippy

Ch. Alistair's Woodland Gael   Ch. Greenglen's Alistair Glory

CH. MACLEOD'S ELECTRA O'CHAPARRAL, CD

AKC No. SB624058-7-78   Whelped 1 May, 1974   Bitch
       Owner: Sanders   Breeder; Corcoran

                  Ch. Afternod Drambuie   Ch. Afternod Buchanan
        Ch. Afternod Callant   Ch. Afternod Sue
                  Ch. Afternod Woodbine   Ch. Afternod Hickory
Dual Ch. Loch Adair Monarch   Ch. Afternod Elgin II
                  Ch. Afternod Hickory   Ch. Page's MacDonegal II
        Loch Adair Diana of Redchico   Afternod Hedera
                  Allspice of Redchico   Ch. Loch Adair Blair
                                              Ch. Afternod Kate

                  Can. & US Ch. Hickory Smoke's Wild'N   Sergeant's Colorful Major, CD
        Ch. Hickory Smoke Black Douglas   Wully,CD   Windy Hill's Zoe
                  Can. & US Ch. Hickory Harvest   Can. & US Ch. Hickory Smoke's Wild
Ch. Windrock Kelly MacLeod   Heslop's ShoField Misty   'N Wully, CD
                  Windrock's Skye MacQueen   Windrock's Wainscot Torgue
        Jon's Majestic Lady   Windrock's Highland Heather
                  Page's Gingerbread Jenny   Talifer's Merry Michael
                                              Page's Miss Ginger

        Dam of 6 Champions: Sired by:

        Ch. Chaparral Able Bodied

        Ch. Chaparral Ablaze Aglory, CD

        Ch. Chaparral Ace's High, CD

        Ch. Chaparral Au Natch O'Ral   Can. & US Ch. MacAlder Mr. Chips

        Ch. Chaparral Amaretta

        Ch. Chaparral Affirmed

CAN., BERM. & US CH. MACNEAL OF ELLICOTT

AKC No. SA 459114-11-69   Whelped 15 November 1966   Dog
          Owner: Monaghan   Breeder: J. Freundel

Ch. Blake's Rogue of Windy Hill	Blake of Windy Hill
Windy Hills Davey B	Heslop's Burnvale Janet
Windy Hills Heidi of Shuriridge	Duncan of Windy Hill
Hugh's Sir Gordieof Windy Hill	Ch. Fast's Faith of Windy Hill
Ch. Star Farm Best Bet	Ch. Fast's Flash of Windy Hill
Abbie of Ann an Charr	Ch. Babs of Windy Hill
Laurel Lane's Cindy Lou	Ch. Windy Hills Satan
	Windy Hills Jennifer
Ch. Afternod Drambuie	Ch. Afternod Buchanan
Ch. Wee Geordie Adair	Ch. Afternod Sue
Loch Adair Diana of Redchico	Ch. Afternod Hickory
Ch. Loch Adair Kate	Allspice of Redchico
Ch. Afternod Drambuie	Ch. Afternod Buchanan
Ch. Afternod Curry	Ch. Afternod Sue
Allspice of Redchico	Ch. Loch Adair Blair
	Ch. Afternod Kate

CAN., BERM., & US CH. MACNEAL OF ELLICOTT

Sire of 46 Champions: Out of:

Ch. Tomar's Cool Hand Luke   ⎤
Ch. Tomar's Parnelli Jones   ⎥
Ch. Tomar's Mighty Mike MacTavish   ⎥   Ch. Vagabond's Yes I Can
Ch. Tomar's Reflection of Beauty   ⎥
Ch. Tomar's Bonnie Bit O'Heather   ⎦
Ch. Kadon's Blue Tango of Warlock   ⎤
Ch. Kadon's Chance Of A Lifetime   ⎦   Ch. Afternod Adair of Ballantrae
Ch. QuanGlo Kadon's Nealson, CD   Lorroy Scot Linnet
Ch. Holly Creek's Elvis   Ch. Stumpy Acres Blandwagin Kate
Ch. Kadon's Idyll of Claymore   ⎤
Ch. Kadon's I'm Bonnie's Clyde   ⎥   Ch. Kadon's Katie Did
Ch. Kadon's I'm Miss MacNeal   ⎦
Ch. Portici's Shade O Flintlok   ⎤
Ch. KaDan's Flintlok Frizzen   ⎥
Ch. Flintlok's Robin MacNeal   ⎥   Ch. Idlenot's Lady Guinevere, CD
Ch. Flintlok's Muffin MacNeal   ⎥
Ch. Flintlok's Mister Peebles   ⎦
Ch. Kadon's Riff Raff   ⎤
Ch. Kadon's Ruff & Ready   ⎥
Ch. Kadon's Robert E. Lee   ⎥   Bonnie Bess MacLean
Ch. Kadon's Robert Redford   ⎦
Ch. Timkaric Merrytail Meg   Ch. Glenalder Upland Lady
Ch. Stawen's Chevis Regal, CD   Bonnie of Stawen, CD
Ch. Stalwart Arwen of Gondor, CD   Flintlok's Misty Lass
Ch. MacMarlen's Black Bear   ⎤
Ch. MacMarlen's Braw Clan Ballad   ⎦   MacGeowl's Valiant Moonbeam
Ch. High Brass Gaelic Brogue   Ch. Afternod Hectate
Ch. MacMarlen Duncan O'Neal   ⎤
Ch. MacMarlen Douglas O'Neal   ⎥   Ch. Kadon's Monday Morning
Ch. MacMarlen Dubh-Linn O'Neal   ⎦
Ch. Mahoghany Acres Abbey, CD   ⎤
Ch. Mahoghany Acres Angus   ⎦   Ledgewood's Diana
Ch. MacBick's Seoras   Ch. Claymore's Autumn Aria
Can. Ch. Bradmar's Devilsome Duchess   Can. Ch. Grianan Fellside Cutty Sark
Ch. Sevshun's Casey MacCoy   ⎤
Ch. Sevshun's Shasta MacKay   ⎥   Ch. Sevshun's Tracy MacKnight
Ch. Sevshun's Hogan MacKay   ⎥
Ch. Erin MacKay, CD   ⎦
Ch. Greycoach Clan Chattan   ⎤
Ch. Greycoach Angus Baird   ⎥   Ch. Greycoach Vis-A-Vis
Ch. Greycoach Dunbar   ⎦
Ch. Sunbree Sinbad of BenWen   Ch. BenWen's Shona Dee
Ch. Braelinn's Lady Scamp   Vagabond's Dark Morning Star
Ch. Gordon Hill Zephyr   ⎤
Ch. Farmholme Practical Angler   ⎦   Can. Ch. Gordon Hill Xcitation, CD
Dual Ch. Shadowmere Scylla Savoy   Field Ch. & Amtr. Field Ch. Springset Lady Bug, CD

CH. MCMAC'S RETURN TO RAVENSCRAIG

AKC No. SB 261014-7-76   Whelped 6 January, 1973   Dog
    Owner: Zak   Breeder: Watson

            Windy Hill's Davey B   Ch. Blake's Rogue of Windy Hill
      Hugh's Sir Gordie of Windy Hill   Windy Hill's Heidi of Shuriridge
           Abbie of Ann an Charr   Ch. Star Farm Best Bet
Ch. Torrance of Ellicott   Laurel Lane's Cindy Lou
           Ch. Wee Geordie Adair   Ch. Afternod Drambuie
      Ch. Loch Adair Kate   Loch Adair Diana of Redchico
           Ch. Afternod Curry   Ch. Afternod Drambuie
                             Allspice of Redchico

            Windy Hill's Atha B   Ch. Blake's Rogue of Windy Hill
      Duke of Timber Lane   Ch. Sycamore Lodge Sue
           Windy Hill's Hilary B   Ch. Blake's Rogue of Windy Hill
Ch. Timberdoodle Thistledown   Windy Hill's Falconess
           Afternod Rockingham   Afternod Fidemac
      Heidi of Blackmore   Ch. Afternod Caramel
           Hewitt's Dutchess   Bud O'Field Brookview
                             Sangerfield Nell

<u>Sire of 11 Champions</u>:   <u>Out of</u>:

Ch. Flintlok's Black Watch Piper, CD
Ch. Flintlok's Bouncing Bette
Ch. Flintlok's Charlie Brown
Ch. Flintlok's Raven Bairn, CD   Ch. Flintlok's Robin MacNeal

Ch. Flintlok's Gloamin' Star

Ch. Flintlok's Piper of River Glen

Ch. Kadon's Tidbit   Ch. Kadon's I'm Miss MacNeal

Ch. O'Eires Lord Black Magic Jason

Ch. Flintlok's Beau O'Shamerin

Ch. Flintlok's Jock of Tanaiste   Ch. Idlenot's Lady Guinevere, CD

Ch. Flintlok's Lady Liza of Teva

CH. NORCOASTERS MACMANUS

AKC No. SB 489723-1-76   Whelped 20 March, 1974   Dog
       Owner: Grimm   Breeder: L. Peaker

                Ch. Wildfire Black Watch   Afternod Fidemac
    Dual Ch. St. Andrew's Gaelic Brogue, CD Ch. Afternod Woodbine
        Ch. St. Andrew's Bonnie Par   Sangerfield Doc Lyte
Ch. Nor'Coasters Glenplaid   Tammy O'Sylvan Lane
        Ch. HiLaway's Fin, CD   Ch. Pinerow's Duncan of Redchico
    Springset Butterscotch   Gay Bonnie Glascott
        Springset Breeze, CD   Mex. & US Ch. Windy Hill's MacGregor
                                            Smoke Signal

                Hugh's Sir Gordie of Windy Hill Windy Hills Davey B
    Ch. Torrance of Ellicott   Abbie of Ann an Charr
        Ch. Loch Adair Kate   Ch. Wee Geordie Adair
Rockaplenty's Good News   Ch. Afternod Curry
        Ch. Afternod MacAlder Tyr   Afternod Fidemac
    Ch. MacAlder Alcy of Rockaplenty, CD   Ch. Afternod Alder
        Ch. Afternod Corrie of Teequinn   Ch. Afternod Anagram
                                                 Afternod Ginger

---

Sire of 15 Champions: Out of:

Ch. Daron Black Diamond of Kymry   Ch. Daron Rainbows N Roses

Can. Ch. Blackloch's Bold Design   Can. Ch. Feathercroft Christmas Carol

Ch. Doggone Classy Chassis   Sutherland Jacinth

Ch. Bo-Cham's Forever Amber   ⎤
Ch. Bo-Cham's Free Spirit   ⎬   Ch. Bo-Cham's Blackberry Brandy
Ch. Bo-Cham's Flyer of Pineglenn, CD ⎦

Can. & US Ch. Clansmen SunYak Ebony ⎤
Can. Ch. Clansmen Black Bond   ⎬   Can. & US Ch. MacAlder Lona
Can. & US Ch. Clansmen Witchcraft   ⎦

Ch. Chawanakee Sagelin Orion   ⎤
Ch. Chawanakee Star Chaser   ⎦   Ch. Lipe's Princess Anna

Can. Ch. Scottland's All About Abbey ⎤
Ch. Harvest Going In Style   ⎦   Ch. Scottland's Glacier Glory, CD

Ch. Kymry Abaigael of Blackthorn   Ch. Sutherland Kymry Sweet Talk, CD

Ch. Bramblebush All That Jazz   Ch. Camptown Bramblebush Brier

CH. ROCKAPLENTY'S BONANZA

AKC No. SA 983048-3-75   Whelped 18 August, 1971   Bitch
       Owner: Clark   Breeder: Clark

                    Windy Hills Davey B
          Hugh's Sir Gordie of Windy Hill
                    Abbie of Ann an Charr
    Ch. Torrance of Ellicott
                    Ch. Wee Geordie Adair
          Ch. Loch Adair Kate
                    Ch. Afternod Curry

Ch. Blake's Rogue of Windy Hill
Windy Hills Heidi of Shuriridge
Ch. Star Farm Best Bet
Laurel Lane's Cindy Lou
Ch. Afternod Drambuie
Loch Adair Diana of Redchico
Ch. Afternod Drambuie
Allspice of Redchico

                    Afternod Fidemac
          Ch. Afternod MacAlder Tyr
                    Ch. Afternod Alder
    Ch. MacAlder's Alcy of Rockaplenty, CD
                    Ch. Afternod Anagram
          Ch. Afternod Corrie of Teequinn
                    Afternod Ginger

Afternod Sumac
Ch. Afternod Fidelia
Ch. Afternod Drambuie
Afternod Kalmia
Ch. Afternod Drambuie
Loch Adair Diana of Redchico
Ch. Afternod Drambuie
Afternod Victoria II

<u>Dam of 6 Champions:</u>   <u>Sired by:</u>

Can. & US Ch. Rockaplenty's Country Redlegs ⎤
                                             ⎥ Ch. Afternod Yank of Rockaplenty
Can. & US Ch. Rockaplenty's Nomad   ⎦

Ch. Rockaplenty's Tiger Rag   ⎤
                                            ⎥   Ch. Rockaplenty Quicksand
Ch. Rockaplenty's Tarragon Vee, CDX   ⎦

Ch. Rockaplenty's Impossible Dream   ⎤
                                            ⎥   Ch. Sutherland Lexington
Ch. Rockaplenty's Indian Summer   ⎦

CAN. & US CH. ROCKAPLENTY'S HANG EM HIGH

AKC No. SB 282572-3-75   Whelped 22 February, 1973   Dog
Owner: Carden   Breeder: Clark, VA.

```
                                          Ch. Afternod Drambuie
              Ch. Afternod Callant        Ch. Afternod Woodbine
        Ch. Wee Jock Adair, CD            Ch. Afternod Hickory
              Loch Adair Diana of Redchico Allspice of Redchico
Ch. Afternod Yank of Rockaplenty          Afternod Sumac
              Afternod Fidemac            Ch. Afternod Fidelia
        Ch. Afternod Ripple               Ch. Afternod Drambuie
              Ch. Afternod Caramel        Ch. Afternod Woodbine


              Hugh's Sir Gordie of Windy Hill Windy Hills Davey B
        Ch. Torrance of Ellicott          Abbie of Ann an Charr
              Ch. Loch Adair Kate         Ch. Wee Geordie Adair
Ch. Rockaplenty's Pit-A-Pat               Ch. Afternod Curry
              Ch. Afternod MacAlder Tyr   Afternod Fidemac
        Ch. MacAlder Alcy of Rockaplenty, CD Ch. Afternod Alder
              Ch. Afternod Corrie of Teequinn Ch. Afternod Anagram
                                          Afternod Ginger
```

Sire of 39 Champions: Out of:

Ch. MacAlder Phoenix

Can. & US Ch. MacAlder Pride of Castle Hill, CD

Ch. MacAlder Penelope

Ch. MacAlder Up N'Coming   Ch. MacAlder Lara

Ch. MacAlder Unforgetable Star

Ch. MacAlder Unforgetable Dream

Ch. MacAlder Unanimous Decision

Ch. O'Hillocks Devine Sarah   Jennifer Gray Lady

Ch. Rockaplenty's Salute To Erik

Ch. Rockaplenty's Sassafras

Ch. Rockaplenty's Sooner Victory

Ch. Rockaplenty's Sunshine   Ch. Rockaplenty's Miss Kitty

Ch. Rockaplenty's Super Skirt

Ch. Rockaplenty's Ultimatum

Ch. Glen Ayr's Moonshadow

Ch. Glen Ayr's Rebel Rouser

Ch. Glen Ayr's Great Expectation   Ch. Flintlok's Muffin MacNeal

Ch. Glen Ayr's Knight of Thunder

Ch. Glen Ayr Timbertrail Star

Ch. Glenwood's High Hopes   Ch. Glenwood's Heavenly Body

Ch. Glenwood's Hung Jury

Ch. Kris' Lightening & Thunder   Ch. MacAlder Ingenue of Chris

Ch. Samson's Sequel To Sassy

Can. & US Ch. Samson's Shojin of Daniel

Ch. Samson's Ms MacDuffy   Ch. Samson's Sweet Sassy For Alan

Ch. Samson's Royal Heritage

Ch. Firebrand Chateau Challenge   Ch. Don-D's Hello Dolly

CAN. & US CH. ROCKAPLENTY'S HANG EM HIGH

, Fieldstone Highlight		
, Fieldstone Halleluiah	} Ch. Rockaplenty's Gaelic Ribbons	
, Doggone Slick Chick		
, Doggone Sassy Chassis	} Ch. Doggone Classy Chassis	
, Doggone Bizi Body		
ı. & US Ch. Heavenly Big Gun of Brighton		
ı. Ch. Heavenly Genesis of Brighton	} Ch. Rockaplenty's Frosty Morn	
, Zephyr's Free Spirit	Ch. Wee Shannon of Berridale	
, Scottland's Double Dare You		
ı. & US Ch. Scottland's De Droit	} Can. & US Ch. Scottland's American Spirit	
Quailwood's Excalibur		
Quailwood Elegant Erica	} Quailwood's Gaelic Sonnet	

CH. ROCKAPLENTY'S MISS KITTY

AKC No. SB 473803-12-75   Whelped 6 January, 1974   Bitch
       Owner: Clark, VA.   Breeder: Bland & Blanco

```
                     Ch. Afternod Callant      Ch. Afternod Drambuie
          Ch. Wee Jock Adair, CD               Ch. Afternod Woodbine
             Loch Adair Diana of Redchico      Ch. Afternod Hickory
Ch. Afternod Yank of Rockaplenty               Allspice of Redchico
             Afternod Fidelia                  Afternod Sumac
          Ch. Afternod Ripple                  Ch. Afternod Fidelia
             Ch. Afternod Caramel              Ch. Afternod Drambuie
                                               Ch. Afternod Woodbine

                     Ch. Bonnie's Macs MacGeowls, CD   Dual Ch. Windy Hills Lucky Chance
          Dual Ch. MacGeowl's MacDougal               Field Ch. Denida's Bonnie Velvet
             Ch. MacGeowls Miss Misty                 Braw Clan Contender
Ch. Stumpy Acres Kadon Katie                          King's Misty's Sweetheart
             Hugh's Sir Gordie of Windy Hill          Windy Hills Davey B
          Ch. Kadon's Katie Did                       Abbie of Ann an Charr
             Ch. Loch Adair Kate                      Ch. Wee Geordie Adair
                                                      Ch. Afternod Curry
```

Dam of 9 Champions: Sired by:

Ch. Rockaplent's Sassafras	
Ch. Rockaplenty's Sooner Victory	
Ch. Rockaplenty's Sunshine	
Ch. Rockaplenty's Salute To Eric	} Ch. Rockaplenty Hang Em High
Ch. Rockaplenty's Super Skirt	
Ch. Rockaplenty's Ultimatum	
Ch. Rockaplenty's Joker's Wild	Ch. Sutherland Lexington
Ch. Rockaplenty's Twice As Nice	
Ch. Rockaplenty's Northern Lights	} Ch. Rockaplenty Grand Slam

CH. ROCKAPLENTY'S PIT-A-PAT

AKC No. SA 682231-11-72   Whelped 12 June, 1969   Bitch
          Owner: Clark, VA.   Breeder: Clark, VA.

                    Windy Hills Davey B   Ch. Blake's Rogue of Windy Hill
          Hugh's Sir Gordie of Windy Hill   Windy Hills Heidi of Shuriridge
                    Abbie of Ann an Charr   Ch. Star Farm Best Bet
Ch. Torrance of Ellicott   Laurel Lane's Cindy Lou
                    Ch. Wee Geordie Adair   Ch. Afternod Drambuie
          Ch. Loch Adair Kate   Loch Adair Diana of Redchico
                    Ch. Afternod Curry   Ch. Afternod Drambuie
                                                    Allspice of Redchico

                    Afternod Fidemac   Afternod Sumac
          Ch. Afternod MacAlder Tyr   Ch. Afternod Fidelia
                    Ch. Afternod Alder   Ch. Afternod Drambuie
Ch. MacAlder's Alcy of Rockaplenty, CD   Afternod Kalmia
                    Ch. Afternod Anagram   Ch. Afternod Drambuie
          Ch. Afternod Corrie of Teequinn   Loch Adair Diana of Redchico
                    Afternod Ginger   Ch. Afternod Drambuie
                                                    Afternod Victoria II

Dam of 16 Champions: Sired by:

Ch. Rockaplenty Pandora's Box, CD ⎫
Ch. Rockaplenty Pillow Talk   ⎪
Ch. Rockaplenty's Peaches N Cream ⎪
Ch. Rockaplenty's Pride N Joy   ⎪
Ch. Rockaplenty Mountain Dew   ⎪
Ch. Rockaplenty's Mish Mash   ⎬   Ch. Afternod Yank of Rockaplenty
Ch. Rockaplenty's Mercury Morris ⎪
Ch. Rockaplenty's Real McCoy, CD ⎪
Ch. Rockaplenty Royall Holy Hell ⎪
Ch. Rockaplenty Honeybee   ⎪
Ch. Rockaplenty's Hang Em High   ⎪
Ch. Rockaplenty's Hibiscus   ⎭

Ch. Rockaplenty Eldorado   ⎫
Ch. Rockaplenty Echo of Kate   ⎪
Ch. Rockaplenty Elspeth of Ayr, CD⎬   Ch. Torrance of Ellicott
Ch. Rockaplenty Black Eagle   ⎭

CH. ROCKAPLENTY'S SASSAFRAS

No. SB 812432-4-77   Whelped 12 July, 1975   Bitch
    Owner: Clark, VA.   Breeder: Clark, VA.

                    Ch. Wee Jock Adair, CD   Ch. Afternod Callant
          Ch. Afternod Yank of Rockaplenty   Loch Adair Diana of Redchico
                    Ch. Afternod Ripple   Afternod Fidemac
Can. & US Ch. Rockaplenty's Hang Em High   Ch. Afternod Caramel
               Ch. Torrance of Ellicott   Hugh's Sir Gordie of Windy Hill
          Ch. Rockaplenty's Pit-A-Pat   Ch. Loch Adair Kate
               Ch. MacAlder Alcy of Rockaplenty, CD Ch. Afternod MacAlder Tyr
                                                     Ch. Afternod Corrie of Teequinn

                    Ch. Wee Jock Adair, CD   Ch. Afternod Callant
          Ch. Afternod Yank of Rockaplenty   Loch Adair Diana of Redchico
                    Ch. Afternod Ripple   Afternod Fidemac
Ch. Rockaplenty's Miss Kitty   Ch. Afternod Caramel
               Dual Ch. MacGeowls MacDougal   Ch. Bonnie's Macs MacGeowls, CD
          Ch. Stumpy Acres Kadon Katie   Ch. MacGeowls Miss Misty
               Ch. Kadon's Katie Did   Hugh's Sir Gordie of Windy Hill
                                                     Ch. Loch Adair Kate

Dam of 6 Champions: Sired by:

Ch. Rockaplenty's Grand Slam   ⎤
Ch. Rockaplenty's Gaelic Ribbons   ⎬   Ch. Sutherland Lexington
Ch. Rockaplenty's Go For Broke   ⎦

Ch. Rockaplenty's Ain't She Sweet   Ch. Torrance of Ellicott

Ch. Rockaplenty's Run For The Roses ⎤
Ch. Rockaplenty's Rainbow   ⎦   Rockaplenty Inherit The Wind

CAN. & US CH. ROGHEATH BEN MACDHUI

AKC No. SA 396770-3-69　　　　Whelped 8 January, 1966　　　　Dog
Owner: Stahl　　　　　　　　　　　　　Breeder: L. Sykes

```
                    Ch. Afternod Buchanan        Ch. EEGs Scotia Nodrog Rettes
          Ch. Afternod Drambuie                  Ch. Wilson's Corrie, CD
                    Ch. Afternod Sue             Ch. Fast's Falcon of Windy Hill
Ch. Afternod Anagram                             Afternod Ember of Gordon Hill
                    Ch. Afternod Hickory         Ch. Page's MacDonegal II
          Loch Adair Diana of Redchico           Afternod Hedera
                    Allspice of Redchico         Ch. Loch Adair Blair
                                                 Ch. Afternod Kate


                    Afternod Sumac               Afternod Hedemac
          Afternod Fidemac                       Ch. Afternod Sue
                    Ch. Afternod Fidelia         Ch. Milestone Monarch
Ch. Afternod Ivy III                             Ch. Wilson's Corrie, CD
                    Ch. Afternod Drambuie        Ch. Afternod Buchanan
          Ch. Afternod Alder                     Ch. Afternod Sue
                    Afternod Kalmia              Afternod Hedemac
                                                 Ch. Afternod Sue
```

CAN.& US CH. ROGHEATH BEN MACDHUI

Sire of 49 Champions: Out of:

Ch. Oakridge Merrydown Mead   ⎤
Ch. Oakridge Mr. Mike of Shinfayne │
Ch. Oakridge Marakesha   │
Ch. Oakridge Magic Marker, CDX   │
Ch. Oakridge Trick Or Treat   │   Ch. Afternod Octavia III
Ch. Oakridge Timbershine, CD   │
Ch. Oakridge Tweed MacDhui   │
Ch. Oakridge Treebeard   │
Ch. Oakridge Tisha of Fiannafail   ⎦
Ch. Kiltklan Regina of Aberdeen   ⎤
Ch. Kiltklan Robbie MacBean   │   Ch. Afternod Robena of Aberdeen
Ch. Kiltklan's McNish   │
Ch. HiLite Delight of Kiltklan   ⎦
Can. Ch. Comfort's Pineview Abbey   Viking Hill's Black Ember
Mex. & US Ch. Kingswood's Fannie of Faraday ⎤
Ch. Country Club's Merry Fargo   ⎦   Duchess of Virginia
Can. & US Ch. Daron Make Mine Scotch   ⎤
German & US Ch. Daron's Majestic Jet   │
Ch. Daron's Mistique Melody   │
Ch. Daron's My Guy McTavish   │
Ch. Daron Monarch   │   Ch. Sangerfield Bonnie of RuBern
Ch. Daron Desert Stardust   │
Ch. Daron Rainbows 'N Roses   │
Ch. Daron Rebel With A Cause   ⎦
Can. Ch. Highcountry's Kalamalka Shuna ⎤
Can. Ch. Highcountry's Black Abbey Morn ⎦ Can. Ch. Madrona's Highcountry Piper
Ch. Smokey Islay Mist of Delta   Country Club Deamon Brew
Ch. Laird Duncan of Berridale   ⎤
Ch. Calderwood Castle   ⎦   Ch. Wee Bonnie Corrie Sue, CD
Ch. Tam O Shanter's Scottish Rogue   Ch. Weaver's TamOShanter, CD
Ch. Newkirk's Black Bart, UD   Ch. St. Andrew's Lady Jessica
Ch. Siobahan's Hope of Blackmagic   Ch. MacAlder Dora of Seneca Hill
Can. Ch. Blackthorn's Lady Alpha   ⎤
Can. & US Ch. Blackthorn's Laird Aaron ⎦ Can. Ch. Madrona Veteran Lady

Can. & US Ch. Inwood Meadow Rue, UD
Ch. Inwood Greenglen, CD   Ch. Cricket of Macalester
Ch. Inwood Windflower

Can. Ch. MacAlder Midnight Piper
Can. & US Ch. MacAlder Mr. Chips
Ch. MacAlder Melody   Ch. MacAlder Dede
Can. & US Ch. MacAlder Merry of Clansmen, CD

Ch. MacAlder Nike Angel Baejacs
Ch. MacAlder Nutmeg of Lodestar, CD   Ch. MacAlder Flame

Can. & US Ch. MacAlder Lona
Ch. MacAlder Lara   MacAlder Beauty

Ch. Ledgewood James Shandygaff
Ch. Ledgewood Annie Get Your Gun, CD   Ch. Loch Adair Quentina, CD

Ch. Marakesh Orion McQ
Ch. McQ Advocate   Ch. Quaco's Magic Negra Marakesh

CH. ST. ANDREW'S BONNIE PAR

AKC No. SA 317289-10-65   Whelped 14 May, 1963   Bitch
      Owner: Bechler   Breeder: King

                Hall's Carolina Ace   Peter's Rob Roy
          Pride of Dixey   Carolina Dinah Lee
                Griffin's Princess Peggy   Pope's Black Bob
ngerfield Doc Lyte   Blackie Lady
                Judge Palmer   Ch. Heslop's Courageous
      Ch. Sangerfield Fly   Tam O'Shanter
                Ch. Look's Carolina Redbird   Ch. Heslop's Criss Cross
                                              Ch. Heslop's Burnvale Dawn

                SunYak Medicine Man   Ch. King of the Palouse
          Dave's Mike   Ch. Rural Rhythm
                Ch. Princess Barbara   El Princepe Valiente
mmy O'Sylvan Lane   Lydia Bell
                Prince of Midcrest Way   Boisen's Thistle One
          Frisco Sheda   Lady Elizabeth
                Sweetie of Midcrest Way   Spinky of Riverside
                                              Highland Mary II

Dam of 6 Champions: Sired by:

Dual Ch. St. Andrew Gaelic Brogue, CD ⎤
Ch. St. Andrew's Jamie Parish |
Ch. St. Andrew's James Daryl | Ch. Wildfire Black Watch
Ch. Rayo Archie   ⎦

Ch. St. Andrew's Kelpie   Stylish Rhythm

Can. Ch. St. Andrew's Georgina   Wildfire Pont Road St. Andrew

CH. SANGERFIELD BONNIE OF RU-BERN

AKC No. SA 595887-9-71   Whelped 19 July, 1968   Bitch
         Owner: Solheim & Wedeman   Breeder: J. Look

Ch. Sangerfield Index	Can. & US Ch. Sangerfield Jed
Ch. George Gordon Sangerfield	Ch. Sangerfield Tracy
Sangerfield Edie	Can. & US Ch. Sangerfield Smokey
Can. & US Ch. Sporting Look	Ch. Sangerfield Tracy
Ch. Sangerfield Index	Can. & US Ch. Sangerfield Jed
Ch. Sangerfield HiJinks	Ch. Sangerfield Tracy
Sangerfield Judy	Ch. Heslop's Burnvale Christopher
	Sanger's Blackberry

Can. & US Ch. Sangerfield Jed	Ch. Sangerfield Peter
Ch. Sangerfield Index	Ch. Sangerfield Tillie
Ch. Sangerfield Tracy	Look's Black Daniel
Ch. Bonnie Gay of RuBern	Ch. Heslop's Burnvale Edie
Ch. Thurston's Stylish Angus	Roevalley Duke
Ch. Alice of Achnacarry	Osborne's Stylish Tammerlane II
Sangerfield Sally	Ch. Sangerfield Peter
	Ch. Sangerfield Tillie

Dam of 8 Champions: Sired by:

Ch. Daron's Desert Stardust

Ch. Daron's Rainbows N Roses

Ch. Daron's Mistique Melody

Ch. Daron's My Guy McTavish

Ch. Daron Monarch   Can.& US Ch. Rogheath Ben MacDhui

Can. & US Ch. Daron Make Mine Scotch

German & US Ch. Daron's Majestic Jet

Ch. Daron Rebel With A Cause

CH. SANGERFIELD INDEX

AKC No. SA79967-1-63   Whelped 4 June, 1960   Dog
      Owner: Sanger, N.Y.   Breeder: Sanger, N.Y.

```
                    Ch. Heslop's Burnvale Christopher   Ch. Heslop's Courageous
           Ch. Sangerfield Peter                        Ch. Heslop's Burnvale Duchess
                    Sandy's Bess                         Long Branch Sandy
  Can. & US Ch. Sangerfield Jed                          Long Branch Bess
                    Judge Palmer                         Ch. Heslop's Courageous
           Ch. Sangerfield Tillie                        Tam O'Shanter
                    Ch. Heslop's Burnvale Dawn           Ch. Heslop's Courageous
                                                         Ch. Heslop's Burnvale Duchess


                    Ch. Heslop's Criss Cross            Ch. Heslop's Courageous
           Look's Black Daniel                           Inglehurst Ingenue
                    Dandy                                Dan O'Field
  Ch. Sangerfield Tracy                                  Major's Bessie O'Field
                    Ch. Heslop's Courageous             Ch. Barnlake Brutus of Salmagundi
           Ch. Heslop's Burnvale Edie                    Ch. Larrabee's Cricket
                    Ch. Heslop's Burnvale Duchess        Ch. Heslop's Crusader
                                                         Ch. Highland Queen of Tweedvale
```

Sire of 10 Champions: Out of:

Ch. Terlo's Lady of Clan Cameron   ⎤
                                        ⎥   Ch. Terlo's Andrea
Ch. Terlo's Laird of Clan Cameron   ⎦

Ch. Bonnie Gay of RuBern   Ch. Alice of Achnacarry

Ch. George Gordon Sangerfield   Sangerfield Edie

Ch. Killiedrum Tag   Ch. Saturday Farm Killiedrum Eve

Ch. Sangerfield HiJinks   Sangerfield Judy

Can. Ch. Hickory Smoke Tay Brodie, CD   ⎤
                                         ⎥
Can. Ch. Hickory Smoke Dirk Brodie   ⎥
                                         ⎥ Can. & US Ch. Hickory Harvest
Can. Ch. Hickory Smoke Morag Brodie, CD ⎥
                                         ⎥
Can. Ch. Hickory Smoke Bonnet Brodie   ⎦

CAN. & US CH. SANGERFIELD PATSY, CD

AKC No. SA 532541-4-70   Whelped 5 November, 1967   Bitch
Owner: Sanderson   Breeder: Itzenplitz

		Ch. Sangerfield Index	Can. & US Ch. Sangerfield Jed
	Ch. George Gordon Sangerfield		Ch. Sangerfield Tracy
		Sangerfield Edie	Can. & US Ch. Sangerfield Smokey
Can. & US Ch. Sporting Look			Ch. Sangerfield Tracy
		Ch. Sangerfield Index	Can. & US Ch. Sangerfield Jed
	Ch. Sangerfield HiJinks		Ch. Sangerfield Tracy
		Sangerfield Judy	Ch. Heslop's Burnvale Christopher
			Sanger's Blackberry
		Ch. Sangerfield Index	Can. & US Ch. Sangerfield Jed
	Ch. George Gordon Sangerfield		Ch. Sangerfield Tracy
		Sangerfield Edie	Can. & US Ch. Sangerfield Smokey
RuBern's Miss Pepper			Ch. Sangerfield Tracy
		Ch. Sangerfield Index	Can. & US Ch. Sangerfield Jed
	Ch. Bonnie Gay of RuBern		Ch. Sangerfield Tracy
		Ch. Alice of Achnacarry	Ch. Thurston's Stylish Angus
			Sangerfield Sally

Dam of 7 Champions: Sired by:

Ch. Sangerfield Rrenamere Tansy ⎤

Ch. Ferguson's Sangerfield Cynde ⎥   Killiedrum Jay of Oak Lynn

Ch. Sangerfield Cymbal ⎦

Ch. Sangerfield Black Dawn, CDX, TD   Ch. Sangerfield Black James

Ch. Sangerfield Sports Fame ⎤

Ch. Sangerfield Sports Index ⎦   Ch. Sportin' Life

Ch. Hirolin Sangerfield Fancy Me   Ch. Peacham's Sangerfield Jack

CH. SANGERFIELD SPORTS INDEX

AKC No. SB30608-6-73   Whelped 9 July, 1971   Dog
        Owner: Look & Chambers   Breeder: J. Look, N.Y.

		Ch. Sangerfield Index
	Ch. George Gordon Sangerfield	Sangerfield Edie
Can. & US Ch. Sporting Look		Ch. Sangerfield Index
	Ch. Sangerfield HiJinks	Sangerfield Judy
Ch. Sportin' Life		Can. & US Ch. Sangerfield Jed
	Ch. Sangerfield Index	Ch. Sangerfield Tracy
	Ch. Terlo's Lady of Clan Cameron	Ch. Denida's Bonnie Rebel, CD
	Ch. Terlo's Andrea	Ch. Look's Carolina Redbird

		Ch. Sangerfield Index
	Ch. George Gordon Sangerfield	Sangerfield Edie
Can. & US Ch. Sporting Look		Ch. Sangerfield Index
	Ch. Sangerfield Hi-Jinks	Sangerfield Judy
Can. & US Ch. Sangerfield Patsy, CD		Ch. Sangerfield Index
	Ch. George Gordon Sangerfield	Sangerfield Edie
Ru-Bern's Miss Pepper		Ch. Sangerfield Index
	Ch. Bonnie Gay of Ru-Bern	Ch. Alice of Achnacarry

Sire of 11 Champions:

Out of:

Can.,US Ch. Gillian of Grianan

           Can.,US Ch. Grianan Victoria Balfour

Ch. Glenwood's Heavenly Body

Ch. Glenwood's Kouhoutek, CD   Ch. Glenwood's Jennifer Pax

Brazilian Ch. Sangerfield Good As Gold   Sangerfield Ginger

Can,US Ch. Indigo's Jasmine

Can . Ch. Indigo's Desert Sky   Can. Ch. Sangerifield Veronica

Can. Ch. Indigo's Mandy Diamond Girl

Can. Ch. Clansmen Cara Mia

Can. Ch. Clansmen Jasper   Can, US Ch. MacAlder Merry of
                              Clansmen, CD

Ch. Clansmen Merriment of Savoy, CDX

Ch. BoCham's Carrioca of Anders   BoCham's Bourbon And Ginger

CH. SANGERFIELD SPORTS DON

AKC No. SB 51009-4-73   Whelped 30 May, 1971   Dog
     Owner: Itzenplitz   Breeder: Look, NY

```
                                          Ch. Sangerfield Index
           Ch. George Gordon Sangerfield  Sangerfield Edie
  Can. & US Ch. Sporting Look             Ch. Sangerfield Index
           Ch. Sangerfield HiJinks        Sangerfield Judy
Ch. Sportin' Life                         Can. & US Ch. Sangerfield Jed
           Ch. Sangerfield Index          Ch. Sangerfield Tracy
  Ch. Terlo's Lady of Clan Cameron        Ch. Denida's Bonnie Rebel, CD
           Ch. Terlo's Andrea             Ch. Look's Carolina Redbird


                                          Ch. Page's MacDonegal II
           Ch. Glascott's Tom O'Shanter   Breadalbane Copper Coin
  Page's Jeffrey of Cranmer               Field Ch. Page's Jock MacBess
           Page's Patti MacBess           Page's Miss Ginger
Sangerfield Ginger                        Can. & US Ch. Sangerfield Smokey
           Sangerfield Spencer            Ch. Sangerfield Tracy
  Sangerfield Mischief                    Ch. Sangerfield Index
           Killiedrum Sangerfield Tess    Ch. Saturday Farm Killiedrum Eve
```

Sire of 11 Champions: Out of:

Ch. Riverbend's Sangerfield Rob ⎤
                              Sangerfield Oriole
Ch. Sangerfield Ardis   ⎦

Ch. Sir Charles Gordon of Henshaw ⎤

Ch. Sangerfield Typology

Can. Ch. Sangerfield Veronica   Ch. Sangerfield Rrenamere Tansy

Ch. Sangerfield Sage

Ch. Sangerfield Verbena, CD   ⎦

Can. Ch. Grianan Hutton Callbeck   Can. Ch. Grianan Felicity

Can. Ch. Gordon Hill Very Special, CD ⎤
                                        HiLaway's Quota of Gordon Hill
Ch. Gordon Hill Virginia Velvet   ⎦

Ch. Haliburton's Artimus Gordon   Amy Luv of Haliburton

CAN. & US CH. SPORTING LOOK

KC No. SA 380116-8-67   Whelped 20 June, 1965   Dog
     Owner; Itzenplitz, N.Y.   Breeder: J. Look, N.Y.

                                           Ch. Sangerfield Peter
          Can. & US Ch. Sangerfield Jed   Ch. Sangerfield Tillie
     Ch. Sangerfield Index   Look's Black Daniel
          Ch. Sangerfield Tracy   Ch. Heslop's Burnvale Edie
Ch. George Gordon Sangerfield   Judge Palmer
          Can. & US Ch. Sangerfield Smokey Holt's Dolly of Greymount
     Sangerfield Edie   Look's Black Daniel
          Ch. Sangerfield Tracy   Ch. Heslop's Burnvale Edie

                                           Ch. Sangerfield Peter
          Can. & US Ch. Sangerfield Jed   Ch. Sangerfield Tillie
     Ch. Sangerfield Index   Look's Black Daniel
          Ch. Sangerfield Tracy   Ch. Heslop's Burnvale Edie
Ch. Sangerfield HiJinks   Ch. Heslop's Courageous
          Ch. Heslop's Burnvale Christopher Ch. Heslop's Burnvale Duchess
     Sangerfield Judy   O'Field's Ready Response
          Sanger's Blackberry   Ch. Heslop's Burnvale Edie

Sire of 14 Champions: Out of:

Ch. Sportin' Life   ⎤

Ch. Sangerfield Portrait   ⎪

Ch. Sangerfield Highland Fling   ⎪

Ch. Sangerfield Cameo   ⎬ Ch. Terlo's Lady of Clan Cameron

Ch. Terlo's Inverness Thistle   ⎪

Can., Mex. & US Ch. Terlo's Briarpatch Dawn, CD ⎦

Ch. Sangerfield Sporting Jenny   Sangerfield Oriole

Can. & US Ch. Sangerfield Patsy, CD   RuBern's Miss Pepper

Can. & US Ch. Sangerfield Sir Clipsby Crew ⎤ Ch. Bonnie Gay of RuBern

Ch. Sangerfield Bonnie of RuBern   ⎦

Ch. DewE's Sangerfield Alfresco   ⎤ Sangerfield Jayne

Ch. DewE's Sangerfield Ameghan   ⎦

Can. Ch. Glenappin Nick of Marwin   ⎤ Can. Ch. Fichtental's Black Princess

Can. Ch. Glenappin Ameera   ⎦

CH. SPORTIN' LIFE

Steve Klein

AKC No. SA501694-10-68   Whelped 20 May, 1967   Dog
         Owner: Itzenplitz   Breeder: Itzenplitz, N.Y.

                    Ch. Sangerfield Index   Can. & US Ch. Sangerfield Jed
        Ch. George Gordon Sangerfield   Ch. Sangerfield Tracy
            Sangerfield Edie   Can. & US Ch. Sangerfield Smokey
Can. & US Ch. Sporting Look   Ch. Sangerfield Tracy
            Ch. Sangerfield Index   Can. & US Ch. Sangerfield Jed
        Ch. Sangerfield HiJinks   Ch. Sangerfield Tracy
            Sangerfield Judy   Ch. Heslop's Burnvale Christopher
                                           Sanger's Blackberry

                    Can. & US Ch. Sangerfield Jed Can. & US Ch. Sangerfield Peter
        Ch. Sangerfield Index   Ch. Sangerfield Tillie
            Ch. Sangerfield Tracy   Look's Black Daniel
Ch. Terlo's Lady of Clan Cameron   Ch. Heslop's Burnvale Edie
            Ch. Denida's Bonnie Rebel,CD   Ch. Pell Mell Bonnie Bruce
        Ch. Terlo's Andrea   Ch. Calvert's Highland Queen
            Ch. Look's Carolina Redbird   Ch. Heslop's Criss Cross
                                           Ch. Heslop's Burnvale Dawn

Sire of 27 Champions: Out of:

Ch. Sangerfield Black James   ⎤
Ch. Mickthea Sporting Lass, CD   │
Ch. Craig A Chalamain   │   Ch. Sangerfield Tam O'Shanter
Ch. Sangerfield Crathe Ben Nevis   ⎦

Ch. DonD's Miss Mischief   Ch. Thurston's R Lady MacTavish

Can. Ch. Grianan Fanny de Courvoisier ⎤
Can. Ch. Grianan Felicity   │
Can. Ch. Grianan Fellside Cutty Sark │   Can. Ch. Grianan Morag MacTay
Can. Ch. Grianan Flint   ⎦

CH. SPORTIN' LIFE

rman & US Ch. Gordon Hill Wilscot Lektor ⎤
⎦ Ch. Gordon Hill Tyrelle MacAlder
i. Wilscot Maclaine of Lochbuie, CD

i. BoCham's Butter Rum ⎤
i. BoCham's Byline On Sports
i. BoCham's Boone Wynds ⎬ Ch. BoCham's Cricket of Cromarty
i. BoCham's Blackwatch Piper
i. BoCham's Blackberry Brandy ⎦

i. Killiedrum Tanist ⎤
i. Sangerfield Deacon Brown ⎬ Ch. Killiedrum Tag
i. Sangerfield Tease ⎦

i. Enterprise Sangerfield Dave   Enterprise Sangerfield Gigi

i. Sangerfield Sports Index ⎤
⎦ Can. & US Ch. Sangerfield Patsy, CD
i. Sangerfield Sports Fame

i. Sangerfield Sports Don ⎤
i. Sangerfield Sports Page, CD ⎬ Sangerfield Ginger
i. Sangerfield Sports Penny, CD, TD ⎦

i. Sangerfield Rowdy West ⎤
⎦ Can. & US Ch. RuBern's Sangerfield Dolly
i. Sangerfield Highland Mary

CAN. CH. SANGERFIELD VERONICA

CKC No. 959544   Whelped   Bitch
      Owner: Harris, B.C.   Breeder:Sanger, N.Y.

                                              Ch. George Gordon Sangerfield
              Can. & US Ch. Sporting Look   Ch. Sangerfield HiJinks
      Ch. Sportin' Life   Ch. Sangerfield Index
              Ch. Terlo's Lady of Clan Cameron Ch. Terlo's Andrea
Ch. Sangerfield Sports Don   Ch. Glascott's Tom O'Shanter
              Page's Jeffrey of Cranmer   Page's Patti MacBess
      Sangerfield Ginger   Sangerfield Spencer
              Sangerfield Mischief   Killiedrum Sangerfield Tess

                                                    Ch. Sangerfield Peter
              Can. & US Ch. Sangerfield Jed   Ch. Sangerfield Tillie
      Killiedrum Jay of Oak Lynn   Eng. Ch. Javelin of Westerdale
              Borderland Taupie   Borderland Quair
Ch. Sangerfield Rrenamere Tansy   Ch. George Gordon Sangerfield
              Can. & US Ch. Sporting Look   Ch. Sangerfield HiJinks
      Can. & US Ch. Sangerfield Patsy, CD   Ch. George Gordon Sangerfield
              RuBern's Miss Pepper   Ch. Bonnie Gay of RuBern

Dam of 7 Champions: Sired by:

Can. & US Ch. Indigo High Times   ⎤

Can. Ch. Indigo Raven   │
                                     │   Can. & US Ch. MacAlder Mr. Chips
Ch. Indigo Moonshine of Inverness, CD│

Ch. Indigo Velvet of Inverness   ⎦

Can. & US Ch. Indigo's Jasmine   ⎤

Can. Ch. Indigo's Desert Sky   │   Ch. Sangerfield Sports Index

Can. Ch. Indigo's Mandy Diamond Girl ⎦

Martin Booth

CH. STILMEADOWS EOLANDE DESMONA

AKC No. SA 971846-1-75   Whelped 4 July, 1971   Bitch
Owner: Gidday, MI   Breeder: Gidday, MI

```
                                                Ch. Afternod Buchanan
                    Ch. Afternod Drambuie       Ch. Afternod Sue
          Ch. Afternod Callant                  Ch. Afternod Hickory
                    Ch. Afternod Woodbine       Ch. Afternod Elgin II
Ch. Wee Jock Adair, CD                          Ch. Page's MacDonegal II
                    Ch. Afternod Hickory        Afternod Hedera
          Loch Adair Diana of Redchico          Ch. Loch Adair Blair
                    Allspice of Redchico        Ch. Afternod Kate


                    Afternod Sumac              Afternod Hedemac
          Afternod Fidemac                      Ch. Afternod Sue
                    Ch. Afternod Fidelia        Ch. Milestone Monarch
Can. & US Ch. Afternod Sybilla                  Ch. Wilson's Corrie, CD
                    Ch. Afternod Drambuie       Ch. Afternod Buchanan
          Ch. Afternod Alder                    Ch. Afternod Sue
                    Afternod Kalmia             Afternod Hedemac
                                                Ch. Afternod Sue
```

Dam of 6 Champions: Sired by:

Ch. Stilmeadows Yesterday's Wish ⎤

Ch. Stilmeadows Lord Flint ⎥   Ch. Stilmeadows Flim Flam Man

Can. Ch. Stilmeadows Uist O'Torridon ⎤

Ch. Stilmeadows Scarlett O'Hara ⎥

Ch. Stilmeadows Echo of Sybilla ⎥   Can. & US Ch. Stilmeadows Kaliber

Ch. Stilmeadows The Devil U Say ⎦

Martin Booth

CH. STILMEADOWS FLIM FLAM MAN

AKC No. SB 57951-11-74   Whelped 1 December, 1971   Dog
Owner: Gidday   Breeder: Gidday

```
                  Windy Hills Davey B          Ch. Blake's Rogue of Windy Hill
         Hugh's Sir Gordie of Windy Hill      Windy Hills Heidi of Shuriridge
                  Abbie of Ann an Charr        Ch. Star Farm Best Bet
Ch. Torrance of Ellicott                       Laurel Lane's Cindy Lou
                  Ch. Wee Geordie Adair        Ch. Afternod Drambuie
         Ch. Loch Adair Kate                   Loch Adair Diana of Redchico
                  Ch. Afternod Curry           Ch. Afternod Drambuie
                                               Allspice of Redchico


                  Ch. Afternod Drambuie        Ch. Afternod Buchanan
         Ch. Afternod Callant                  Ch. Afternod Sue
                  Ch. Afternod Woodbine        Ch. Afternod Hickory
Ch. Stilmeadows Aragant Angie                  Ch. Afternod Elgin II
                  Afternod Fidemac             Afternod Sumac
         Can. & US Ch. Afternod Sybilla        Ch. Afternod Fidelia
                  Ch. Afternod Alder           Ch. Afternod Drambuie
                                               Afternod Kalmia
```

<u>Sire of 11 Champions:</u>   <u>Out of</u>:

Ch. Stilmeadows Lord Flint

Can. & US Ch. Stilmeadows Yesterday's Wish   Ch. Stilmeadows Eolande Desmona

Ch. Stilmeadows Kaliber

Ch. Stilmeadows Patriot   Ch. Stilmeadows Dara Dundrenan

Ch. Kadan Lane's Bebhin

Ch. Kadan Lane's Bhaird   Ch. Stilmeadows Jenny Leigh

Ch. Kadan Kelly Girl

Ch. Woodsage's Ace In The Hole
                                               Ch. Stilmeadows Indika Moria
Ch. Woodsage's Abigail of Ivanhoe

Ch. Tarbaby's Freedom Fighter
                                               Ch. Tarbaby's Cuss of Cabin Creek, CD, TD
Ch. Tarbaby's Flying Colors

CH. STUMPY ACRE'S KADON KATIE

AKC No. SA 719570-12-71   Whelped 12 July, 1969   Bitch
          Owner: Blanco   Breeder: Monaghan, MD.

```
                                                    Ch. Fast's Falcon of Windy Hill
                    Dual Ch. Windy Hill's Lucky Chance
                                                    Windy Hill's Double Scotch
        Ch. Bonnie's Macs MacGeowls, CD
                                                    Ch. Pell Mell Bonnie Bruce
                    Field Ch. Denida's Bonnie Velvet
                                                    Ch. Calvert's Highland Queen
Dual Ch. MacGeowl's MacDougal
                                                    Braw Clan Animation
                    Braw Clan Contender
                                                    Braw Clan Becky
        Ch. MacGeowls Miss Misty
                                                    Windy Hill's Davey B
                    King's Misty's Sweetheart
                                                    Falcon's Misty's Sweetheart


                                                    Ch. Blake's Rogue of Windy Hill
                    Windy Hill's Davey B
                                                    Windy Hill's Heidi of Shuriridge
        Hugh's Sir Gordie of Windy Hill
                                                    Ch. Star Farm Best Bet
                    Abbie of Ann an Charr
                                                    Laurel Lane's Cindy Lou
Ch. Kadon's Katie Did
                                                    Ch. Afternod Drambuie
                    Ch. Wee Geordie Adair
                                                    Loch Adair Diana of Redchico
        Ch. Loch Adair Kate
                                                    Ch. Afternod Drambuie
                    Ch. Afternod Curry
                                                    Allspice of Redchico
```

Dam of 6 Champions: Out of:

Ch. Stumpy Acres Blandwagin Kate   ⎤

Ch. Stumpy Acres Blandwagin Al |

Ch. Rockaplenty's Miss Kitty |

Ch. Rockaplenty's Abigail | Ch. Afternod Yank of Rockaplenty

Can. & US Ch. Rockaplenty's Gunsmoke   ⎦

Ch. Criston's Temperance   Ch. Loch Adair Ripple's Rumpus

CH. SUTHERLAND DUNIDEER WALTZ

AKC No. SA 828904-11-71 Whelped 26 August, 1969   Bitch
   Owner: Buletza   Breeder: J. Lawrence

```
                    Ch. Afternod Buchanan          Ch. EEGs Scotia Nodrog Rettes
      Ch. Afternod Drambuie                        Ch. Wilson's Corrie, CD
                    Ch. Afternod Sue               Ch. Fast's Falcon of Windy Hill
Ch. Afternod Anagram                               Afternod Ember of Gordon Hill
                    Ch. Afternod Hickory           Ch. Page's MacDonegal II
      Loch Adair Diana of Redchico                 Afternod Hedera
                    Allspice of Redchico           Ch. Loch Adair Blair
                                                   Ch. Afternod Kate


                    Ch. Afternod Buchanan          Ch. EEGs Scotia Nodrog Rettes
      Ch. Afternod Drambuie                        Ch. Wilson's Corrie, CD
                    Ch. Afternod Sue               Ch. Fast's Falcon of Windy Hill
Ch. HiLaway's Calopin                              Afternod Ember of Gordon Hill
                    Resthaven's Hill Artist        Bud O'Field Brookview
      Gay Bonnie Glascott                          Blarney Stone's Bonnie Belle
                    Field Ch. Denida's Bonnie Velvet  Ch. Pell Mell Bonnie Bruce
                                                   Ch. Calvert's Highland Queen
```

Dam of 11 Champions: Sired by:

Ch. Dunnideer Dana   ⎤
Ch. Dunnideer Dugan, CD   Ch. Afternod Kyle of Sutherland
Ch. Dunnideer Dendraxon
Ch. Sutherland Squaredance ⎦

Ch. Dunnideer Example   ⎤
Ch. Dunnideer Excalibur   Ch. Sutherland Talisman
Ch. Sutherland Saber, CD ⎦

Ch. Sutherland MacDuff   ⎤
Ch. Sutherland Mariah   Dual Ch. Loch Adair Monarch
Ch. Sutherland Maid O'Siobahan ⎦

Ch. Sutherland General Jackson ⎤
               Ch. Sutherland Odds On
Ch. Sutherland Felicity O'Samson ⎦

CH. SUTHERLAND'S LASS OF SHAMBRAY

AKC No. SB 233433-11-74   Whelped 8 May, 1972   Bitch
    Owner: J. Lawrence   Breeder: J. Lawrence

```
                  Afternod Sumac                Afternod Hedemac
           Afternod Fidemac                     Ch. Afternod Sue
                  Ch. Afternod Fidelia          Ch. Milestone Monarch
Ch. Loch Adair Peer of Sutherland, CD           Ch. Wilson's Corrie, CD
                  Ch. Afternod Callant          Ch. Afternod Drambuie
           Ch. Wee Laurie Adair                 Ch. Afternod Woodbine
                  Loch Adair Diana of Redchico  Ch. Afternod Hickory
                                                Allspice of Redchico

                  Ch. Afternod Drambuie         Ch. Afternod Buchanan
           Ch. Afternod Callant                 Ch. Afternod Sue
                  Ch. Afternod Woodbine         Ch. Afternod Hickory
Ch. Afternod Karma                              Ch. Afternod Elgin II
                  Ch. Afternod Drambuie         Ch. Afternod Buchanan
           Ch. Afternod Amber                   Ch. Afternod Sue
                  Ch. Afternod Kate             Afternod Hedemac
                                                Ch. Afternod Sue
```

Dam of 10 Champions: Sired by:

Ch. Sutherland Delilah ┐

Ch. Sutherland Lesson of Maryvan │

Ch. Sutherland Lexington │

Ch. Sutherland Lennox │   Ch. Sutherland Gallant

Ch. Sutherland Leading Lady │

Ch. Sutherland Leaps And Bounds │

Ch. Loch Adair Firefly ┘

Ch. Sutherland Shambray Accent   Sutherland Ian of Lewis

Ch. Sutherland Balarran Ofelia ┐

Ch. Sutherland Ogilvy Bran ┘   Ch. Sutherland MacDuff

CH. SUTHERLAND LEXINGTON

AKC No. SC 180943-11-77   Whelped 23 May, 1976   Dog
         Owner: Clark, VA   Breeder: Lawrence, WA.

                                              Ch. Afternod Callant
                Dual Ch. Loch Adair Monarch   Loch Adair Diana of Redchico
        Ch. Sutherland MacDuff   Ch. Afternod Anagram
                Ch. Sutherland Dunnideer Waltz Ch. HiLaway's Calopin
Ch. Sutherland Gallant   Ch. Afternod Callant
                Ch. Afternod Kyle of Sutherland Ch. Afternod Amber
        Ch. Sutherland Pavane   Ch. Wee Jock Adair, CD
                Ch. Sutherland Xenia   Ch. HiLaway's Calopin

                                              Afternod Sumac
                Afternod Fidemac   Ch. Afternod Fidelia
        Ch. Loch Adair Peer of Sutherland, CD Ch. Afternod Callant
                Ch. Wee Laurie Adair   Loch Adair Diana of Redchico
Ch. Sutherland's Lass of Shambray   Ch. Afternod Drambuie
                Ch. Afternod Callant   Ch. Afternod Woodbine
        Ch. Afternod Karma   Ch. Afternod Drambuie
                Ch. Afternod Amber   Ch. Afternod Kate

Sire of 12 Champions: Out of:

Ch. Fieldstone Serenade   ⎤

Ch. Fieldstone Swashbuckler   ⎥   Ch. Fieldstone Warlock Sweet Sue

Ch. Fieldstone Gordon Delight   ⎦

Ch. Dunsmuir Makaua   ⎤
                                     ⎥   Ch. Sutherland Daer of Dunsmuir
Ch. Dunsmuir Molly of Kiloh   ⎦

Ch. Rockaplenty's Grandslam   ⎤

Ch. Rockaplenty's Gaelic Ribbons   ⎥   Ch. Rockaplenty's Sassafras

Ch. Rockaplenty's Go For Broke   ⎦

Ch. Rockaplenty's Jokers Wild   Ch. Rockaplenty's Miss Kitty

Ch. Rockaplenty's Patriotic   Ch. Rockaplenty's Abigail

Ch. Rockaplenty's Impossible Dream   ⎤
                                     ⎥   Ch. Rockaplenty's Bonanza
Ch. Rockaplenty's Indian Summer   ⎦

CH. SUTHERLAND MACDUFF

AKC No. SB 154204-11-73   Whelped 10 February, 1972   Dog
          Owner: J. Lawrence   Breeder: J. Lawrence

                                          Ch. Afternod Buchanan
           Ch. Afternod Drambuie   Ch. Afternod Sue
     Ch. Afternod Callant   Ch. Afternod Hickory
           Ch. Afternod Woodbine   Ch. Afternod Elgin II
Dual Ch. Loch Adair Monarch   Ch. Page's MacDonegal II
           Ch. Afternod Hickory   Afternod Hedera
     Loch Adair Diana of Redchico   Ch. Loch Adair Blair
           Allspice of Redchico   Ch. Afternod Kate

                                          Ch. Afternod Buchanan
           Ch. Afternod Drambuie   Ch. Afternod Sue
     Ch. Afternod Anagram   Ch. Afternod Hickory
           Loch Adair Diana of Redchico   Allspice of Redchico
Ch. Sutherland Dunnideer Waltz   Ch. Afternod Buchanan
           Ch. Afternod Drambuie   Ch. Afternod Sue
     Ch. HiLaway's Calopin   Resthaven's Hill Artist
           Gay Bonnie Glascott   Field Ch. Denida's Bonnie Velvet

Sire of 20 Champions: Out of:

Ch. Kendelee Pearl Of A Girl   ⎤

Ch. Kendelee Pendragon   │

Ch. Kendelee Penelope   │   Ch. Afternod Nighean Kendelee

Ch. Sutherland Scala of Huntly   │

Ch. Kendelee Alleluia Jubilation   ⎦

Ch. Sutherland Kymry Sweet Talk, CD ⎤

Ch. Loch Loin's Ebisu Ginger, CD   │

Ch. Loch Loin's Eve Mandy   │   Ch. Sutherland Vaillance Gilda

Ch. Loch Loin's Ebon of Penmar   │

Ch. Loch Loin's Excalibur   │

Ch. Loch Loin's Corinne   ⎦

Ch. Sutherland Galloway Kate   ⎤

Ch. Sutherland Gallant   │   Ch. Sutherland Pavane

Ch. Sutherland Chisai Gamasach   │

Ch. Sutherland Gavotte   ⎦

Ch. Sutherland Venture   Ch. Sutherland Xenia

Ch. Sutherland Balarran Ofelia   ⎤
                                    │   Ch. Sutherland Lass of Shambray
Ch. Sutherland Ogilvy Bran   ⎦

Ch. Sutherland Hallmark   Ch. Sutherland Sybil

Ch. Sutherland Jessica   Ch. Sutherland Damask Rose

CH. SUTHERLAND VAILLANCE GILDA

AKC No. SA 829380-11-72   Whelped 25 October, 1969   Bitch
     Owner: Brun   Breeder: Lawrence

```
                    Afternod Sumac            Afternod Hedemac
          Afternod Fidemac                    Ch. Afternod Sue
                    Ch. Afternod Fidelia      Ch. Milestone Monarch
Ch. Loch Adair Peer of Sutherland, CD         Ch. Wilson's Corrie, CD
                    Ch. Afternod Callant      Ch. Afternod Drambuie
          Ch. Wee Laurie Adair                Ch. Afternod Woodbine
                    Loch Adair Diana of Redchico  Ch. Afternod Hickory
                                              Allspice of Redchico


                    Ch. Afternod Drambuie     Ch. Afternod Buchanan
          Ch. Afternod Callant                Ch. Afternod Sue
                    Ch. Afternod Woodbine     Ch. Afternod Hickory
Ch. Afternod Karma                            Ch. Afternod Elgin II
                    Ch. Afternod Drambuie     Ch. Afternod Buchanan
          Ch. Afternod Amber                  Ch. Afternod Sue
                    Ch. Afternod Kate         Afternod Hedemac
                                              Ch. Afternod Sue
```

Dam of 7 Champions: Sired by:

Ch. Loch Loin's Bacus   Ch. Sutherland Pan of Loch Loin

Ch. Sutherland Kymry Sweet Talk, CD ⎤

Ch. Loch Loin's Corinne |

Ch. Loch Loin's Ebisu Ginger |

Ch. Loch Loin's Excalibur | Ch. Sutherland MacDuff

Ch. Loch Loin's Eve Mandy |

Ch. Loch Loin's Ebon of Penmar ⎦

CH. SUTHERLAND XENIA

AKC No. SA713888-1-72   Whelped 3 February, 1969   Bitch
     Owner: Lawrence, WA.   Breeder: Lawrence, WA.

```
                    Ch. Afternod Drambuie     Ch. Afternod Buchanan
          Ch. Afternod Callant                Ch. Afternod Sue
                    Ch. Afternod Woodbine     Ch. Afternod Hickory
Ch. Wee Jock Adair, CD                        Ch. Afternod Elgin II
                    Ch. Afternod Hickory      Ch. Page's MacDonegal II
          Loch Adair Diana of Redchico        Afternod Hedera
                    Allspice of Redchico      Ch. Loch Adair Blair
                                              Ch. Afternod Kate


                    Ch. Afternod Buchanan     Ch. EEGs Scotia Nodrog Rettes
          Ch. Afternod Drambuie               Ch. Wilson's Corrie, CD
                    Ch. Afternod Sue          Ch. Fast's Falcon of Windy Hill
Ch. HiLaway's Calopin                         Afternod Ember of Gordon Hill
                    Resthaven's Hill Artist   Bud O'Field Brookview
          Gay Bonnie Glascott                 Blarney Stone's Bonnie Belle
                    Field Ch. Denida's Bonnie Velvet  Ch. Pell Mell Bonnie Bruce
                                              Ch. Calvert's Highland Queen
```

Dam of 7 Champions: Sired by:

Ch. Sutherland Pavane   ⎤

Ch. Sutherland Pan of Loch Loin |

Ch. Sutherland Pathfinder   ⎦   Ch. Afternod Kyle of Sutherland

Ch. Sutherland Venture   Ch. Sutherland MacDuff

Ch. Sutherland Katrine   Ch. Sutherland Talisman

Ch. Sutherland Daer of Dunsmuir ⎤

Ch. Sutherland Damask Rose   ⎦   Ch. Loch Adair Peer of Sutherland

CH. TERLO'S LADY OF CLAN CAMERON

AKC No. SA 287056-9-66   Whelped 13 October, 1964   Bitch
        Owner: Ellis, PA.   Breeder: Ellis, PA.

                    Ch. Sangerfield Peter   Ch. Heslop's Burnvale Christopher
        Can. & US Ch. Sangerfield Jed   Sandy's Bess
                    Ch. Sangerfield Tillie   Judge Palmer
Ch. Sangerfield Index   Ch. Heslop's Burnvale Dawn
                    Look's Black Daniel   Ch. Heslop's Criss Cross
        Ch. Sangerfield Tracy   Dandy
                    Ch. Heslop's Burnvale Edie   Ch. Heslop's Courageous
                                                 Ch. Heslop's Burnvale Duchess

                    Ch. Pell Mell Bonnie Bruce   Gabriel of Serlway
        Ch. Denida's Bonnie Rebel, CD   Ch. Pell Mell Penelope
                    Ch. Calvert's Highland Queen Ch. Heslop's Stylish Lad
Ch. Terlo's Andrea   Mississippi Valley Jet
                    Ch. Heslop's Criss Cross   Ch. Heslop's Courageous
        Ch. Look's Carolina Redbird   Inglehurst Ingenue
                    Ch. Heslop's Burnvale Dawn   Ch. Heslop's Courageous
                                                 Ch. Heslop's Burnvale Duchess

    Dam of 6 Champions: Sired by:

    Ch. Sportin' Life

    Ch. Sangerfield Portrait

    Ch. Sangerfield Highland Fling

    Ch. Sangerfield Cameo   Can. & US Ch. Sporting Look

    Ch. Terlo's Inverness Thistle

    Can, Mex. & US Ch. Terlo's Briarpatch Dawn, CD

CH. TIMBERDOODLE THISTLEDOWN

AKC No. SA 624272-3-71   Whelped 26 August, 1968   Bitch
          Owner: Watson   Breeder: Hobbs

                    Ch. Blake's Rogue of Windy Hill Blake of Windy Hill
          Windy Hill's Atha B   Heslop's Burnvale Janet
                    Ch. Sycamore Lodge Sue   Ch. Fast's Falcon of Windy Hill
Duke of Timber Lane   Ravenall BonBon
                    Ch. Blake's Rogue of Windy Hill Blake of Windy Hill
          Windy Hill's Hilary B   Heslop's Burnvale Janet
                    Windy Hill's Falconess   Ch. Fast's Falcon of Windy Hill
                                                      Jill of Windy Hill

                    Afternod Fidemac   Afternod Sumac
          Afternod Rockingham   Ch. Afternod Fidelia
                    Ch. Afternod Caramel   Ch. Afternod Drambuie
Heidi of Blackmore   Ch. Afternod Woodbine
                    Bud O'Field Brookview   Piper's Don O'Field
          Hewitt's Dutchess   Debonair Patty O'Field
                    Sangerfield Nell   Pride of Dixey
                                                      Sangerfield Fly

Dam of 11 Champions: Sired by:

Ch. McMac's Fred

Ch. McMac's September Morn   ]   Ch. Saturday Farm MacIntosh

Ch. McMac's O'Dorsey's Lamont   ]

Ch. McMac's Return To Ravenscraig

Ch. McMac's Miss Torrance

Can. & US Ch. McMac's George

Ch. McMac's Mary Anne   Ch. Torrance of Ellicott

Mex. & US Ch. McMac's Blackjack of Sungold

Ch. McMac's Dixie Lee of Creek Farm

Mex. & US Ch. McMac's Miranda of Siobahan

Ch. McMac's Murphy of Rusmar   ]

CH. TORRANCE OF ELLICOTT

AKC No. SA 459115-6-68   Whelped 15 November 1966   Dog
        Owner: Clark & Freundel   Breeder: J. Freundel

		Blake of Windy Hill
	Ch. Blake's Rogue of Windy Hill	Heslop's Burnvale Janet
	Windy Hills Davey B	Duncan of Windy Hill
Hugh's Sir Gordie of Windy Hill	Windy Hills Heidi of Shuriridge	Ch. Fast's Faith of Windy Hill
	Ch. Star Farm Best Bet	Ch. Fast's Flash of Windy Hill
	Abbie of Ann an Charr	Ch. Babs of Windy Hill
	Laurel Lane's Cindy Lou	Ch. Windy Hills Satan
		Windy Hills Jennifer

		Ch. Afternod Buchanan
	Ch. Afternod Drambuie	Ch. Afternod Sue
	Ch. Wee Geordie Adair	Ch. Afternod Hickory
Ch. Loch Adair Kate	Loch Adair Diana of Redchico	Allspice of Redchico
	Ch. Afternod Drambuie	Ch. Afternod Buchanan
	Ch. Afternod Curry	Ch. Afternod Sue
	Allspice of Redchico	Ch. Loch Adair Blair
		Ch. Afternod Kate

CH. TORRANCE OF ELLICOTT

Sire of 50 Champions: Out of:

Ch. McMac's O'Dorseys Lamont

Ch. McMac's Return To Ravenscraig

Ch. McMac's Miss Torrance

Can. & US Ch. McMac's George

Ch. McMac's Mary Anne   Ch. Timberdoodle Thistledown

Mex. & US Ch. McMac's Blackjack ofSungold

Ch. McMac's Dixie Lee of Creek Farm

Mex. & US Ch. McMac's Miranda ofSiobahan

Ch. McMac's Murphy of Rusmar

Can. Ch. Feathercroft Christmas Carol   Can. Ch. Highcountry Moon Wind

Ch. Blackaders Anna
                                               Ch. Rockaplenty's Cinnamon
Ch. Blackaders Andrea

Ch. Stilmeadows Flim Flam Man
                                               Ch. Stilmeadows Aragant Angie
Ch. Stilmeadows Fenella

Ch. Brodalyn Fieldstone Momento
                                               Ch. Kris' Keepsake of Fieldstone
Ch. Fieldstone Mandy of Foxhall

Ch. Scottland CB Supersport

Ch. Scottland CB Lark's Angel, CDX   Can. & US Ch. Vagabond Lark of
                                                              Rockaplenty,CD
Ch. Scottland CB Movin On Misty

Can., Berm, and US Ch. Jadehill Ashran of   Cannon Hill Abby of Jade Hill
                              TriSett, CD
Ch. Holyrood's Bedegraine
                                               Mt. Mansfield's Little Egypt
Ch. Holyrood's Black Sambo of Delta

Ch. Princemoor's Borne On The Wind

P.R., Dom, & US Ch. Princemoor's Bannok of   Ch. Princemoor's McMac Ebonymist
                              Moroco
Ch. Rockaplenty's Pit-A-Pat

Ch. Rockaplenty's Black Jack

Ch. Rockaplenty's Bill Bailey

Ch. Rockaplenty's Band Wagon

Ch. Rockaplenty's Blackberry

Ch. Rockaplenty's Beau Brunnell

Ch. Rockaplenty's Bonanza   Ch. MacAlder Alcy of Rockaplenty, CD

Ch. Rockaplenty's Whangdoodle

Ch. Rockaplenty's Wheeler Dealer

Ch. Rockaplenty's Move Em Out

Ch. Rockaplenty's Dandy Virgil

Ch. Rockaplenty's Rack On

Ch. Rockaplenty's Razzledazzle

Ch. Rockaplenty's Rugged But Rite

Ch. Rockaplenty's Glory Bound

Ch. Rockaplenty's Black Eagle ⎤
Ch. Rockaplenty's Elspeth of Ayr, CD ⎥   Ch. Rockaplenty's Pit-A-Pat
Ch. Rockaplenty's Echo of Kate ⎥
Ch. Rockaplenty's Eldorado ⎦
Ch. Rockaplenty's Zembezi ⎤
Ch. Rockaplenty's Zuider Zee ⎥   Rockaplenty's Lonesome Me
Ch. Rockaplenty's Zig-Zag ⎥
Ch. Rockaplenty's Zephyr ⎦
Ch. Rockaplenty's Winchester   Ch. Rockaplenty's Move Em Out
Ch. Rockaplenty's Frosty Morn   Ch. Criston's Temperance
Ch. Rockaplenty's Ain't She Sweet   Ch. Rockaplenty's Sassafras

CAN. & US CH. VAGABOND LARK OF ROCKAPLENTY, CD

AKC No. SB130509-2-76   Whelped 10 July, 1972   Bitch
Owner: Scott   Breeder: Weber

Ch. Afternod Callant	Ch. Afternod Drambuie
Ch. Wee Jock Adair, CD	Ch. Afternod Woodbine
Loch Adair Diana of Redchico	Ch. Afternod Hickory
Ch. Afternod Yank of Rockaplenty	Allspice of Redchico
Afternod Fidemac	Afternod Sumac
Ch. Afternod Ripple	Ch. Afternod Fidelia
Ch. Afternod Caramel	Ch. Afternod Drambuie
	Ch. Afternod Woodbine
Hugh's Sir Gordie of Windy Hill	Windy Hill's Davey B
Ch. Torrance of Ellicott	Abbie of Ann an Charr
Ch. Loch Adair Kate	Ch. Wee Geordie Adair
Ch. Rockaplenty Rugged But Rite	Ch. Afternod Curry
Ch. Afternod MacAlder Tyr	Afternod Fidemac
Ch. MacAlder Alcy of Rockaplenty, CD	Ch. Afternod Alder
Ch. Afternod Corrie of Teequinn	Ch. Afternod Anagram
	Afternod Ginger

Dam of 12 Champions: Sired by:

Can & US Ch. Afternod Ace of Lochiel   Ch. Afternod Simon

Ch. Scottland's American Patriot

Can & US Ch. Scottland's Eagle of Jayvana   Can. & US Ch. Johnston's Highland Storm

Can.& US Ch. Scottland's Great American

Can. Ch. Scottland's Liberty Belle

Can & US Ch. Scottland's American Spirit

Can & US Ch. Scottland's Martha Custis, CDX

Ch. Scottland's Glacier Glory, CD

Ch. Scottland's Blackthorn Leigh

Ch. Scottland's CB Supersport, CD

Ch. Scottland's CB Movin On Misty   Ch. Torrance of Ellicott

Can. & US Ch. Scottland's CB Lark's Angel, CDX

CH. WEE JOCK ADAIR, C.D.

AKC No. SA 296212-12-67   Whelped 23 September, 1964   Dog
Owner: Carol Chevalier, CT.   Breeder: Carol Chevalier, CT.

Ch. Afternod Buchanan	Ch. EEG's Scotia Nodrog Rettes
Ch. Afternod Drambuie	Ch. Wilson's Corrie, CD
Ch. Afternod Sue	Ch. Fast's Falcon of Windy Hill
Ch. Afternod Callant	Afternod Ember of Gordon Hill
Ch. Afternod Hickory	Ch. Page's MacDonegal II
Ch. Afternod Woodbine	Afternod Hedera
Ch. Afternod Elgin II	Ch. Afternod Buchanan
	Afternod Ember of Gordon Hill
Ch. Page's MacDonegal II	Page's MacDonegal, CD
Ch. Afternod Hickory	Mace's Old Bessie
Afternod Hedera	Ch. Heslop's Burnvale Piper
Loch Adair Diana of Redchico	Afternod Benbecula
Ch. Loch Adair Blair	Ch. Halenfred Robin Adair,CD
Allspice of Redchico	Ch. Afternod Fidelia
Ch. Afternod Kate	Afternod Hedemac
	Ch. Afternod Sue

Sire of 33 Champions: Out of:

Ch. Idlenot's Honey v.Heddenhof   Bianka vom Silbersee

Ch. Idlenot's Satin Doll, CD

Ch. Idlenot's Gracious Lady   Ch. Idlenot's Black Thistle

Ch. Mylord Andrew

Ch. Mylord Astrid   Braw Clan's Harmony

Ch. Afternod Yank of Rockaplenty

Ch. Afternod Yauld MacKenzie

Ch. Loch Adair Ripple's Rumpus   Ch. Afternod Ripple

Ch. Loch Adair Ripple's Regal Aire

Can. & US Ch. Loch Adair Dyce

Ch. Afternod Young Jock Dyson, CD

Can. Ch. Afternod Yon MacDuff Dyson   Highland Meg of Wynding Hills

Can. & US Ch. Loch Adair Jasmine

CH. WEE JOCK ADAIR, CD

Can. Ch. Afternod Victoria IV	Ch. Afternod Kippa
Ch. Afternod Zed II	Afternod April of Ballantrae
Ch. Afternod Jean	Ch. Afternod Ellen of Teequinn
Ch. Premonition Royal Cashmere	
Ch. Macarron's Regal Premonition	Ch. Olon Henley
Can. & US Ch. Afternod Nimrod Nuggets	
Ch. Afternod Nighean Kendelee	
Ch. Afternod Nigella	Ch. Afternod Wendee
Ch. Loch Adair Justin	
Ch. Afternod Dylan of Duart	Afternod Paisley of Duart
Can. Ch. Afternod Rona of Lochiel	Ch. Afternod Alexandra
Ch. Sutherland Xenia	
Ch. Sutherland Xenophanes, CD	Ch. HiLaway's Calopin
Ch. Loch Adair Statesman	Ch. Afternod Adair of Ballantrae
Ch. Gordon Hill Scaramouche	Ch. Gordon Hill Tyrelle MacAlder
Can. & US Ch. Stilmeadows Elgin	
Can. & US Ch. Stilmeadows Elegant Erica	
Ch. Stilmeadows Elegant Ephraim	Can. & US Ch. Afternod Sybilla
Ch. Stilmeadows Encore	
Ch. Stilmeadows Eolande Desmona	

CH. WEE LAURIE ADAIR

AKC No. SA 324001-8-67 Whelped 23 April, 1965 Bitch
Owner: Chevalier, CT. Breeder: Chevalier, CT.

Ch. Afternod Buchanan	Ch. EEG's Scotia Nodrog Rettes
Ch. Afternod Drambuie	Ch. Wilson's Corrie, CD.
Ch. Afternod Sue	Ch. Fast's Falcon of Windy Hill
Ch. Afternod Callant	Afternod Ember of ·Gordon Hill
Ch. Afternod Hickory	Ch. Page's MacDonegal II
Ch. Afternod Woodbine	Afternod Hedera
Ch. Afternod Elgin II	Ch. Afternod Buchanan
	Afternod Ember of Gordon Hill
Ch. Page's MacDonegal II	Page's MacDonegal, CD
Ch. Afternod Hickory	Mace's Old Bessie
Afternod Hedera	Ch. Heslop's Burnvale Piper
Loch Adair Diana of Redchico	Afternod Benbecula
Ch. Loch Adair Blair	Ch. Halenfred Robin Adair,CD
Allspice of Redchico	Ch. Afternod Fidelia
Ch. Afternod Kate	Afternod Hedemac
	Ch. Afternod Sue

Dam of 8 Champions: Sired by:

Ch. Loch Adair Pilot	
Ch. Loch Adair Peer of Sutherland, CD	
Ch. Loch Adair Neil	Afternod Fidemac
Can. Ch. Loch Adair Nabob's Flip	
Ch. Loch Adair Vagabond	Dual Ch. Glenraven Autumn Smoke
Ch. Loch Adair John Quincy	
Ch. Loch Adair Quentina, CD	Mylord Arthur
Ch. Loch Adair Titan of Tedmar	Ch. Afternod Simon

CH. WILDFIRE BLACK WATCH

AKC No. SA 168323-5-67   Whelped 22 October, 1962   Dog
      Owner: Martin   Breeder: Freedman, TX.

```
                Afternod Hedemac          Ch. Page's MacDonegal II
        Afternod Sumac                    Afternod Hedera
                Ch. Afternod Sue          Ch. Fast's Falcon of Windy Hill
Afternod Fidemac                          Afternod Ember of Gordon Hill
                Ch. Milestone Monarch     Ch. Great Scot of Blakeen
        Ch. Afternod Fidelia              Loch Ridge Reckless Lady
                Ch. Wilson's Corrie, CD   Loch Ridge Major Rogue
                                          Loch Ridge Victoria


                Ch. Page's MacDonegal, II    Page's MacDonegal, CD
        Ch. Afternod Hickory                 Mace's Old Bessie
                Afternod Hedera              Ch. Heslop's Burnvale Piper
Ch. Afternod Woodbine                        Afternod Benbecula
                Ch. Afternod Buchanan        Ch. EEG's Scotia Nodrog Reetes
        Ch. Afternod Elgin, II               Ch. Wilson's Corrie, CD
                Afternod Ember of Gordon Hill Ch. Scotia Nod'g Duncan, CD
                                             Ch. Heslop's Burnvale Bonnie, CD
```

Sire of 10 Champions: Out of:

Dual Ch. St. Andrew Gaelic Brogue, CD ⎤

Ch. St. Andrew's Jamie Parish   ⎥

Ch. Rayo Archie   Ch. St. Andrew's Bonnie Par

Ch. St. Andrew's James Daryl   ⎦

Can. & US Ch. Tam O'Shanter's Proud Piper, CD Can. & US Ch. Weaver's Tam O'Shanter, CD

Ch. Lochbar Lochleven   ⎤

Ch. Lochbar Lady Bristol   ⎦ Ch. Rogheath Ben Brooke

Can. & US Ch. Heathero Amber Velvet, CD ⎤

Ch. Heathero Arran Ben Ayr   ⎥ Dual Ch. & Can.Ch. Chance's National

Ch. Heathero Aristocrat   ⎦   Velvet, CD

Wm. Brown

DUAL CH. WINDY HILL'S LUCKY CHANCE

AKC No. S690030-8-57   Whelped 5 April, 1954   Dog
        Owner: Putchat   Breeder: Poisker, PA.

```
                                          Inglehurst Gillette, Jr.
              Ch. Ginger                  Inglehurst Minnie HaHa
       Ch. Gregorach Fast                 Stylish Lion
            Stylish Madame                Stylish Mine
Ch. Fast's Falcon of Windy Hill           Ch. Barnlake Brutus of Salmagundi
            Ch. Heslop's Courageous        Ch. Larrabee's Cricket
       Heslop's Burnvale Janet            Ch. Heslop's Crusader
            Ch. Heslop's Burnvale Duchess  Ch. Highland Queen of Tweedvale


                                          Ch. Gregorach Fast
            Ch. Fast's Flash of Windy Hill  Heslop's Burnvale Janet
       Flash's Craig of Windy Hill        Ch. Gregorach Fast
            Fast's Glory of Windy Hill     Jill of Windy Hill
Windy Hill's Double Scotch                Ch. Gregorach Fast
            Ch. Fast's Falcon of Windy Hill  Heslop's Burnvale Janet
       Ch. Sycamore Lodge Sue             Blake of Windy Hill
            Ravenall BonBon               Ch. Coulton's Cherry Ace
```

Sire of 10 Champions: Out of:

Ch. Bonnie's Macs MacGeowls, CD

Can. Ch. & Dual Ch. Chance's National Velvet, CD   Field Ch. Denida's Bonnie Velvet

Ch. Hacasak Inca's Bonnie Velvet

Dual Ch. Glascott's Scottish Majesty   Breadalbane Copper Coin

Ch. Chance's Lucky Ace   Ch. Aberdeen Artemis

Ch. Windy Hill's Gypsy Rose Levy   Ch. Windy Hill's Shiloh Gypsy

Ch. Windy Hill's Sadie B   Ch. Windy Hill's Drusie B

Ch. Hacasak Sioux's Chance

Ch. Chance's Lucky Buck   Ch. Windy Hill's Regina

Can. & US Ch. Chance's Lucky Lady